SWORD ART ONLINE
fairy dance

001

ART: TSUBASA HADUKI
ORIGINAL STORY: REKI KAWAHARA
CHARACTER DESIGN: abec

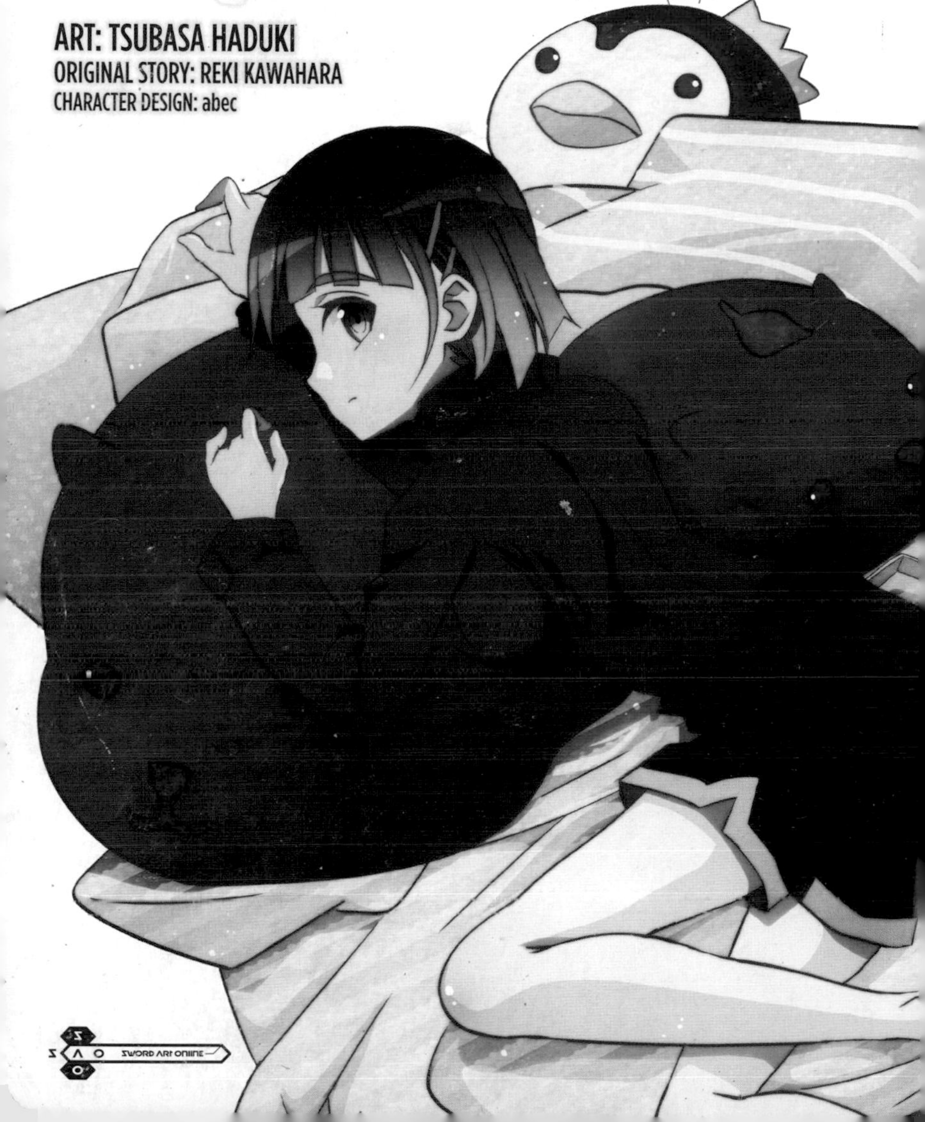

contents

date : 20 jan 2025 mon

rct progress alfheim online

001

SWORD ART ONLINE fairy dance

art : tsubasa haduki

original story : reki kawahara

character design : abec

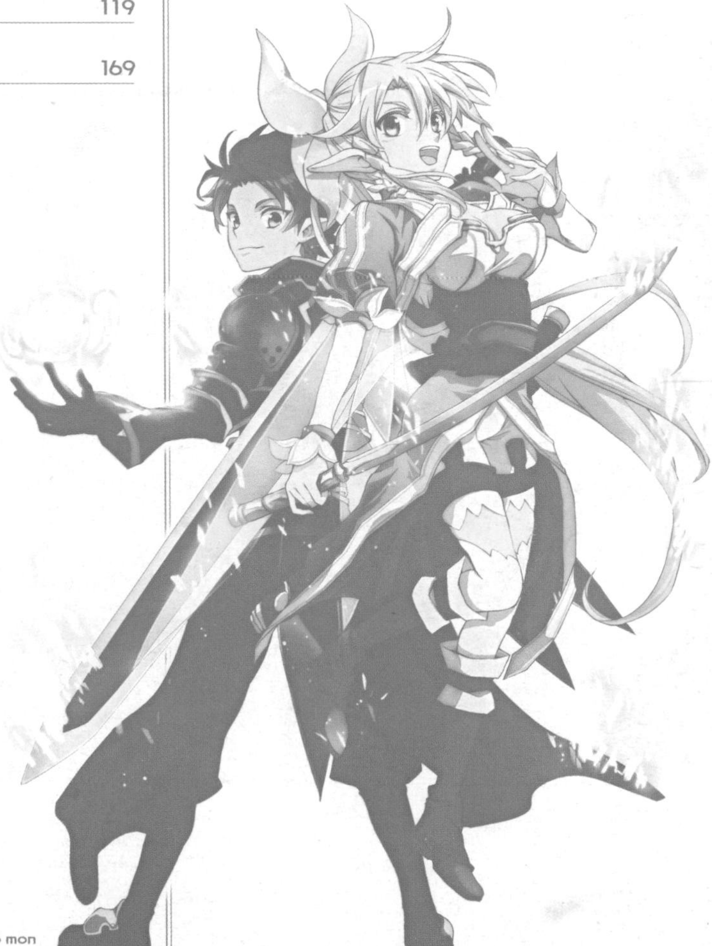

SWORD ART ONLINE

SWORD ART ONLINE fairy dance

001

SWORD ART ONLINE fairy dance

art : tsubasa haduki
original story : reki kawahara
character design : abec

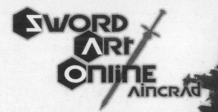

SWORD ART ONLINE AINCRAD

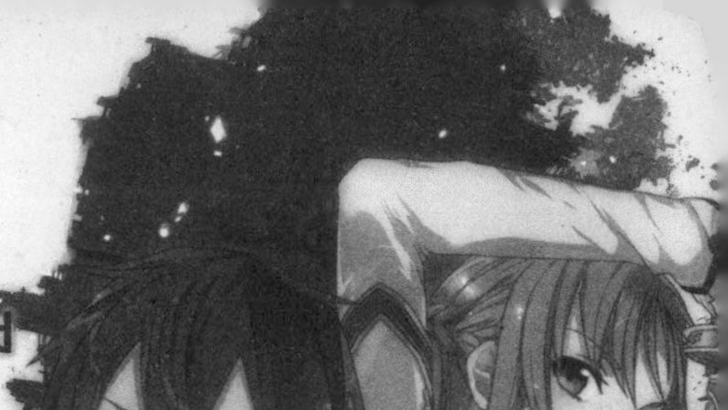

STORY SUMMARY

SWORD ART ONLINE IS A GAME OF DEATH DEVISED BY BRILLIANT PROGRAMMER AKIHIKO KAYABA. BUT THE FAIRY DANCE ARC BEGINS AFTER SAO WAS BEATEN...WHEN KIRITO, THE BLACK SWORDSMAN, LIVES A NORMAL LIFE AGAIN AS KAZUTO KIRIGAYA. LET'S REVISIT THE EVENTS OF WHAT HAPPENED IN AINCRAD TO PREPARE FOR KIRITO'S NEW JOURNEY!

THE GAME OF DEATH BEGINS 001

SWORD ART ONLINE AINCRAD

SWORD ART ONLINE, WHERE ESCAPE IS IMPOSSIBLE UNTIL THE CASTLE IS BEATEN AND GAME OVER MEANS REAL DEATH... THE DEADLY GAME BEGINS WITH 10,000 HELPLESS VICTIMS TRAPPED INSIDE. KIRITO ACCEPTS THE CHALLENGE BEFORE ANYONE ELSE AND HEADS OUT TO CONQUER THE GAME AS A SOLO PLAYER!

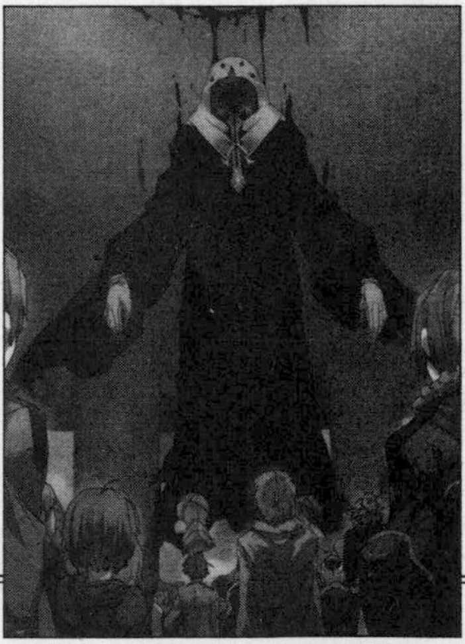

A ROBED FIGURE CLAIMING TO BE AKIHIKO KAYABA. AFTER HIS SPEECH, SAO IS NO LONGER JUST A GAME.

MEETING ASUNA 002

SWORD ART ONLINE AINCRAD

AFTER SURVIVING COUNTLESS BATTLES, KIRITO BECOMES FRIENDS WITH A FELLOW PLAYER. SHE IS ASUNA, NICKNAMED "THE FLASH," A TALENTED FIGHTER EVERY BIT KIRITO'S EQUAL. THEY DISAGREE AT TIMES, BUT AS THEY BATTLE TOGETHER, THEY GROW STEADILY CLOSER...

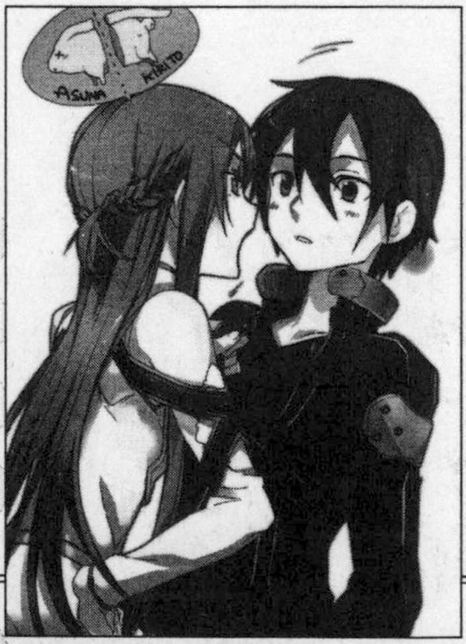
ASUNA
KIRITO

KIRITO REQUESTS A MEAL FROM ASUNA, WHO HAS MASTERED THE COOKING SKILL. HER PRICE: "H-A-L-F!"

MARRIAGE 003

SWORD ART ONLINE Aincrad

KIRITO AND ASUNA BARELY ESCAPE A DEVIOUS TRAP SET BY A CONNIVING FELLOW MEMBER OF HER GUILD, KURADEEL. THEY SWEAR TO PROTECT ONE ANOTHER AND SPEND THE NIGHT TOGETHER, THEN DECIDE TO LEAVE THE FRONT LINE OF SAO...AFTER GETTING "MARRIED," THEY START ON A NEW LIFE TOGETHER.

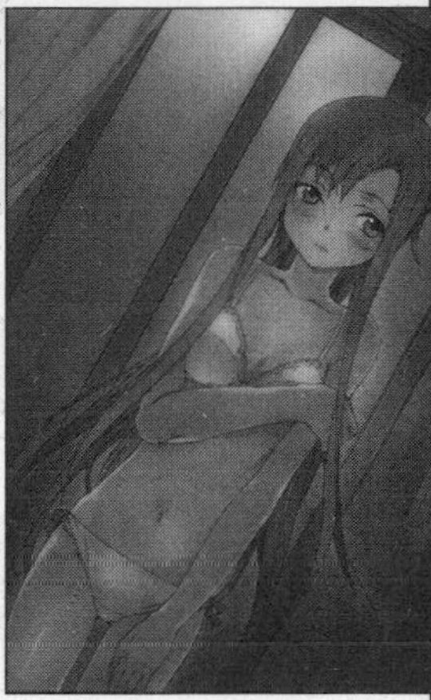

ASUNA MAKES THE BIGGEST DECISION OF HER LIFE. BUT KIRITO'S SO THICK, HER EFFORT IS WASTED...

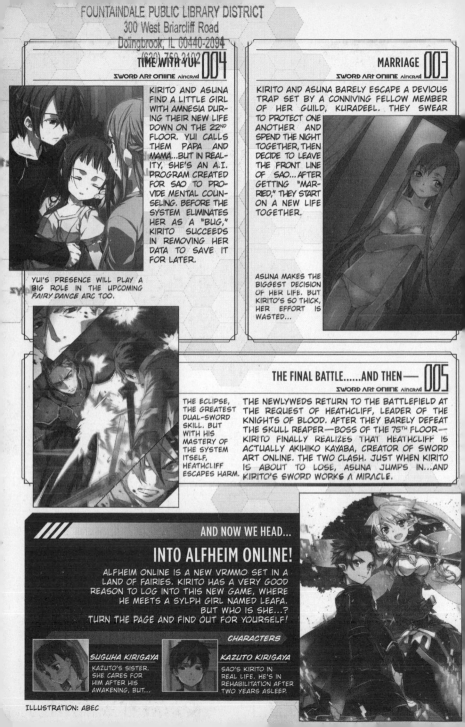

TIME WITH YUI 004

SWORD ART ONLINE Aincrad

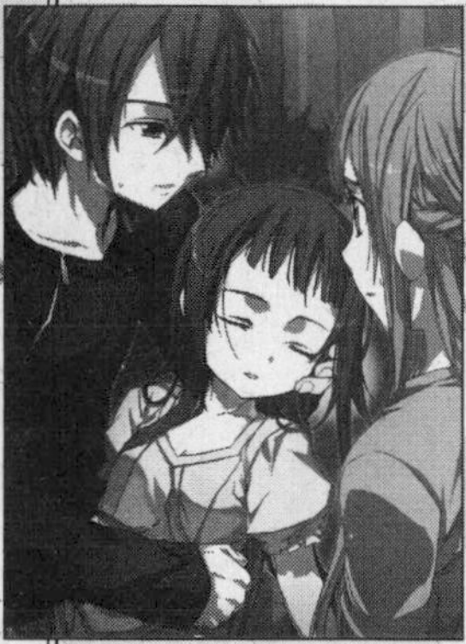

KIRITO AND ASUNA FIND A LITTLE GIRL WITH AMNESIA DURING THEIR NEW LIFE DOWN ON THE 22ND FLOOR. YUI CALLS THEM PAPA AND MAMA...BUT IN REALITY, SHE'S AN A.I. PROGRAM CREATED FOR SAO TO PROVIDE MENTAL COUNSELING. BEFORE THE SYSTEM ELIMINATES HER AS A "BUG," KIRITO SUCCEEDS IN REMOVING HER DATA TO SAVE IT FOR LATER.

YUI'S PRESENCE WILL PLAY A BIG ROLE IN THE UPCOMING *FAIRY DANCE* ARC TOO.

THE FINAL BATTLE......AND THEN— 005

SWORD ART ONLINE Aincrad

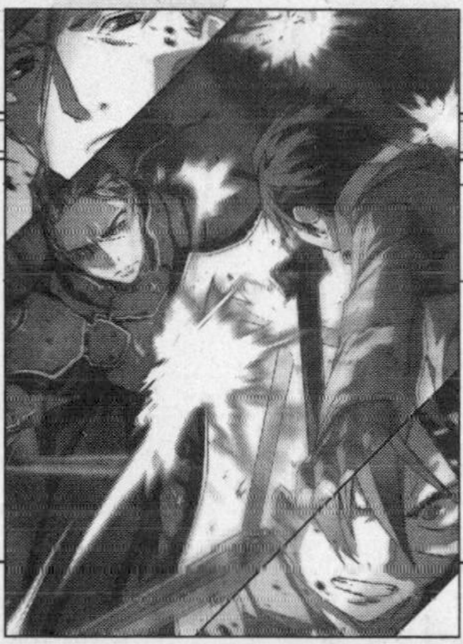

THE ECLIPSE, THE GREATEST DUAL-SWORD SKILL. BUT WITH HIS MASTERY OF THE SYSTEM ITSELF, HEATHCLIFF ESCAPES HARM.

THE NEWLYWEDS RETURN TO THE BATTLEFIELD AT THE REQUEST OF HEATHCLIFF, LEADER OF THE KNIGHTS OF BLOOD. AFTER THEY BARELY DEFEAT THE SKULL REAPER—BOSS OF THE 75TH FLOOR—KIRITO FINALLY REALIZES THAT HEATHCLIFF IS ACTUALLY AKIHIKO KAYABA, CREATOR OF SWORD ART ONLINE. THE TWO CLASH. JUST WHEN KIRITO IS ABOUT TO LOSE, ASUNA JUMPS IN...AND KIRITO'S SWORD WORKS A MIRACLE.

AND NOW WE HEAD...

INTO ALFHEIM ONLINE!

ALFHEIM ONLINE IS A NEW VRMMO SET IN A LAND OF FAIRIES. KIRITO HAS A VERY GOOD REASON TO LOG INTO THIS NEW GAME, WHERE HE MEETS A SYLPH GIRL NAMED LEAFA. BUT WHO IS SHE...? TURN THE PAGE AND FIND OUT FOR YOURSELF!

CHARACTERS

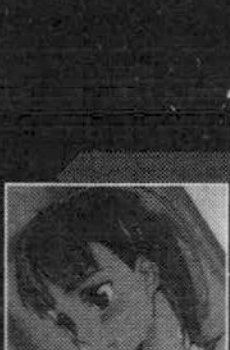

SUGUHA KIRIGAYA

KAZUTO'S SISTER. SHE CARES FOR HIM AFTER HIS AWAKENING, BUT...

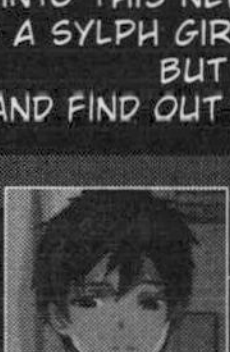

KAZUTO KIRIGAYA

SAO'S KIRITO IN REAL LIFE. HE'S IN REHABILITATION AFTER TWO YEARS ASLEEP.

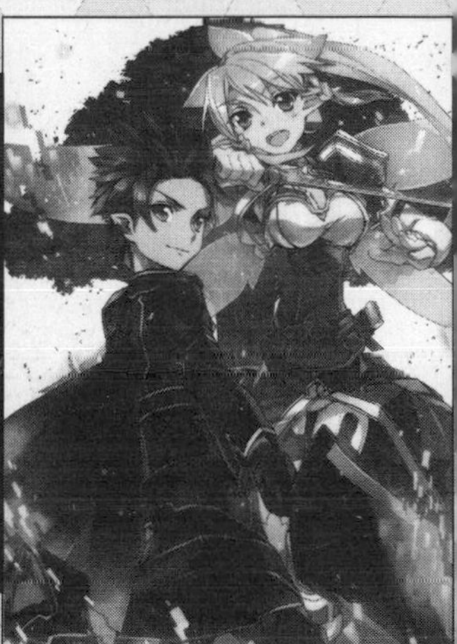

ILLUSTRATION: ABEC

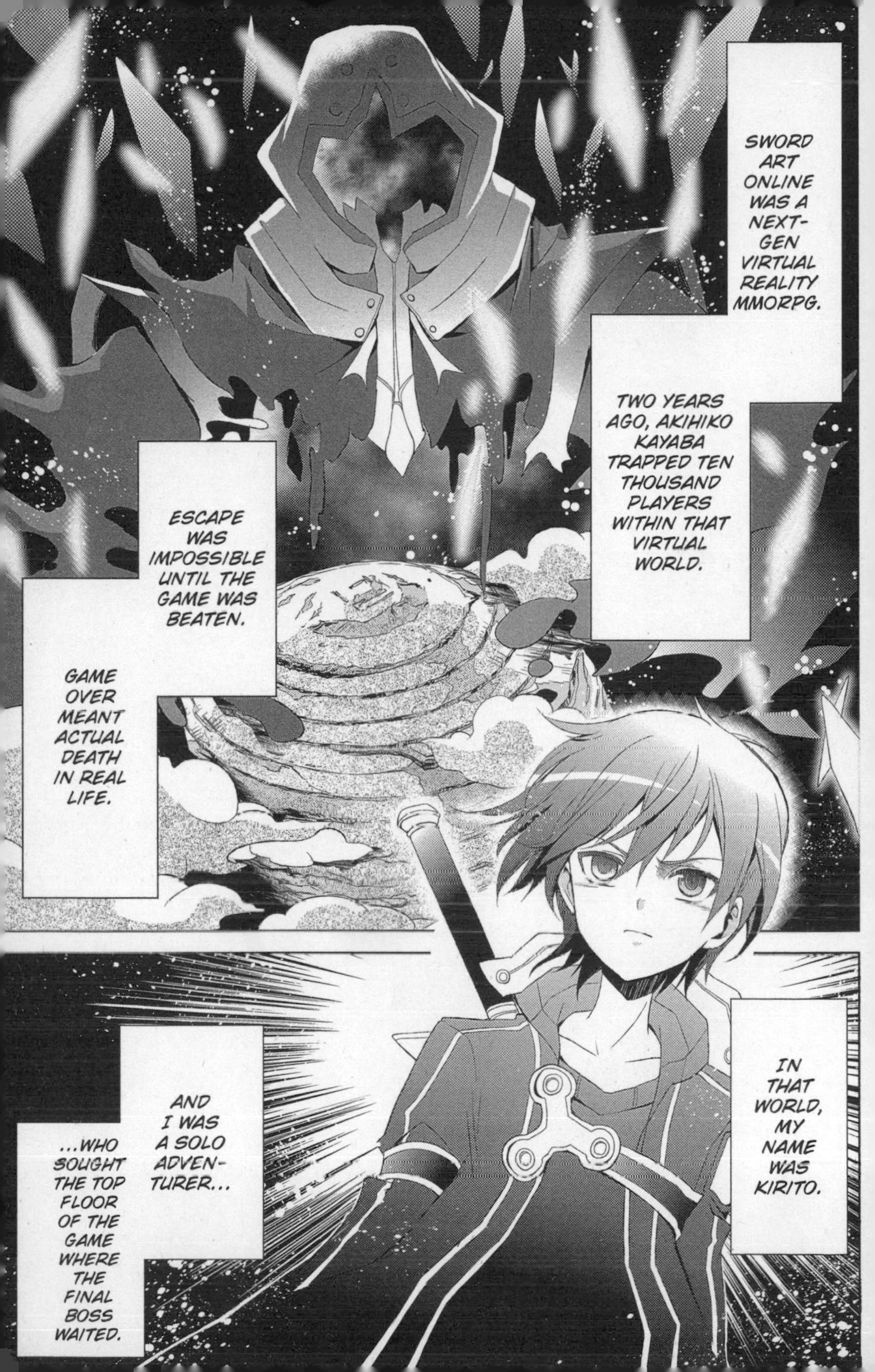
SWORD ART ONLINE WAS A NEXT-GEN VIRTUAL REALITY MMORPG.
TWO YEARS AGO, AKIHIKO KAYABA TRAPPED TEN THOUSAND PLAYERS WITHIN THAT VIRTUAL WORLD.
ESCAPE WAS IMPOSSIBLE UNTIL THE GAME WAS BEATEN.
GAME OVER MEANT ACTUAL DEATH IN REAL LIFE.
IN THAT WORLD, MY NAME WAS KIRITO.
AND I WAS A SOLO ADVEN-TURER...
...WHO SOUGHT THE TOP FLOOR OF THE GAME WHERE THE FINAL BOSS WAITED.

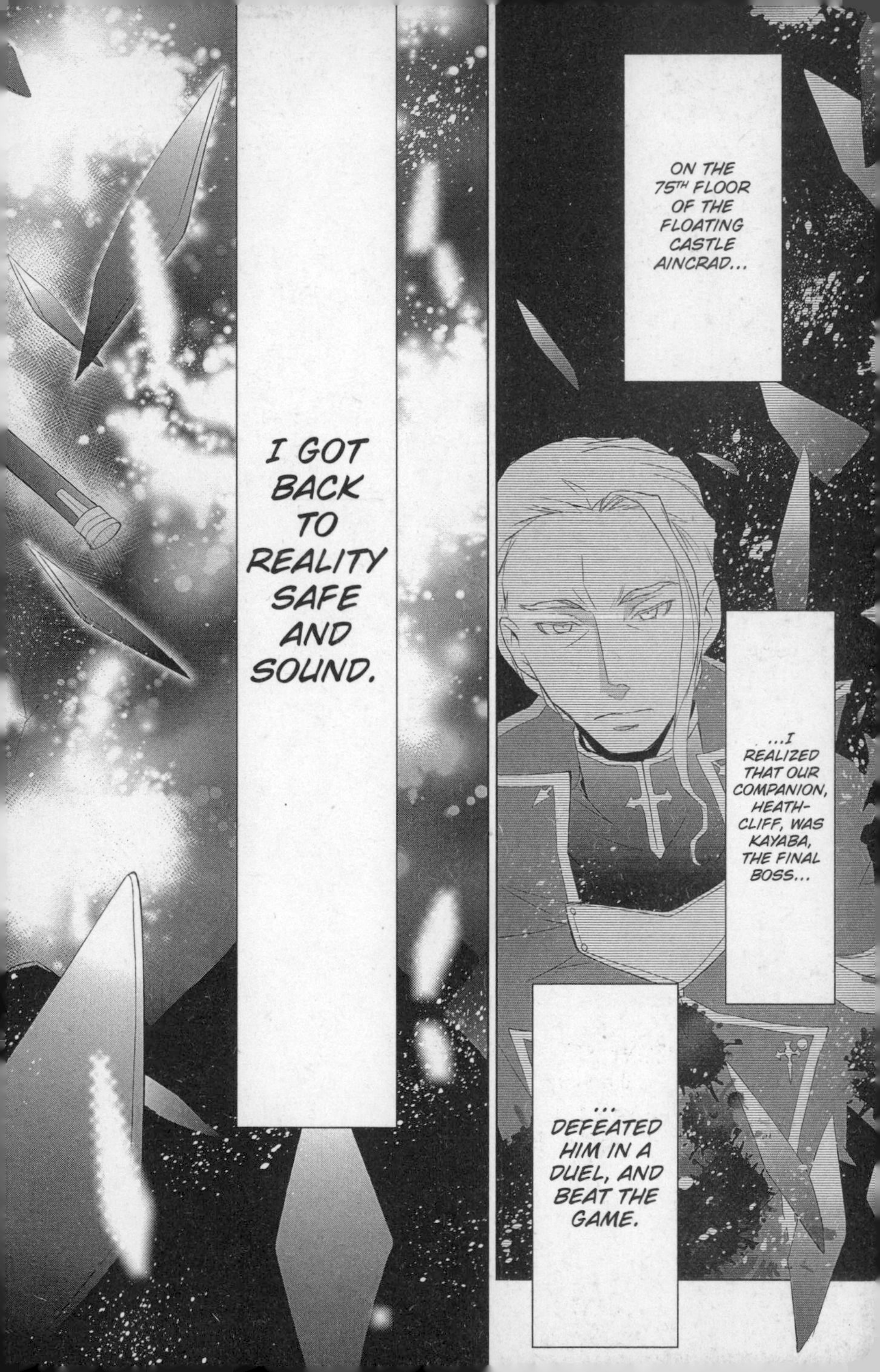
ON THE 75TH FLOOR OF THE FLOATING CASTLE AINCRAD...
...I REALIZED THAT OUR COMPANION, HEATH-CLIFF, WAS KAYABA, THE FINAL BOSS...
...DEFEATED HIM IN A DUEL, AND BEAT THE GAME.
I GOT BACK TO REALITY SAFE AND SOUND.

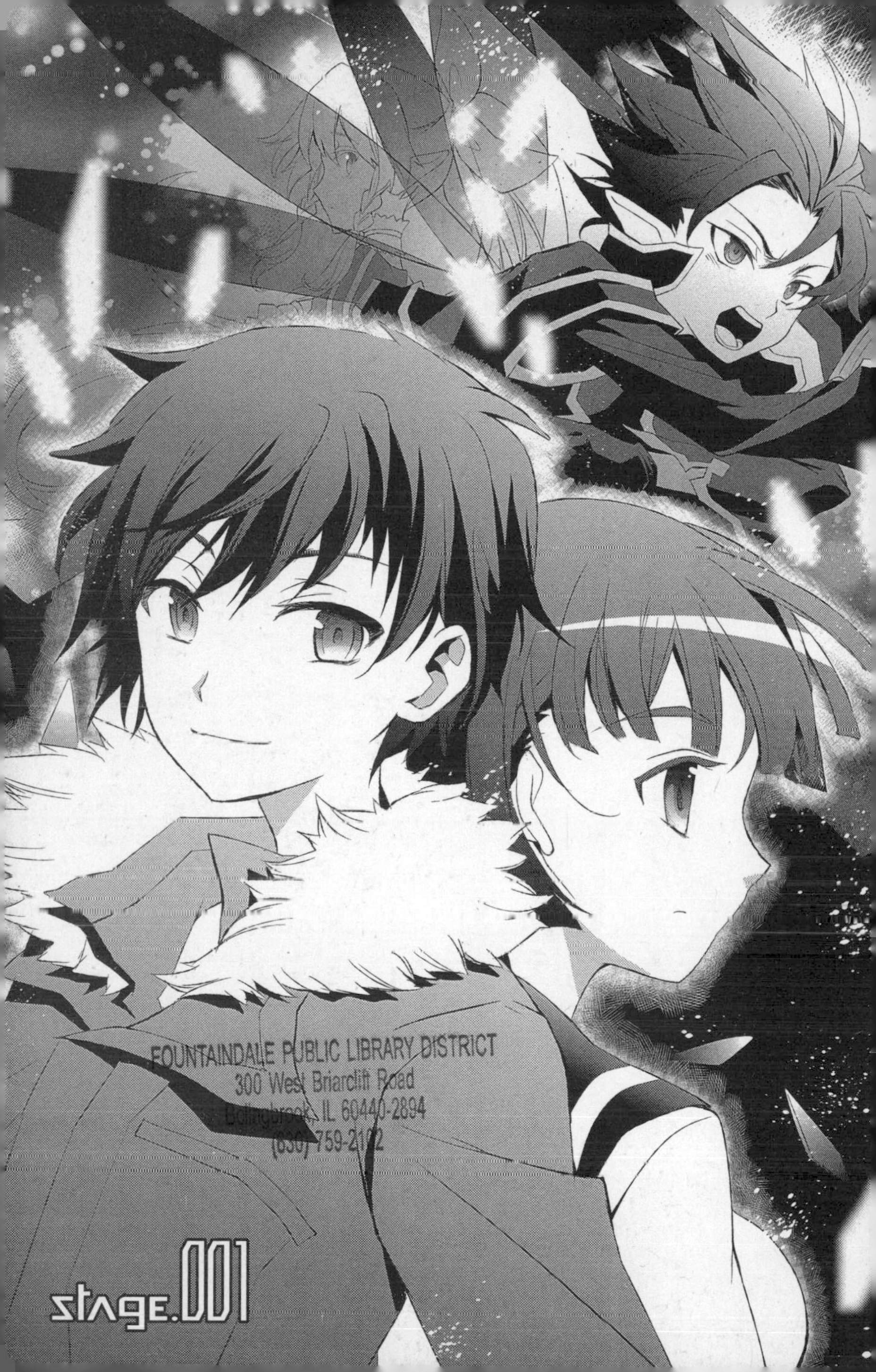
stage.001

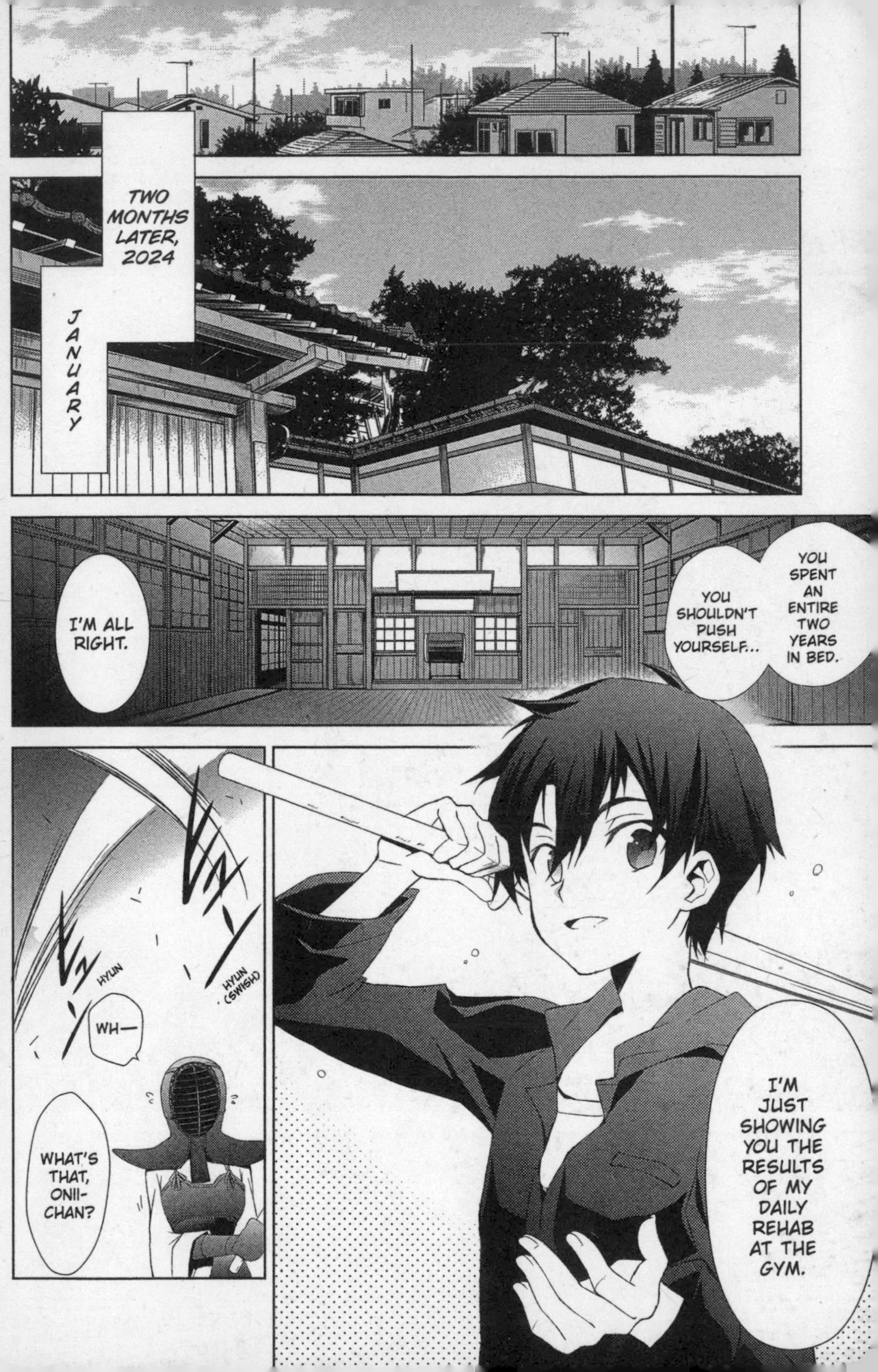
TWO MONTHS LATER, 2024
JANUARY
YOU SPENT AN ENTIRE TWO YEARS IN BED.
YOU SHOULDN'T PUSH YOURSELF...
I'M ALL RIGHT.
I'M JUST SHOWING YOU THE RESULTS OF MY DAILY REHAB AT THE GYM.
HYUN (SWISH)
HYUN
WH—
WHAT'S THAT, ONII-CHAN?

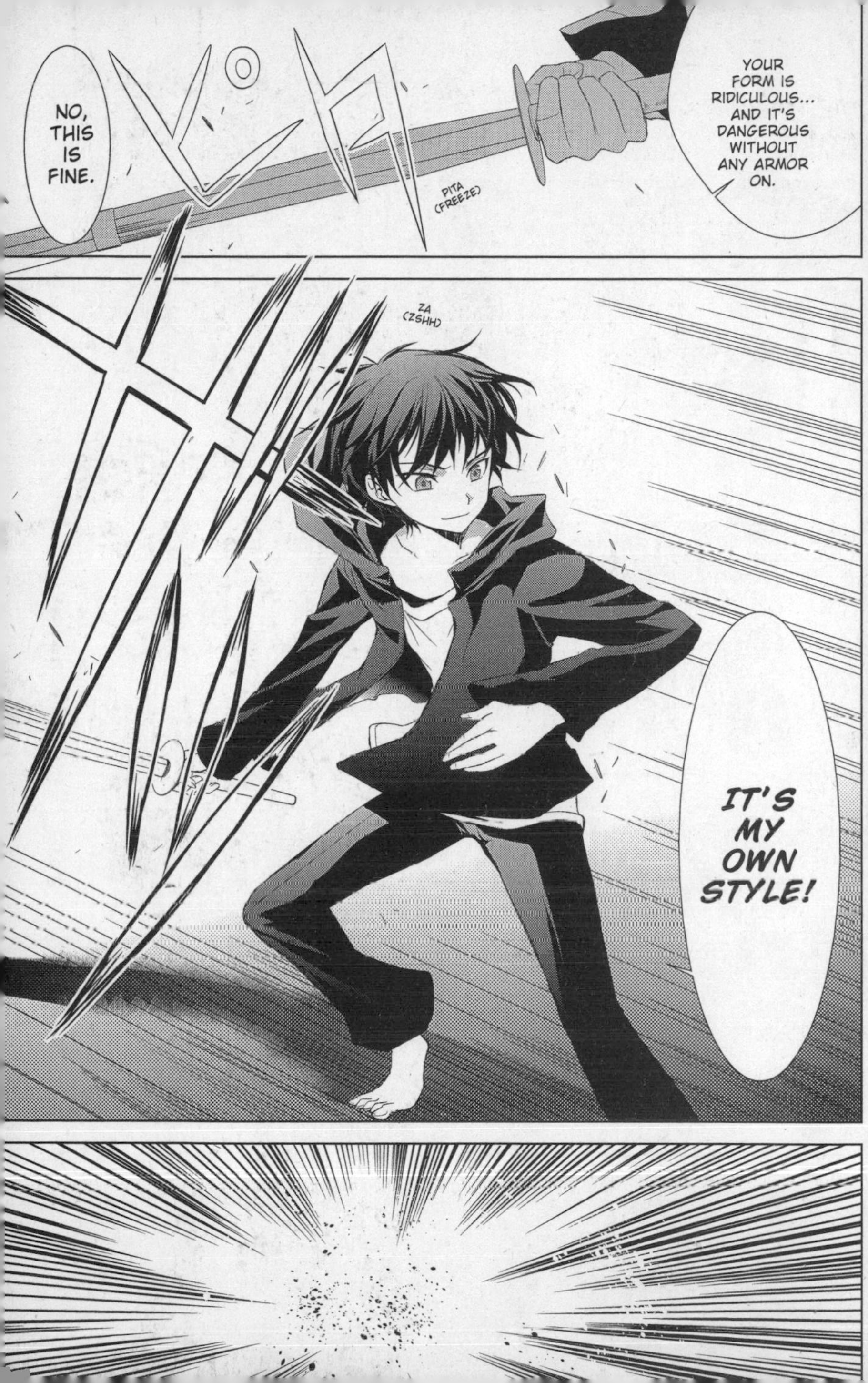
YOUR FORM IS RIDICULOUS... AND IT'S DANGEROUS WITHOUT ANY ARMOR ON.
PITA (FREEZE)
NO, THIS IS FINE.
ZA (ZSHH)
IT'S MY OWN STYLE!

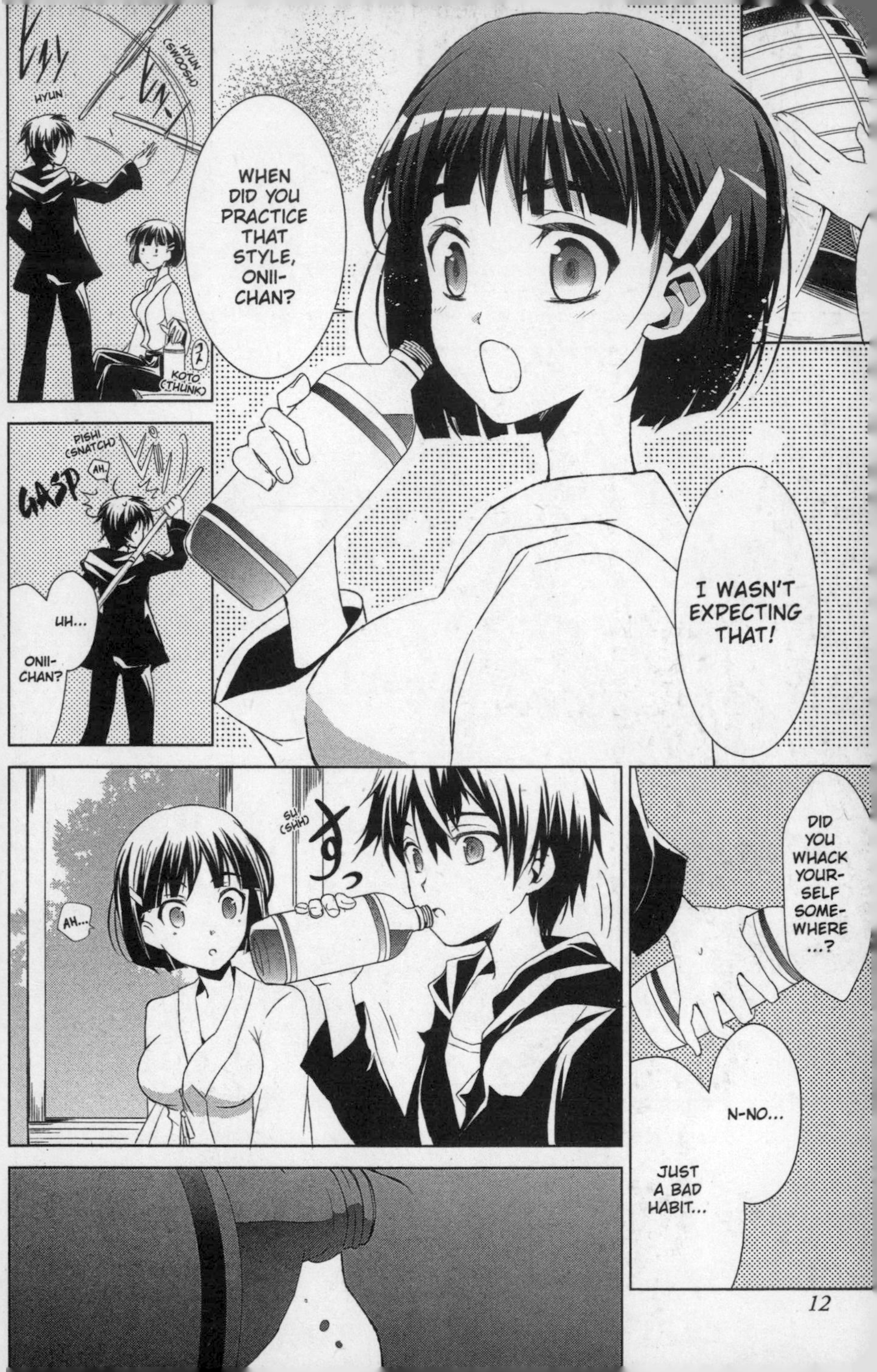
WHEN DID YOU PRACTICE THAT STYLE, ONII-CHAN?
I WASN'T EXPECTING THAT!
HYUN (SWOOSH)
HYUN
KOTO (THUNK)
PISHI (SNATCH)
AH.
GASP
UH...
ONII-CHAN?
DID YOU WHACK YOURSELF SOMEWHERE...?
N-NO...
JUST A BAD HABIT...
SU (SHH)
AH...

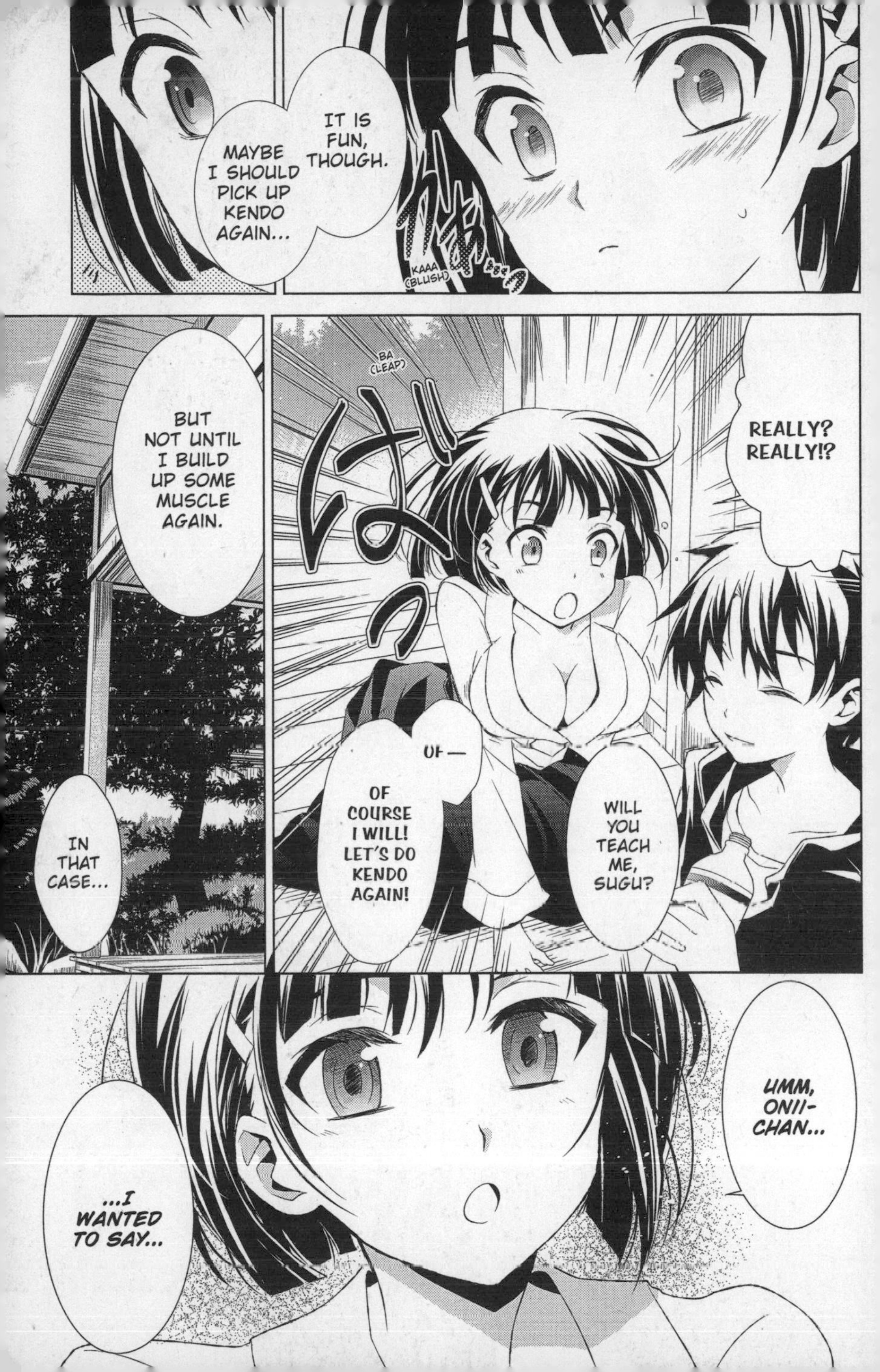
IT IS FUN, THOUGH.
KAAA (BLUSH)
MAYBE I SHOULD PICK UP KENDO AGAIN...
REALLY? REALLY!?
BA (LEAP)
WILL YOU TEACH ME, SUGU?
OF—
OF COURSE I WILL! LET'S DO KENDO AGAIN!
BUT NOT UNTIL I BUILD UP SOME MUSCLE AGAIN.
IN THAT CASE...
UMM, ONII-CHAN...
...I WANTED TO SAY...

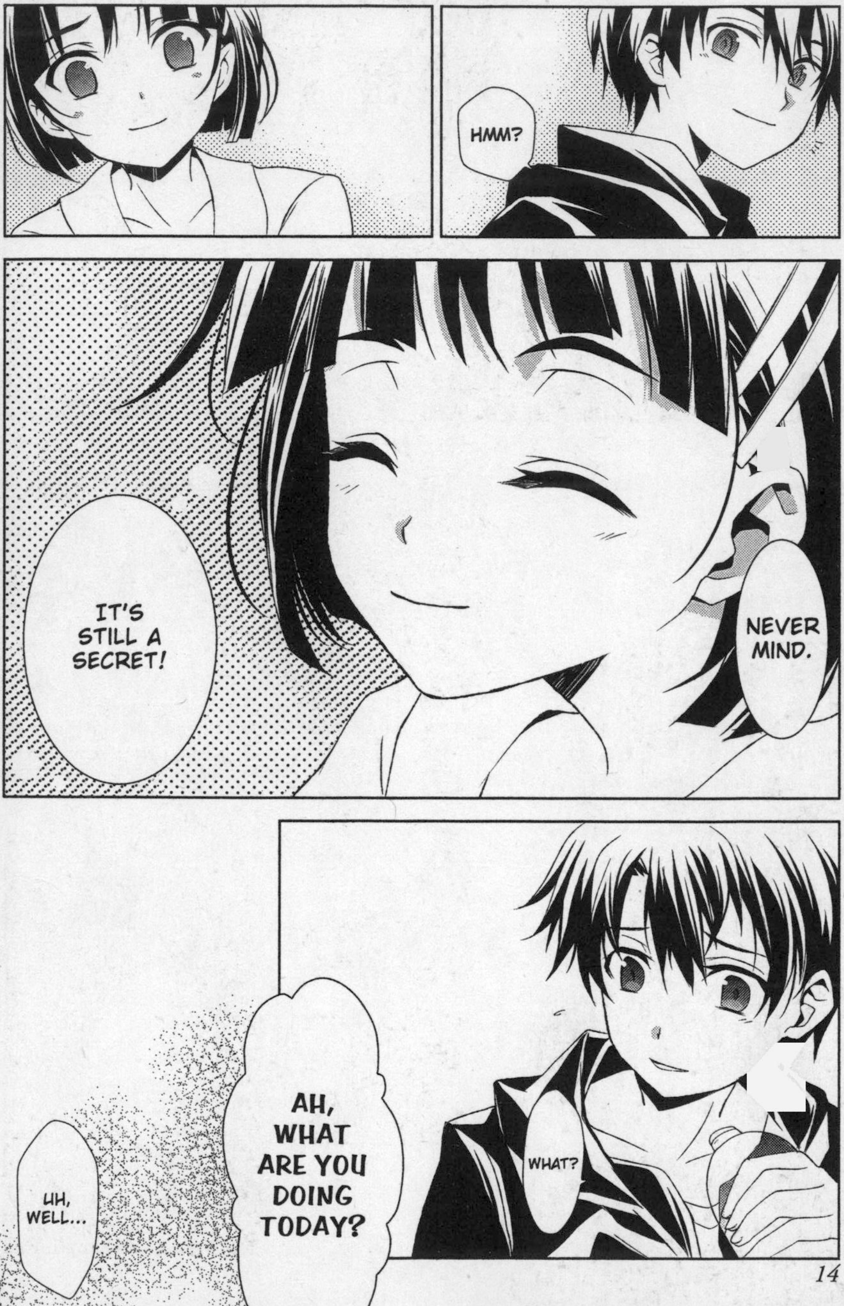
HMM?
NEVER MIND.
IT'S STILL A SECRET!
WHAT?
AH, WHAT ARE YOU DOING TODAY?
UH, WELL...

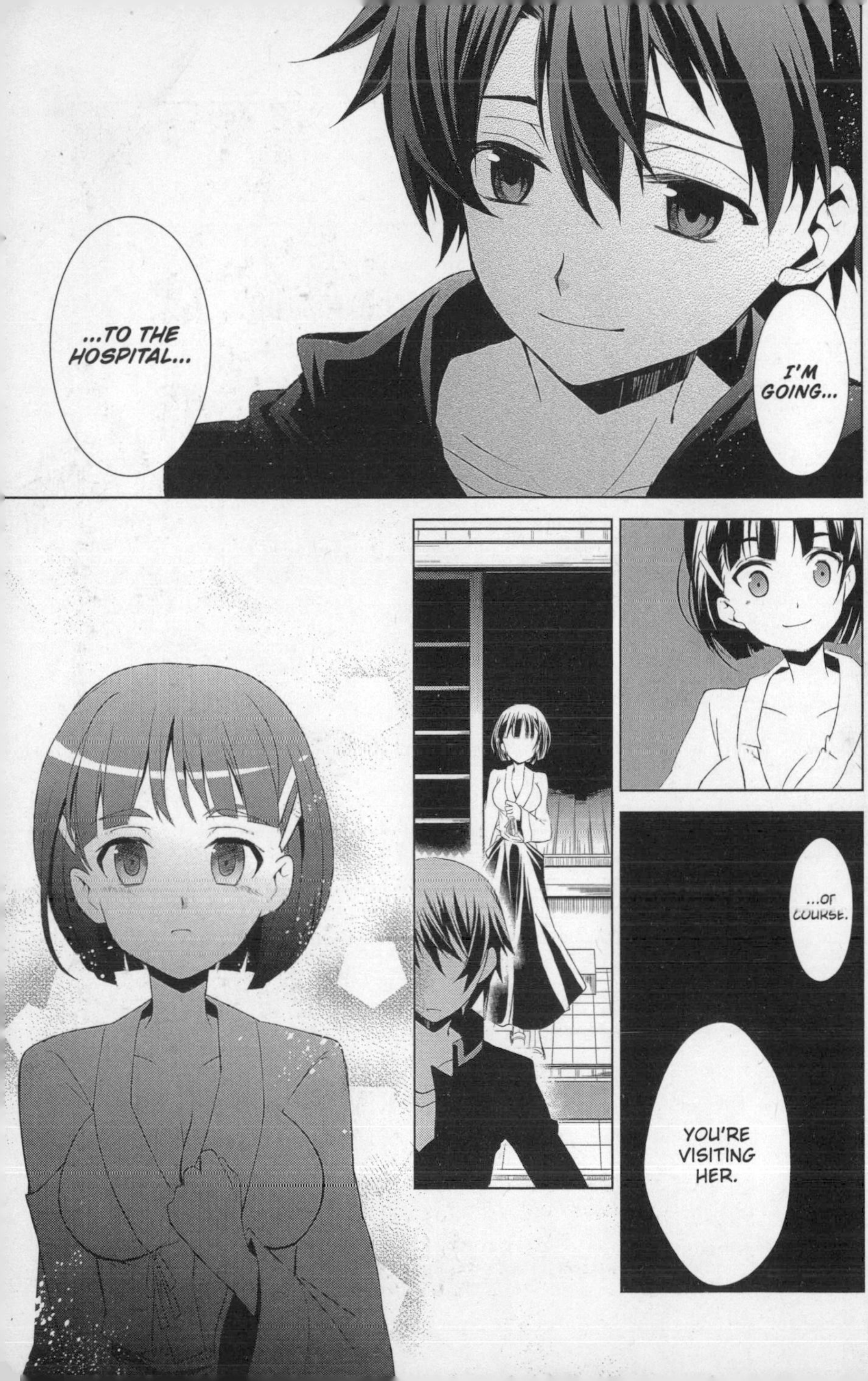
I'M GOING...
...TO THE HOSPITAL...
...OF COURSE.
YOU'RE VISITING HER.

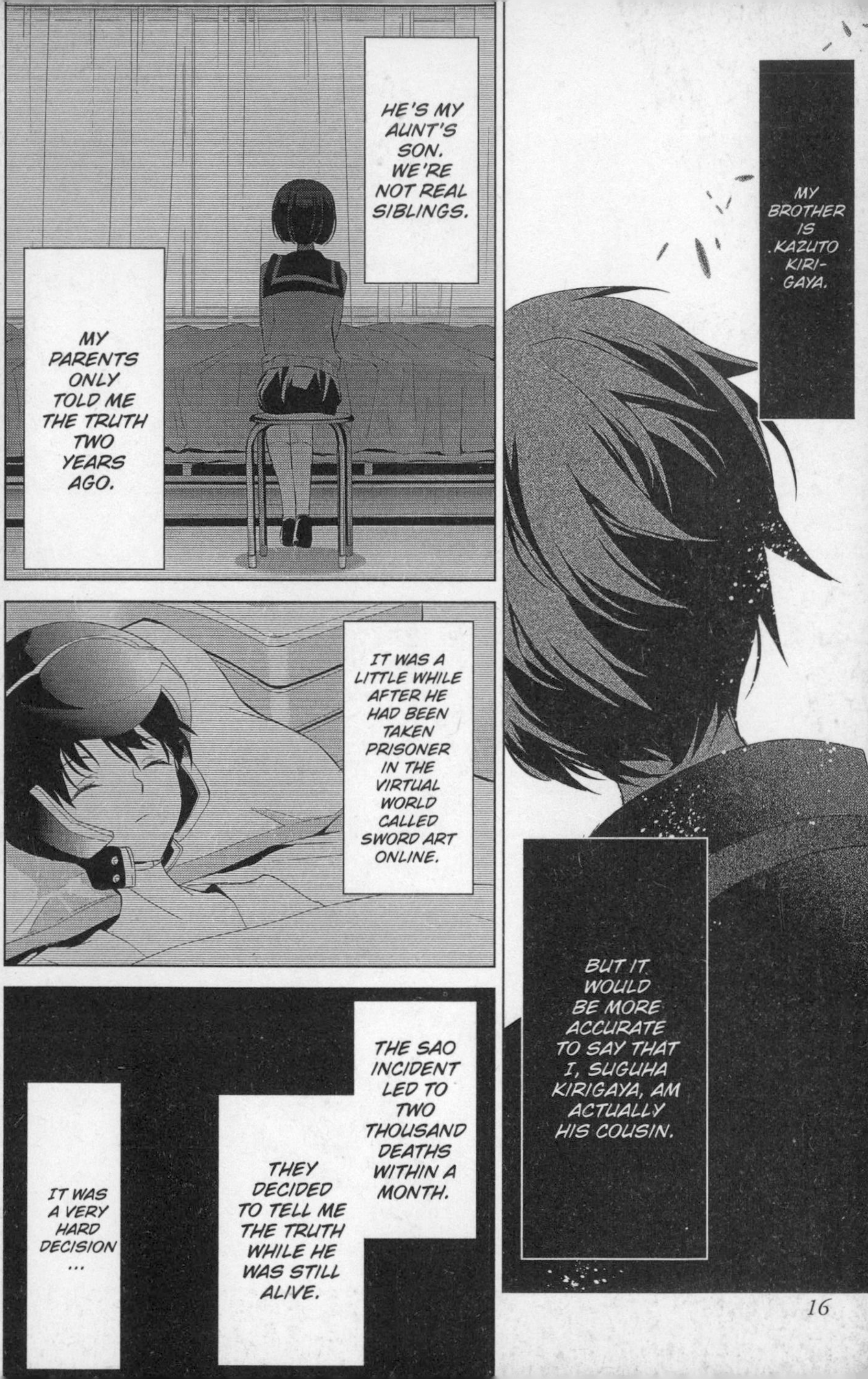
MY BROTHER IS KAZUTO KIRIGAYA.
BUT IT WOULD BE MORE ACCURATE TO SAY THAT I, SUGUHA KIRIGAYA, AM ACTUALLY HIS COUSIN.
HE'S MY AUNT'S SON. WE'RE NOT REAL SIBLINGS.
MY PARENTS ONLY TOLD ME THE TRUTH TWO YEARS AGO.
IT WAS A LITTLE WHILE AFTER HE HAD BEEN TAKEN PRISONER IN THE VIRTUAL WORLD CALLED SWORD ART ONLINE.
THE SAO INCIDENT LED TO TWO THOUSAND DEATHS WITHIN A MONTH.
THEY DECIDED TO TELL ME THE TRUTH WHILE HE WAS STILL ALIVE.
IT WAS A VERY HARD DECISION ...

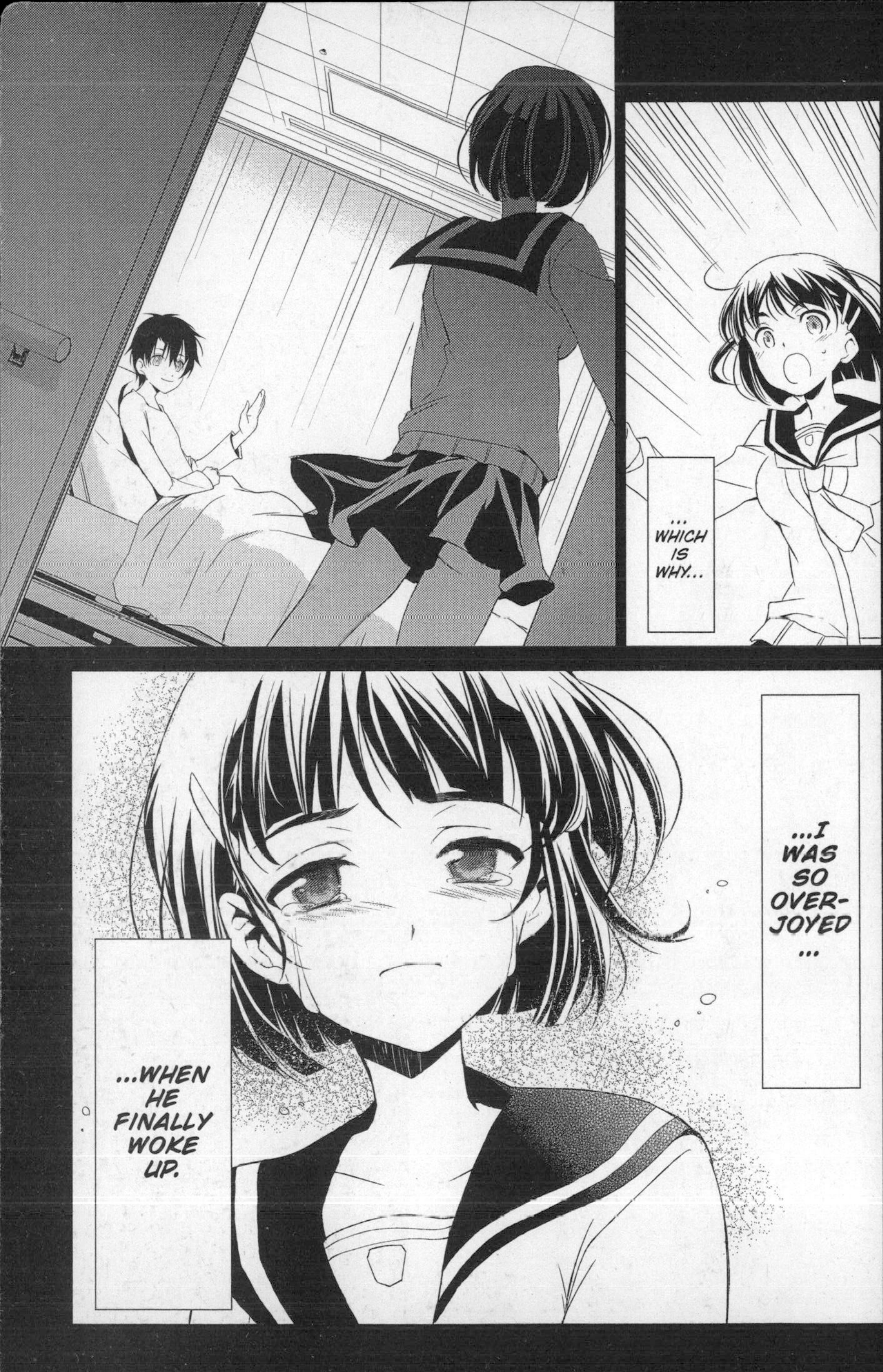
...WHICH IS WHY...
...I WAS SO OVER-JOYED...
...WHEN HE FINALLY WOKE UP.

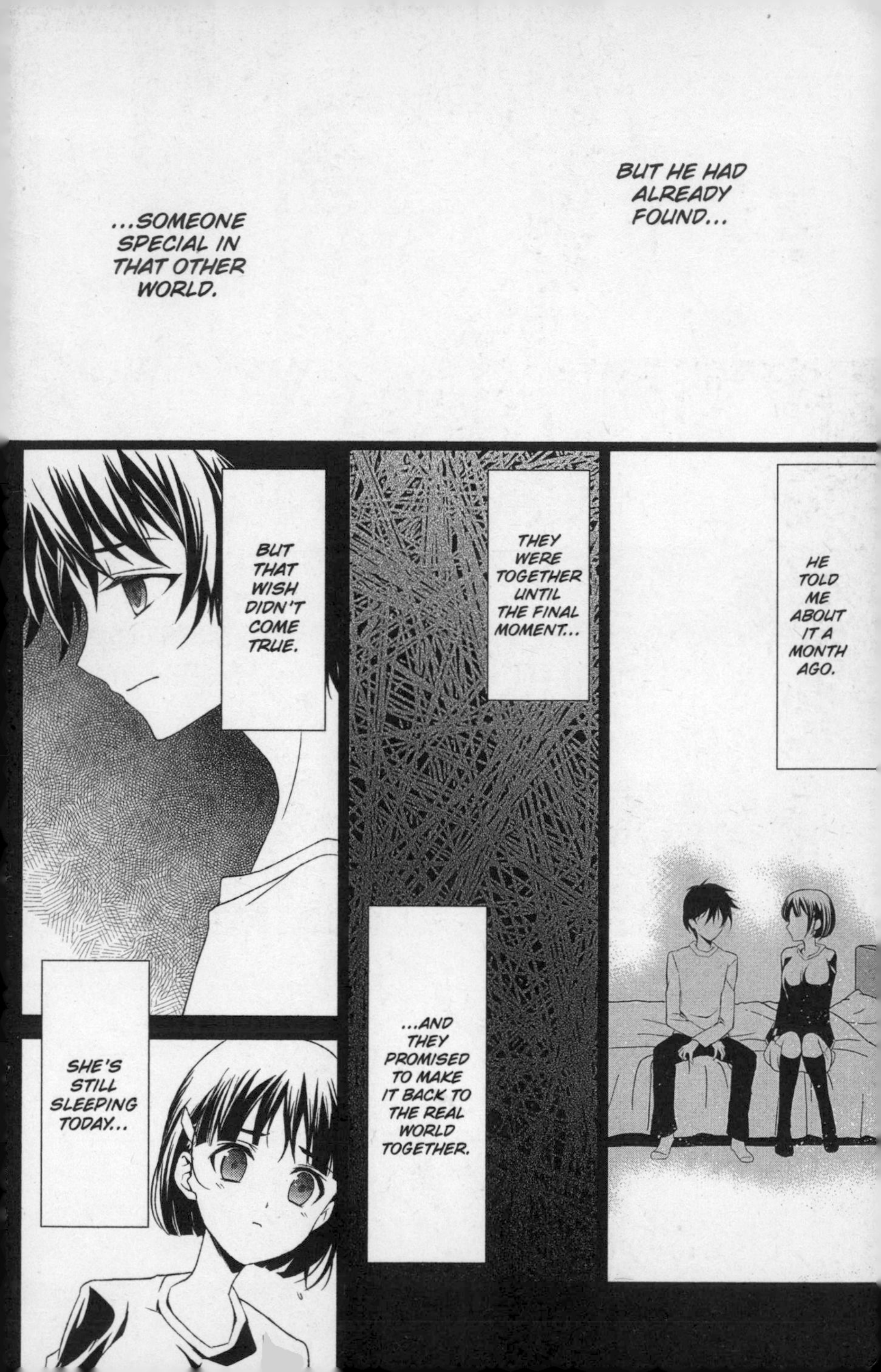
BUT HE HAD ALREADY FOUND...
...SOMEONE SPECIAL IN THAT OTHER WORLD.
HE TOLD ME ABOUT IT A MONTH AGO.
THEY WERE TOGETHER UNTIL THE FINAL MOMENT...
...AND THEY PROMISED TO MAKE IT BACK TO THE REAL WORLD TOGETHER.
BUT THAT WISH DIDN'T COME TRUE.
SHE'S STILL SLEEPING TODAY...

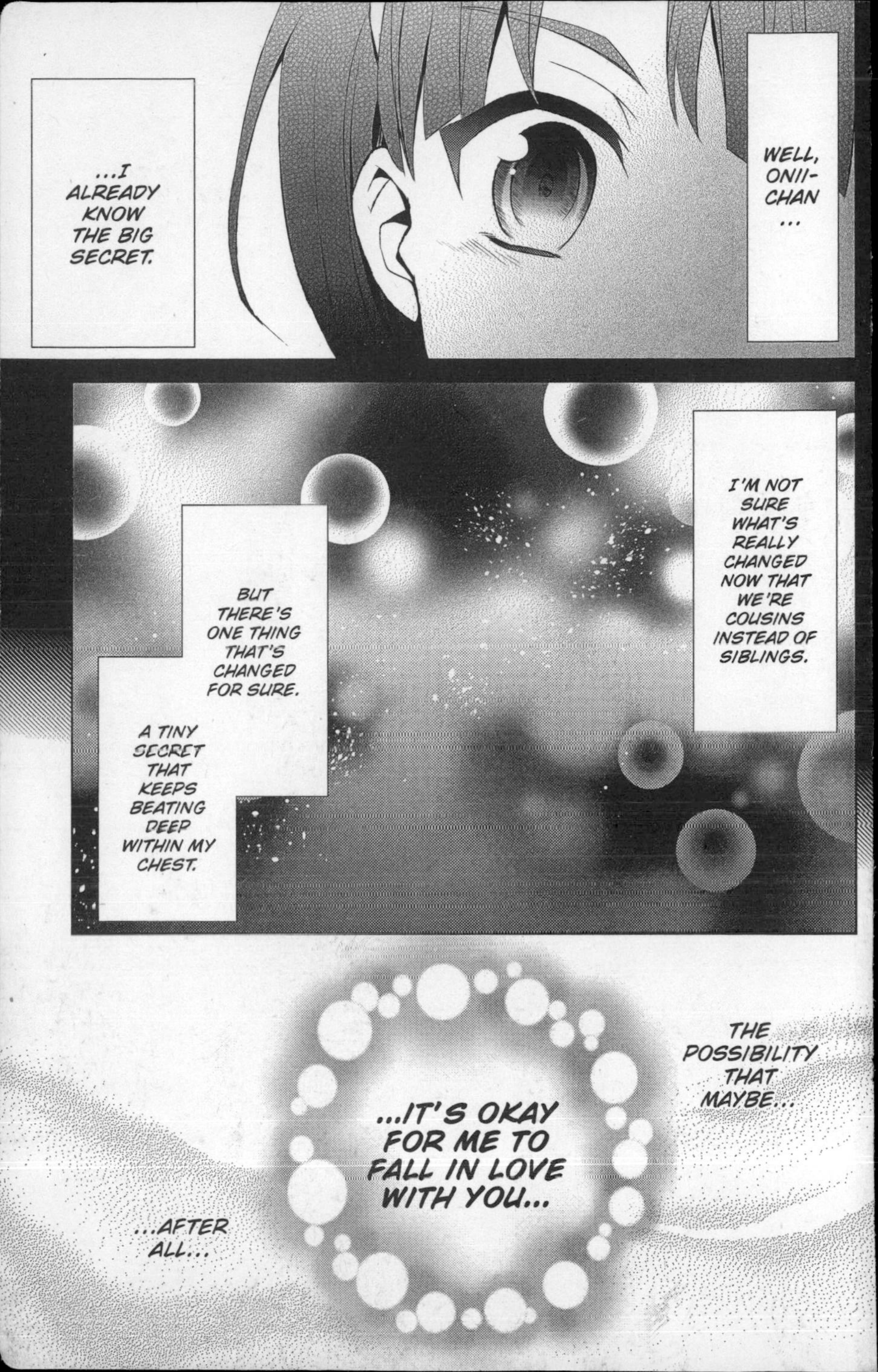
WELL, ONII-CHAN...
...I ALREADY KNOW THE BIG SECRET.
I'M NOT SURE WHAT'S REALLY CHANGED NOW THAT WE'RE COUSINS INSTEAD OF SIBLINGS.
BUT THERE'S ONE THING THAT'S CHANGED FOR SURE.
A TINY SECRET THAT KEEPS BEATING DEEP WITHIN MY CHEST.
THE POSSIBILITY THAT MAYBE...
...IT'S OKAY FOR ME TO FALL IN LOVE WITH YOU...
...AFTER ALL...

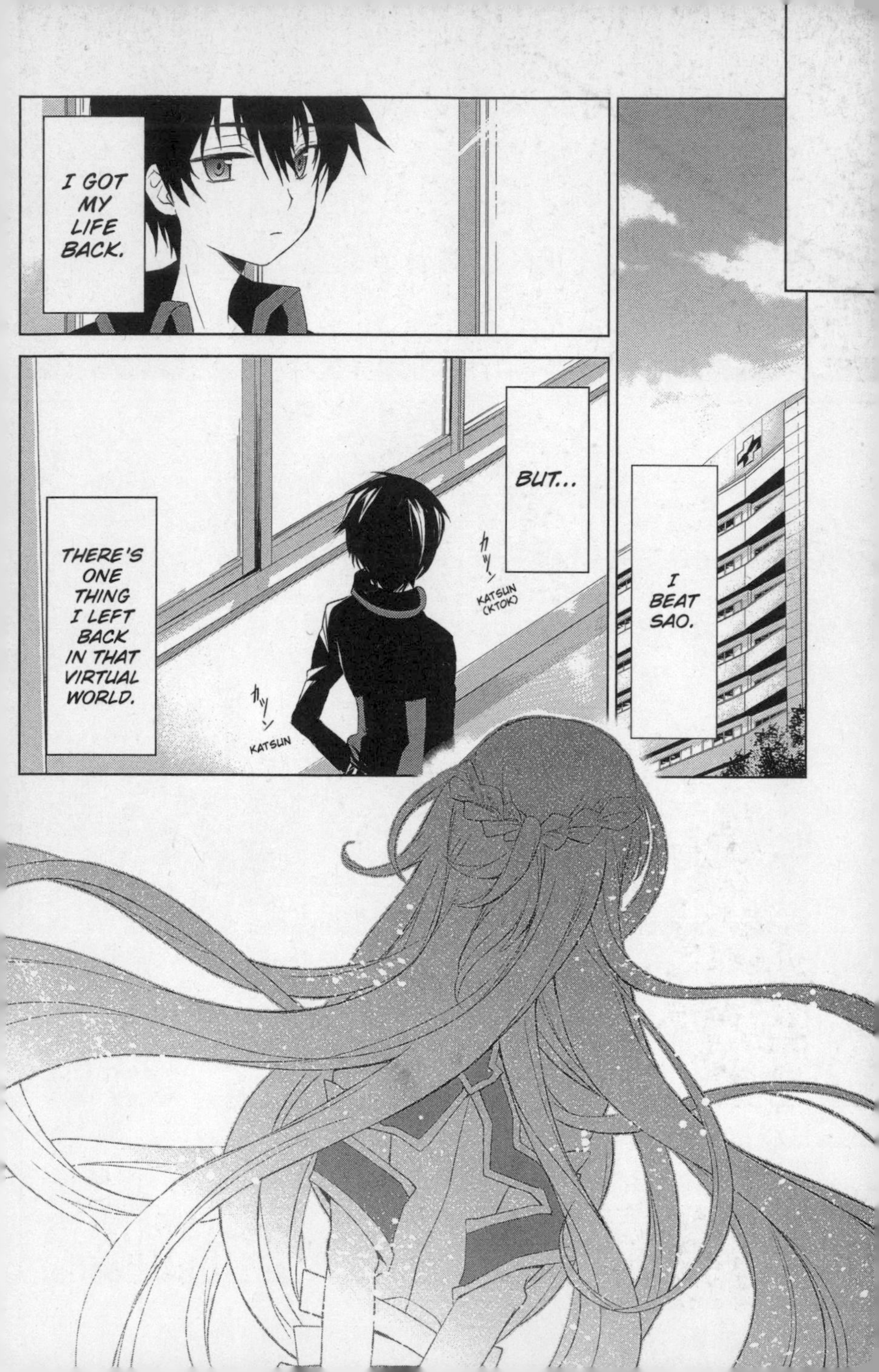
I BEAT SAO.
I GOT MY LIFE BACK.
BUT...
カツン
KATSUN (KTOK)
THERE'S ONE THING I LEFT BACK IN THAT VIRTUAL WORLD.
カツン
KATSUN

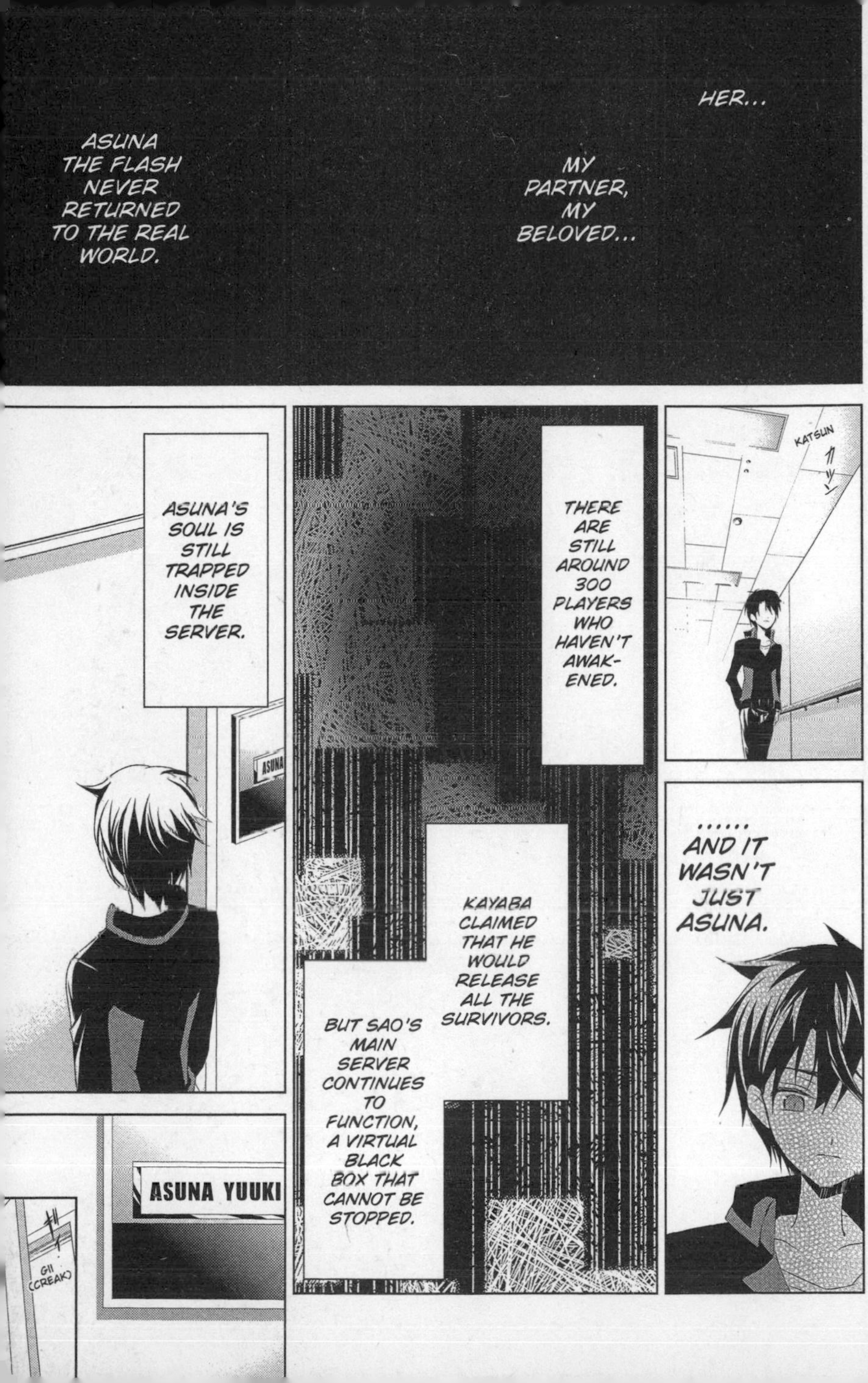
HER...
MY PARTNER, MY BELOVED...
ASUNA THE FLASH NEVER RETURNED TO THE REAL WORLD.
KATSUN
...... AND IT WASN'T JUST ASUNA.
THERE ARE STILL AROUND 300 PLAYERS WHO HAVEN'T AWAKENED.
KAYABA CLAIMED THAT HE WOULD RELEASE ALL THE SURVIVORS.
BUT SAO'S MAIN SERVER CONTINUES TO FUNCTION, A VIRTUAL BLACK BOX THAT CANNOT BE STOPPED.
ASUNA'S SOUL IS STILL TRAPPED INSIDE THE SERVER.
ASUNA YUUKI
GII (CREAK)

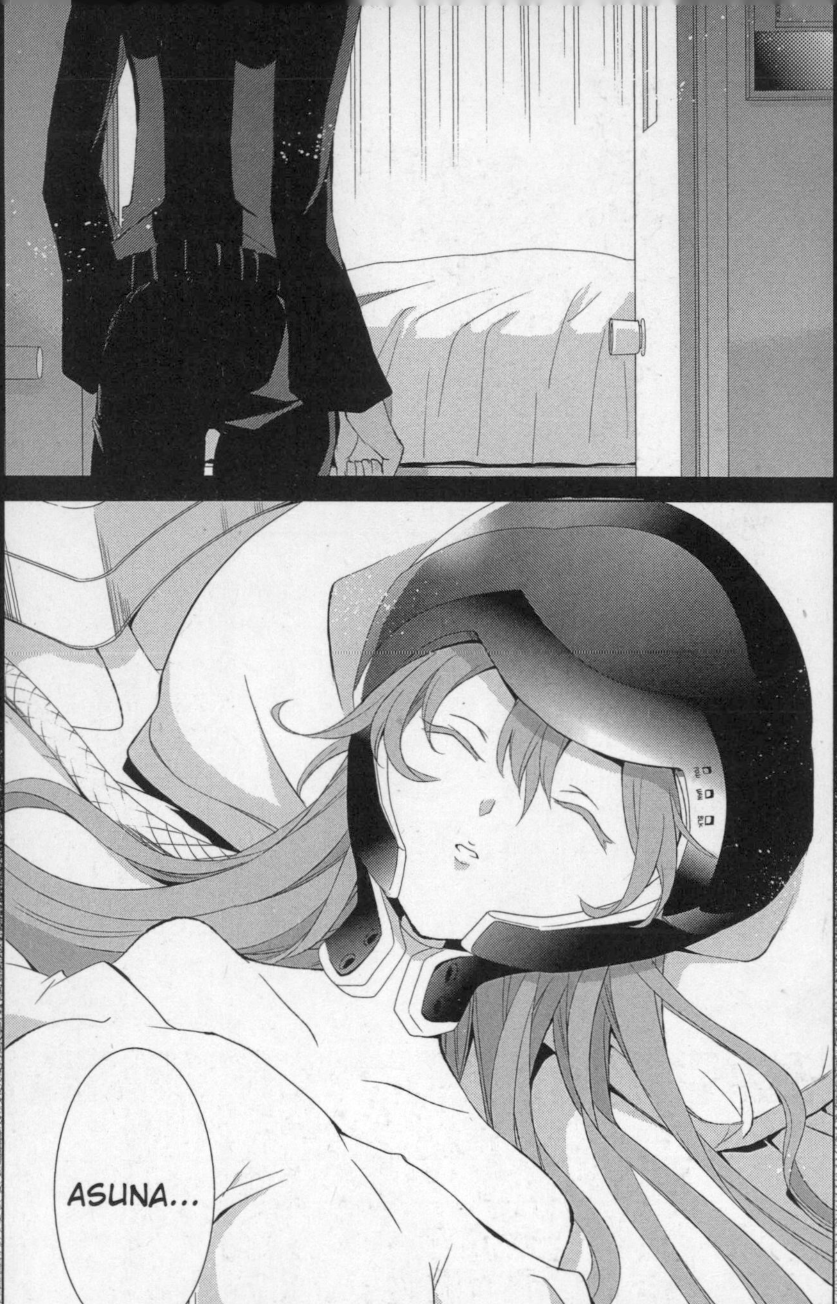
ASUNA...

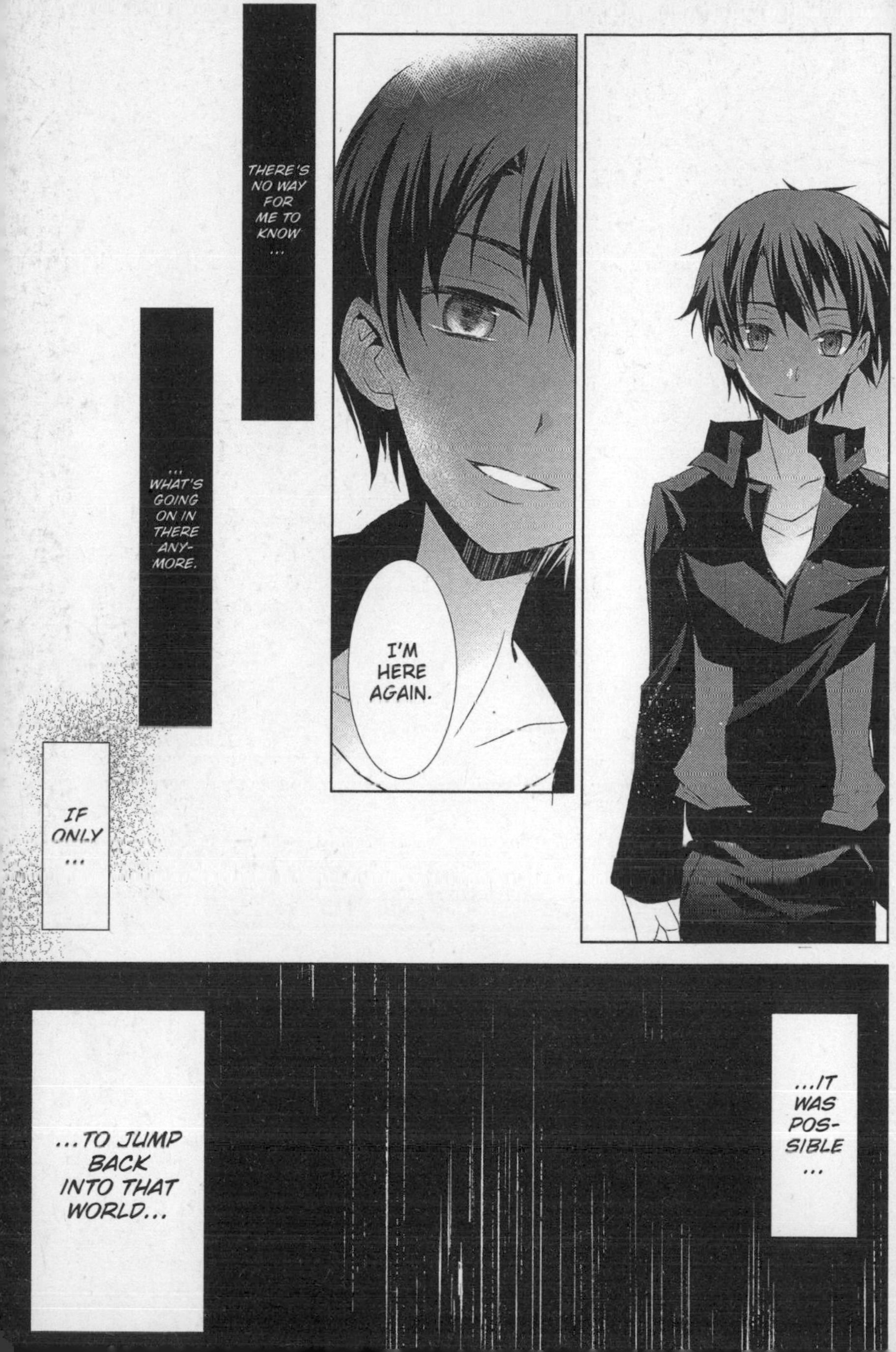
I'M HERE AGAIN.
THERE'S NO WAY FOR ME TO KNOW...
...WHAT'S GOING ON IN THERE ANYMORE.
IF ONLY...
...IT WAS POSSIBLE...
...TO JUMP BACK INTO THAT WORLD...

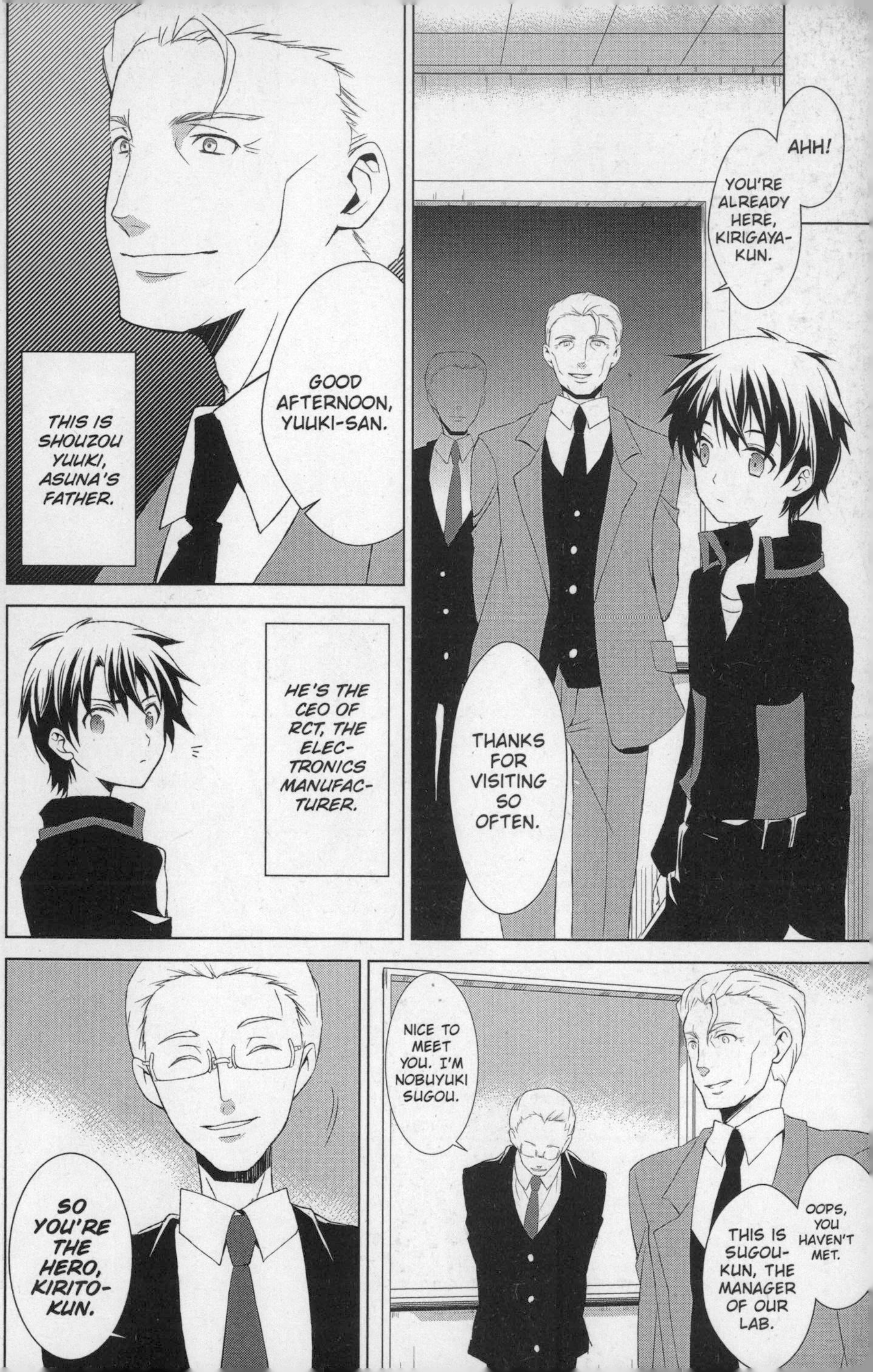
AHH! YOU'RE ALREADY HERE, KIRIGAYA-KUN.
THANKS FOR VISITING SO OFTEN.
GOOD AFTERNOON, YUUKI-SAN.
THIS IS SHOUZOU YUUKI, ASUNA'S FATHER.
HE'S THE CEO OF RCT, THE ELEC-TRONICS MANUFAC-TURER.
OOPS, YOU HAVEN'T MET.
THIS IS SUGOU-KUN, THE MANAGER OF OUR LAB.
NICE TO MEET YOU. I'M NOBUYUKI SUGOU.
SO YOU'RE THE HERO, KIRITO-KUN.

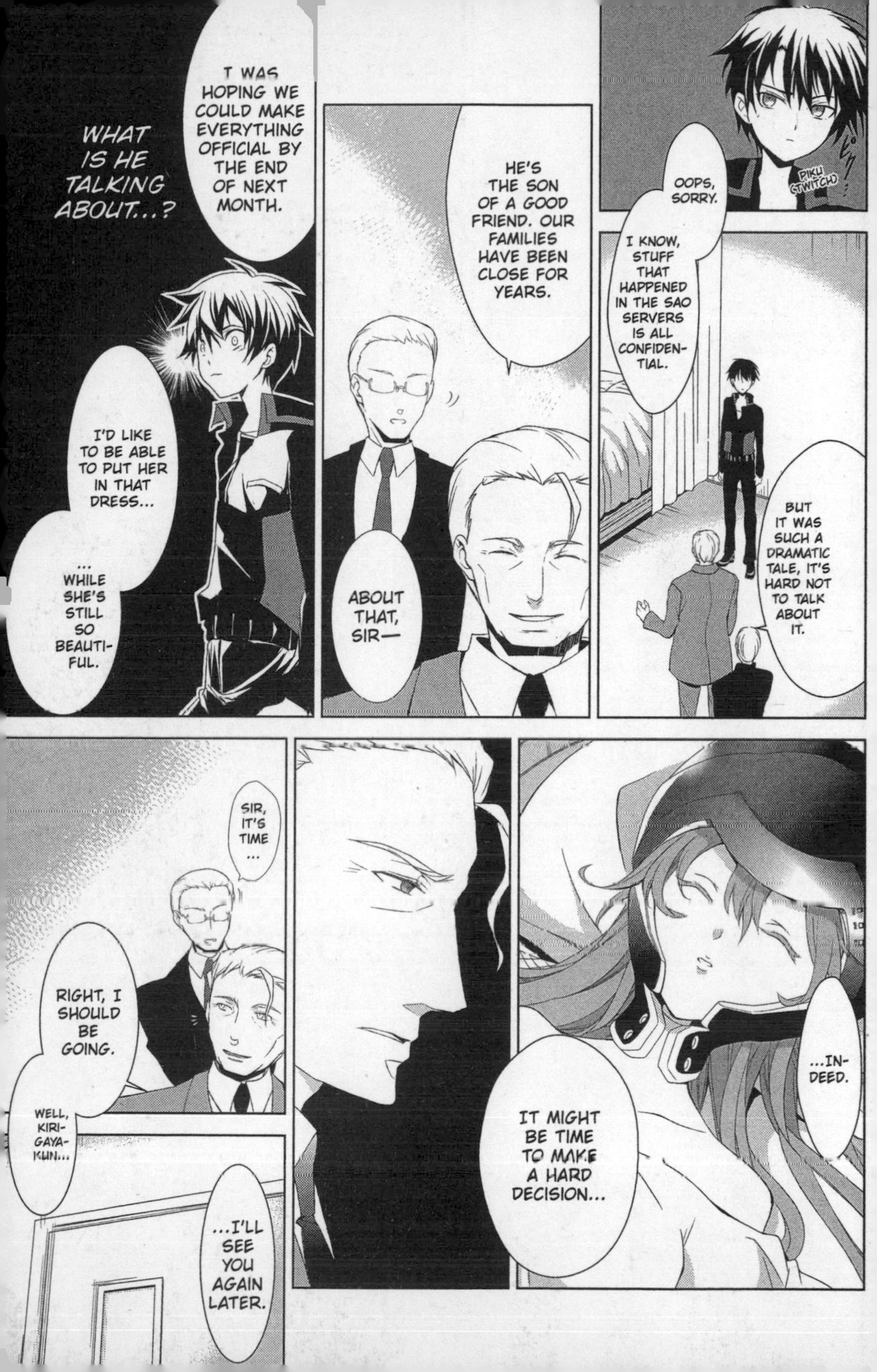

PIKU (TWITCH)
OOPS, SORRY.
I KNOW, STUFF THAT HAPPENED IN THE SAO SERVERS IS ALL CONFIDEN-TIAL.
BUT IT WAS SUCH A DRAMATIC TALE, IT'S HARD NOT TO TALK ABOUT IT.
HE'S THE SON OF A GOOD FRIEND. OUR FAMILIES HAVE BEEN CLOSE FOR YEARS.
ABOUT THAT, SIR—
I WAS HOPING WE COULD MAKE EVERYTHING OFFICIAL BY THE END OF NEXT MONTH.
WHAT IS HE TALKING ABOUT...?
I'D LIKE TO BE ABLE TO PUT HER IN THAT DRESS...
...WHILE SHE'S STILL SO BEAUTI-FUL.
...IN-DEED.
IT MIGHT BE TIME TO MAKE A HARD DECISION...
SIR, IT'S TIME...
RIGHT, I SHOULD BE GOING.
WELL, KIRI-GAYA-KUN...
...I'LL SEE YOU AGAIN LATER.

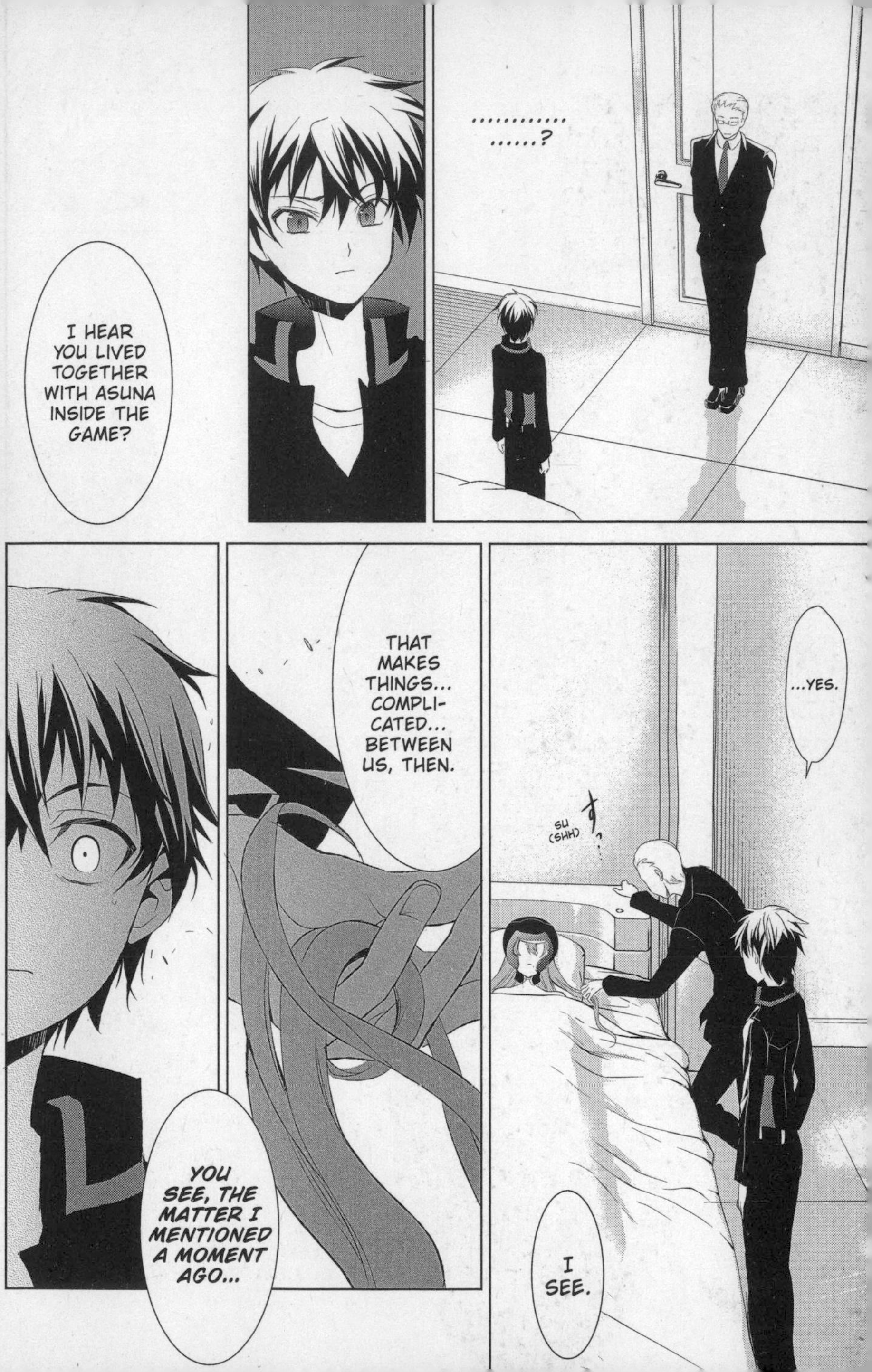
....
......?
I HEAR YOU LIVED TOGETHER WITH ASUNA INSIDE THE GAME?
...YES.
SU (SHH)
I SEE.
THAT MAKES THINGS... COMPLICATED... BETWEEN US, THEN.
YOU SEE, THE MATTER I MENTIONED A MOMENT AGO...

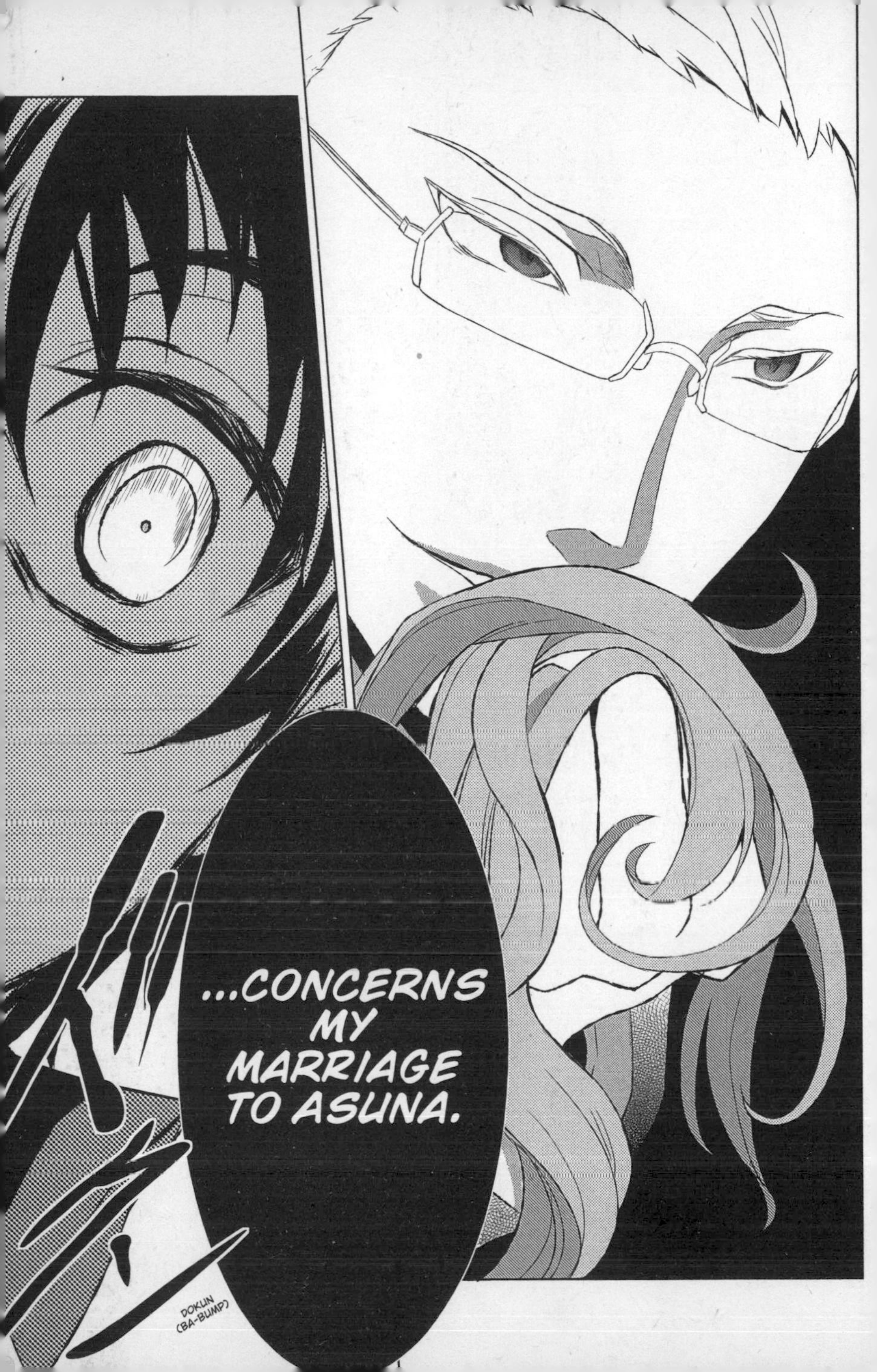
...CONCERNS MY MARRIAGE TO ASUNA.
DOKUN (BA-BUMP)

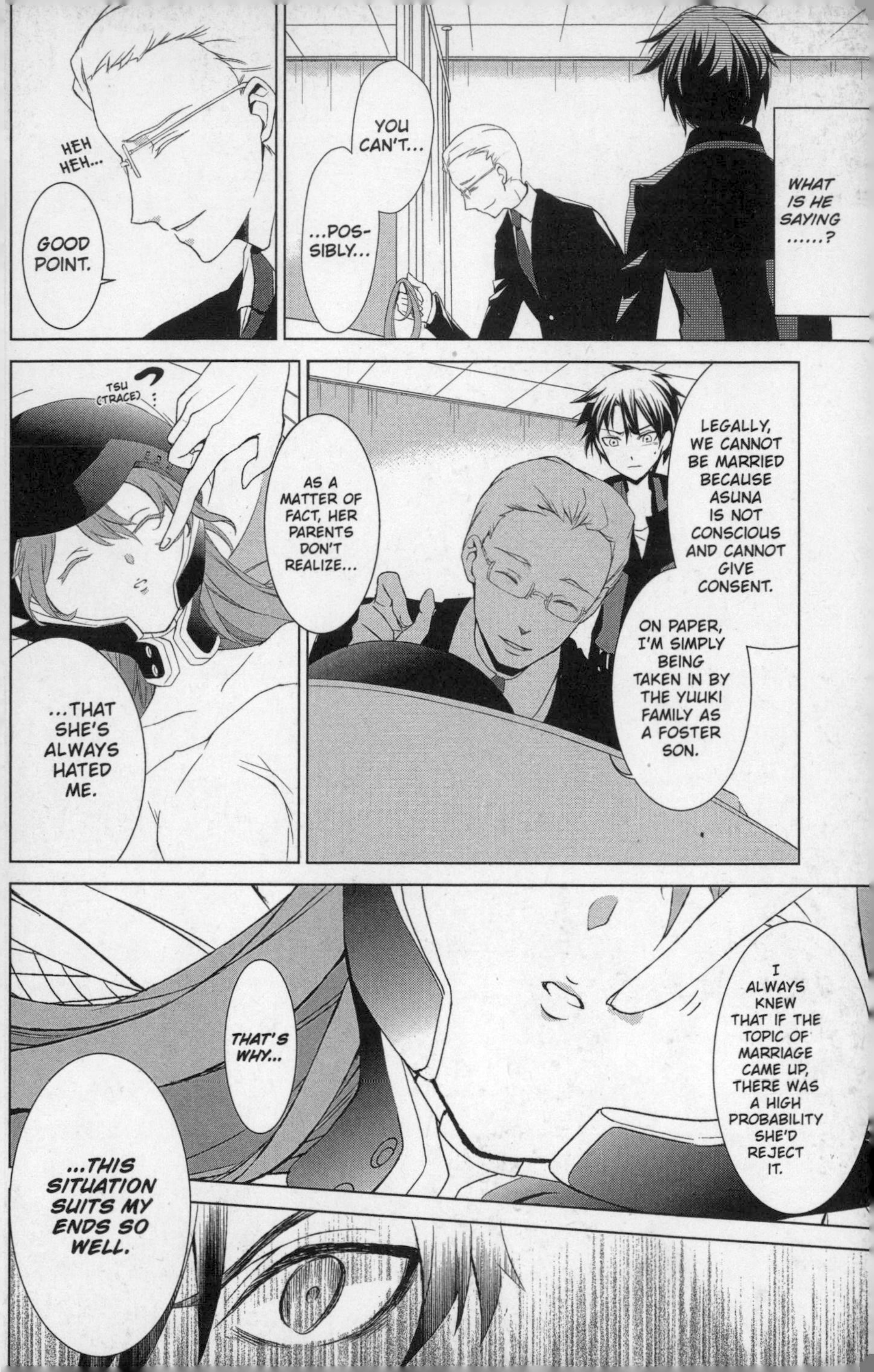
WHAT IS HE SAYING ......?
YOU CAN'T...
...POS-SIBLY...
HEH HEH...
GOOD POINT.
LEGALLY, WE CANNOT BE MARRIED BECAUSE ASUNA IS NOT CONSCIOUS AND CANNOT GIVE CONSENT.
ON PAPER, I'M SIMPLY BEING TAKEN IN BY THE YUUKI FAMILY AS A FOSTER SON.
AS A MATTER OF FACT, HER PARENTS DON'T REALIZE...
TSU (TRACE)
...THAT SHE'S ALWAYS HATED ME.
I ALWAYS KNEW THAT IF THE TOPIC OF MARRIAGE CAME UP, THERE WAS A HIGH PROBABILITY SHE'D REJECT IT.
THAT'S WHY...
...THIS SITUATION SUITS MY ENDS SO WELL.

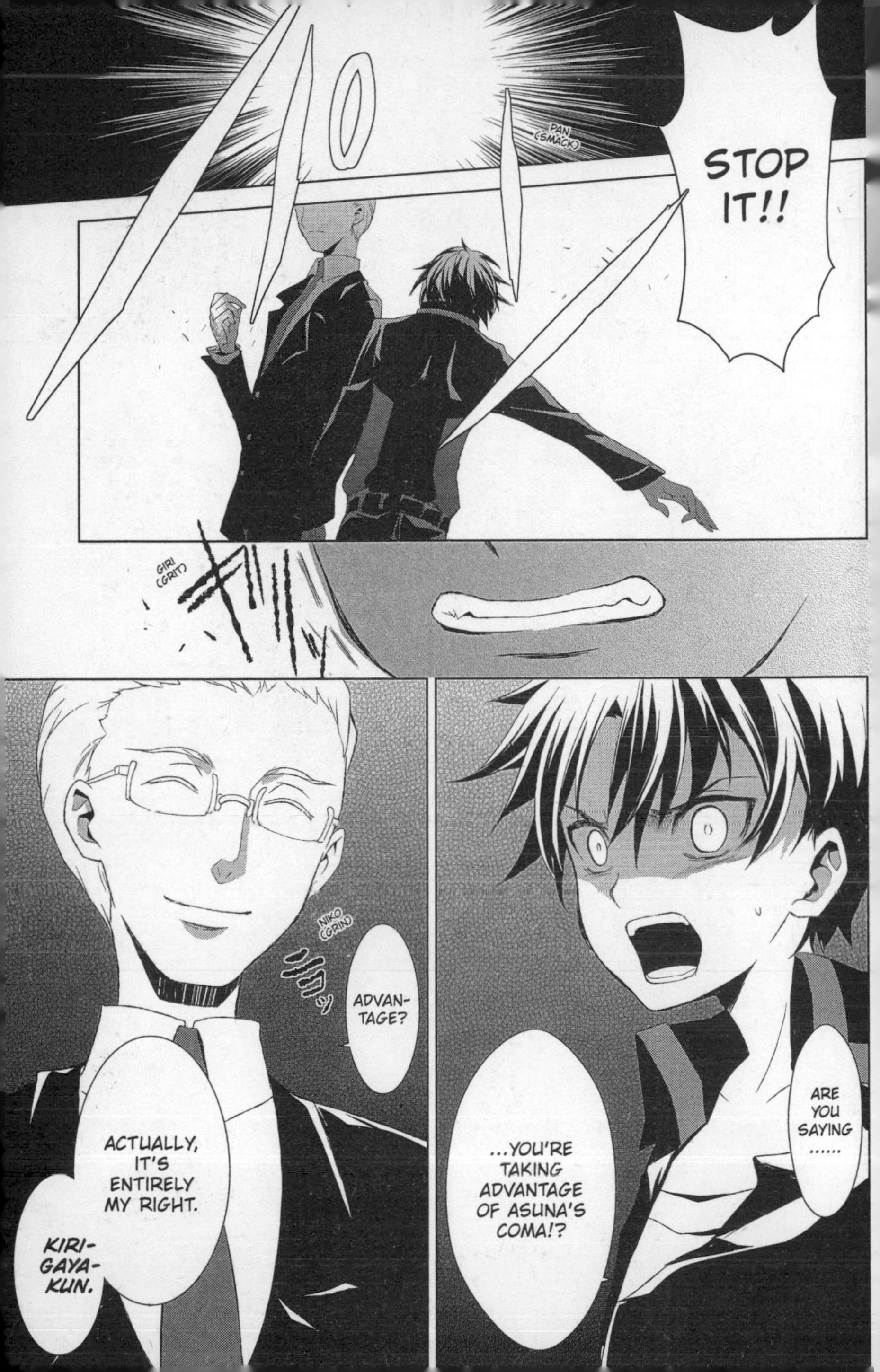
STOP IT!!
PAN (SMACK)
GIRI (GRIT)
ARE YOU SAYING……
…YOU'RE TAKING ADVANTAGE OF ASUNA'S COMA!?
NIKO (GRIN)
ADVANTAGE?
ACTUALLY, IT'S ENTIRELY MY RIGHT.
KIRI-GAYA-KUN.

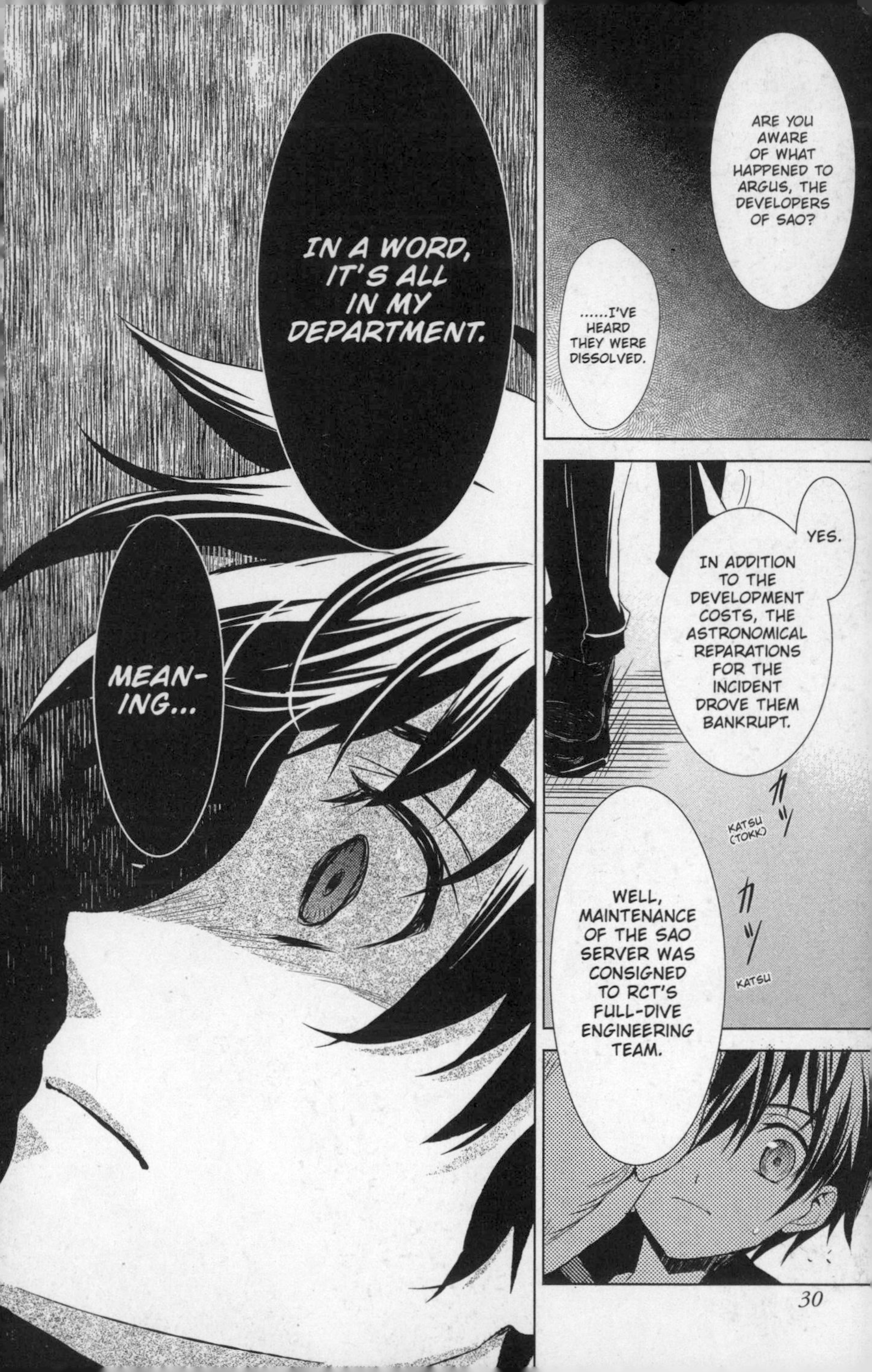

ARE YOU AWARE OF WHAT HAPPENED TO ARGUS, THE DEVELOPERS OF SAO?
......I'VE HEARD THEY WERE DISSOLVED.
YES.
IN ADDITION TO THE DEVELOPMENT COSTS, THE ASTRONOMICAL REPARATIONS FOR THE INCIDENT DROVE THEM BANKRUPT.
KATSU (TOKK)
KATSU
WELL, MAINTENANCE OF THE SAO SERVER WAS CONSIGNED TO RCT'S FULL-DIVE ENGINEERING TEAM.
IN A WORD, IT'S ALL IN MY DEPARTMENT.
MEAN-ING...

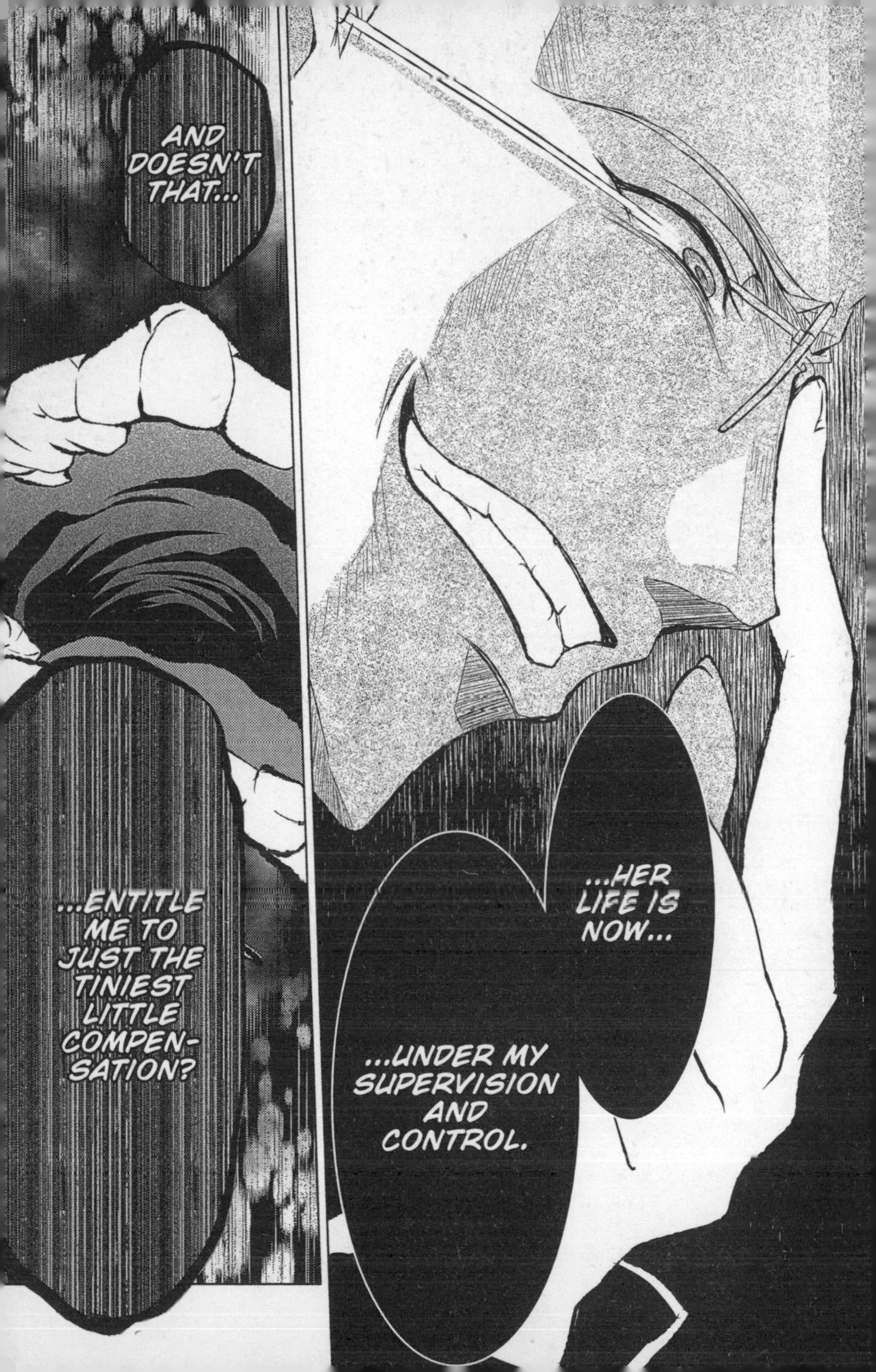
...HER LIFE IS NOW...
...UNDER MY SUPERVISION AND CONTROL.
AND DOESN'T THAT...
...ENTITLE ME TO JUST THE TINIEST LITTLE COMPEN-SATION?

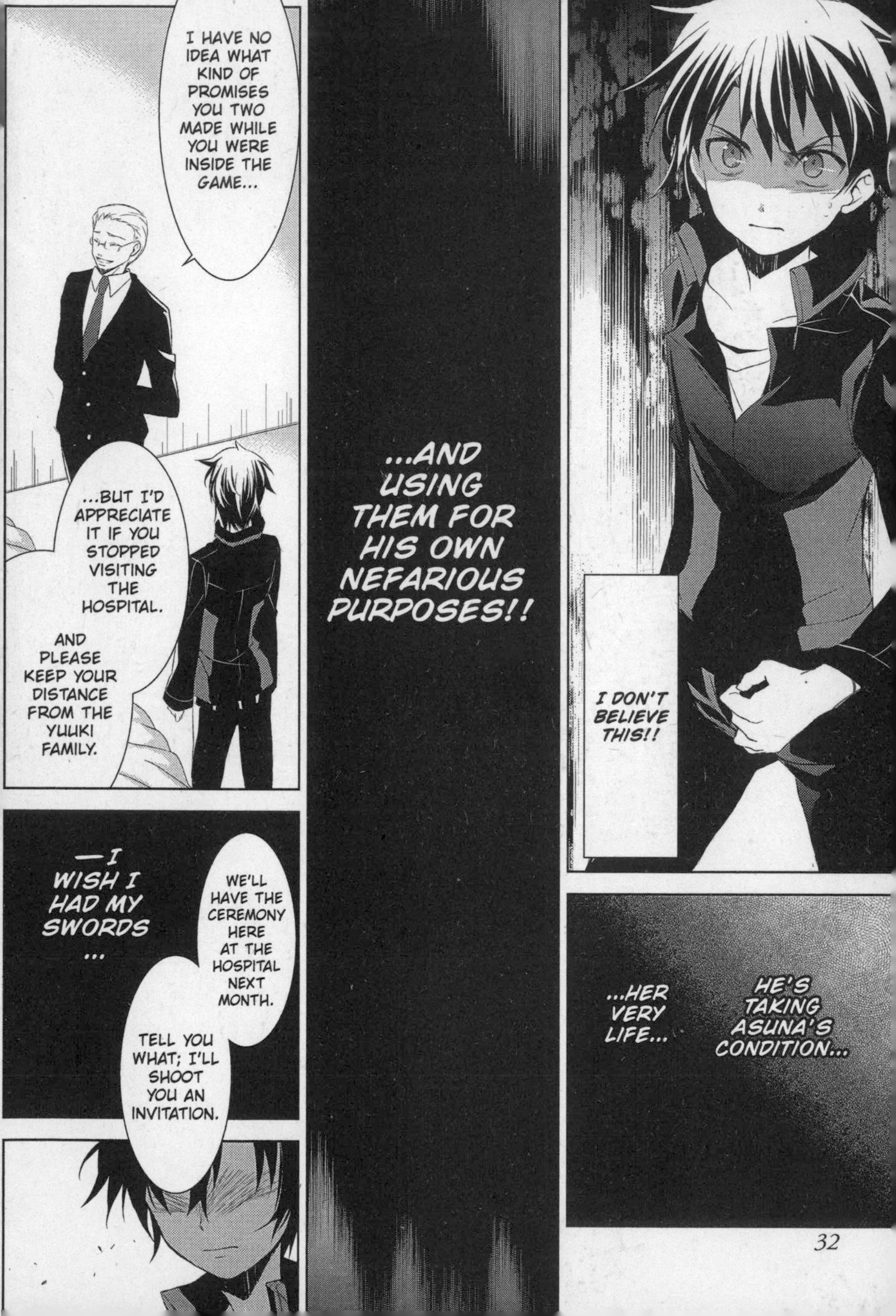
I DON'T BELIEVE THIS!!
HE'S TAKING ASUNA'S CONDITION...
...HER VERY LIFE...
...AND USING THEM FOR HIS OWN NEFARIOUS PURPOSES!!
I HAVE NO IDEA WHAT KIND OF PROMISES YOU TWO MADE WHILE YOU WERE INSIDE THE GAME...
...BUT I'D APPRECIATE IT IF YOU STOPPED VISITING THE HOSPITAL.
AND PLEASE KEEP YOUR DISTANCE FROM THE YUUKI FAMILY.
WE'LL HAVE THE CEREMONY HERE AT THE HOSPITAL NEXT MONTH.
TELL YOU WHAT; I'LL SHOOT YOU AN INVITATION.
—I WISH I HAD MY SWORDS...

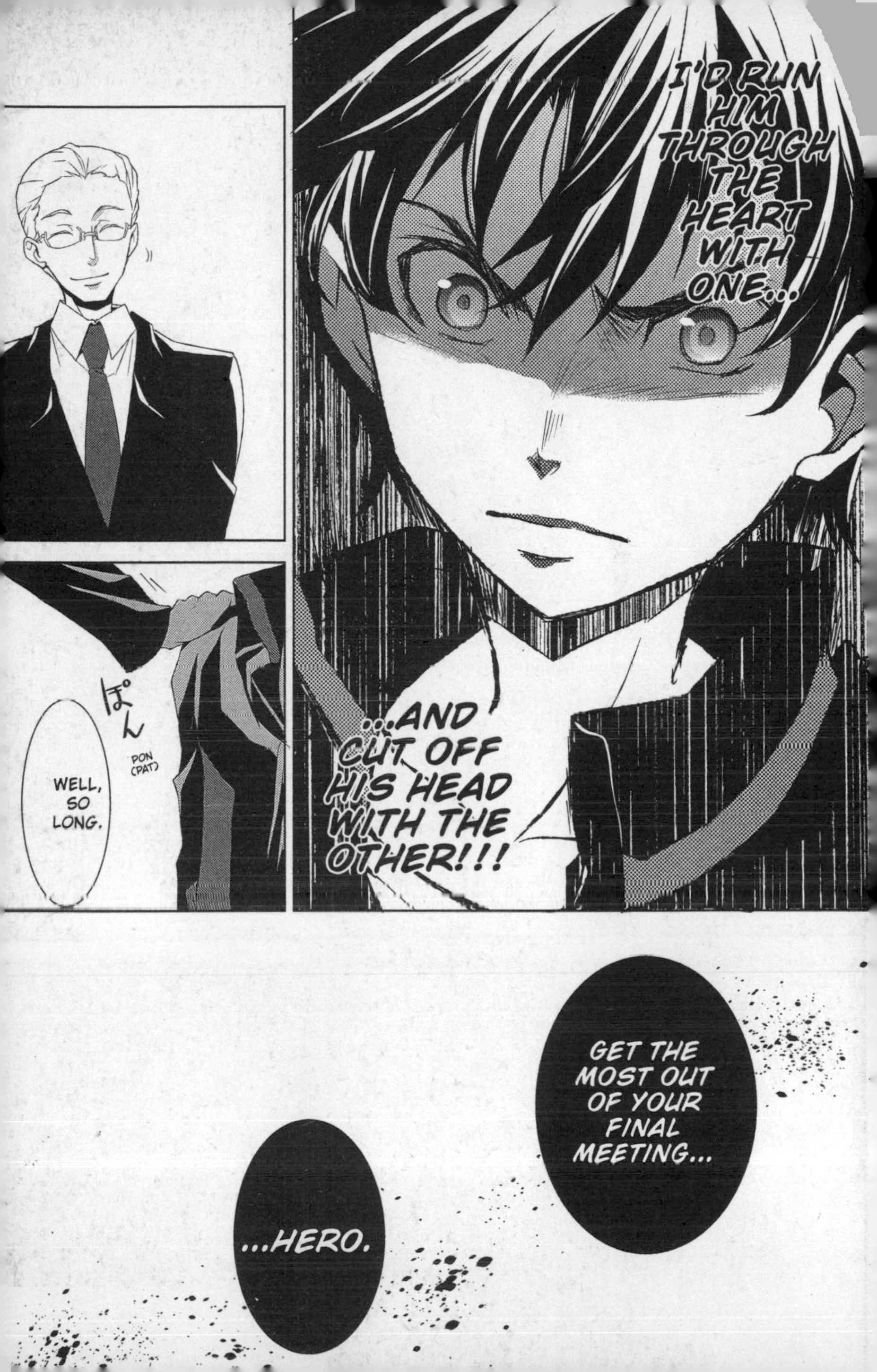
I'D RUN HIM THROUGH THE HEART WITH ONE...
...AND CUT OFF HIS HEAD WITH THE OTHER!!!
ぽん
PON (PAT)
WELL, SO LONG.
GET THE MOST OUT OF YOUR FINAL MEETING...
...HERO.

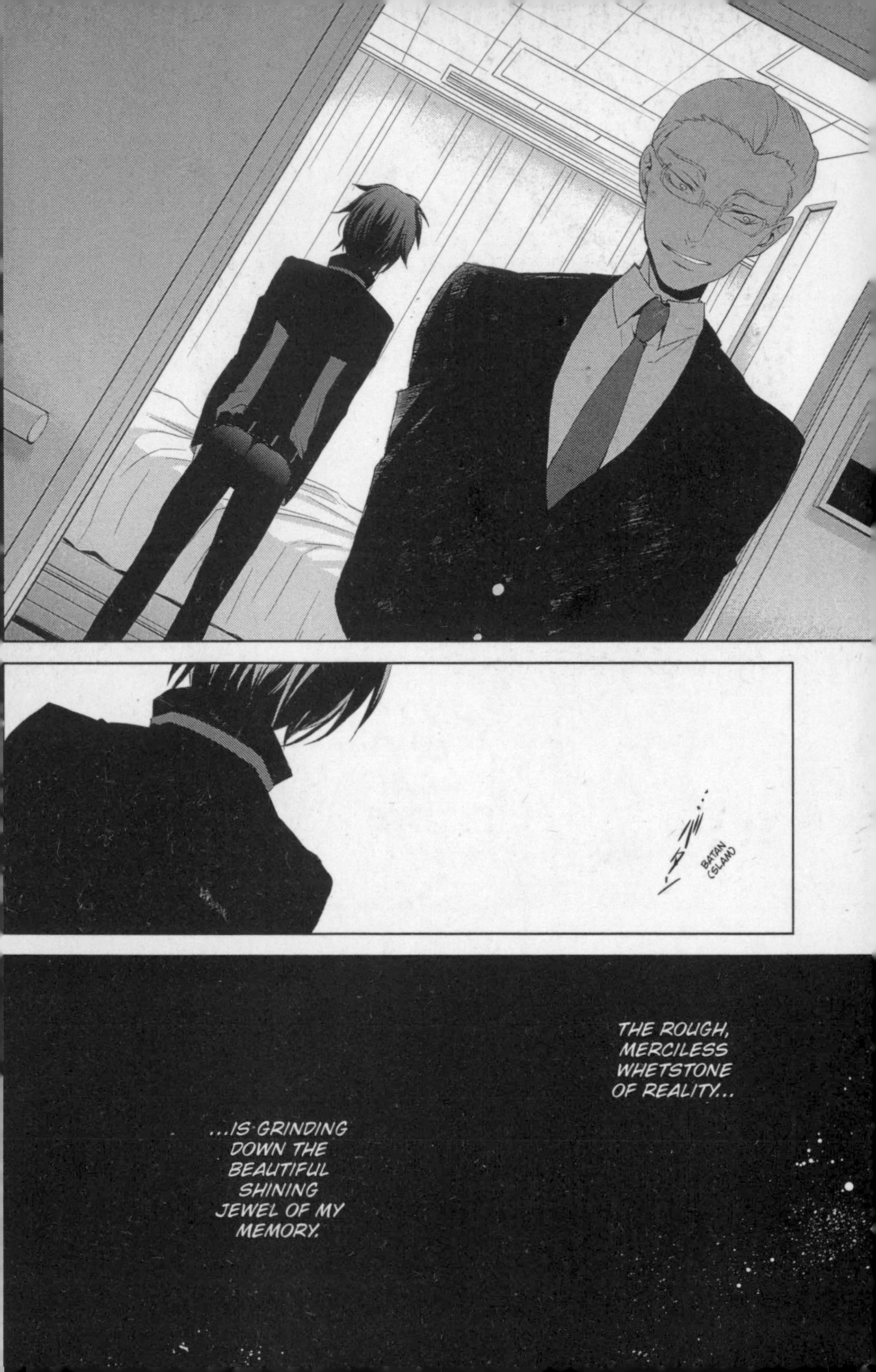
BATAN (SLAM)
THE ROUGH, MERCILESS WHETSTONE OF REALITY...
...IS GRINDING DOWN THE BEAUTIFUL SHINING JEWEL OF MY MEMORY.

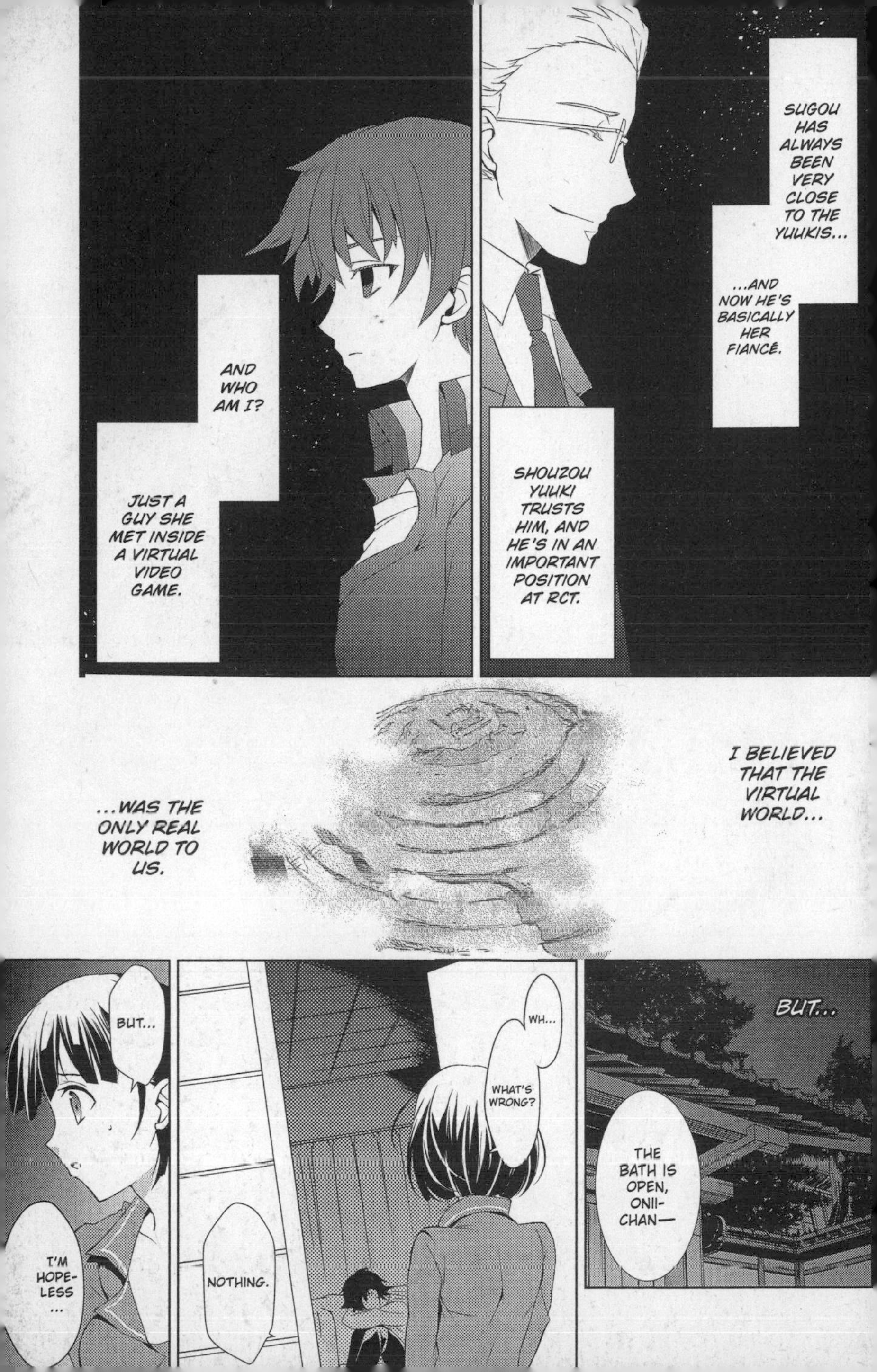
SUGOU HAS ALWAYS BEEN VERY CLOSE TO THE YUUKIS...
...AND NOW HE'S BASICALLY HER FIANCÉ.
SHOUZOU YUUKI TRUSTS HIM, AND HE'S IN AN IMPORTANT POSITION AT RCT.
AND WHO AM I?
JUST A GUY SHE MET INSIDE A VIRTUAL VIDEO GAME.
I BELIEVED THAT THE VIRTUAL WORLD...
...WAS THE ONLY REAL WORLD TO US.
BUT...
THE BATH IS OPEN, ONII-CHAN—
WH...
WHAT'S WRONG?
NOTHING.
BUT...
I'M HOPELESS...

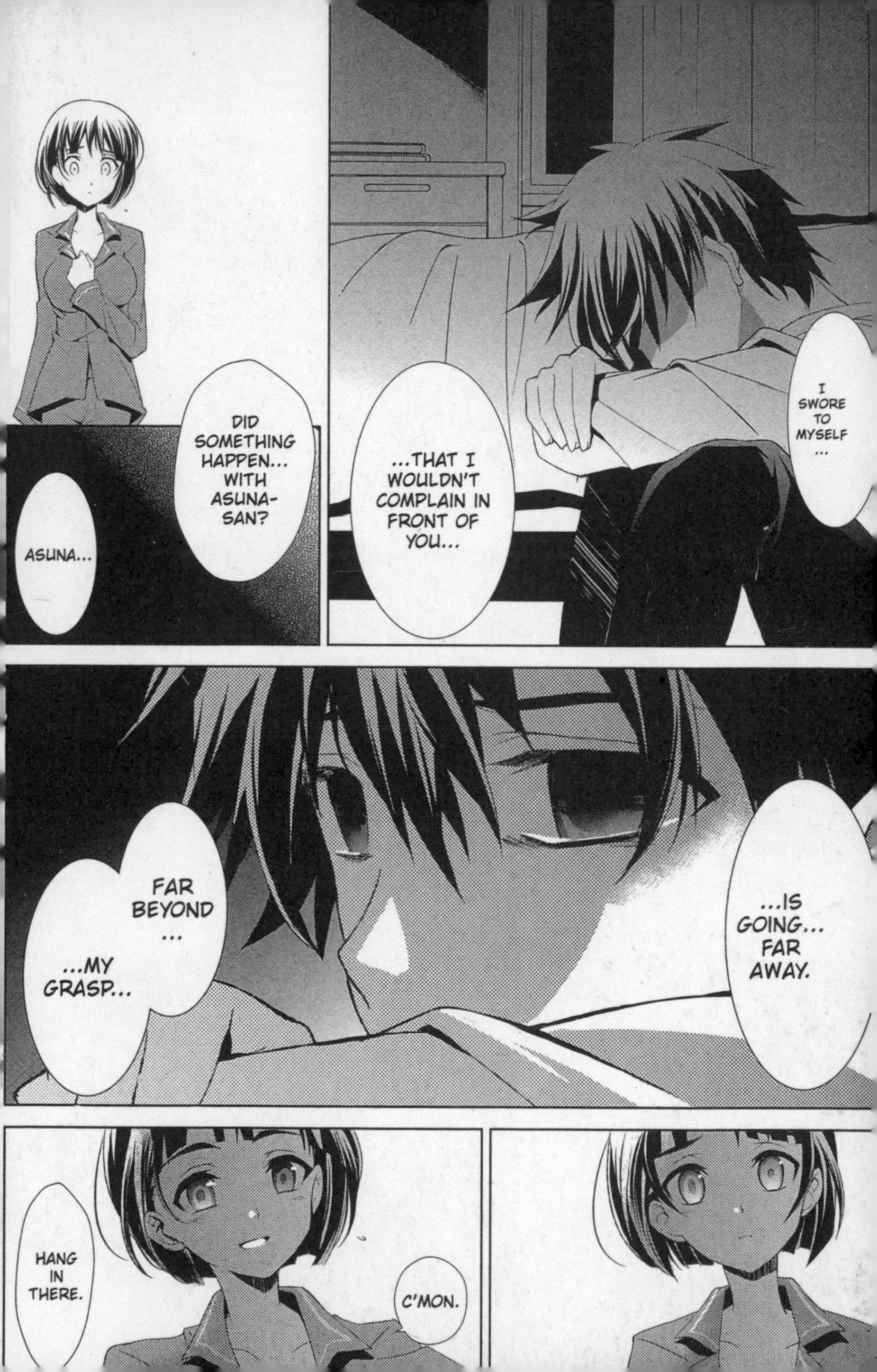
I SWORE TO MYSELF...
...THAT I WOULDN'T COMPLAIN IN FRONT OF YOU...
DID SOMETHING HAPPEN... WITH ASUNA-SAN?
ASUNA...
...IS GOING... FAR AWAY.
FAR BEYOND...
...MY GRASP...
C'MON.
HANG IN THERE.

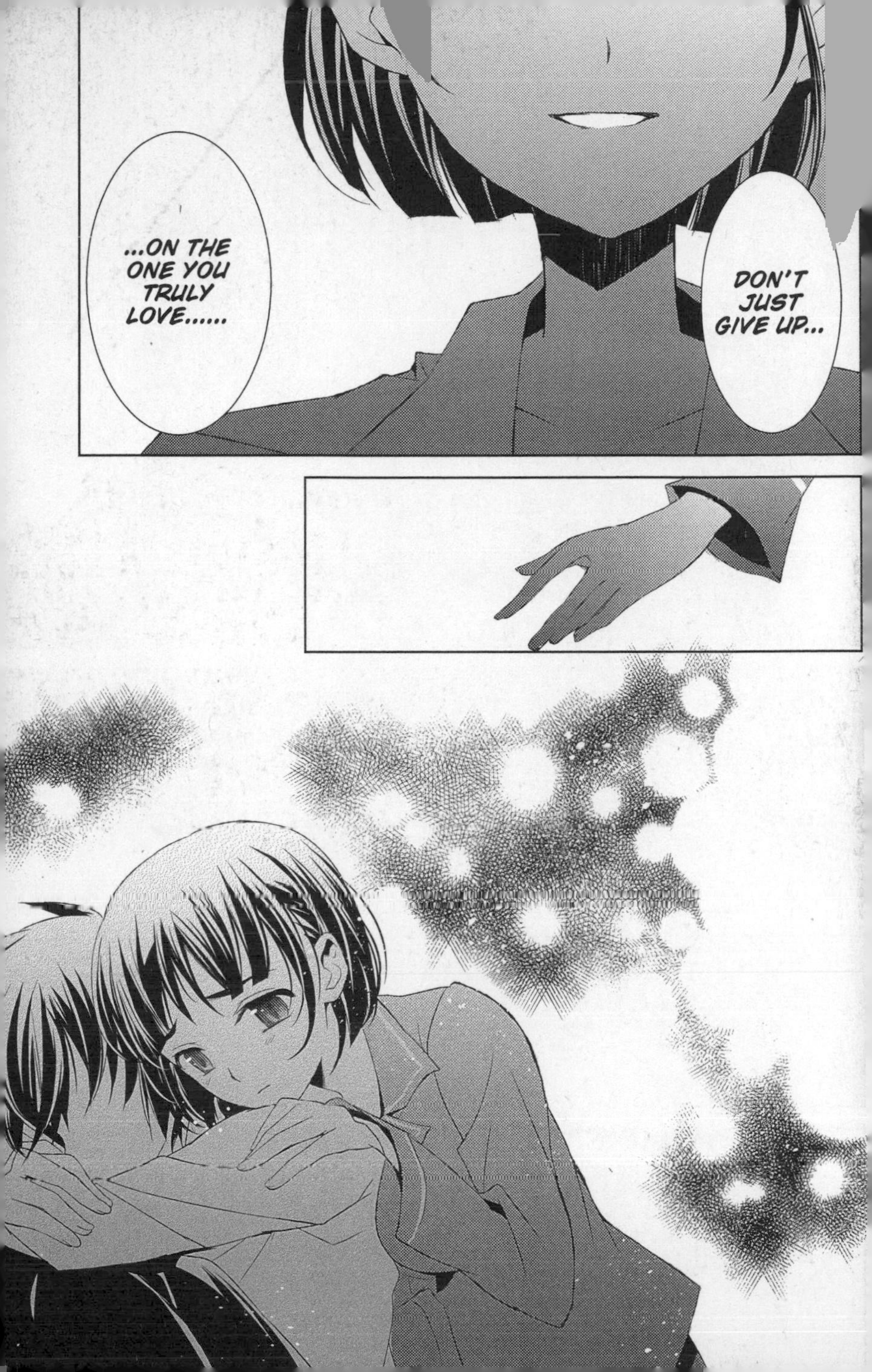
DON'T JUST GIVE UP...
...ON THE ONE YOU TRULY LOVE......

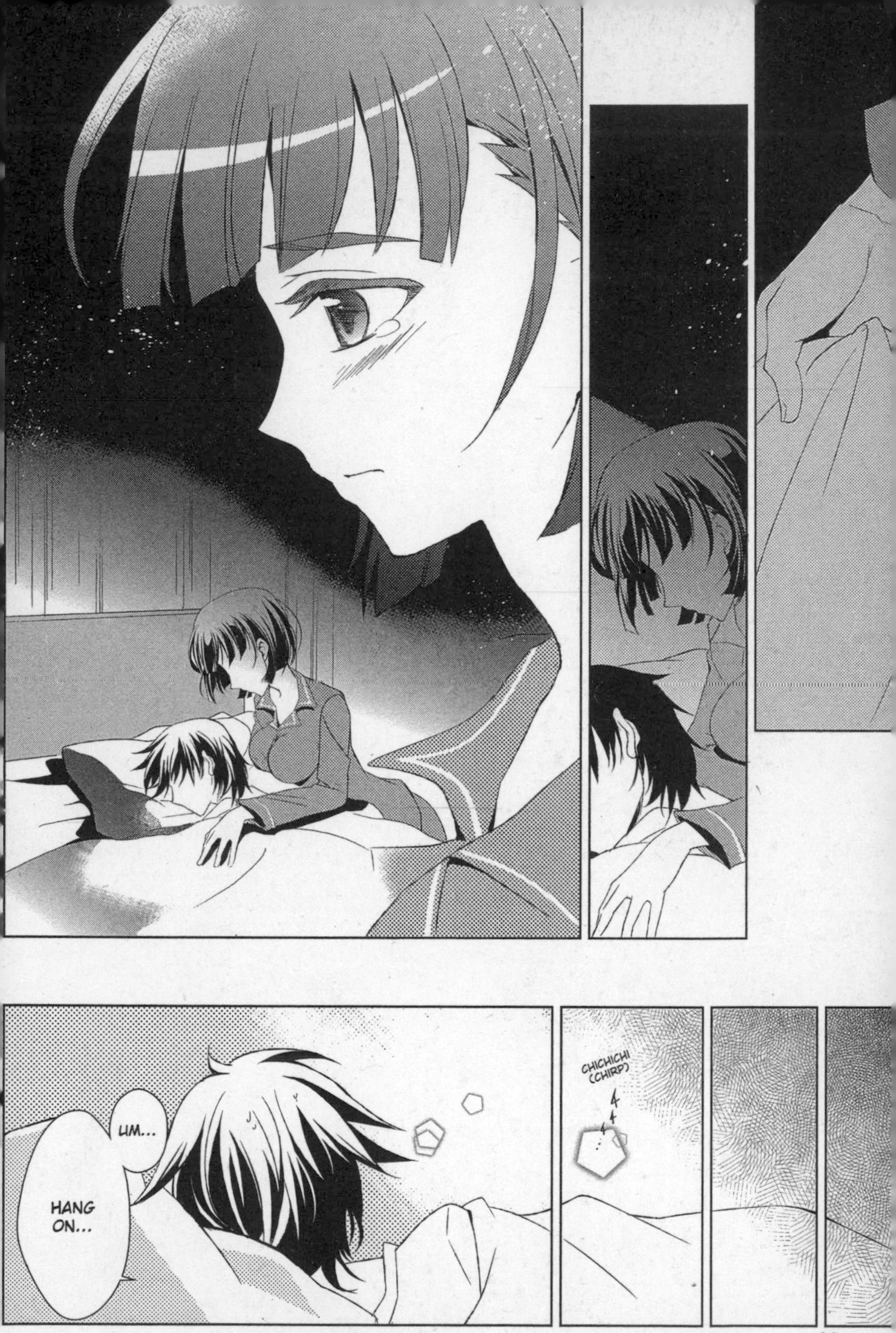
CHICHI
(CHIRP)
UM...
HANG ON...

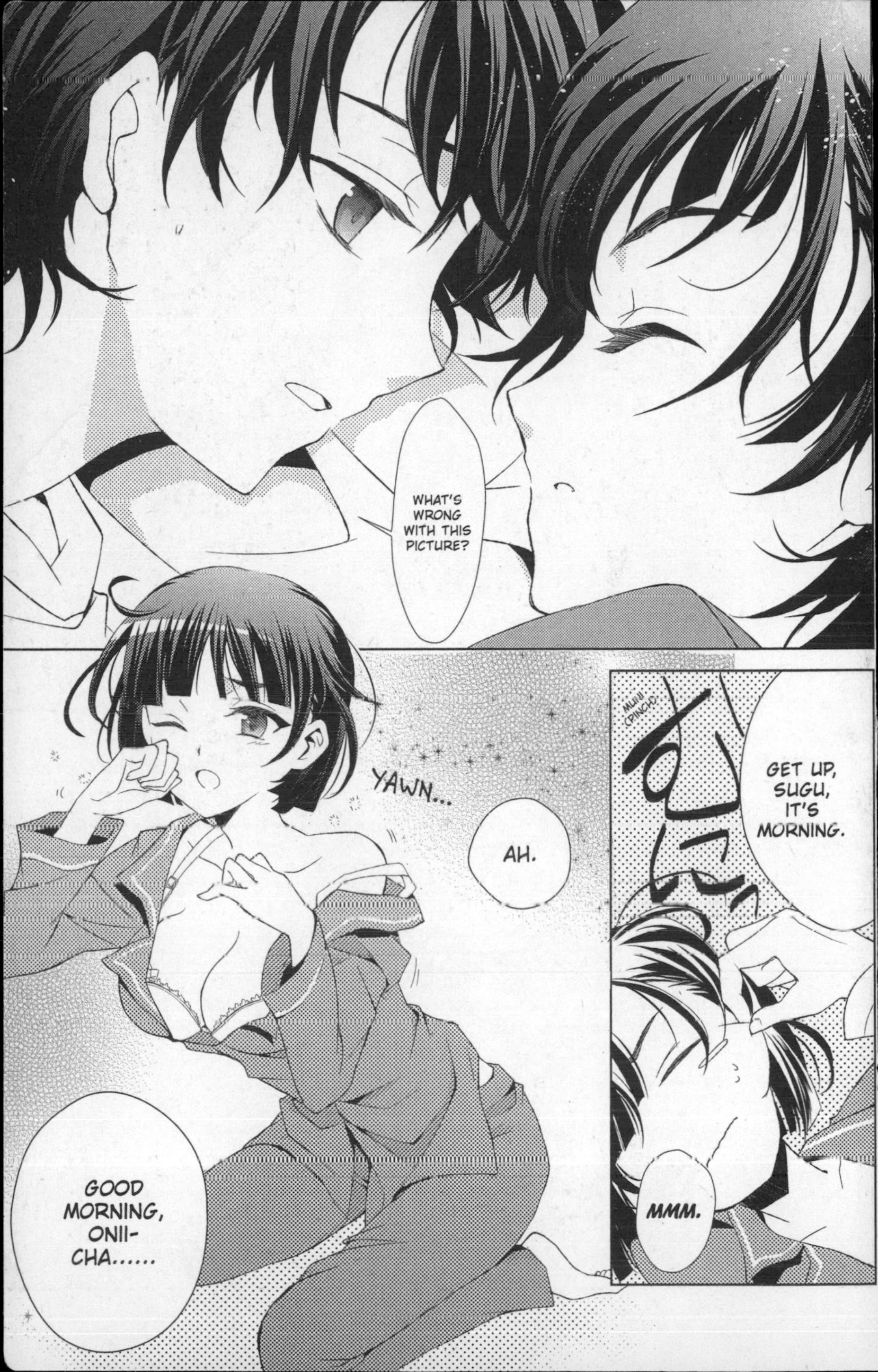
WHAT'S WRONG WITH THIS PICTURE?
MUNI (PINCH)
GET UP, SUGU, IT'S MORNING.
MMM.
YAWN...
AH.
GOOD MORNING, ONII-CHA......

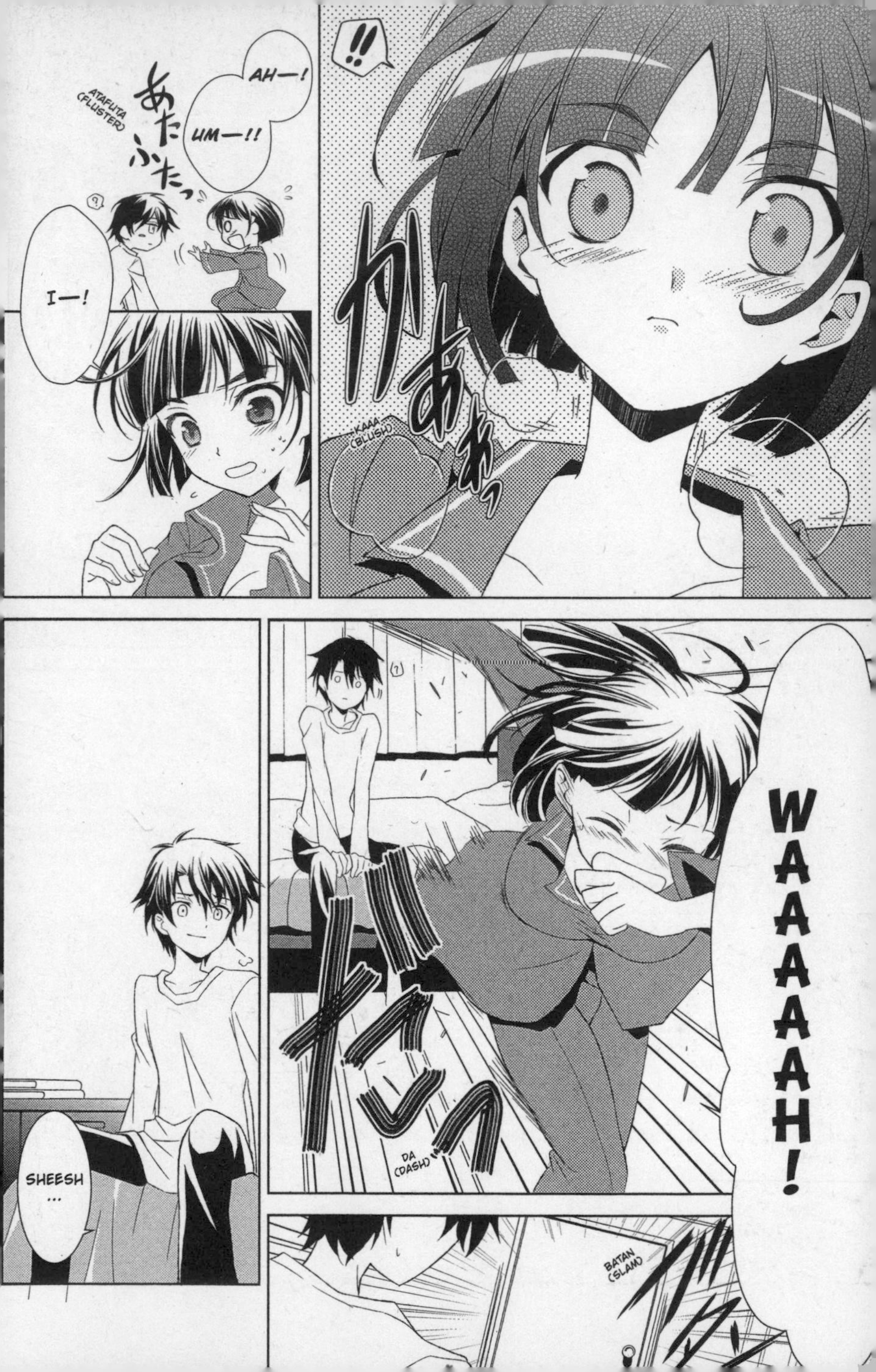
!!
かあぁっ
KAAA (BLUSH)
AH—!
UM—!!
あたふたっ
ATAFUTA (FLUSTER)
?
I—!
WAAAAAAH!
?
ダッ
DA (DASH)
BATAN (SLAM)
SHEESH …

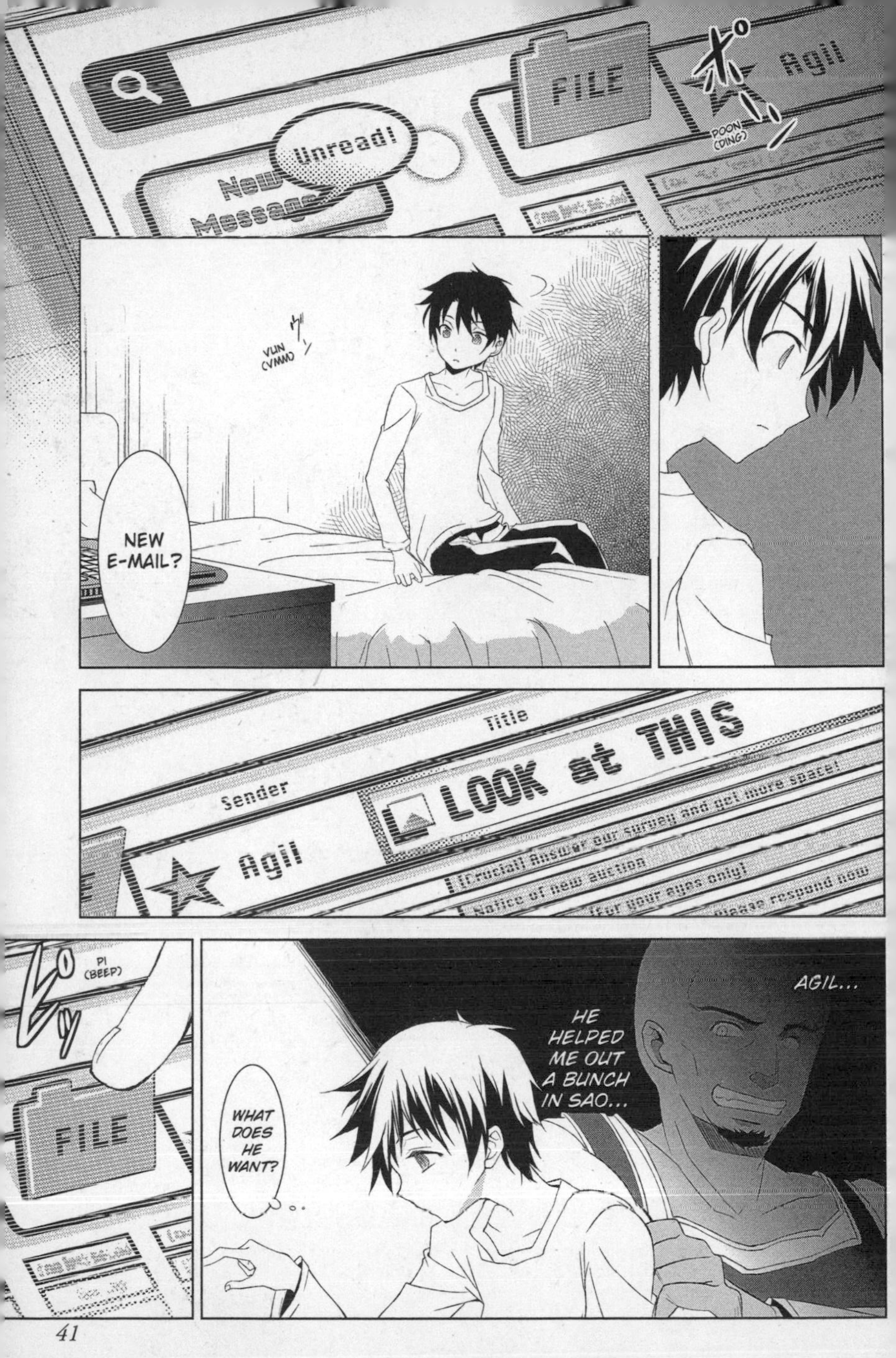

Agil
POON (DING)
FILE
Unread!
New Message
VUN (VMMM)
NEW E-MAIL?
Title
LOOK at THIS
Sender
Agil
[Crucial] Answer our survey and get more space!
Notice of new auction
[For your eyes only]
Please respond now
AGIL...
HE HELPED ME OUT A BUNCH IN SAO...
WHAT DOES HE WANT?
PI (BEEP)
FILE

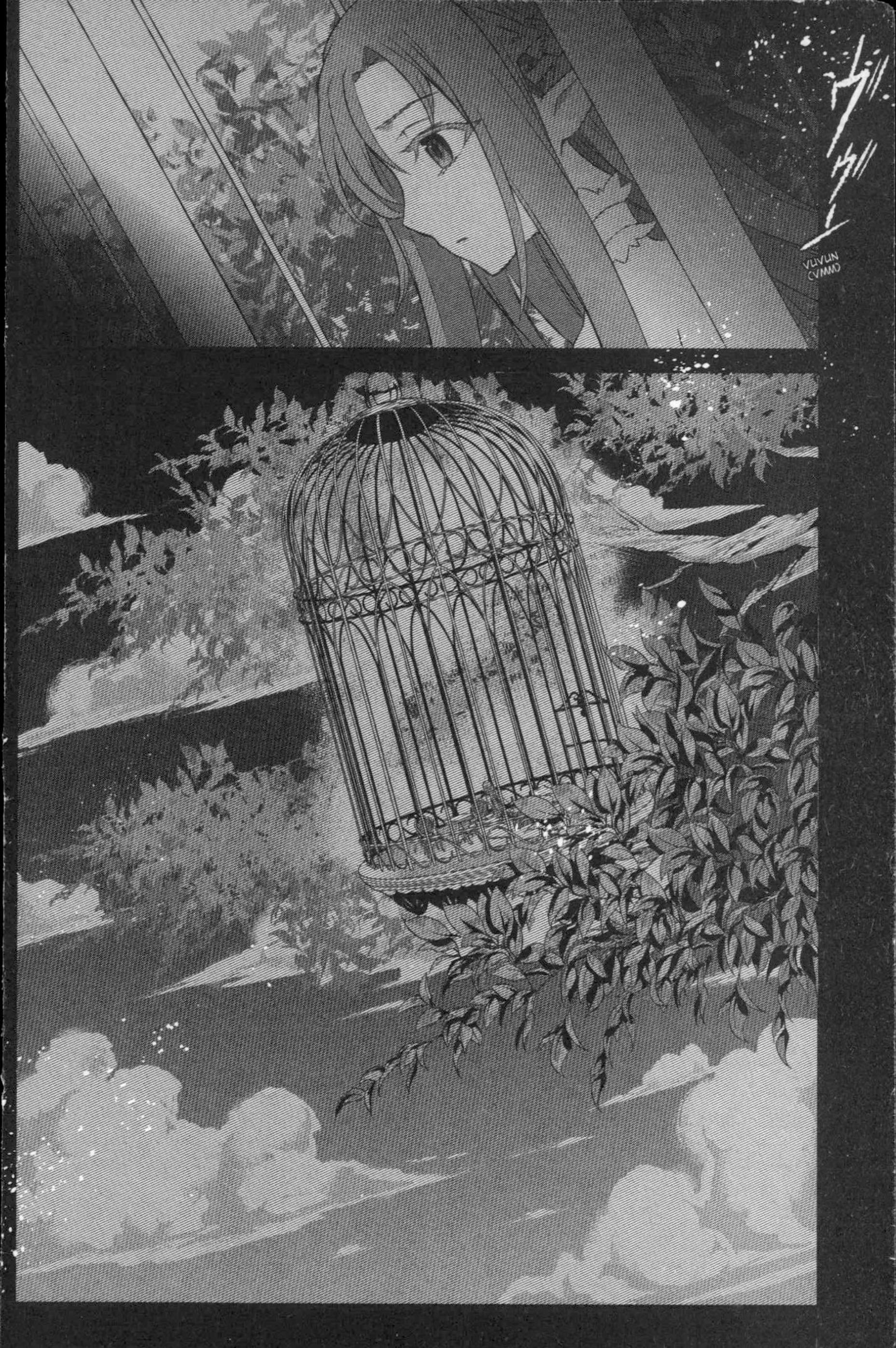
ヴゥゥン
VUVUN
(VMM)

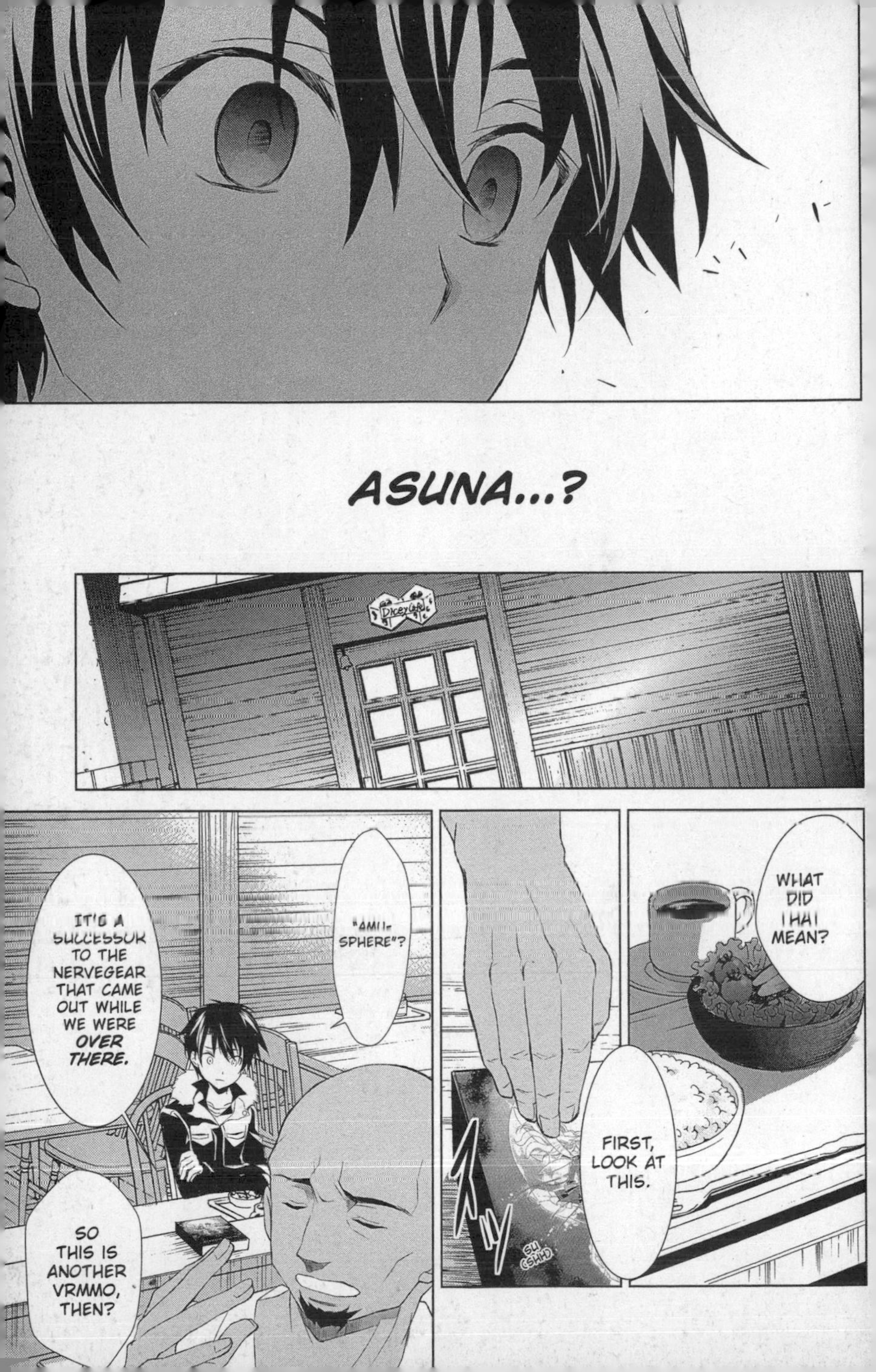
ASUNA...?
Dicey Café
WHAT DID THAT MEAN?
FIRST, LOOK AT THIS.
SU (SHH)
"AMU-SPHERE"?
IT'S A SUCCESSOR TO THE NERVEGEAR THAT CAME OUT WHILE WE WERE OVER THERE.
SO THIS IS ANOTHER VRMMO, THEN?

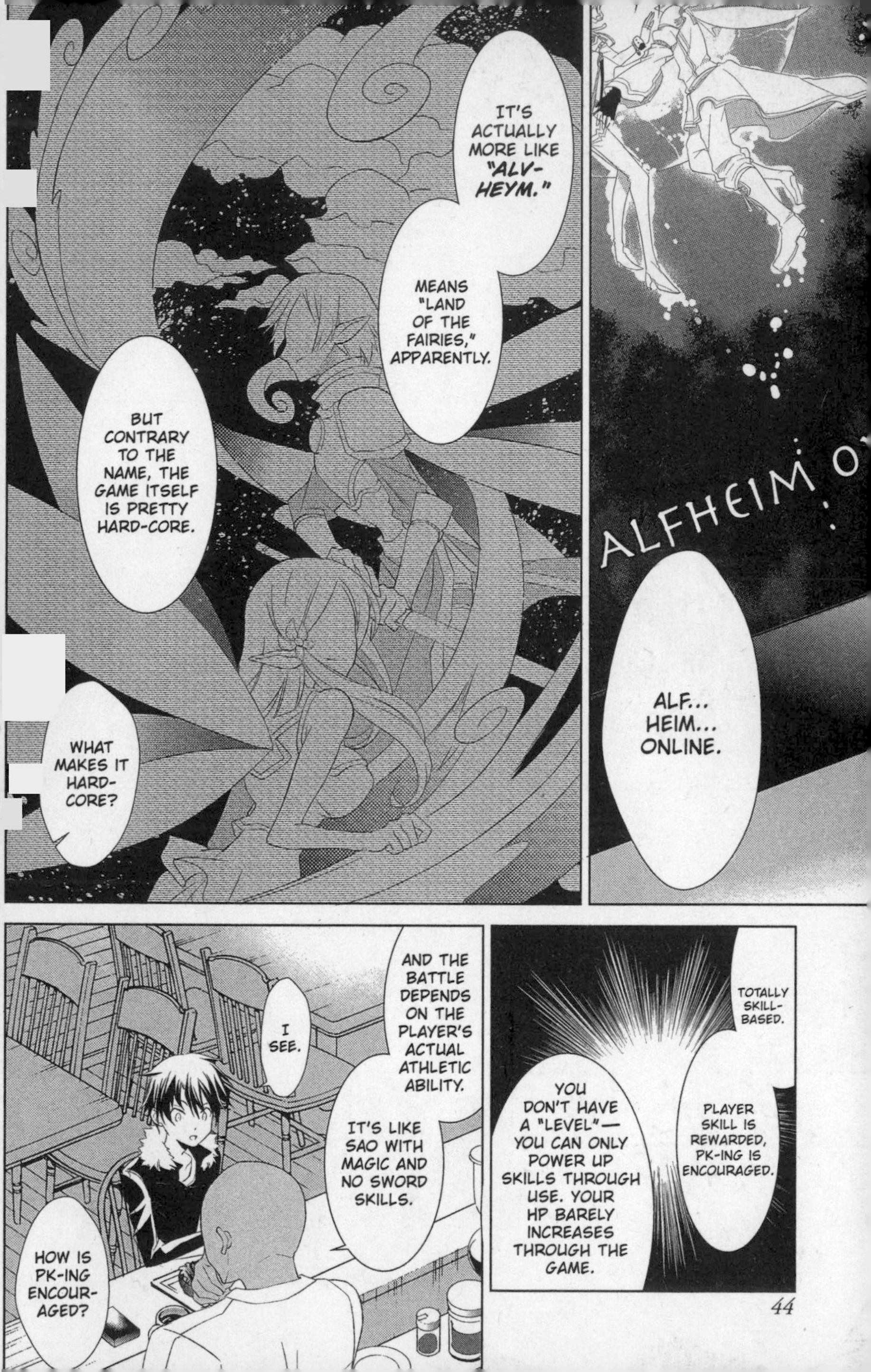
ALFHEIM
ALF... HEIM... ONLINE.
IT'S ACTUALLY MORE LIKE "ALV-HEYM."
MEANS "LAND OF THE FAIRIES," APPARENTLY.
BUT CONTRARY TO THE NAME, THE GAME ITSELF IS PRETTY HARD-CORE.
WHAT MAKES IT HARD-CORE?
TOTALLY SKILL-BASED.
PLAYER SKILL IS REWARDED, PK-ING IS ENCOURAGED.
YOU DON'T HAVE A "LEVEL"—YOU CAN ONLY POWER UP SKILLS THROUGH USE. YOUR HP BARELY INCREASES THROUGH THE GAME.
AND THE BATTLE DEPENDS ON THE PLAYER'S ACTUAL ATHLETIC ABILITY.
I SEE.
IT'S LIKE SAO WITH MAGIC AND NO SWORD SKILLS.
HOW IS PK-ING ENCOURAGED?

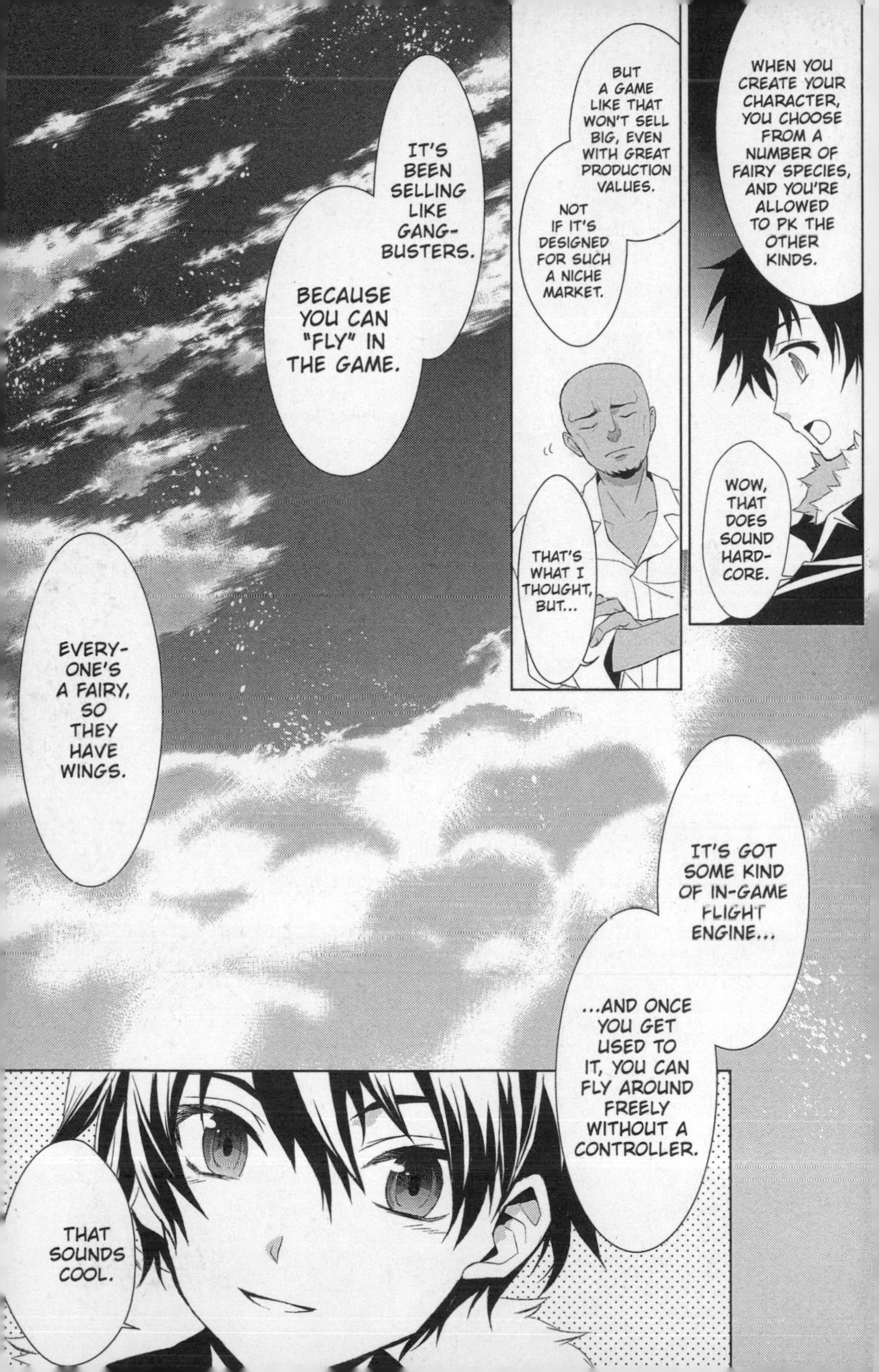
WHEN YOU CREATE YOUR CHARACTER, YOU CHOOSE FROM A NUMBER OF FAIRY SPECIES, AND YOU'RE ALLOWED TO PK THE OTHER KINDS.
WOW, THAT DOES SOUND HARD-CORE.
BUT A GAME LIKE THAT WON'T SELL BIG, EVEN WITH GREAT PRODUCTION VALUES.
NOT IF IT'S DESIGNED FOR SUCH A NICHE MARKET.
THAT'S WHAT I THOUGHT, BUT...
IT'S BEEN SELLING LIKE GANG-BUSTERS.
BECAUSE YOU CAN "FLY" IN THE GAME.
EVERY-ONE'S A FAIRY, SO THEY HAVE WINGS.
IT'S GOT SOME KIND OF IN-GAME FLIGHT ENGINE...
...AND ONCE YOU GET USED TO IT, YOU CAN FLY AROUND FREELY WITHOUT A CONTROLLER.
THAT SOUNDS COOL.

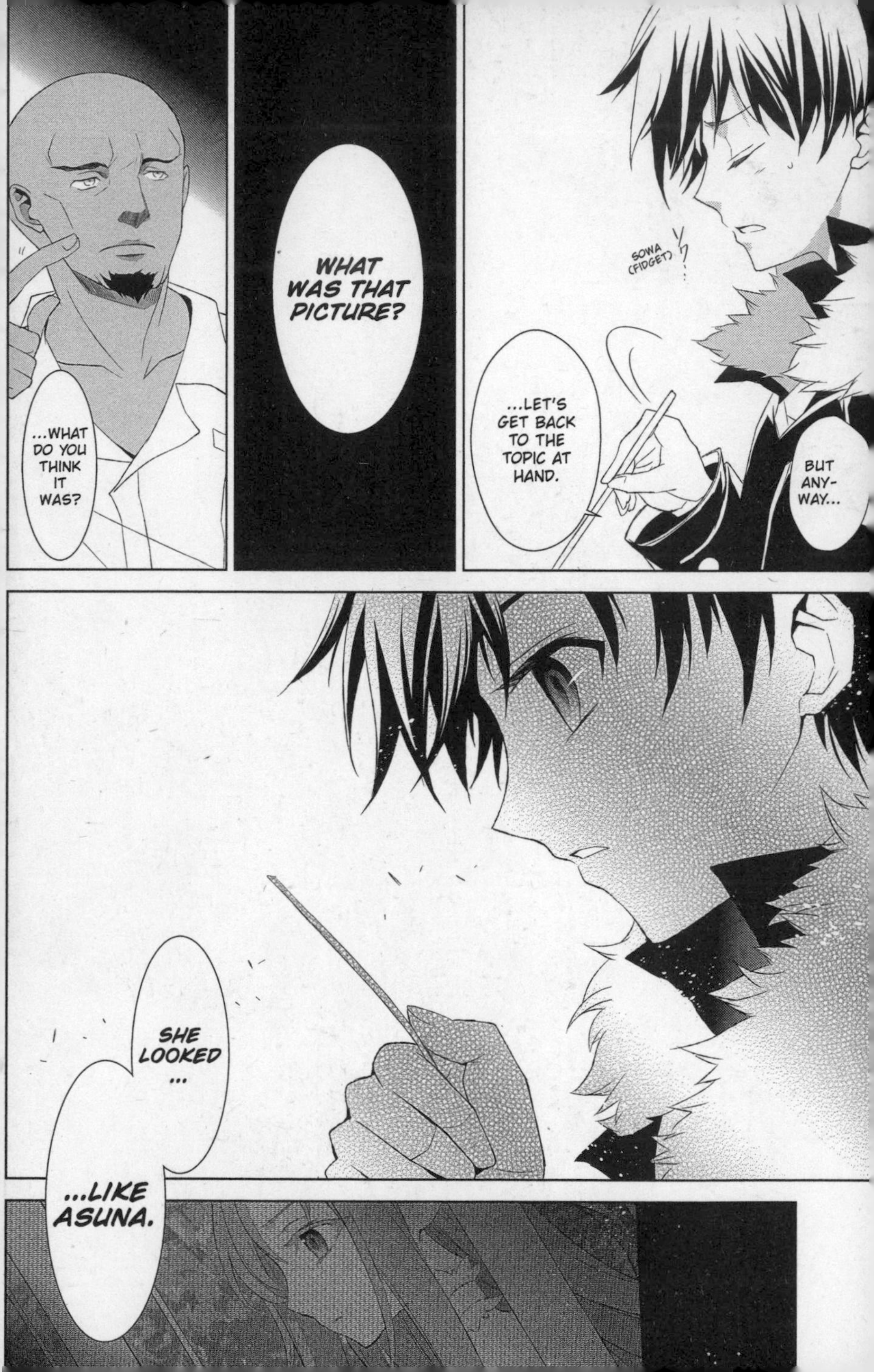
BUT ANYWAY...
SOWA (FIDGET)
...LET'S GET BACK TO THE TOPIC AT HAND.
WHAT WAS THAT PICTURE?
...WHAT DO YOU THINK IT WAS?
SHE LOOKED ...
...LIKE ASUNA.

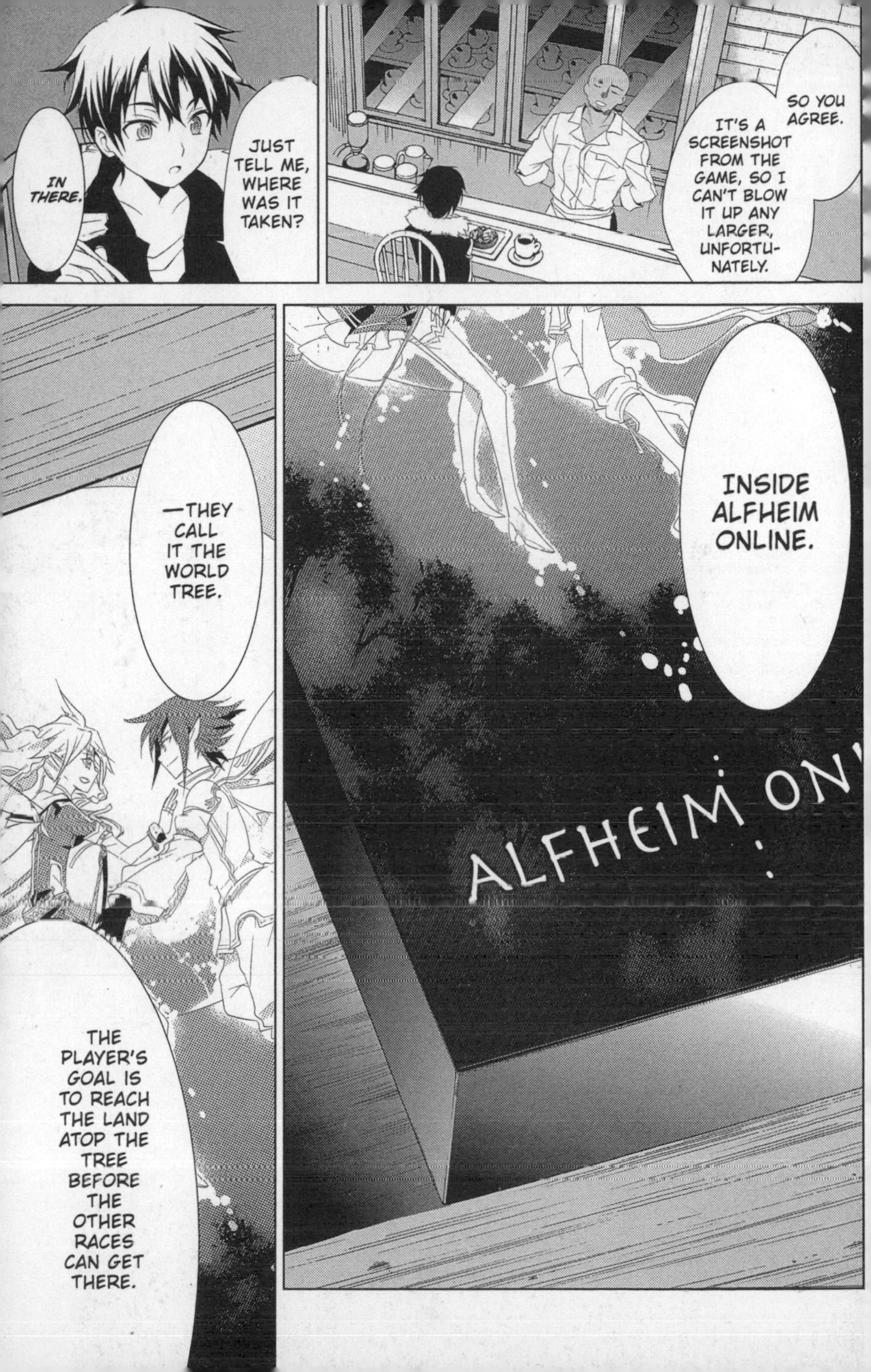
SO YOU AGREE.
IT'S A SCREENSHOT FROM THE GAME, SO I CAN'T BLOW IT UP ANY LARGER, UNFORTUNATELY.
JUST TELL ME, WHERE WAS IT TAKEN?
IN THERE.
INSIDE ALFHEIM ONLINE.
ALFHEIM ON
—THEY CALL IT THE WORLD TREE.
THE PLAYER'S GOAL IS TO REACH THE LAND ATOP THE TREE BEFORE THE OTHER RACES CAN GET THERE.

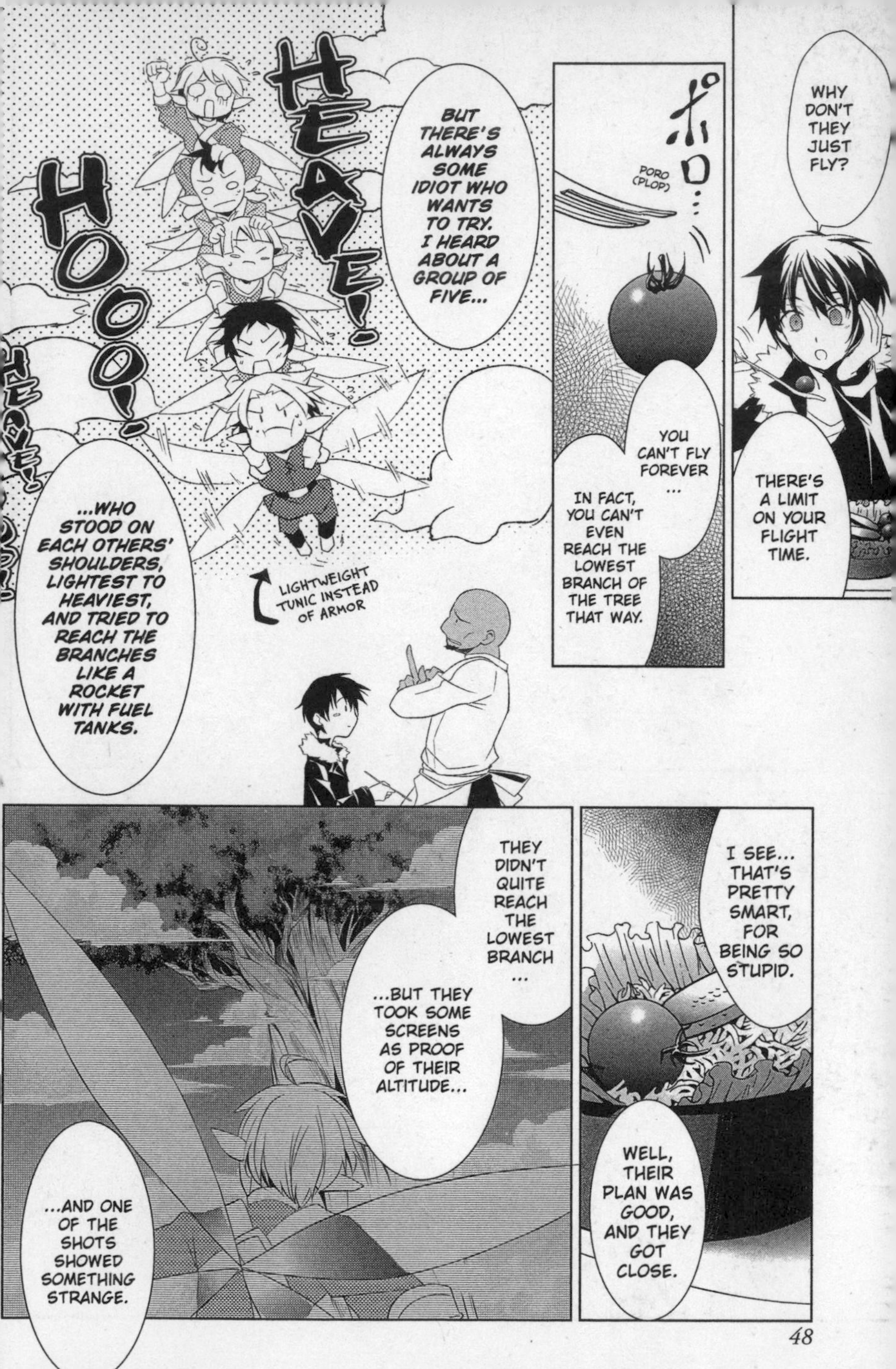

WHY DON'T THEY JUST FLY?
THERE'S A LIMIT ON YOUR FLIGHT TIME.
ポロ…
PORO (PLOP)
YOU CAN'T FLY FOREVER ...
IN FACT, YOU CAN'T EVEN REACH THE LOWEST BRANCH OF THE TREE THAT WAY.
BUT THERE'S ALWAYS SOME IDIOT WHO WANTS TO TRY. I HEARD ABOUT A GROUP OF FIVE...
HEAVE!
HOOOO!
...WHO STOOD ON EACH OTHERS' SHOULDERS, LIGHTEST TO HEAVIEST, AND TRIED TO REACH THE BRANCHES LIKE A ROCKET WITH FUEL TANKS.
LIGHTWEIGHT TUNIC INSTEAD OF ARMOR
I SEE... THAT'S PRETTY SMART, FOR BEING SO STUPID.
WELL, THEIR PLAN WAS GOOD, AND THEY GOT CLOSE.
THEY DIDN'T QUITE REACH THE LOWEST BRANCH ...
...BUT THEY TOOK SOME SCREENS AS PROOF OF THEIR ALTITUDE...
...AND ONE OF THE SHOTS SHOWED SOMETHING STRANGE.

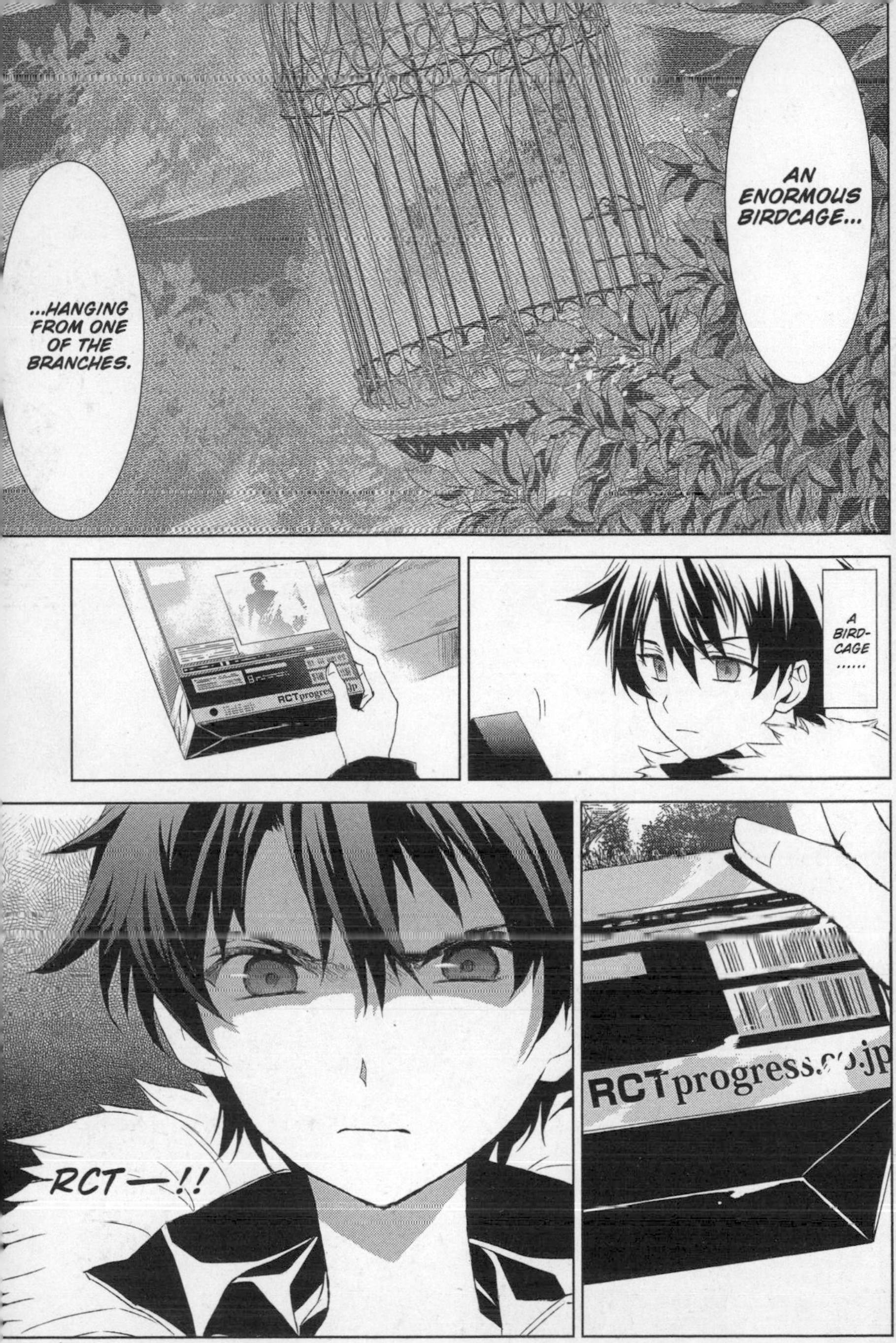
AN ENORMOUS BIRDCAGE...
...HANGING FROM ONE OF THE BRANCHES.
A BIRD-CAGE ......
RCTprogress.co.jp
RCT—!!

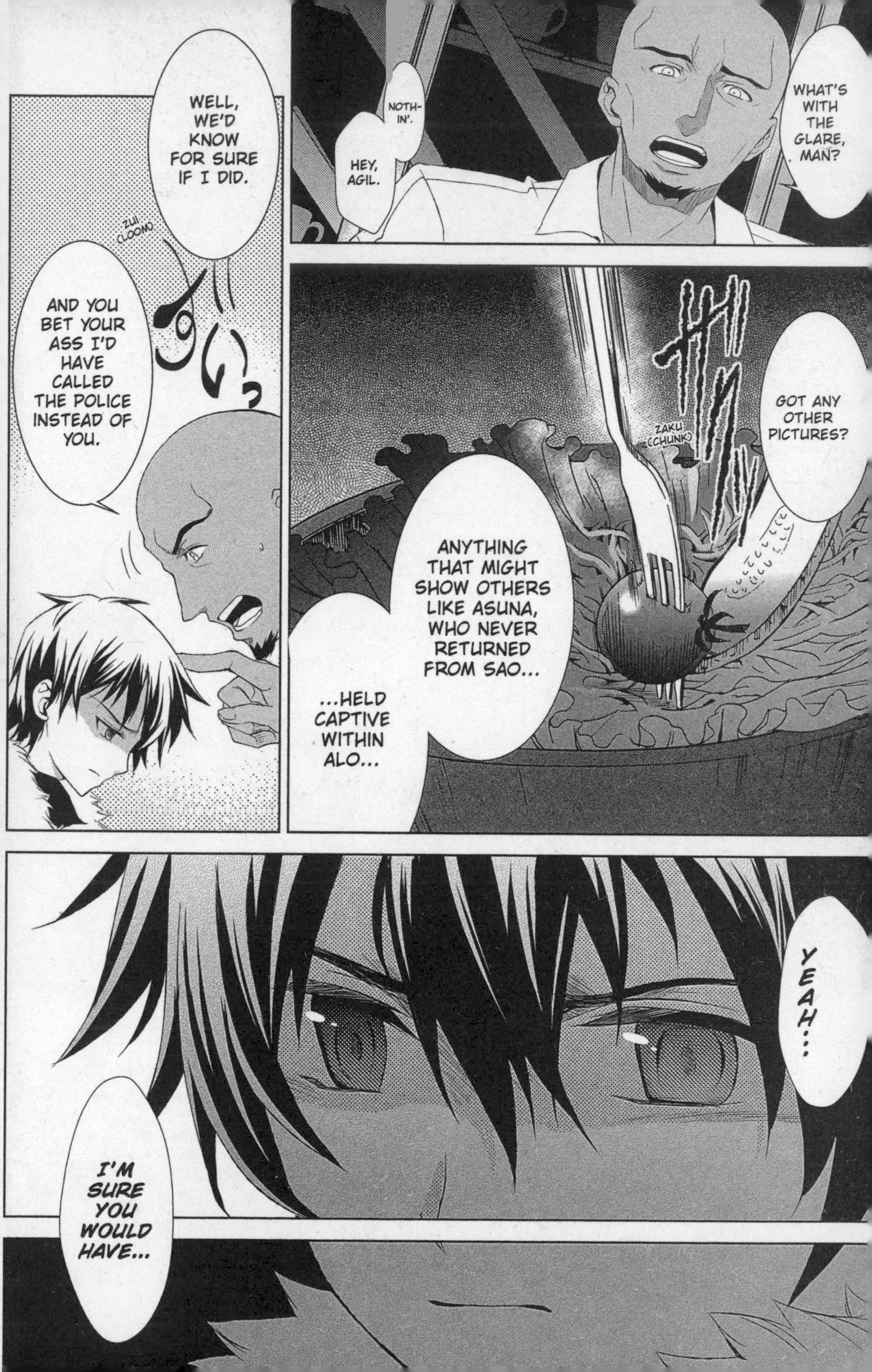
WHAT'S WITH THE GLARE, MAN?
NOTH-IN'.
HEY, AGIL.
GOT ANY OTHER PICTURES?
ZAKU (CHUNK)
ANYTHING THAT MIGHT SHOW OTHERS LIKE ASUNA, WHO NEVER RETURNED FROM SAO...
...HELD CAPTIVE WITHIN ALO...
WELL, WE'D KNOW FOR SURE IF I DID.
ZUI (CLOOM)
AND YOU BET YOUR ASS I'D HAVE CALLED THE POLICE INSTEAD OF YOU.
YEAH...
I'M SURE YOU WOULD HAVE...

SUGOU HIMSELF CLAIMED THAT HE WAS MANAGING THE SAO SERVER.

A GIRL RESEMBLING ASUNA WAS SEEN WITHIN A NEW VRMMO...

...BEING MANAGED BY RCT.

IT'S ALL A LITTLE TOO CONVENIENT FOR HIS PURPOSES...

CAN IT REALLY JUST BE A COINCIDENCE?

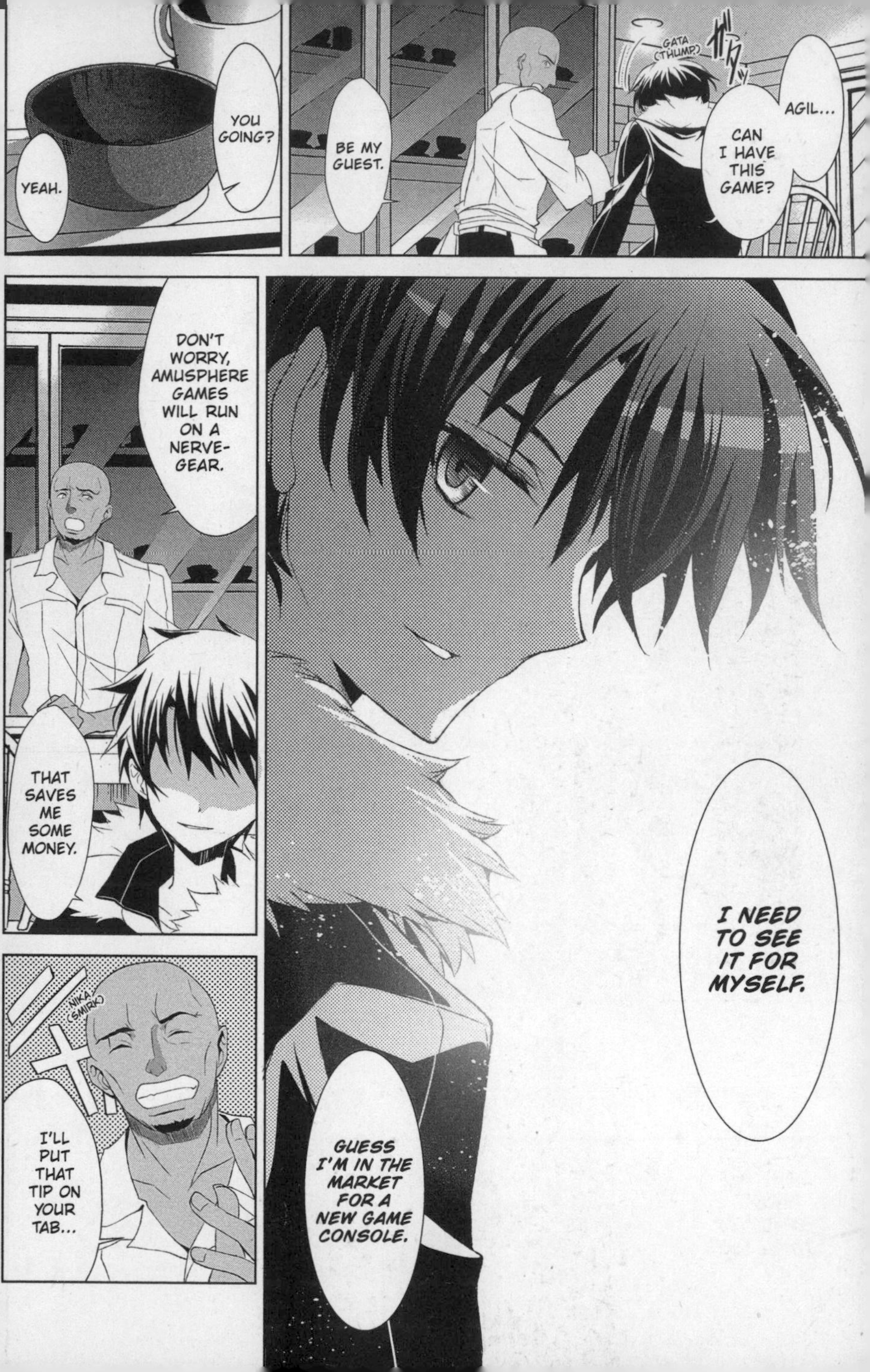
GATA (THUMP)
AGIL...
CAN I HAVE THIS GAME?
BE MY GUEST.
YOU GOING?
YEAH.
I NEED TO SEE IT FOR MYSELF.
GUESS I'M IN THE MARKET FOR A NEW GAME CONSOLE.
DON'T WORRY, AMUSPHERE GAMES WILL RUN ON A NERVE-GEAR.
THAT SAVES ME SOME MONEY.
NIKA (SMIRK)
I'LL PUT THAT TIP ON YOUR TAB...

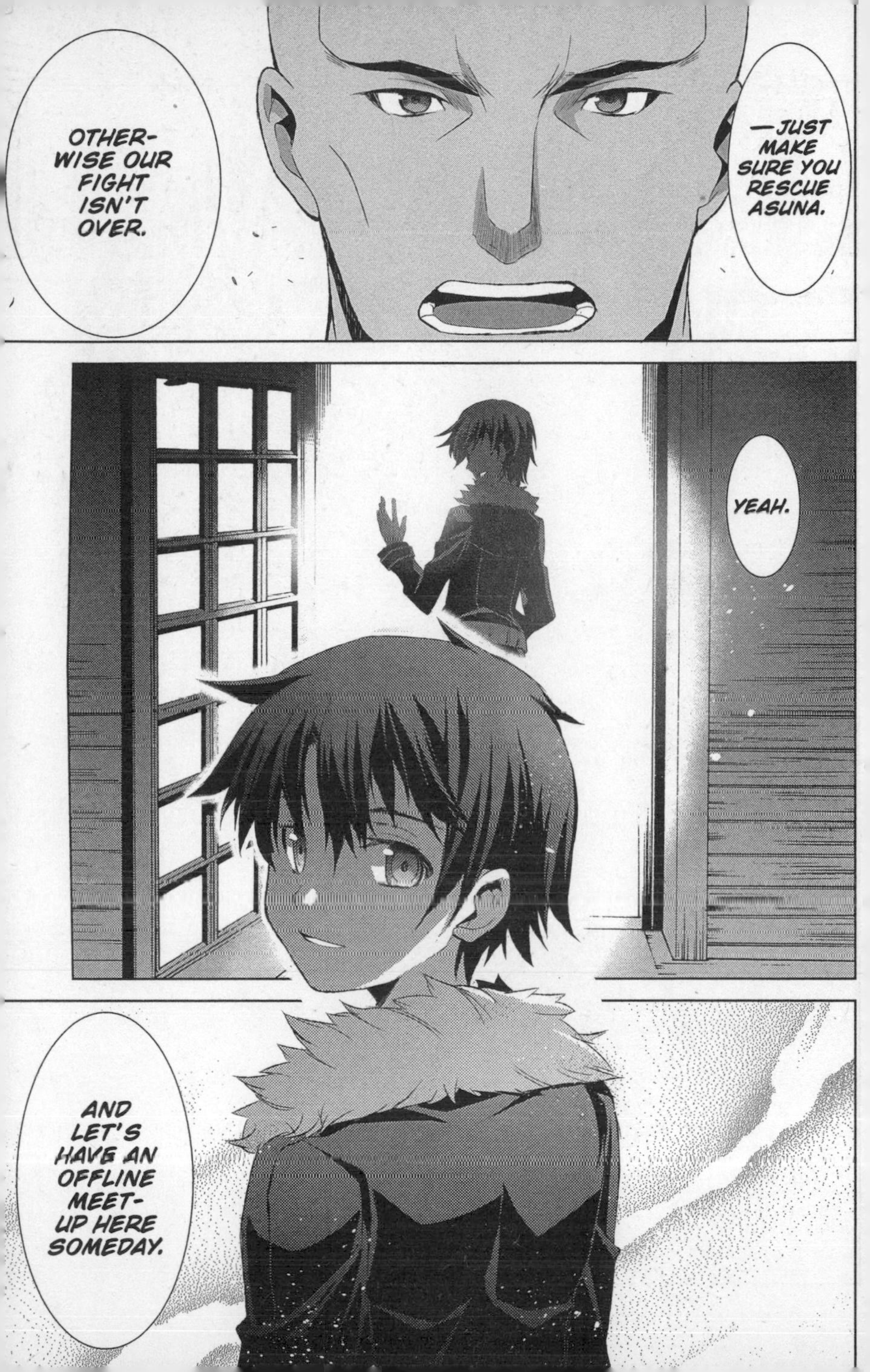
—JUST MAKE SURE YOU RESCUE ASUNA.
OTHER-WISE OUR FIGHT ISN'T OVER.
YEAH.
AND LET'S HAVE AN OFFLINE MEET-UP HERE SOMEDAY.

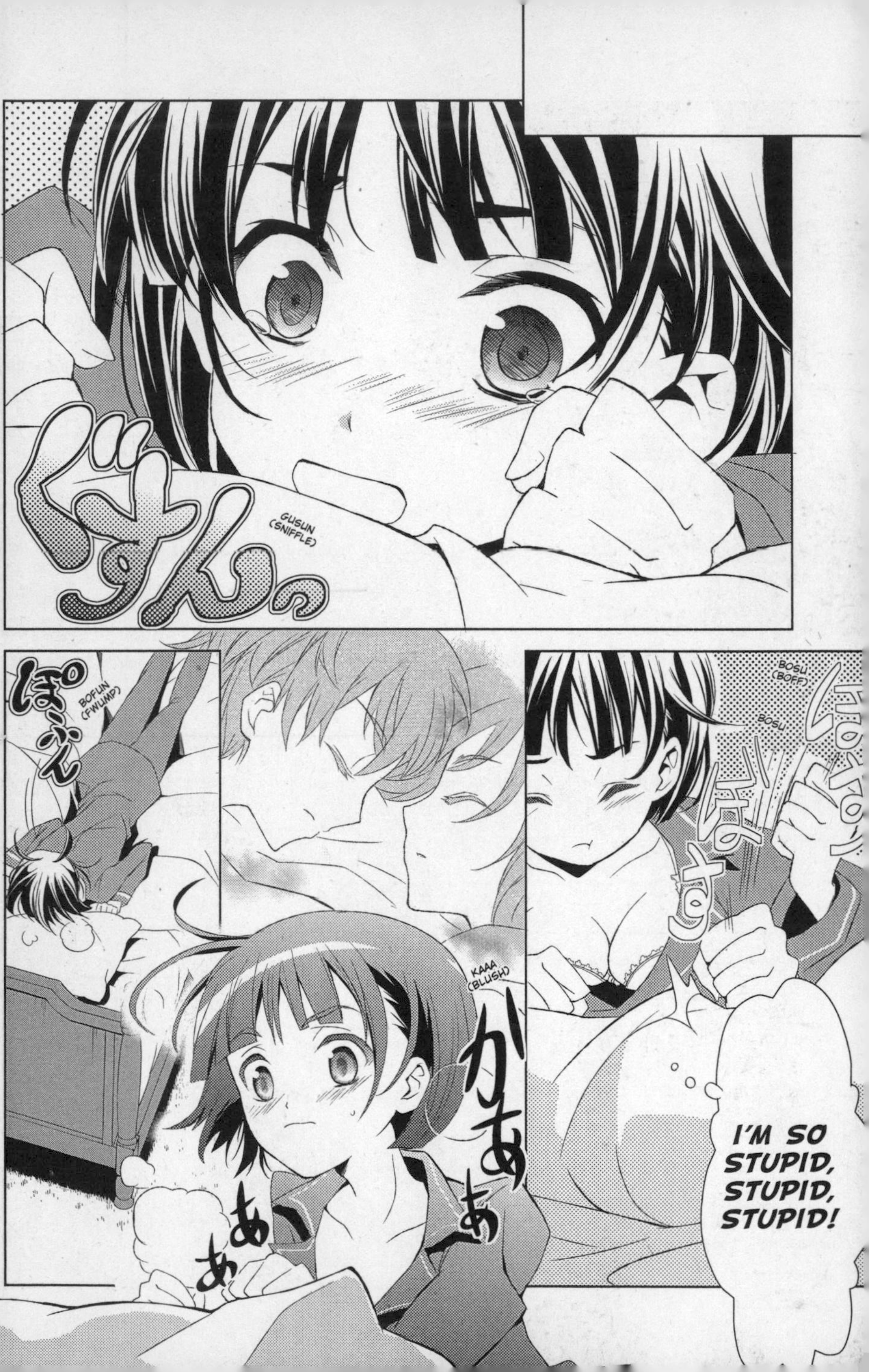
GUSUN (SNIFFLE)
BOSU (BOFF)
BOSU
I'M SO STUPID, STUPID, STUPID!
KAAA (BLUSH)
BOFUN (FWUMP)

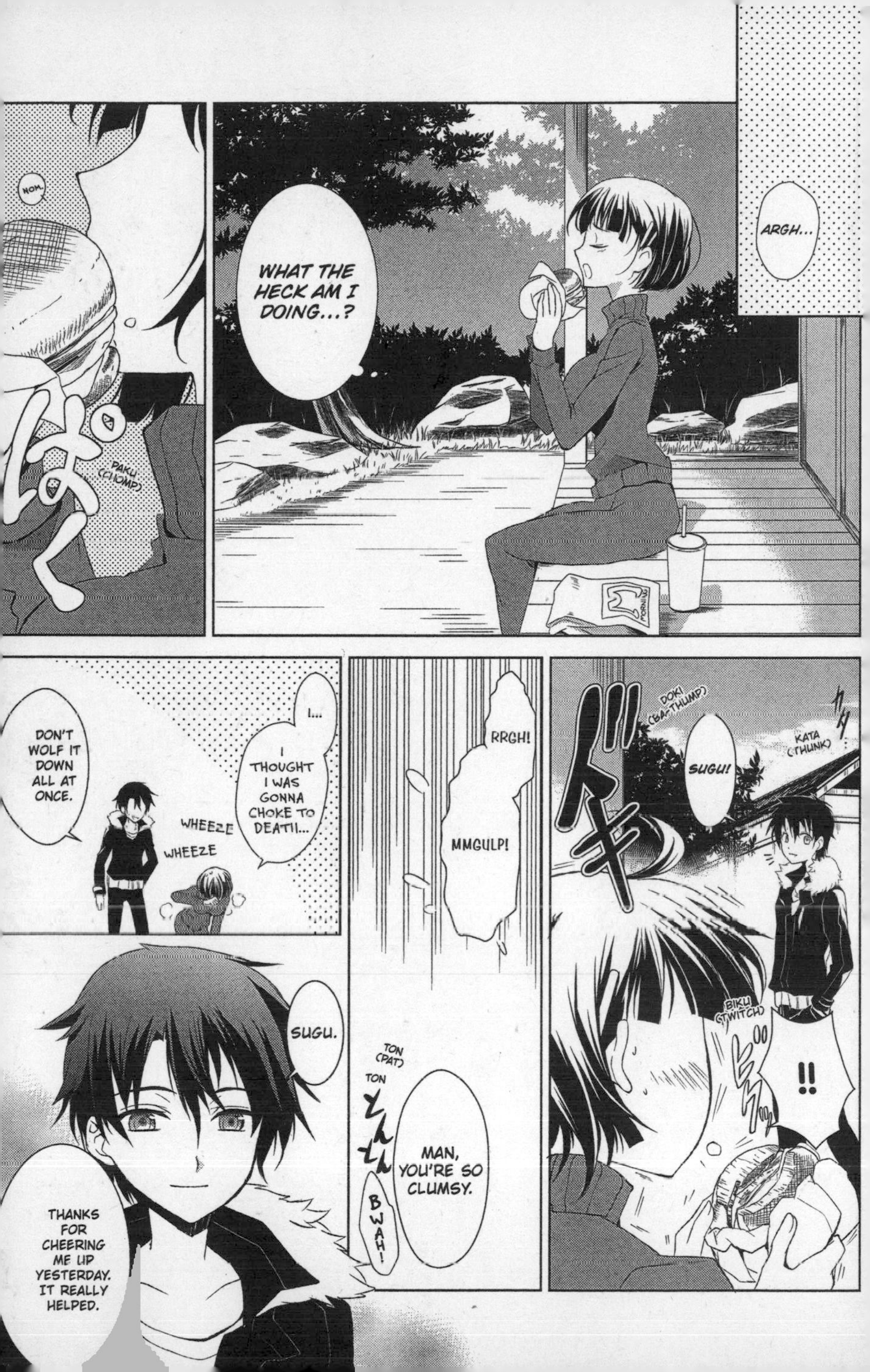
ARGH...
WHAT THE HECK AM I DOING...?
NOM.
PAKU (CHOMP)
DOKI (BA-THUMP)
KATA (THUNK)
SUGU!
BIKU (TWITCH)
!!
RRGH!
MMGULP!
TON (PAT) TON
MAN, YOU'RE SO CLUMSY.
BWAH!
I...
I THOUGHT I WAS GONNA CHOKE TO DEATH...
WHEEZE
WHEEZE
DON'T WOLF IT DOWN ALL AT ONCE.
SUGU.
THANKS FOR CHEERING ME UP YESTERDAY. IT REALLY HELPED.

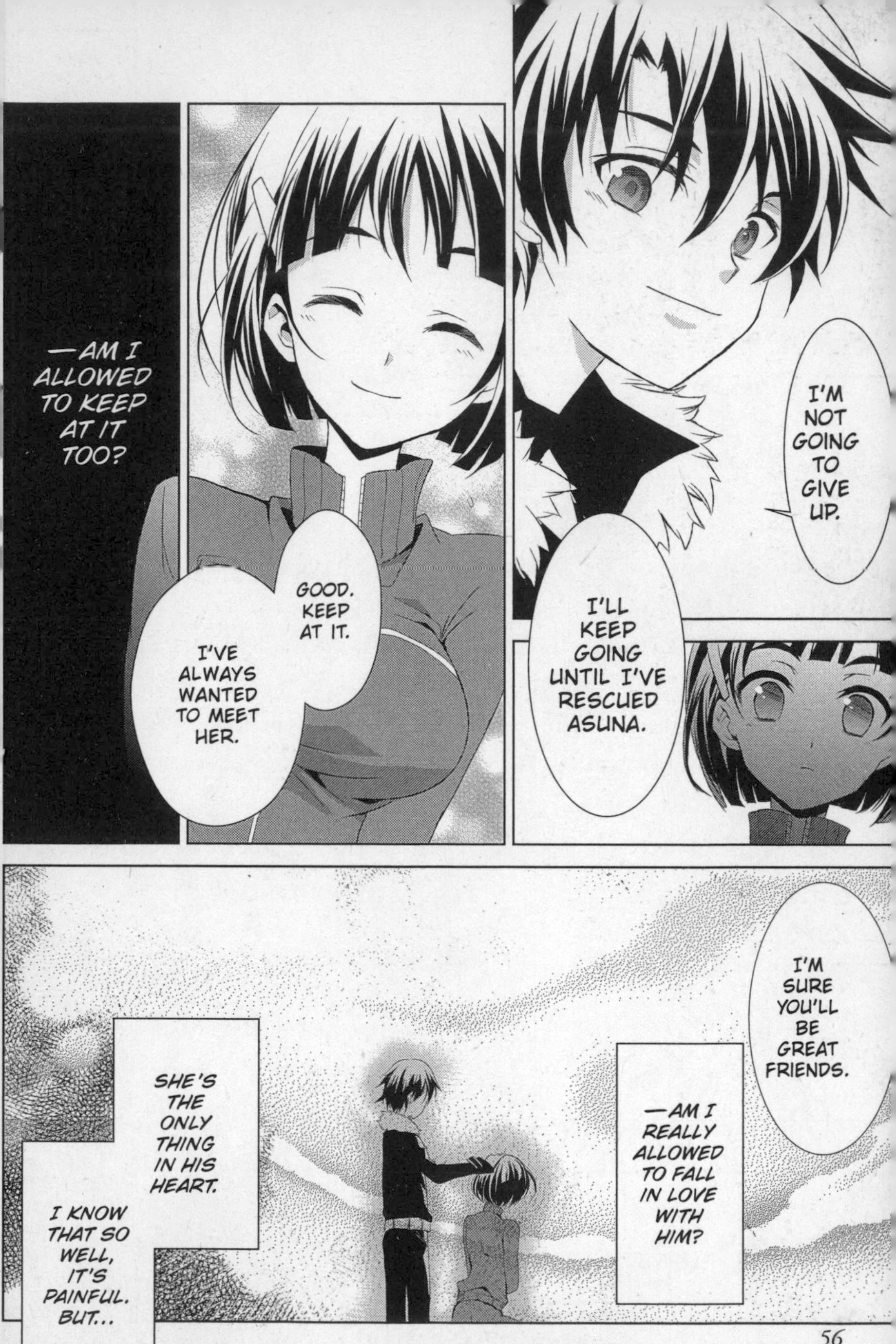
I'M NOT GOING TO GIVE UP.
I'LL KEEP GOING UNTIL I'VE RESCUED ASUNA.
GOOD. KEEP AT IT.
I'VE ALWAYS WANTED TO MEET HER.
—AM I ALLOWED TO KEEP AT IT TOO?
I'M SURE YOU'LL BE GREAT FRIENDS.
—AM I REALLY ALLOWED TO FALL IN LOVE WITH HIM?
SHE'S THE ONLY THING IN HIS HEART.
I KNOW THAT SO WELL, IT'S PAINFUL. BUT...

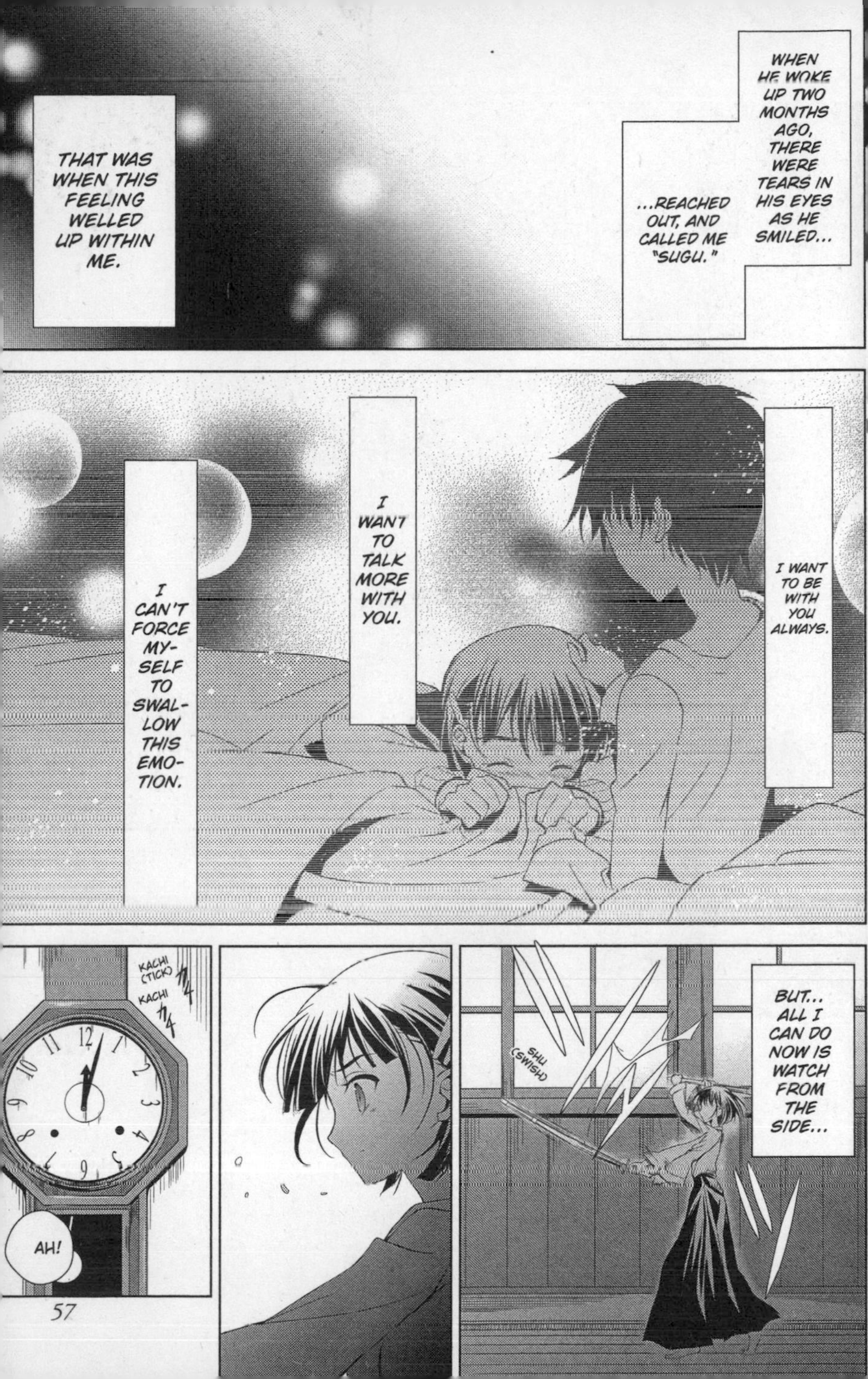
WHEN HE WOKE UP TWO MONTHS AGO, THERE WERE TEARS IN HIS EYES AS HE SMILED...
...REACHED OUT, AND CALLED ME "SUGU."
THAT WAS WHEN THIS FEELING WELLED UP WITHIN ME.
I WANT TO BE WITH YOU ALWAYS.
I WANT TO TALK MORE WITH YOU.
I CAN'T FORCE MY-SELF TO SWAL-LOW THIS EMO-TION.
BUT... ALL I CAN DO NOW IS WATCH FROM THE SIDE...
SHU (SWISH)
KACHI (TICK)
KACHI
AH!

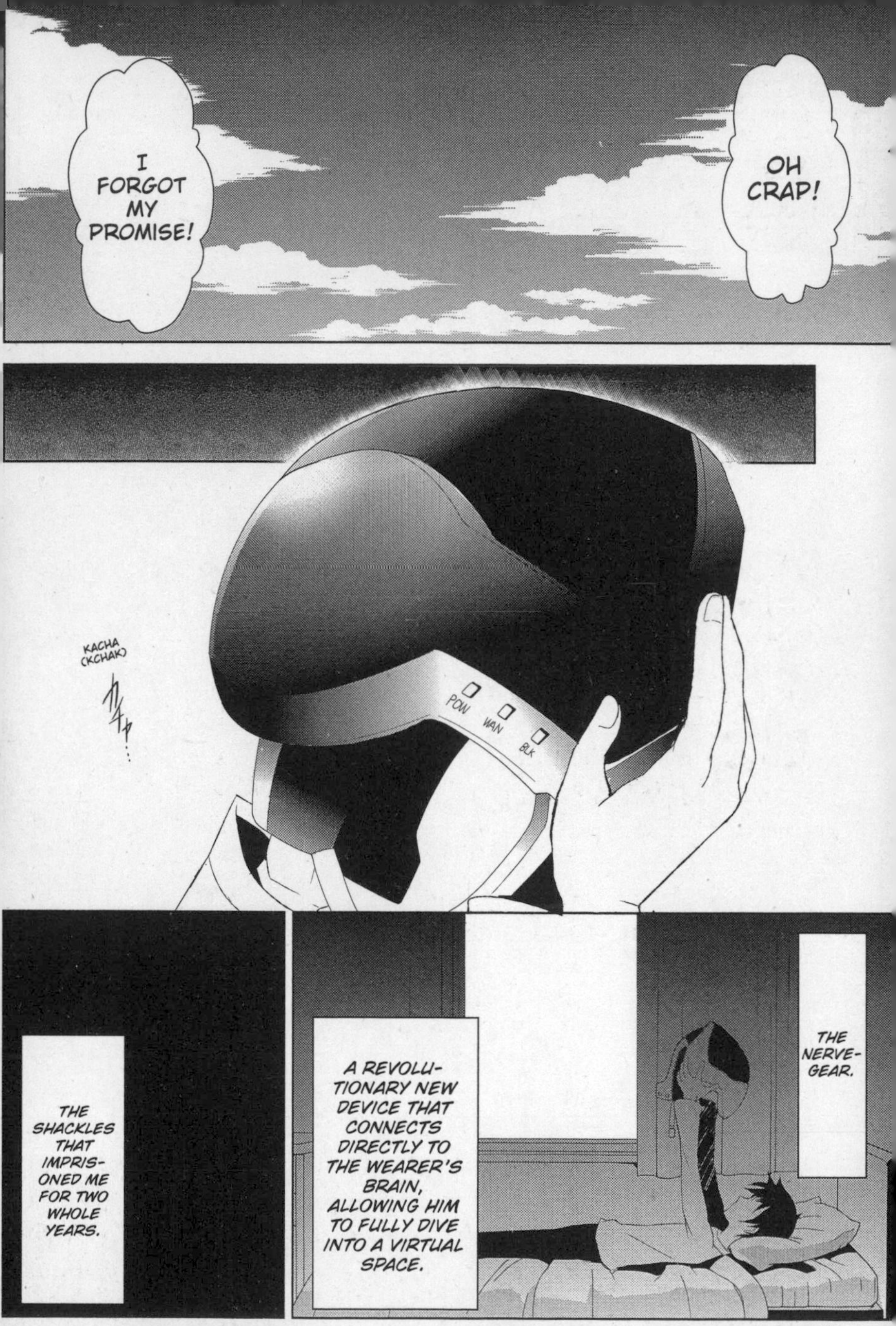
OH CRAP!
I FORGOT MY PROMISE!
POW
WAN
BLK
KACHA (KCHAK)
カチャ…
THE NERVE-GEAR.
A REVOLUTIONARY NEW DEVICE THAT CONNECTS DIRECTLY TO THE WEARER'S BRAIN, ALLOWING HIM TO FULLY DIVE INTO A VIRTUAL SPACE.
THE SHACKLES THAT IMPRISONED ME FOR TWO WHOLE YEARS.

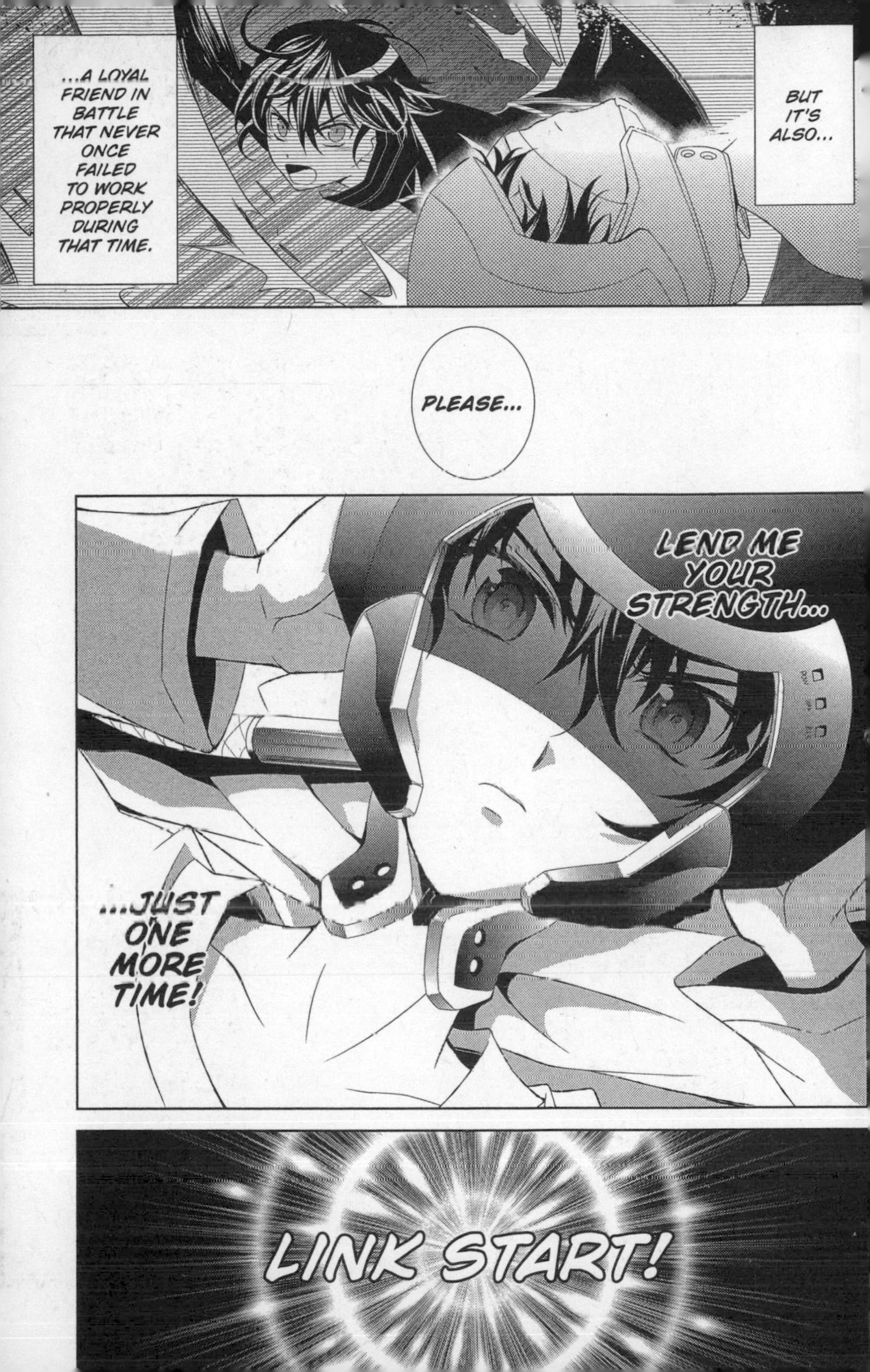
BUT IT'S ALSO...
...A LOYAL FRIEND IN BATTLE THAT NEVER ONCE FAILED TO WORK PROPERLY DURING THAT TIME.
PLEASE...
LEND ME YOUR STRENGTH...
...JUST ONE MORE TIME!
LINK START!

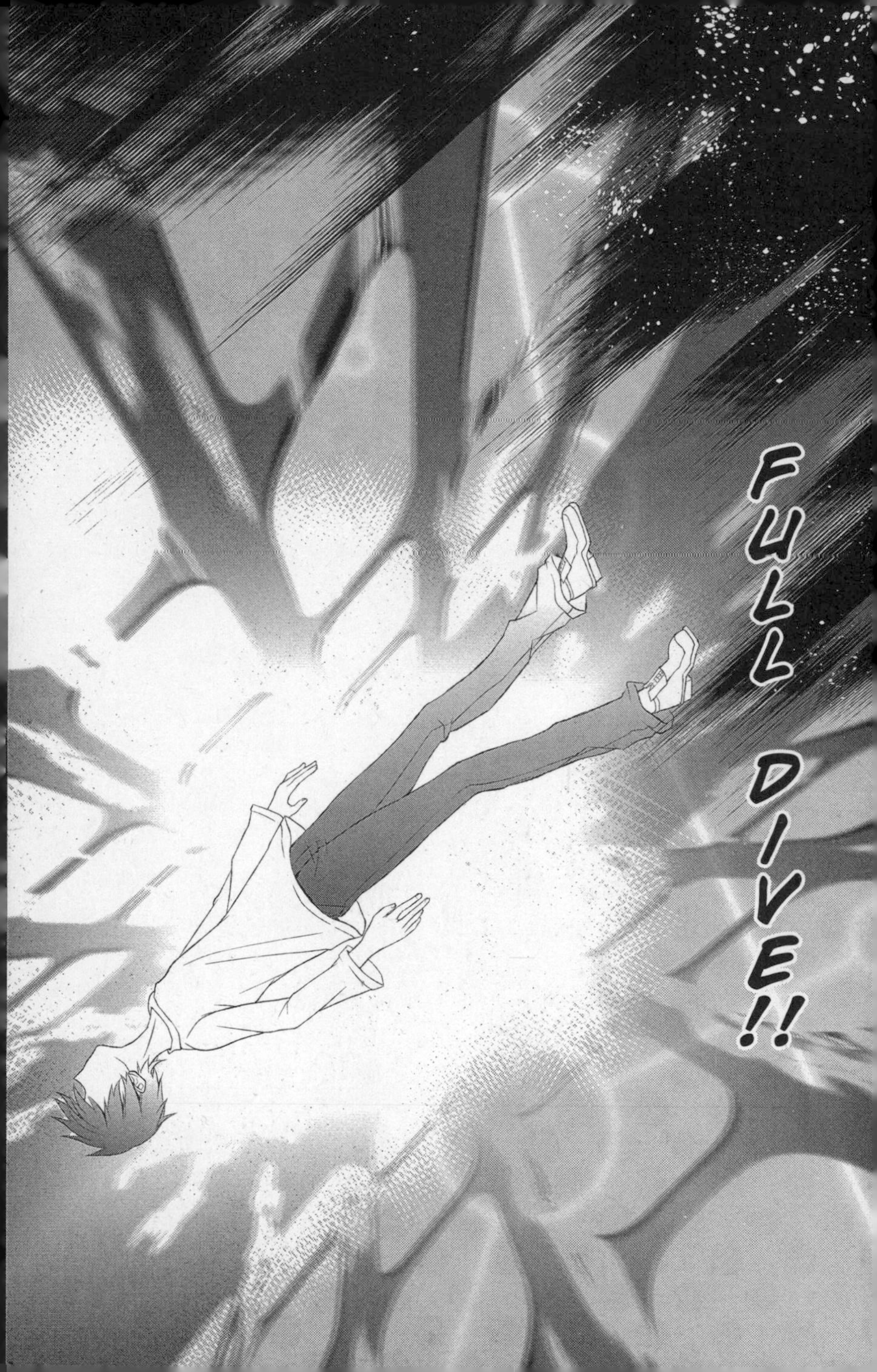
FULL DIVE!!

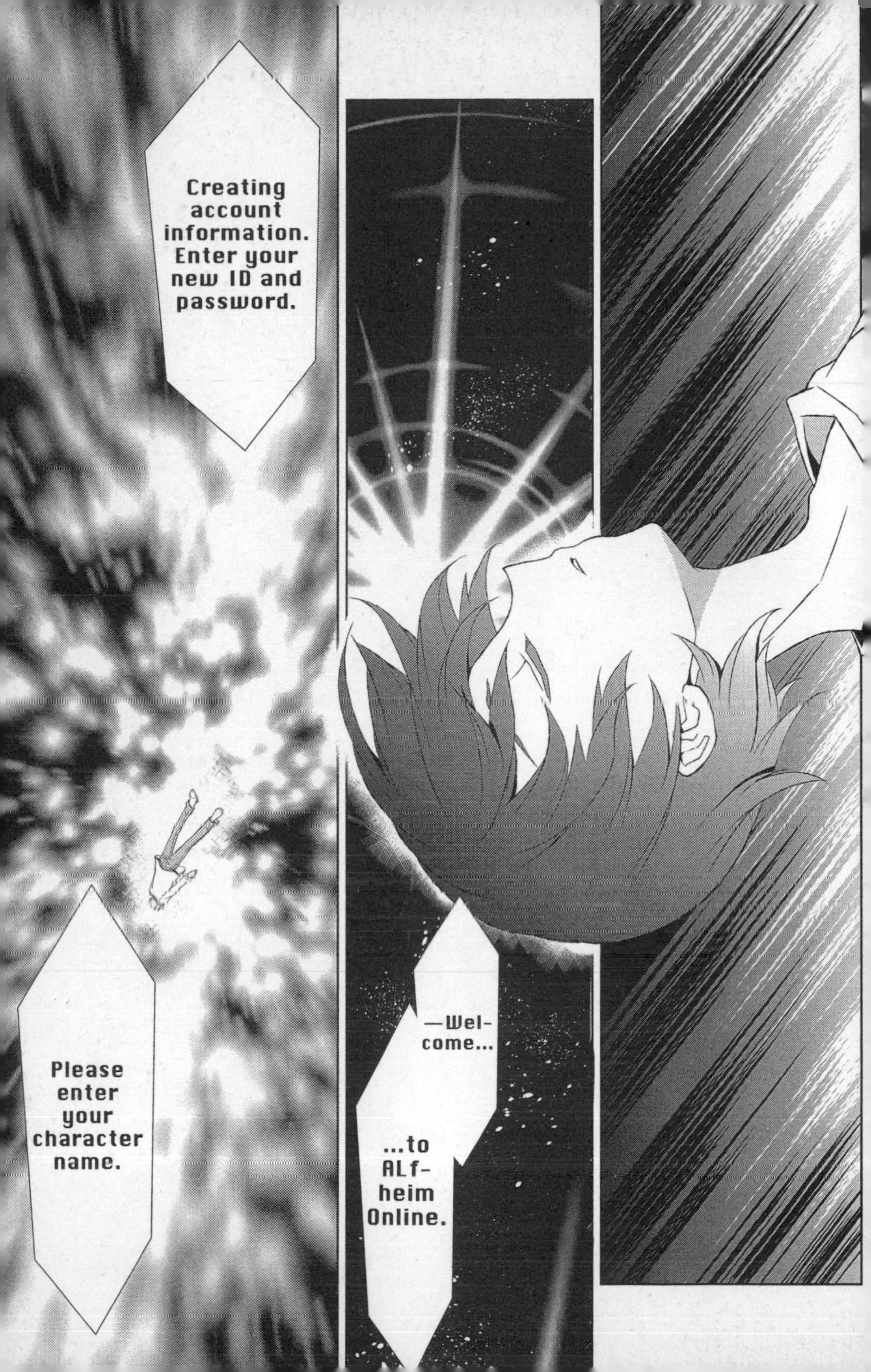
—Wel-come...
...to ALf-heim Online.
Creating account information. Enter your new ID and password.
Please enter your character name.

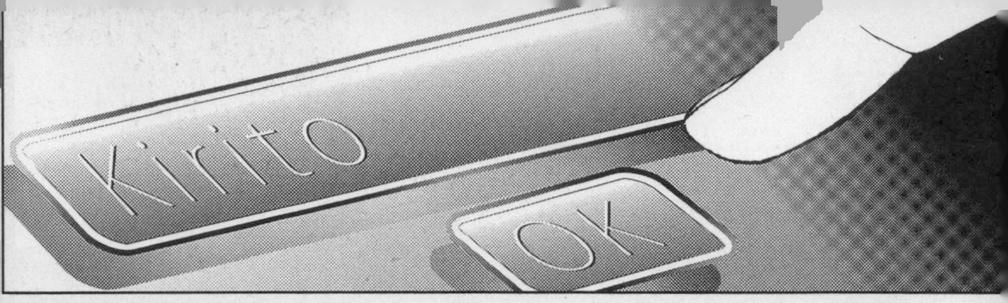
Kirito
OK

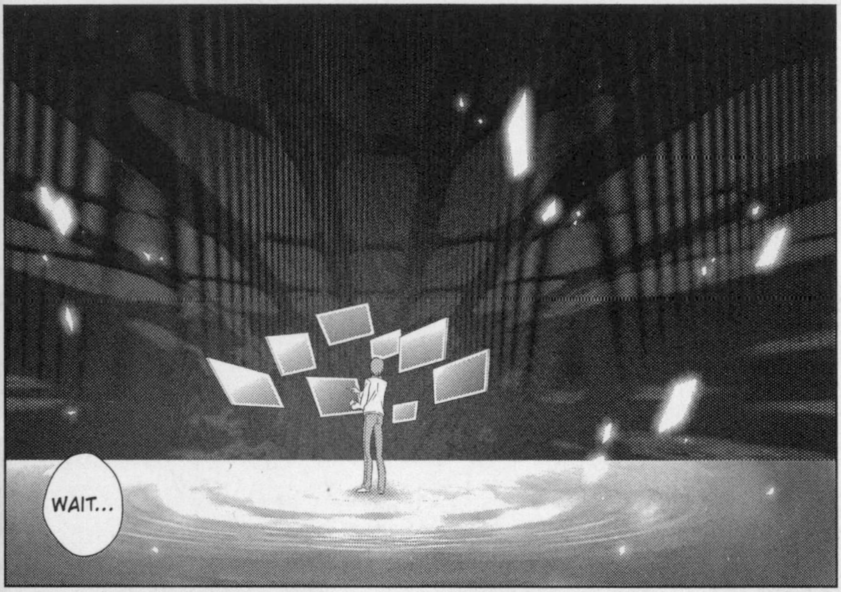
WAIT...

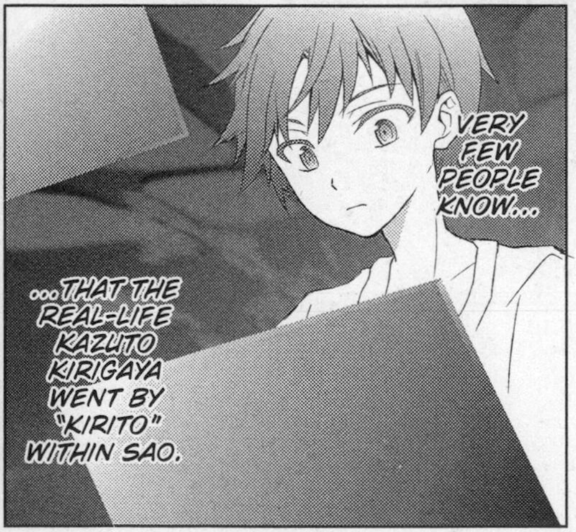
VERY FEW PEOPLE KNOW...
...THAT THE REAL-LIFE KAZUTO KIRIGAYA WENT BY "KIRITO" WITHIN SAO.

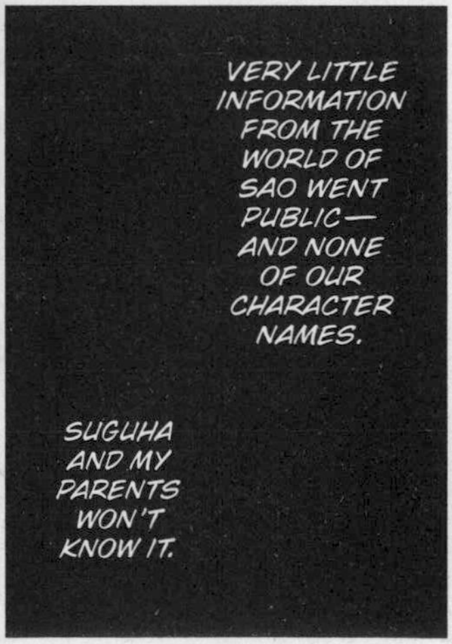
VERY LITTLE INFORMATION FROM THE WORLD OF SAO WENT PUBLIC— AND NONE OF OUR CHARACTER NAMES.
SUGUHA AND MY PARENTS WON'T KNOW IT.

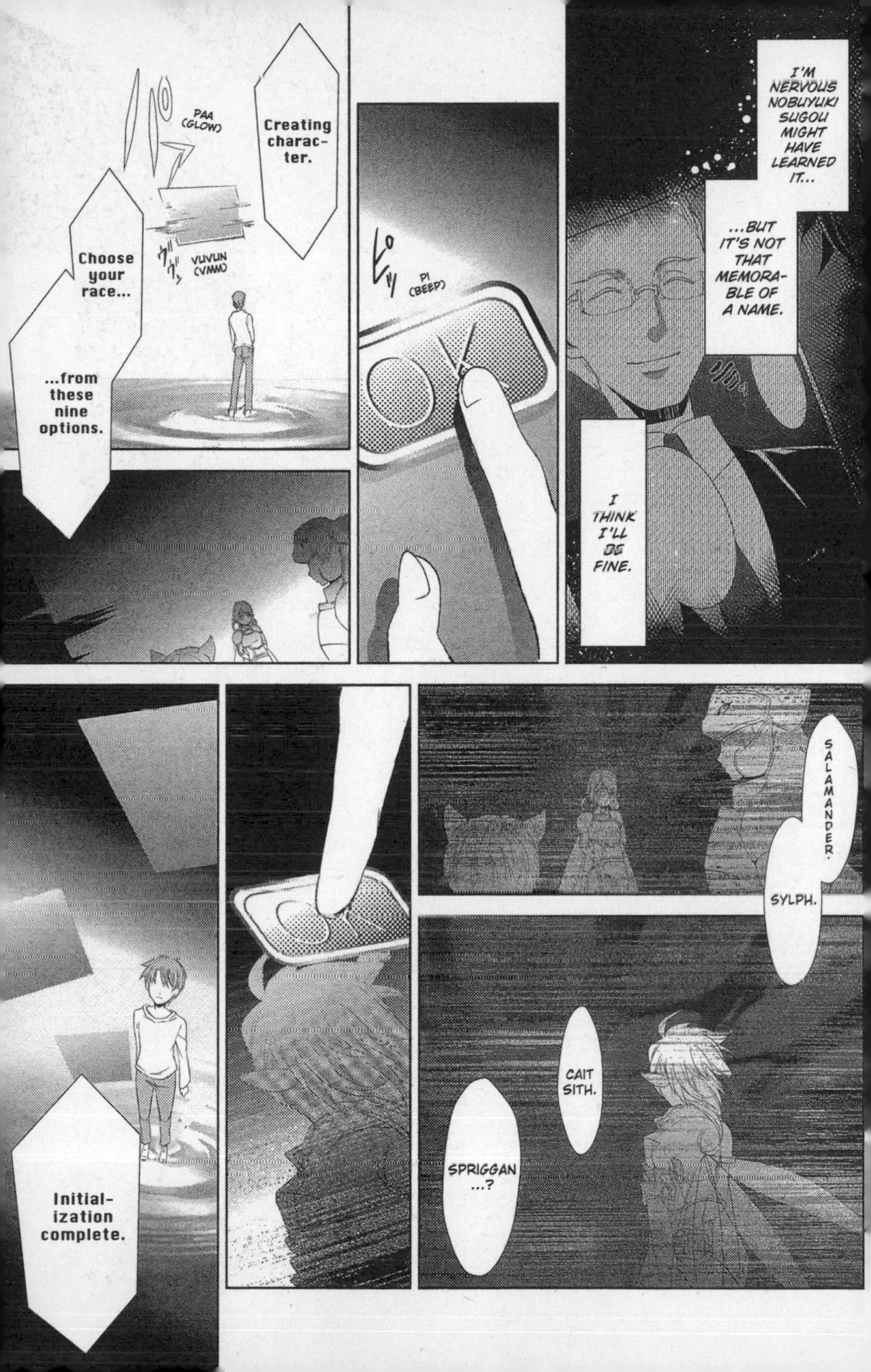
I'M NERVOUS NOBUYUKI SUGOU MIGHT HAVE LEARNED IT...
...BUT IT'S NOT THAT MEMORABLE OF A NAME.
I THINK I'LL BE FINE.
PI (BEEP)
Creating character.
PAA (GLOW)
VUVUN (VMM)
Choose your race...
...from these nine options.
SALAMANDER.
SYLPH.
CAIT SITH.
SPRIGGAN ...?
Initialization complete.

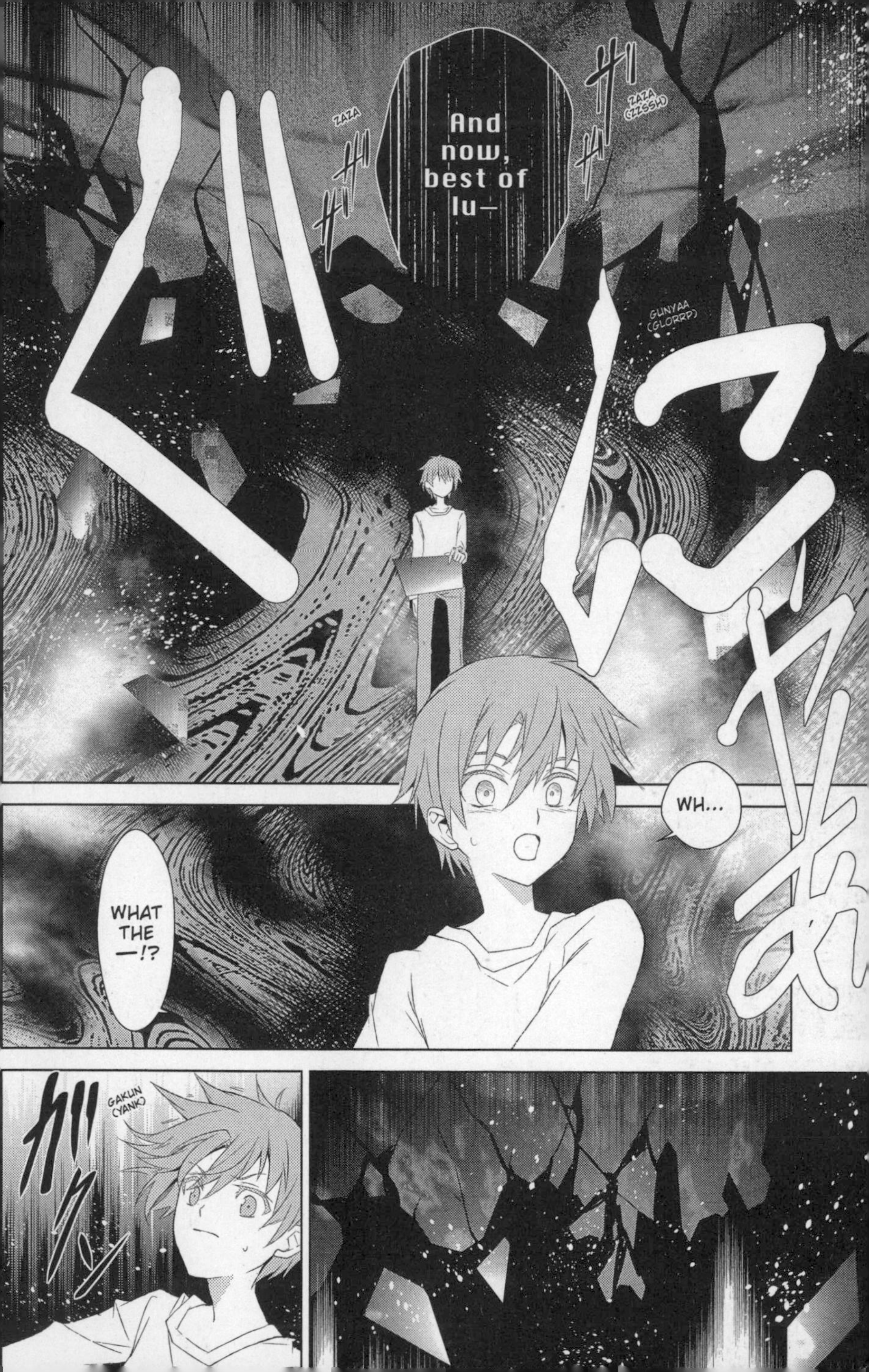
ZAZA (ZZSSH)
And now, best of lu—
ZAZA
GUNYAA (GLORRP)
WH...
WHAT THE—!?
GAKUN (YANK)

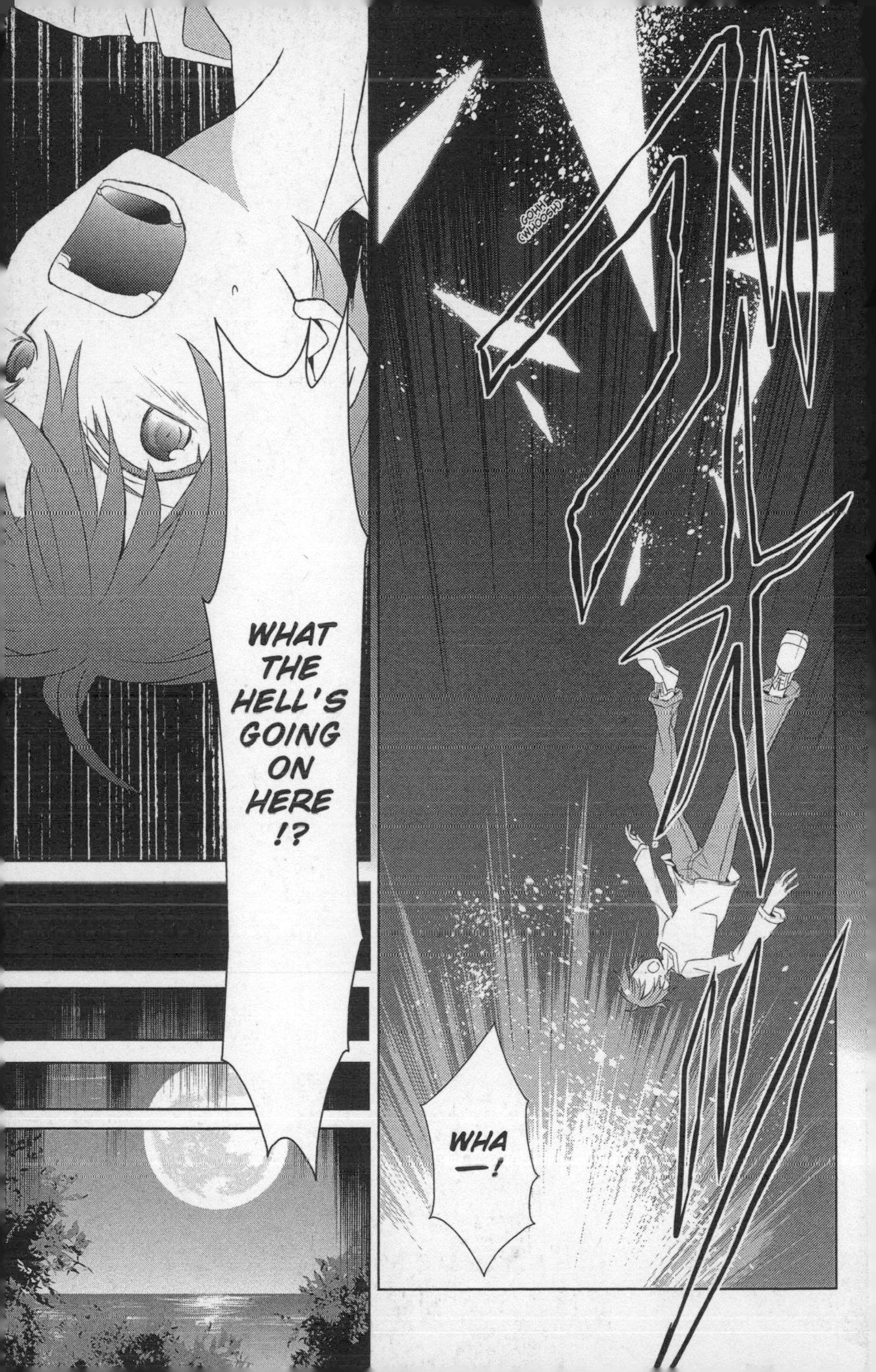
GOHH (WHOOSH)
WHA—!
WHAT THE HELL'S GOING ON HERE!?

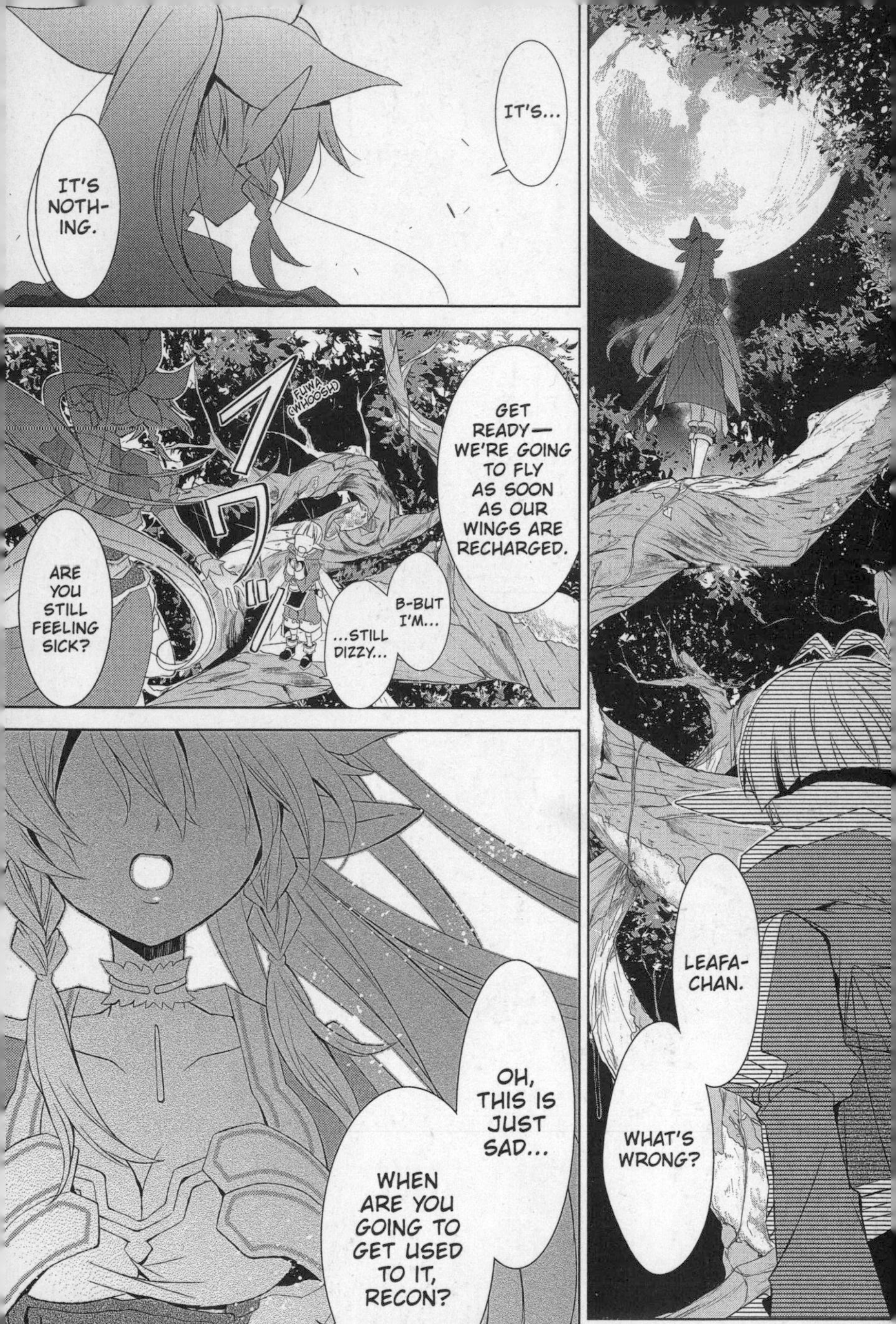
LEAFA-CHAN.
WHAT'S WRONG?
IT'S...
IT'S NOTHING.
FUWA (WHOOSH)
GET READY—WE'RE GOING TO FLY AS SOON AS OUR WINGS ARE RECHARGED.
B-BUT I'M...
...STILL DIZZY...
ARE YOU STILL FEELING SICK?
OH, THIS IS JUST SAD...
WHEN ARE YOU GOING TO GET USED TO IT, RECON?

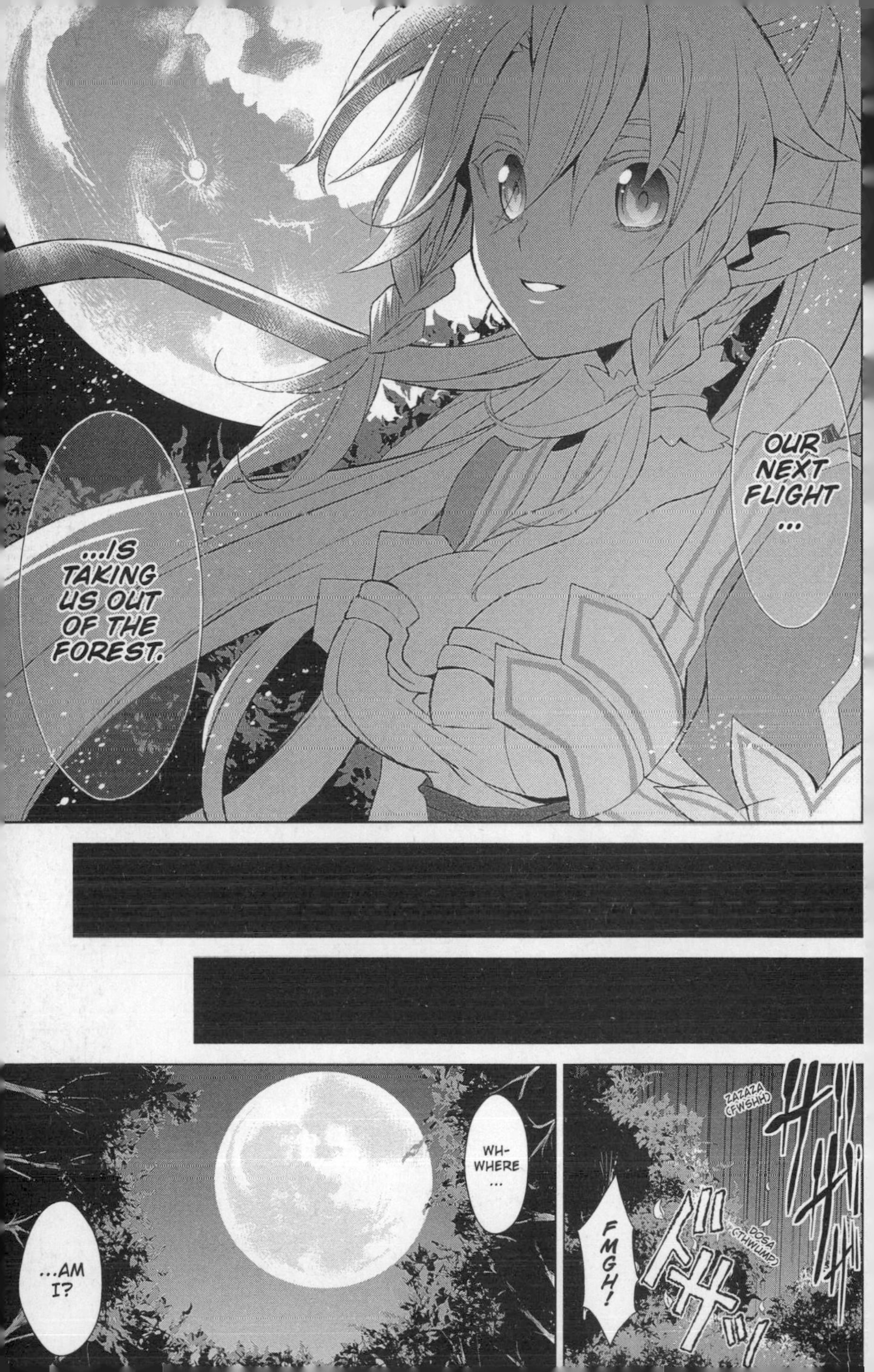
OUR NEXT FLIGHT ...
...IS TAKING US OUT OF THE FOREST.
ZAZAZA (FWSHH)
DOSA (THWUMP)
FMGH!
WH-WHERE ...
...AM I?

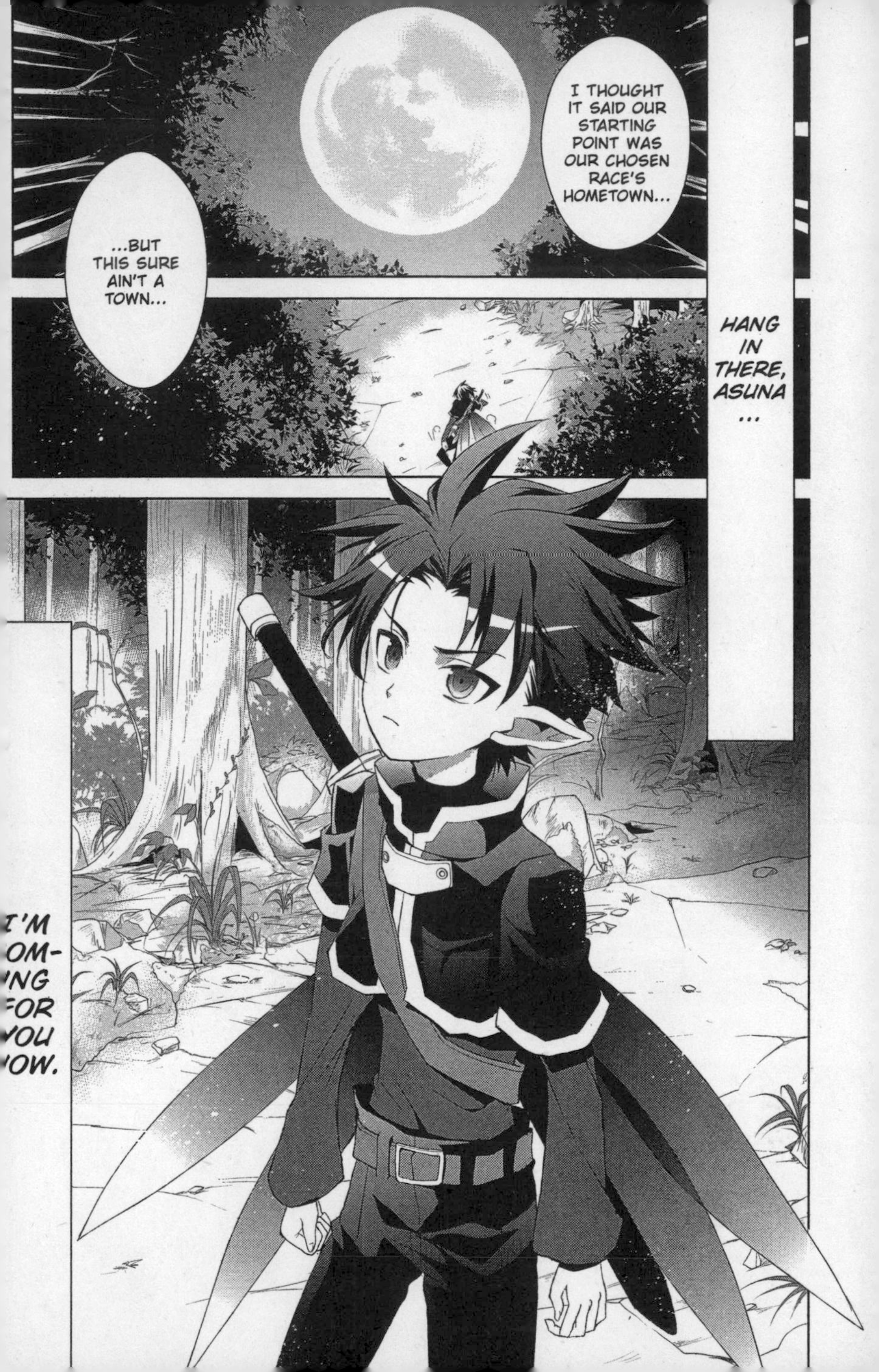
I THOUGHT IT SAID OUR STARTING POINT WAS OUR CHOSEN RACE'S HOMETOWN...
...BUT THIS SURE AIN'T A TOWN...
HANG IN THERE, ASUNA...
I'M OM- NG FOR YOU OW.

SWORD ART ONLINE
FAIRY DANCE

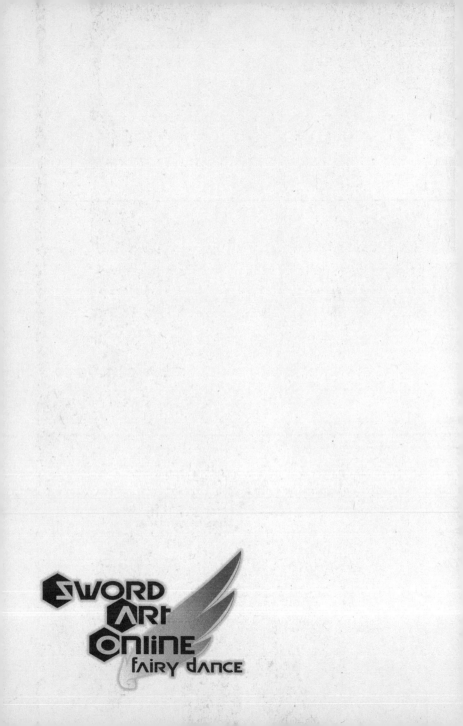

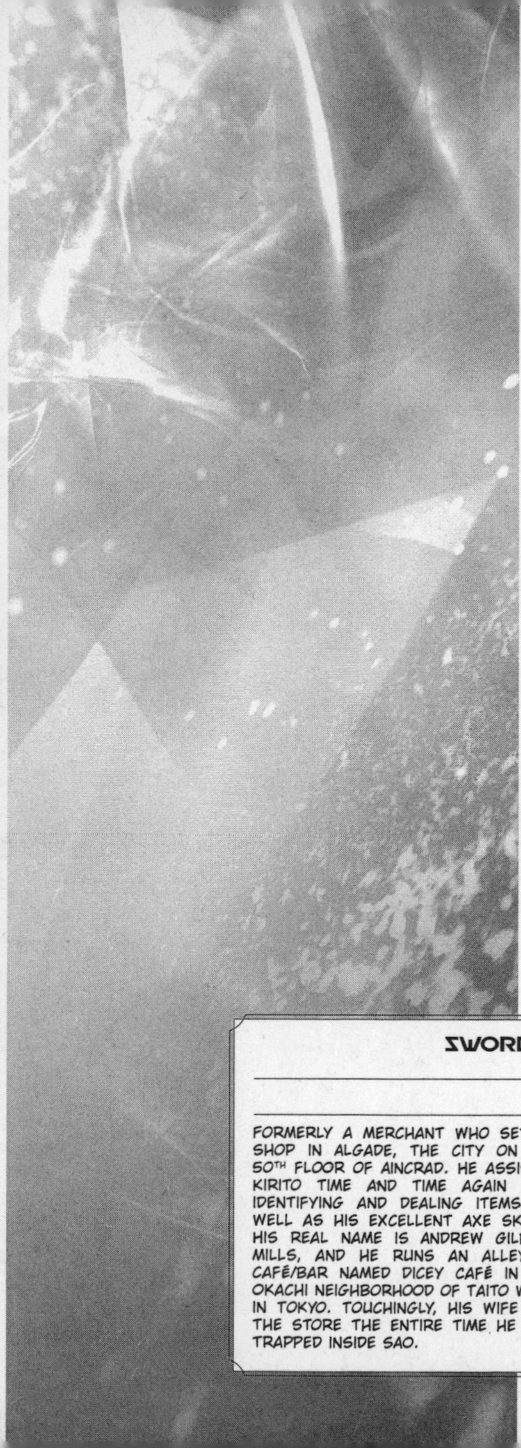

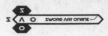

SWORD ART ONLINE fairy dance 01
BACKGROUND GUIDE

AGIL

FORMERLY A MERCHANT WHO SET UP SHOP IN ALGADE, THE CITY ON THE 50TH FLOOR OF AINCRAD. HE ASSISTED KIRITO TIME AND TIME AGAIN WITH IDENTIFYING AND DEALING ITEMS, AS WELL AS HIS EXCELLENT AXE SKILLS. HIS REAL NAME IS ANDREW GILBERT MILLS, AND HE RUNS AN ALLEYWAY CAFÉ/BAR NAMED DICEY CAFÉ IN THE OKACHI NEIGHBORHOOD OF TAITO WARD IN TOKYO. TOUCHINGLY, HIS WIFE RAN THE STORE THE ENTIRE TIME HE WAS TRAPPED INSIDE SAO.

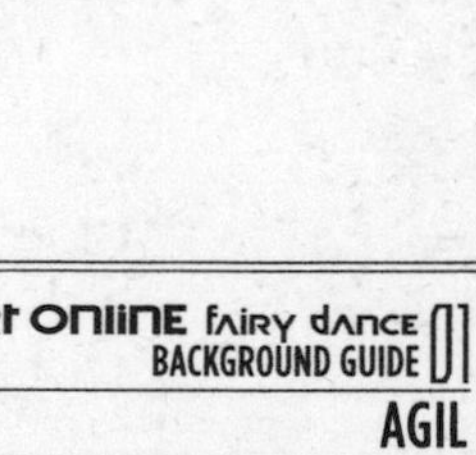

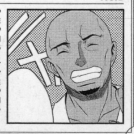

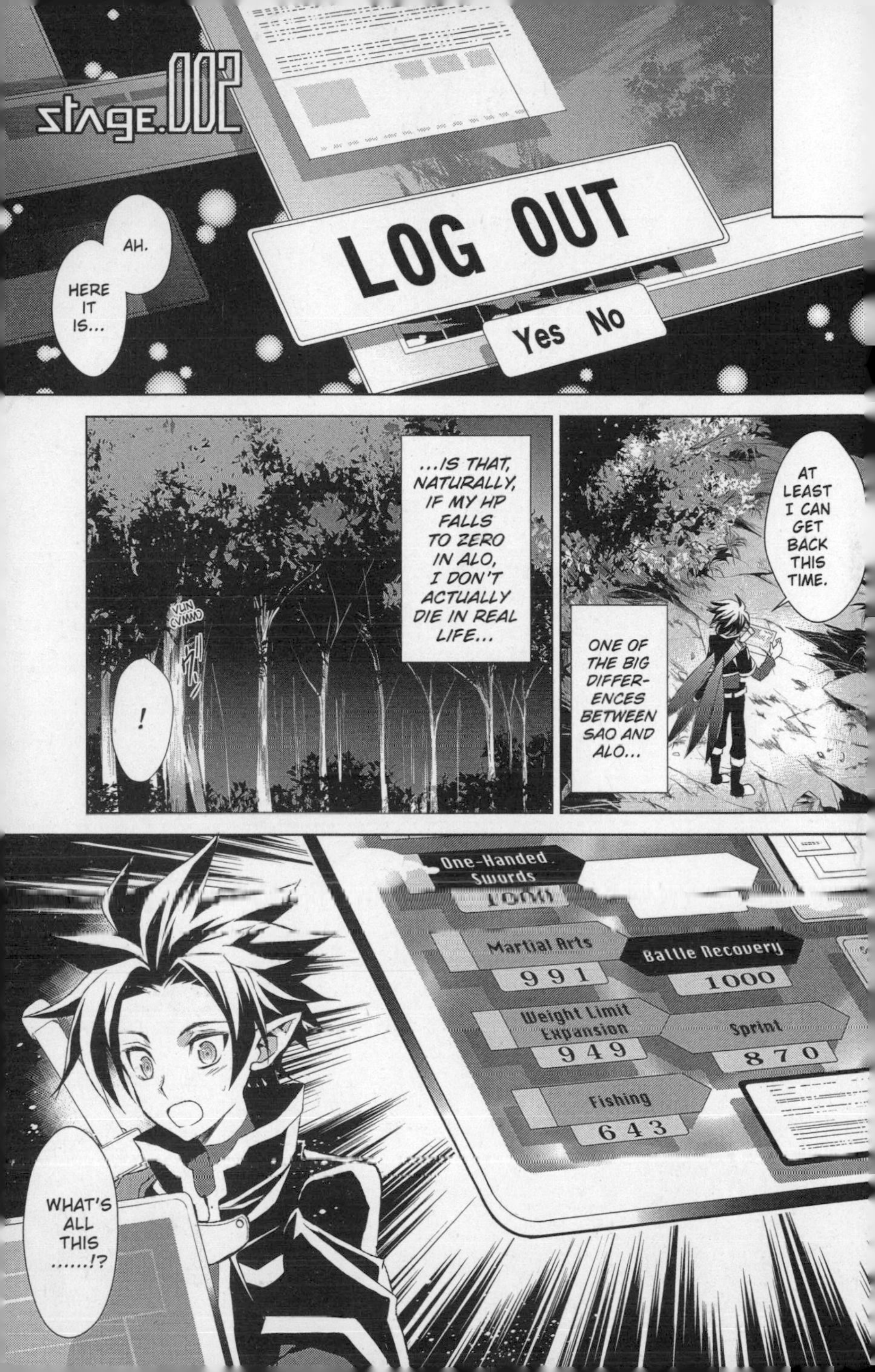
stage.002
LOG OUT
Yes No
AH.
HERE IT IS...
AT LEAST I CAN GET BACK THIS TIME.
ONE OF THE BIG DIFFERENCES BETWEEN SAO AND ALO...
...IS THAT, NATURALLY, IF MY HP FALLS TO ZERO IN ALO, I DON'T ACTUALLY DIE IN REAL LIFE...
VUN VIMM
!
One-Handed Swords
Martial Arts
991
Battle Recovery
1000
Weight Limit Expansion
949
Sprint
870
Fishing
643
WHAT'S ALL THIS ......!?

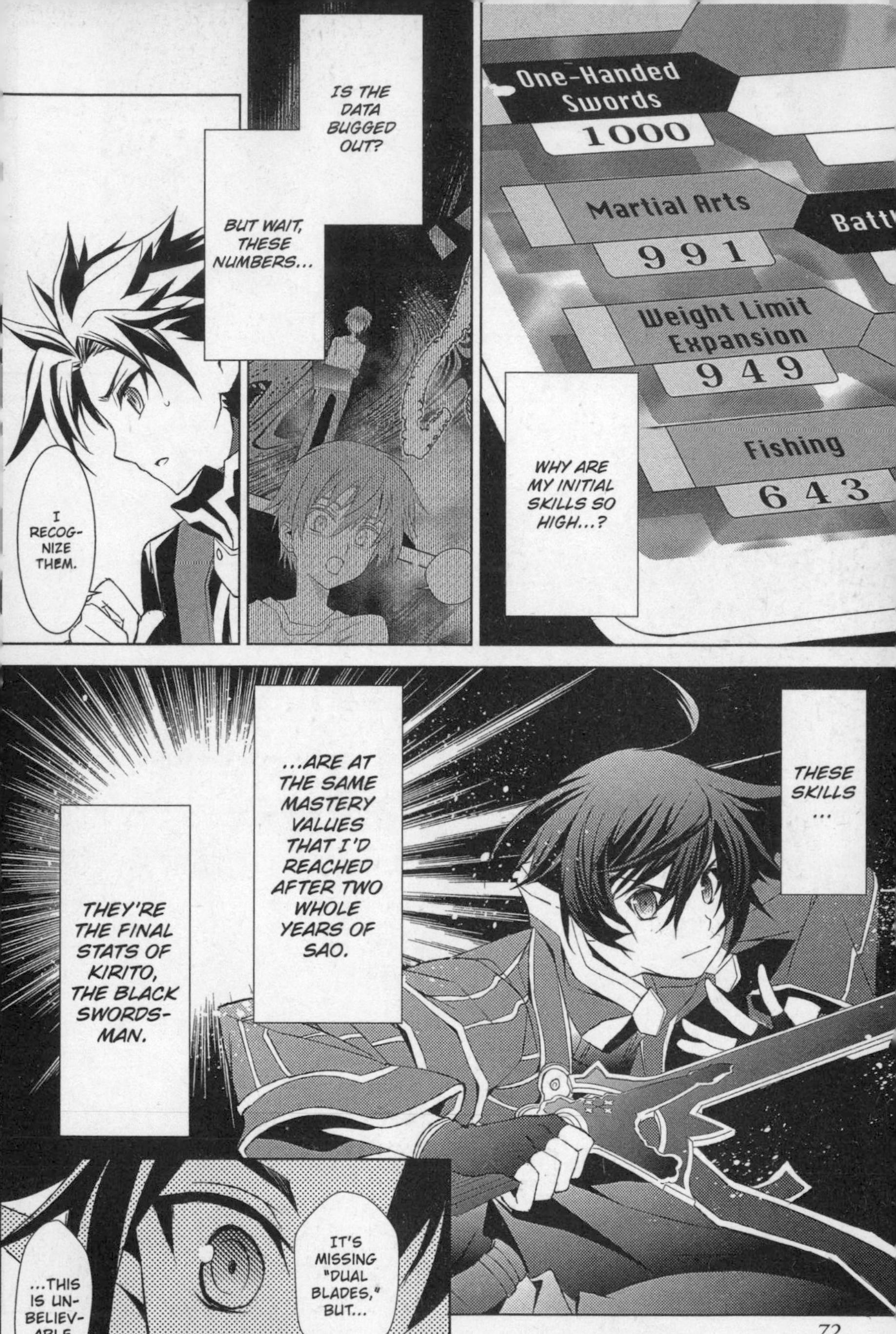

One-Handed Swords
1000
Martial Arts
991
Weight Limit Expansion
949
Fishing
643
WHY ARE MY INITIAL SKILLS SO HIGH...?
IS THE DATA BUGGED OUT?
BUT WAIT, THESE NUMBERS...
I RECOGNIZE THEM.
THESE SKILLS...
...ARE AT THE SAME MASTERY VALUES THAT I'D REACHED AFTER TWO WHOLE YEARS OF SAO.
THEY'RE THE FINAL STATS OF KIRITO, THE BLACK SWORDSMAN.
IT'S MISSING "DUAL BLADES," BUT...
...THIS IS UNBELIEVABLE.

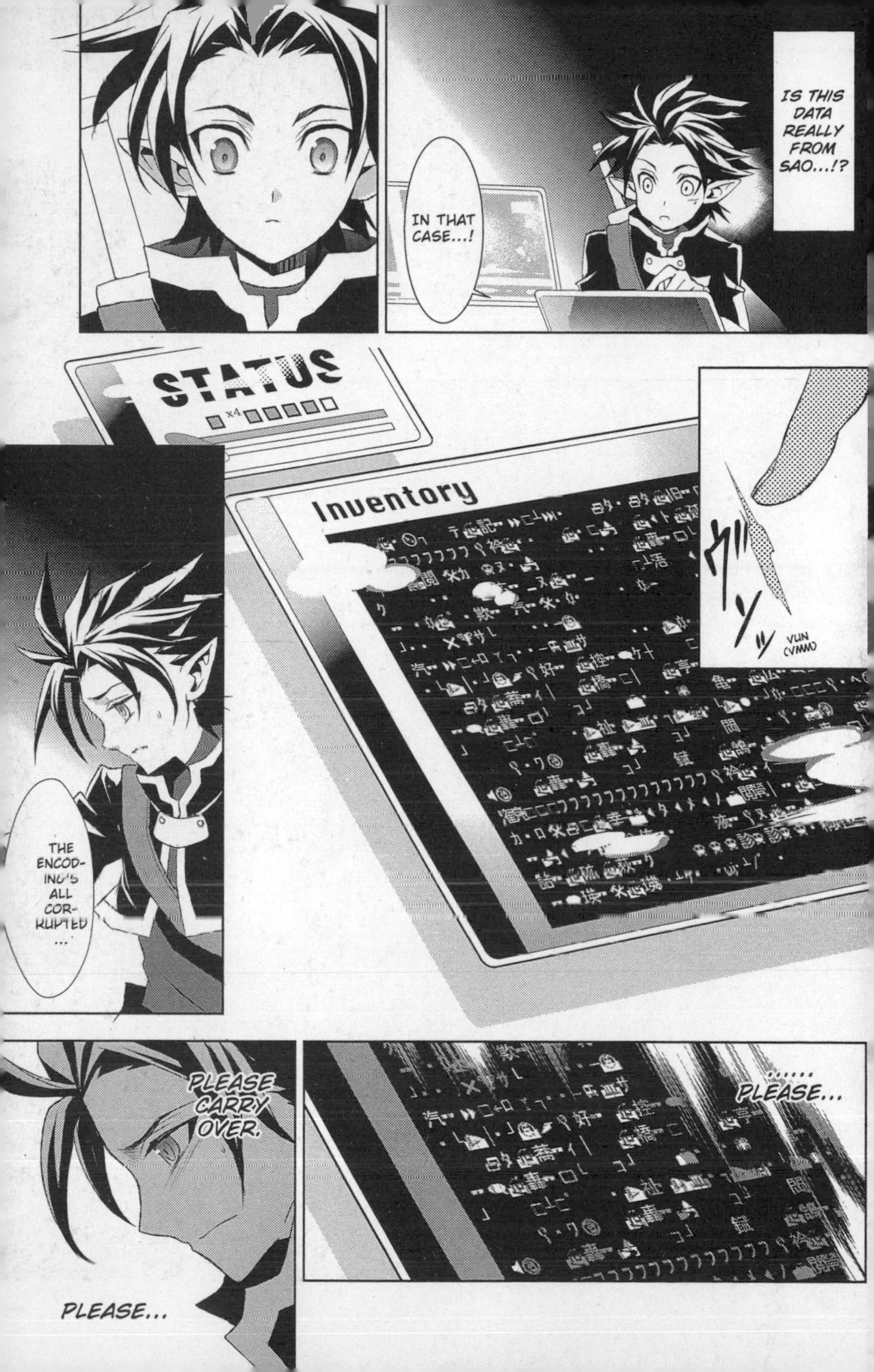
IS THIS DATA REALLY FROM SAO...!?
IN THAT CASE...!
VUN (VMMM)
STATUS
Inventory
THE ENCODING'S ALL CORRUPTED...
......PLEASE...
PLEASE CARRY OVER.
PLEASE...

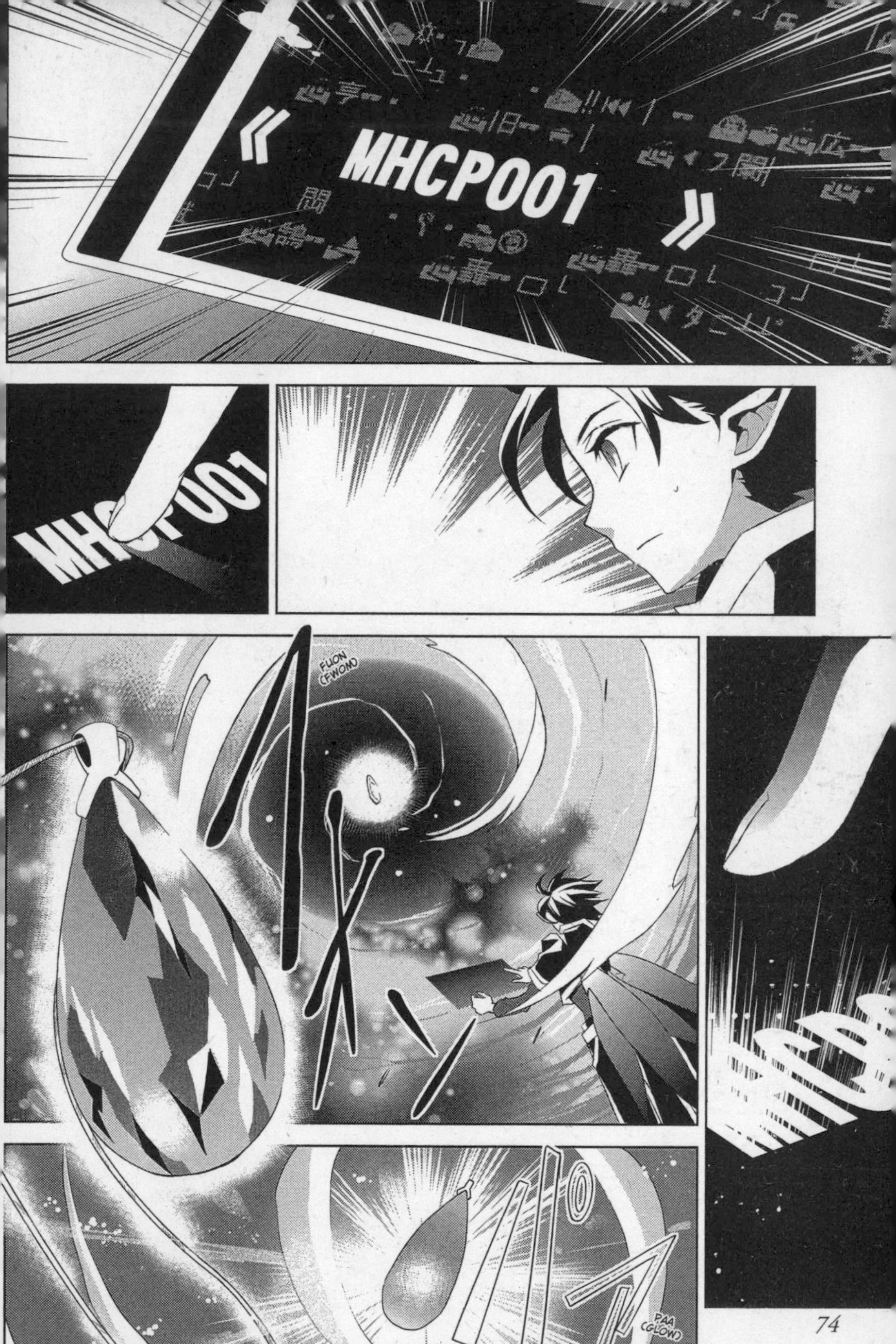
« MHCP001 »
FUON (FWOM)
PAA (GLOW)

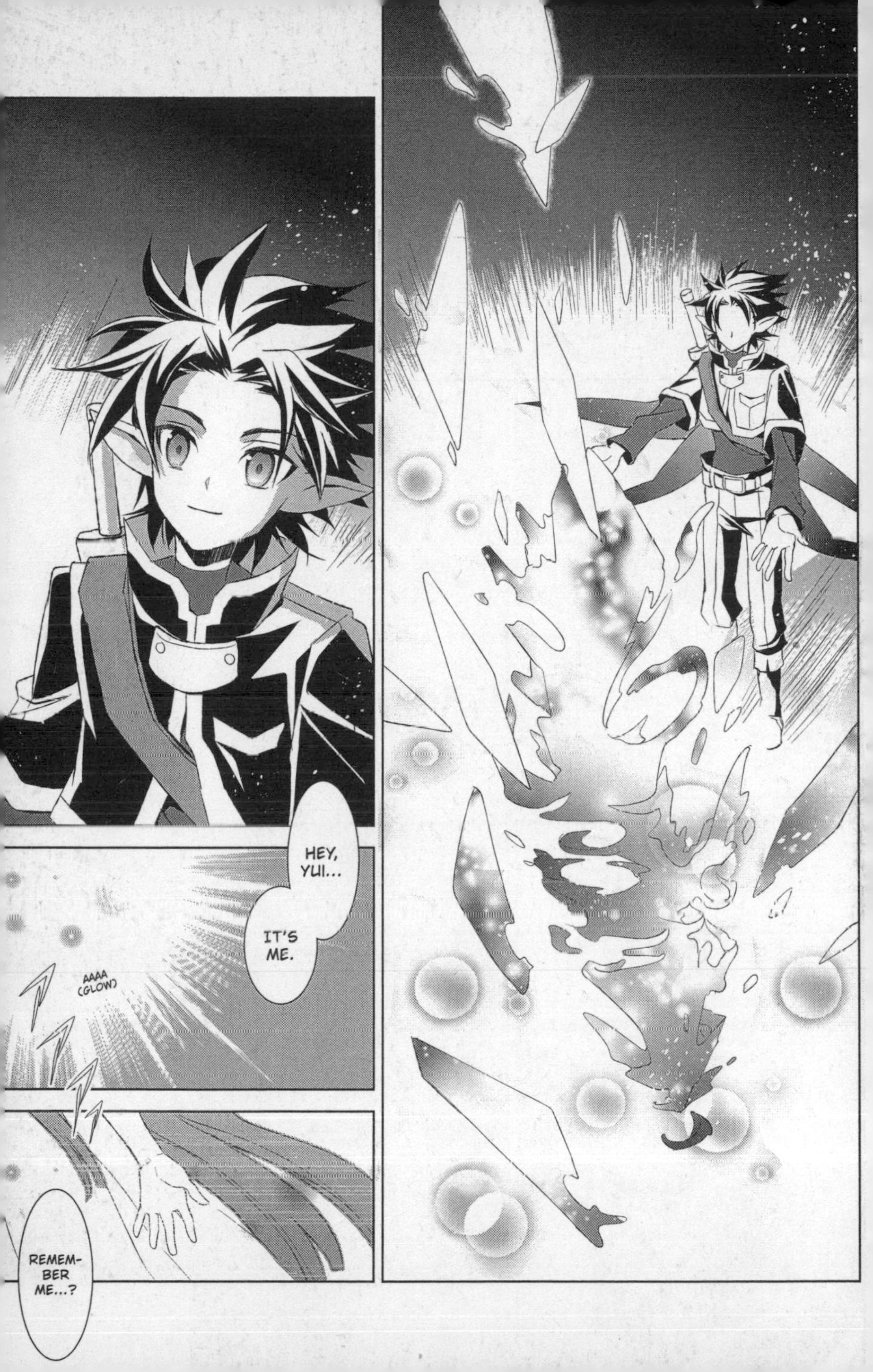
HEY, YUI...
IT'S ME.
AAAA (GLOW)
REMEMBER ME...?

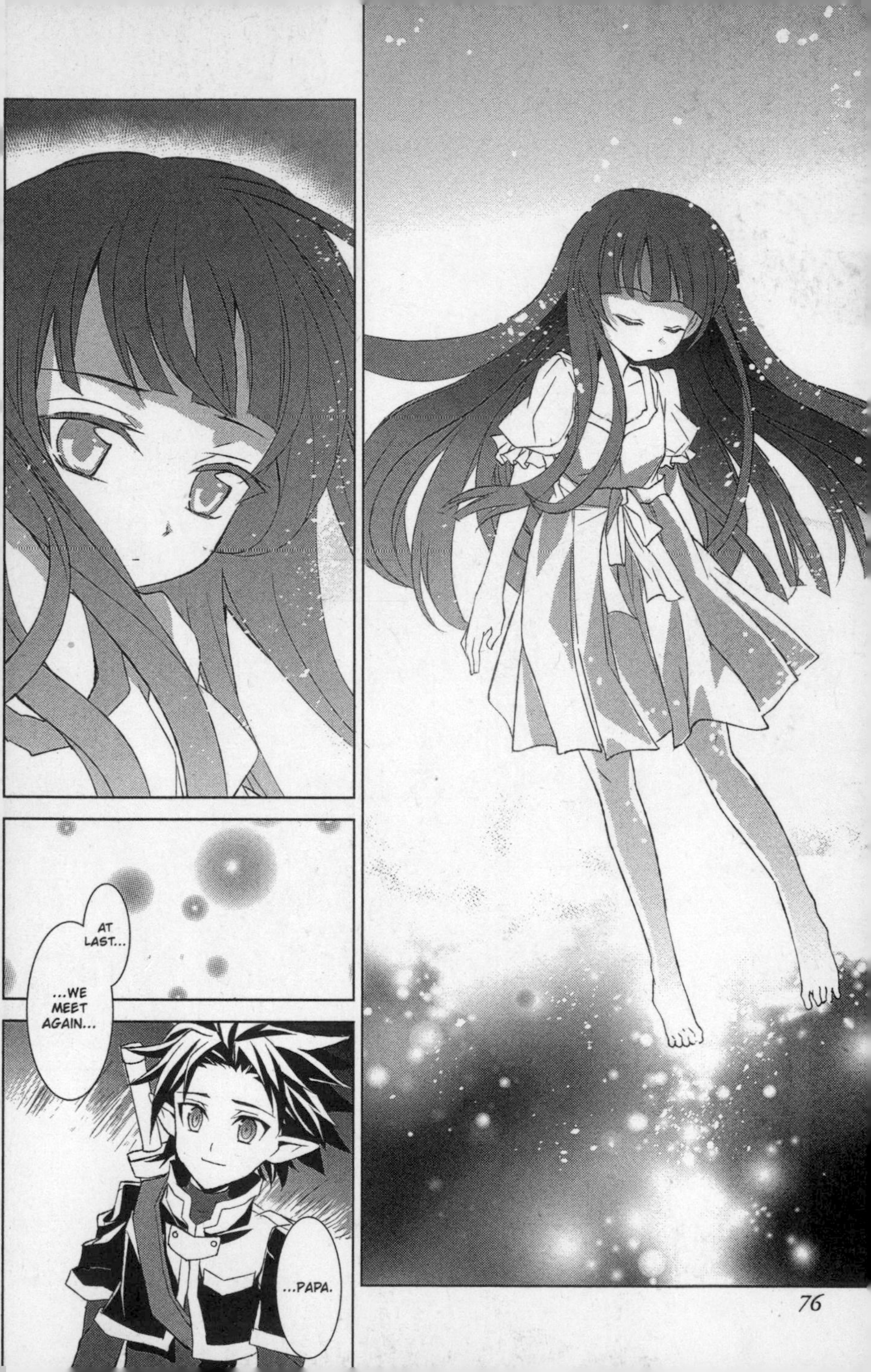
AT LAST...
...WE MEET AGAIN...
...PAPA.

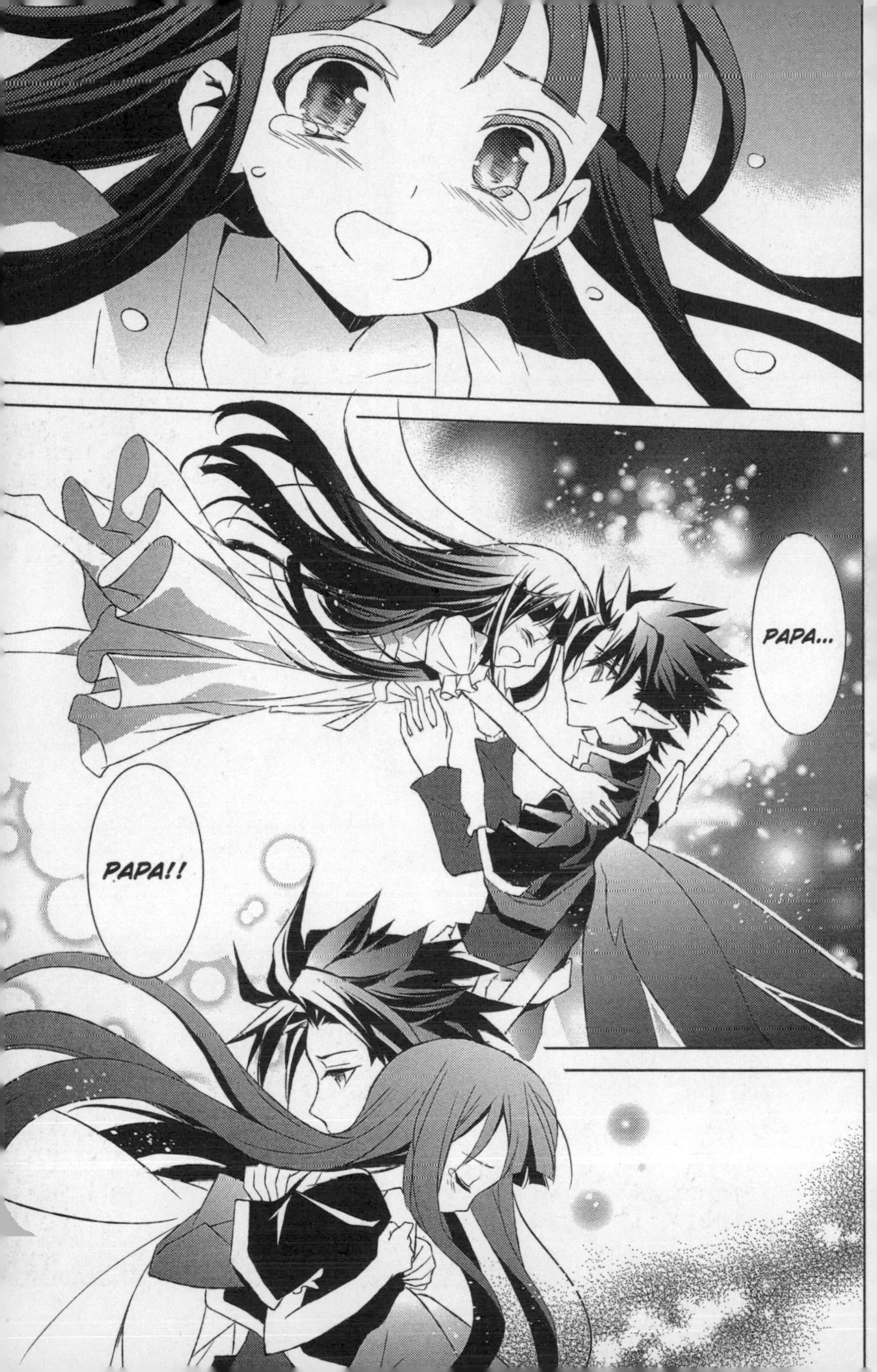
PAPA...
PAPA!!

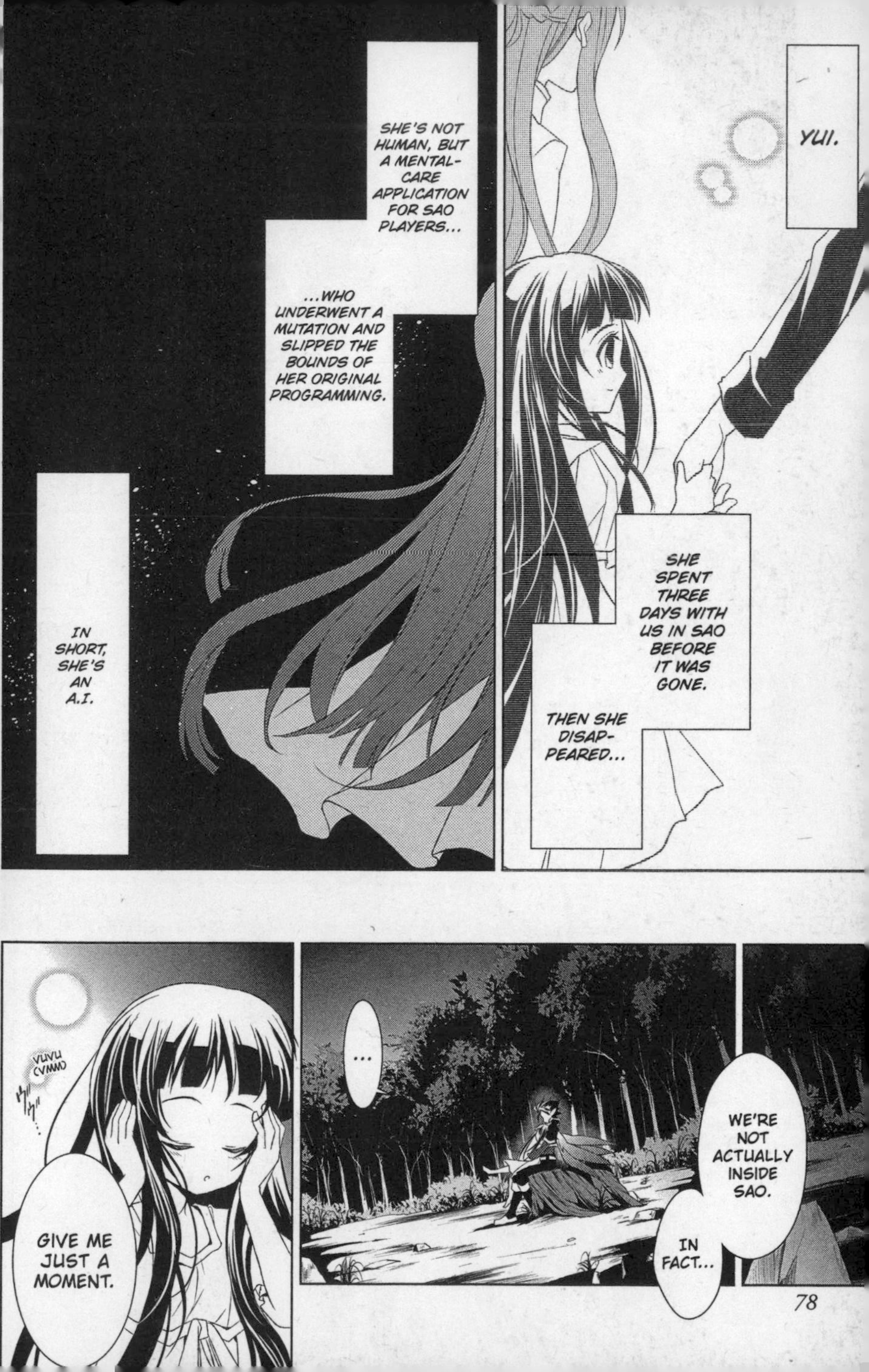
YUI.
SHE SPENT THREE DAYS WITH US IN SAO BEFORE IT WAS GONE.
THEN SHE DISAPPEARED...
SHE'S NOT HUMAN, BUT A MENTAL-CARE APPLICATION FOR SAO PLAYERS...
...WHO UNDERWENT A MUTATION AND SLIPPED THE BOUNDS OF HER ORIGINAL PROGRAMMING.
IN SHORT, SHE'S AN A.I.
WE'RE NOT ACTUALLY INSIDE SAO.
IN FACT...
...
VUVU (VMM)
GIVE ME JUST A MOMENT.

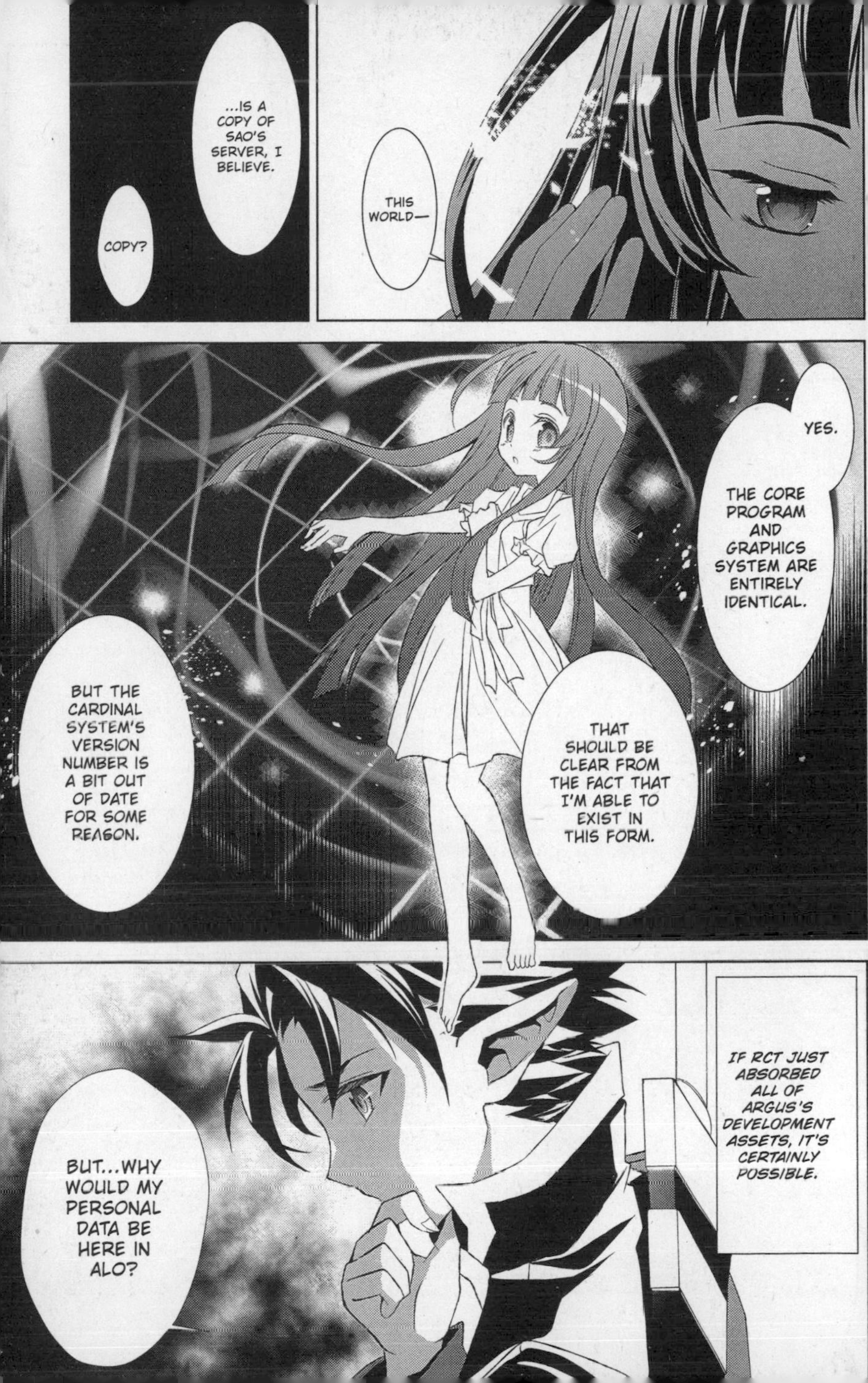
THIS WORLD—
...IS A COPY OF SAO'S SERVER, I BELIEVE.
COPY?
YES.
THE CORE PROGRAM AND GRAPHICS SYSTEM ARE ENTIRELY IDENTICAL.
THAT SHOULD BE CLEAR FROM THE FACT THAT I'M ABLE TO EXIST IN THIS FORM.
BUT THE CARDINAL SYSTEM'S VERSION NUMBER IS A BIT OUT OF DATE FOR SOME REASON.
IF RCT JUST ABSORBED ALL OF ARGUS'S DEVELOPMENT ASSETS, IT'S CERTAINLY POSSIBLE.
BUT...WHY WOULD MY PERSONAL DATA BE HERE IN ALO?

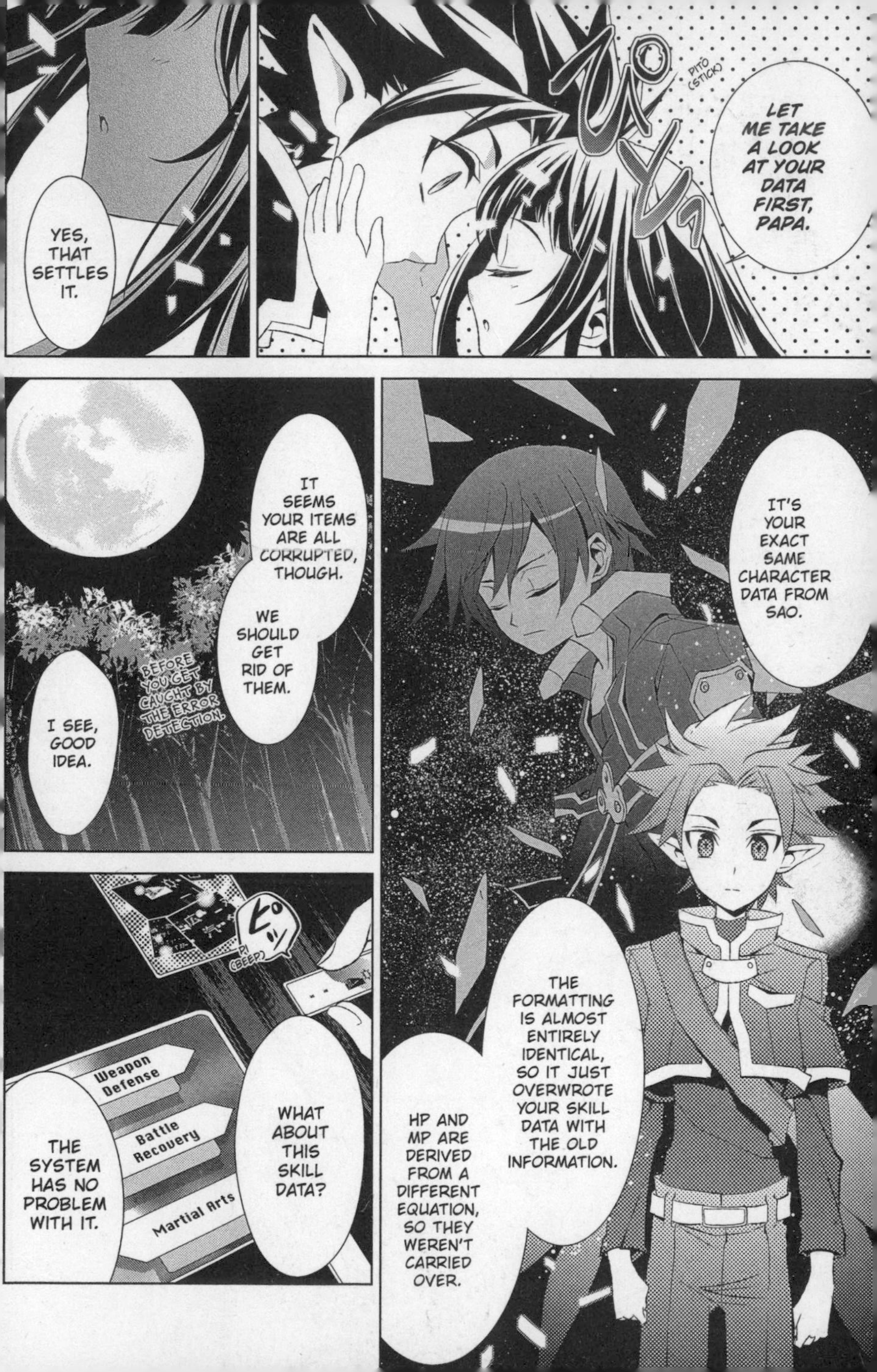
PITŌ (STICK)
LET ME TAKE A LOOK AT YOUR DATA FIRST, PAPA.
YES, THAT SETTLES IT.
IT'S YOUR EXACT SAME CHARACTER DATA FROM SAO.
THE FORMATTING IS ALMOST ENTIRELY IDENTICAL, SO IT JUST OVERWROTE YOUR SKILL DATA WITH THE OLD INFORMATION.
HP AND MP ARE DERIVED FROM A DIFFERENT EQUATION, SO THEY WEREN'T CARRIED OVER.
IT SEEMS YOUR ITEMS ARE ALL CORRUPTED, THOUGH.
WE SHOULD GET RID OF THEM.
BEFORE YOU GET CAUGHT BY THE ERROR DETECTION.
I SEE, GOOD IDEA.
PI (BEEP)
WHAT ABOUT THIS SKILL DATA?
Weapon Defense
Battle Recovery
Martial Arts
THE SYSTEM HAS NO PROBLEM WITH IT.

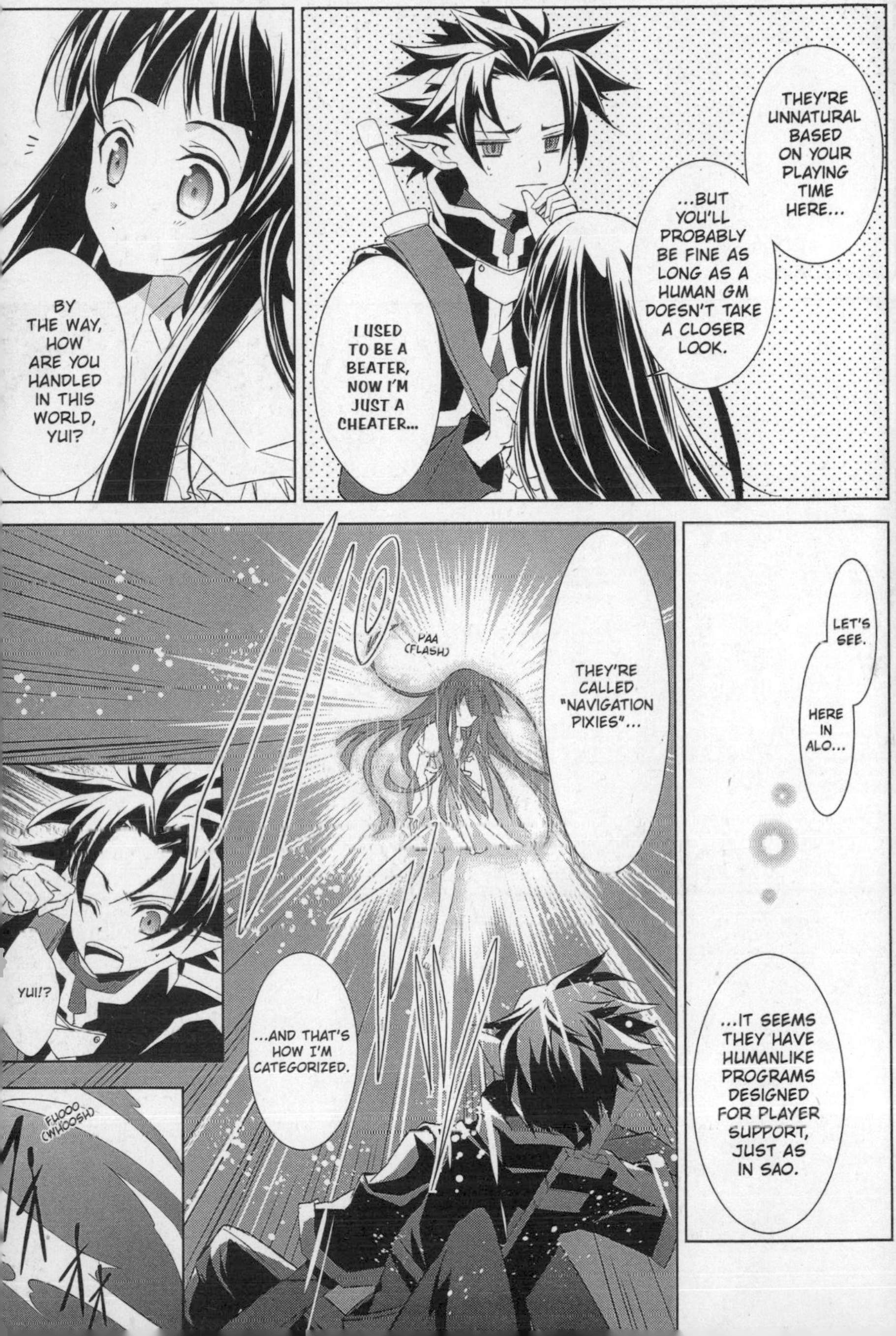
THEY'RE UNNATURAL BASED ON YOUR PLAYING TIME HERE...
...BUT YOU'LL PROBABLY BE FINE AS LONG AS A HUMAN GM DOESN'T TAKE A CLOSER LOOK.
I USED TO BE A BEATER, NOW I'M JUST A CHEATER...
BY THE WAY, HOW ARE YOU HANDLED IN THIS WORLD, YUI?
LET'S SEE.
HERE IN ALO...
...IT SEEMS THEY HAVE HUMANLIKE PROGRAMS DESIGNED FOR PLAYER SUPPORT, JUST AS IN SAO.
THEY'RE CALLED "NAVIGATION PIXIES"...
PAA (FLASH)
...AND THAT'S HOW I'M CATEGORIZED.
YUI!?
FUOOO (WHOOSH)

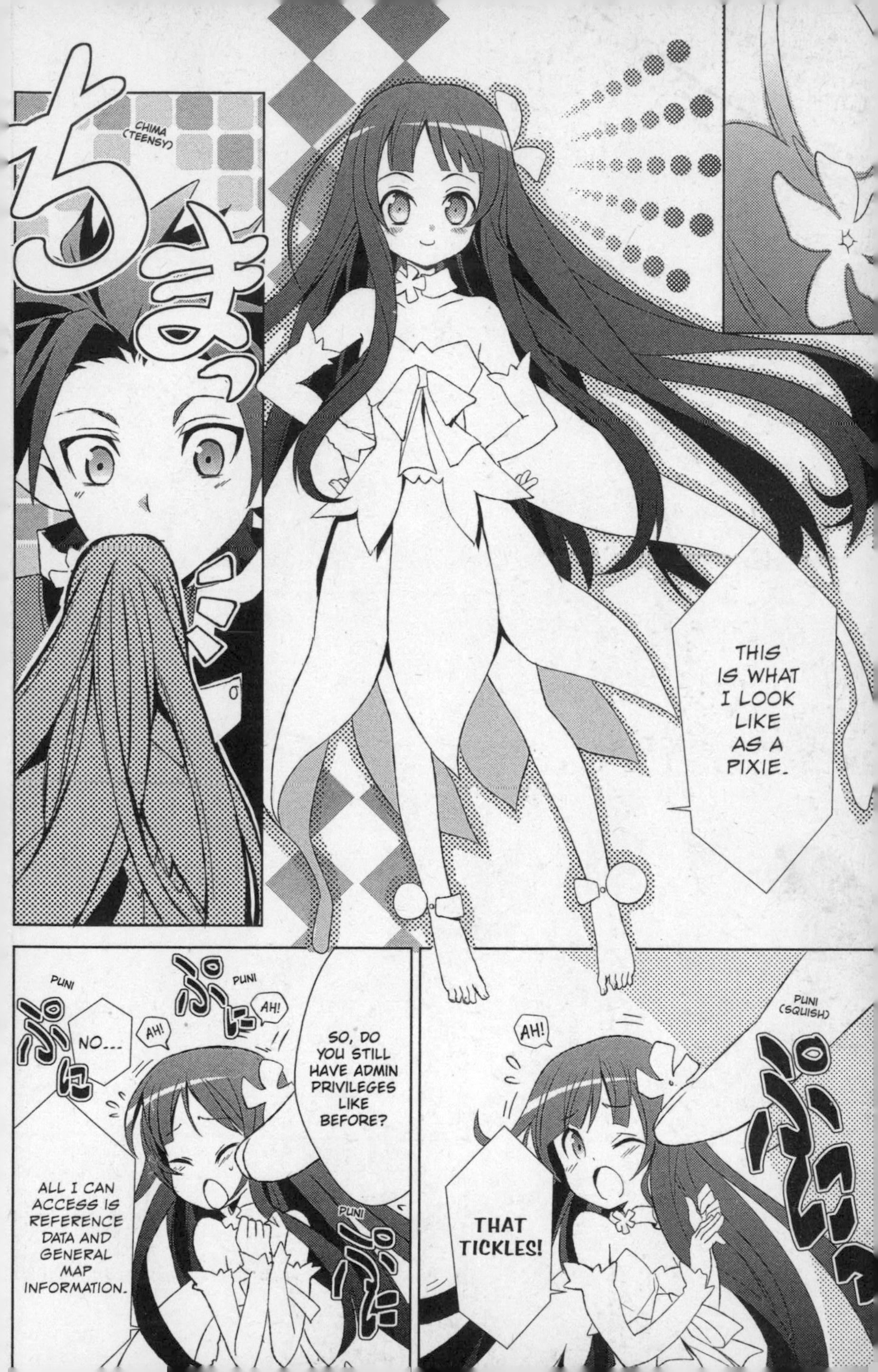
THIS IS WHAT I LOOK LIKE AS A PIXIE.
CHIMA (TEENSY)
PUNI (SQUISH)
AH!
THAT TICKLES!
SO, DO YOU STILL HAVE ADMIN PRIVILEGES LIKE BEFORE?
PUNI
AH!
PUNI
NO...
AH!
ALL I CAN ACCESS IS REFERENCE DATA AND GENERAL MAP INFORMATION.
PUNI

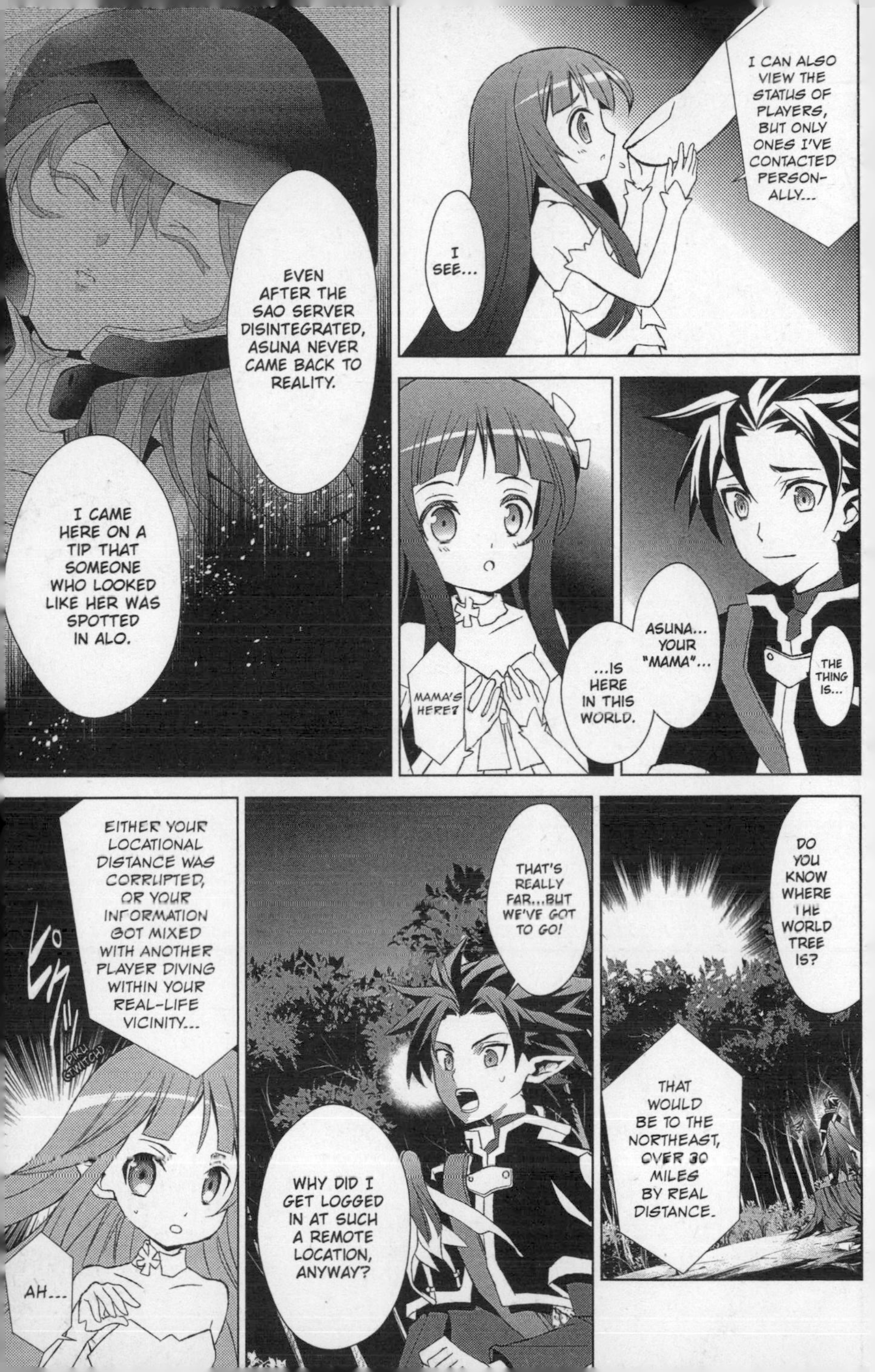
I CAN ALSO VIEW THE STATUS OF PLAYERS, BUT ONLY ONES I'VE CONTACTED PERSON-ALLY...
I SEE...
THE THING IS...
ASUNA... YOUR "MAMA"...
...IS HERE IN THIS WORLD.
MAMA'S HERE?
EVEN AFTER THE SAO SERVER DISINTEGRATED, ASUNA NEVER CAME BACK TO REALITY.
I CAME HERE ON A TIP THAT SOMEONE WHO LOOKED LIKE HER WAS SPOTTED IN ALO.
DO YOU KNOW WHERE THE WORLD TREE IS?
THAT WOULD BE TO THE NORTHEAST, OVER 30 MILES BY REAL DISTANCE.
THAT'S REALLY FAR...BUT WE'VE GOT TO GO!
WHY DID I GET LOGGED IN AT SUCH A REMOTE LOCATION, ANYWAY?
EITHER YOUR LOCATIONAL DISTANCE WAS CORRUPTED, OR YOUR INFORMATION GOT MIXED WITH ANOTHER PLAYER DIVING WITHIN YOUR REAL-LIFE VICINITY...
PIKU (TWITCH)
AH...

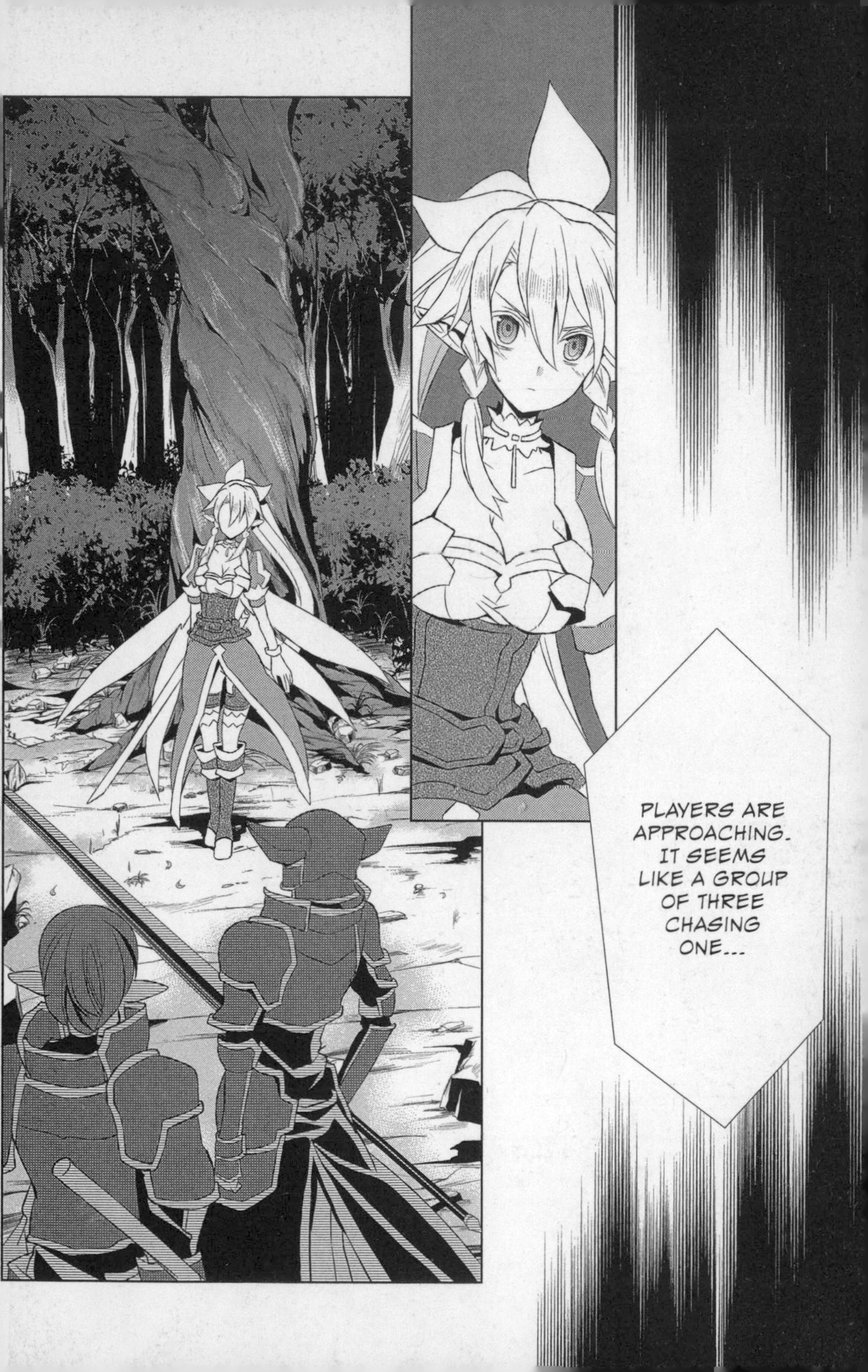
PLAYERS ARE APPROACHING. IT SEEMS LIKE A GROUP OF THREE CHASING ONE...

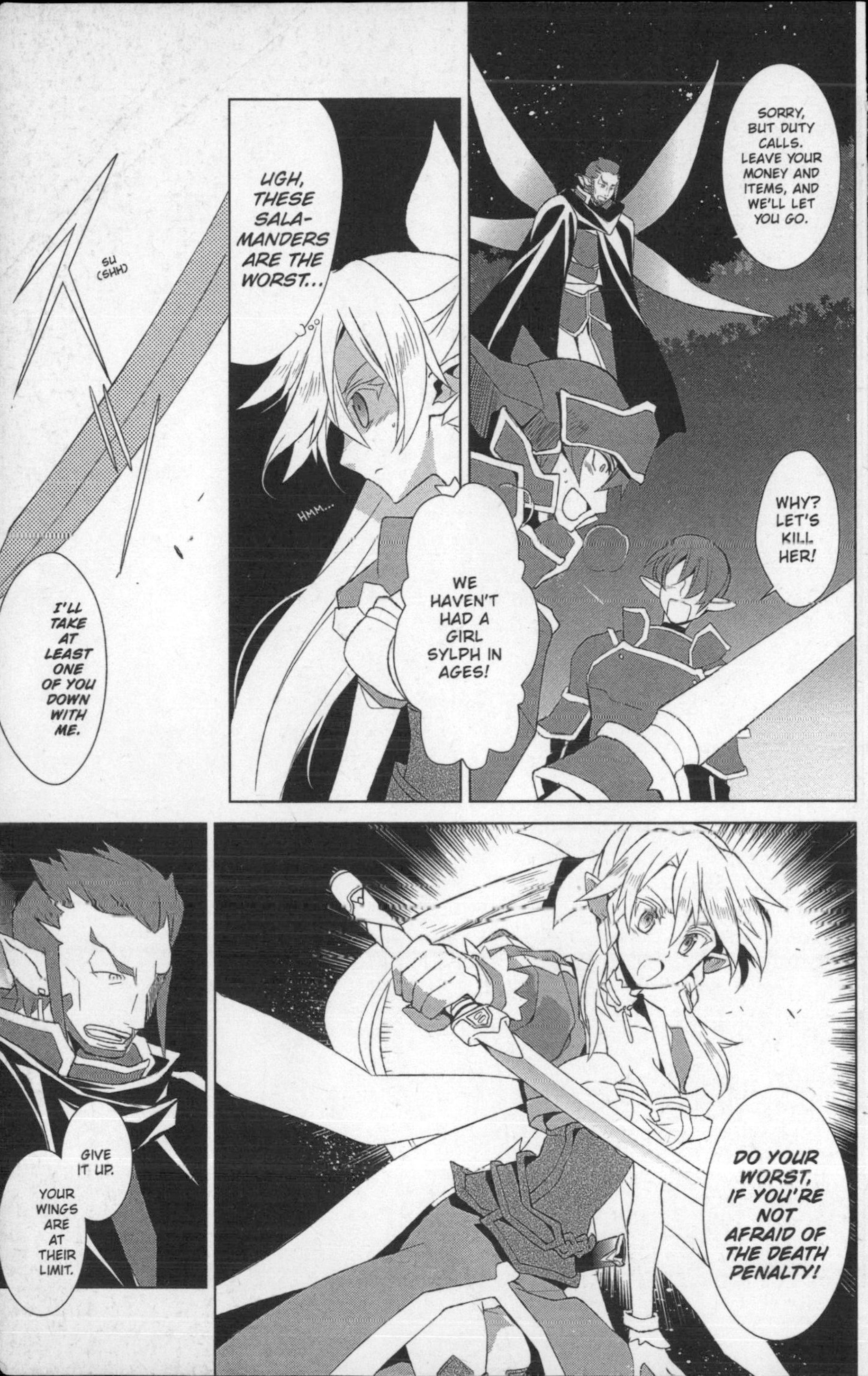
SORRY, BUT DUTY CALLS. LEAVE YOUR MONEY AND ITEMS, AND WE'LL LET YOU GO.
WHY? LET'S KILL HER!
WE HAVEN'T HAD A GIRL SYLPH IN AGES!
UGH, THESE SALAMANDERS ARE THE WORST...
HMM...
SU (SHH)
I'LL TAKE AT LEAST ONE OF YOU DOWN WITH ME.
DO YOUR WORST, IF YOU'RE NOT AFRAID OF THE DEATH PENALTY!
GIVE IT UP.
YOUR WINGS ARE AT THEIR LIMIT.

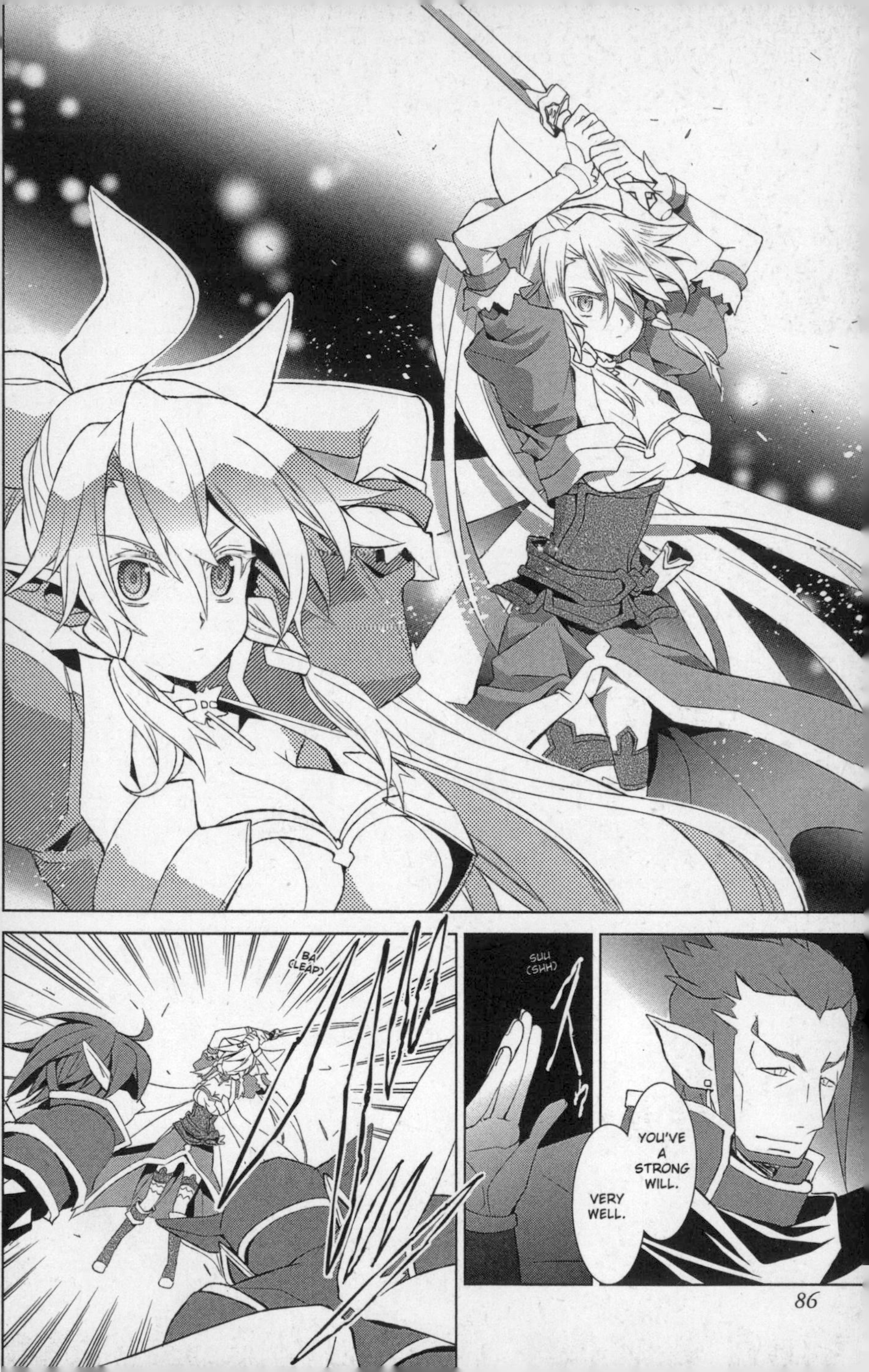
YOU'VE A STRONG WILL.
VERY WELL.
SUU (SHH)
BA (LEAP)

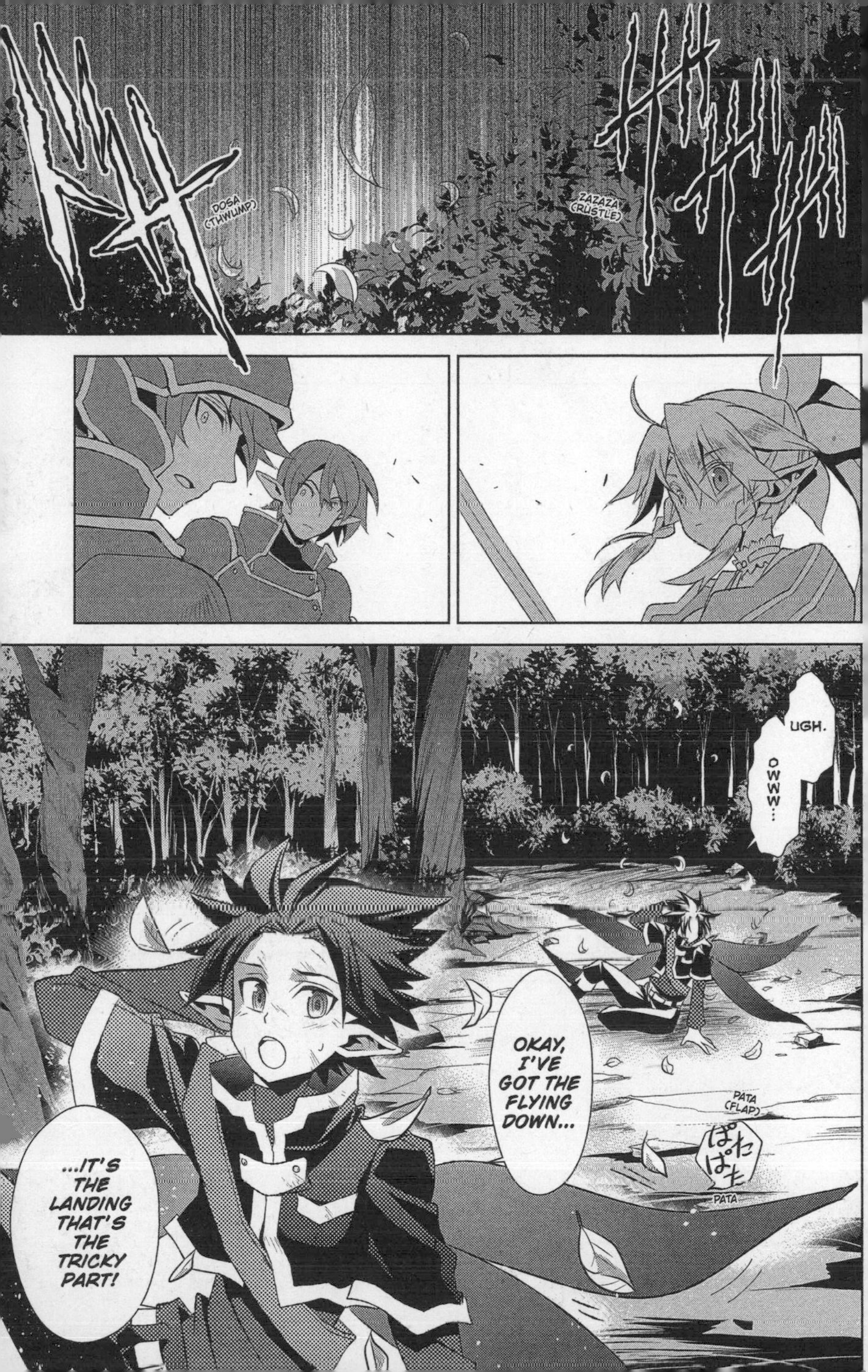
ZAZAZA (RUSTLE)
DOSA (THWUMP)
UGH.
OWWW...
PATA (FLAP)
ぱたぱた
PATA
OKAY, I'VE GOT THE FLYING DOWN...
...IT'S THE LANDING THAT'S THE TRICKY PART!

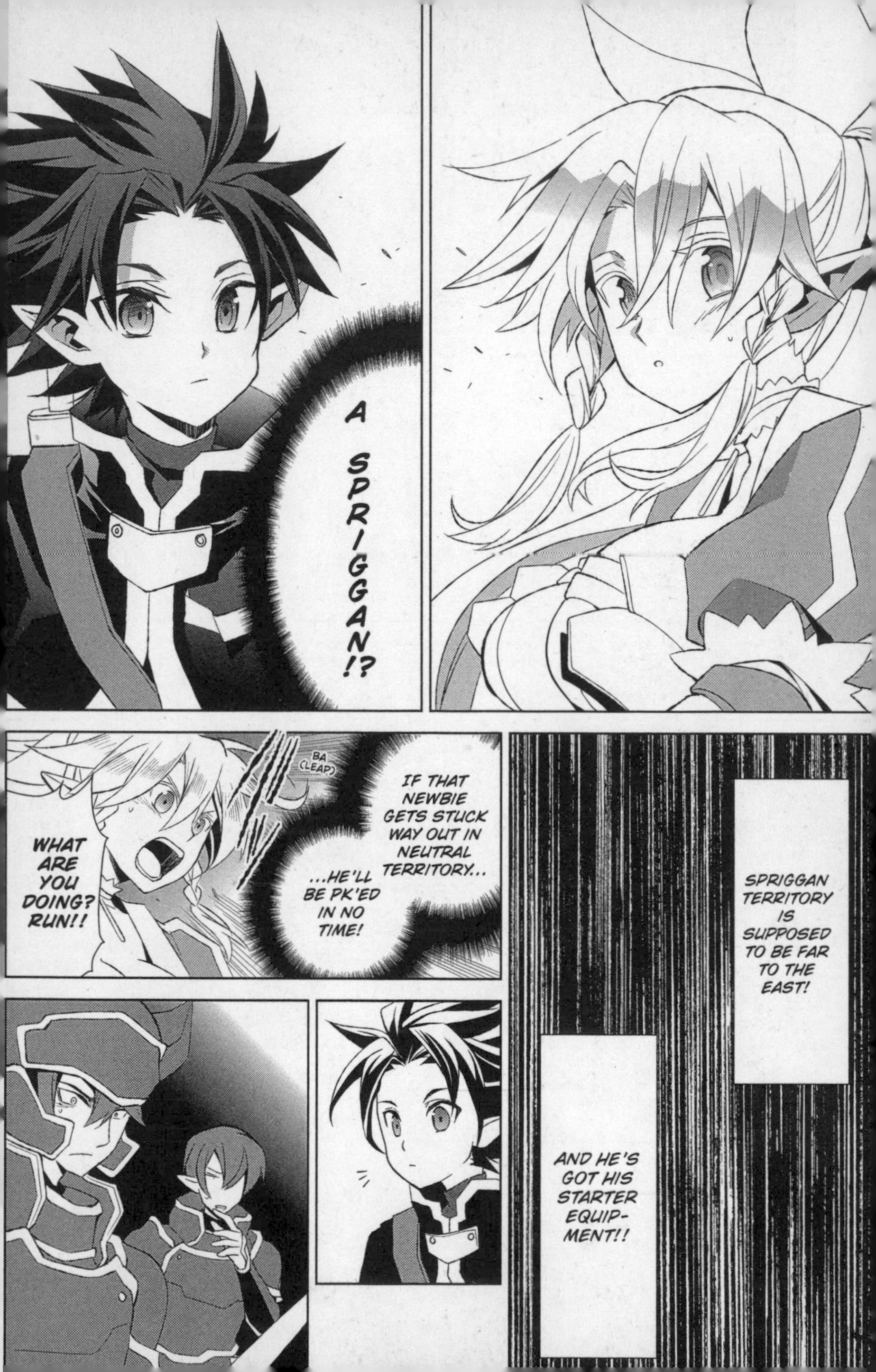
A SPRIGGAN!?
SPRIGGAN TERRITORY IS SUPPOSED TO BE FAR TO THE EAST!
AND HE'S GOT HIS STARTER EQUIP-MENT!!
IF THAT NEWBIE GETS STUCK WAY OUT IN NEUTRAL TERRITORY...
...HE'LL BE PK'ED IN NO TIME!
BA (LEAP)
WHAT ARE YOU DOING? RUN!!

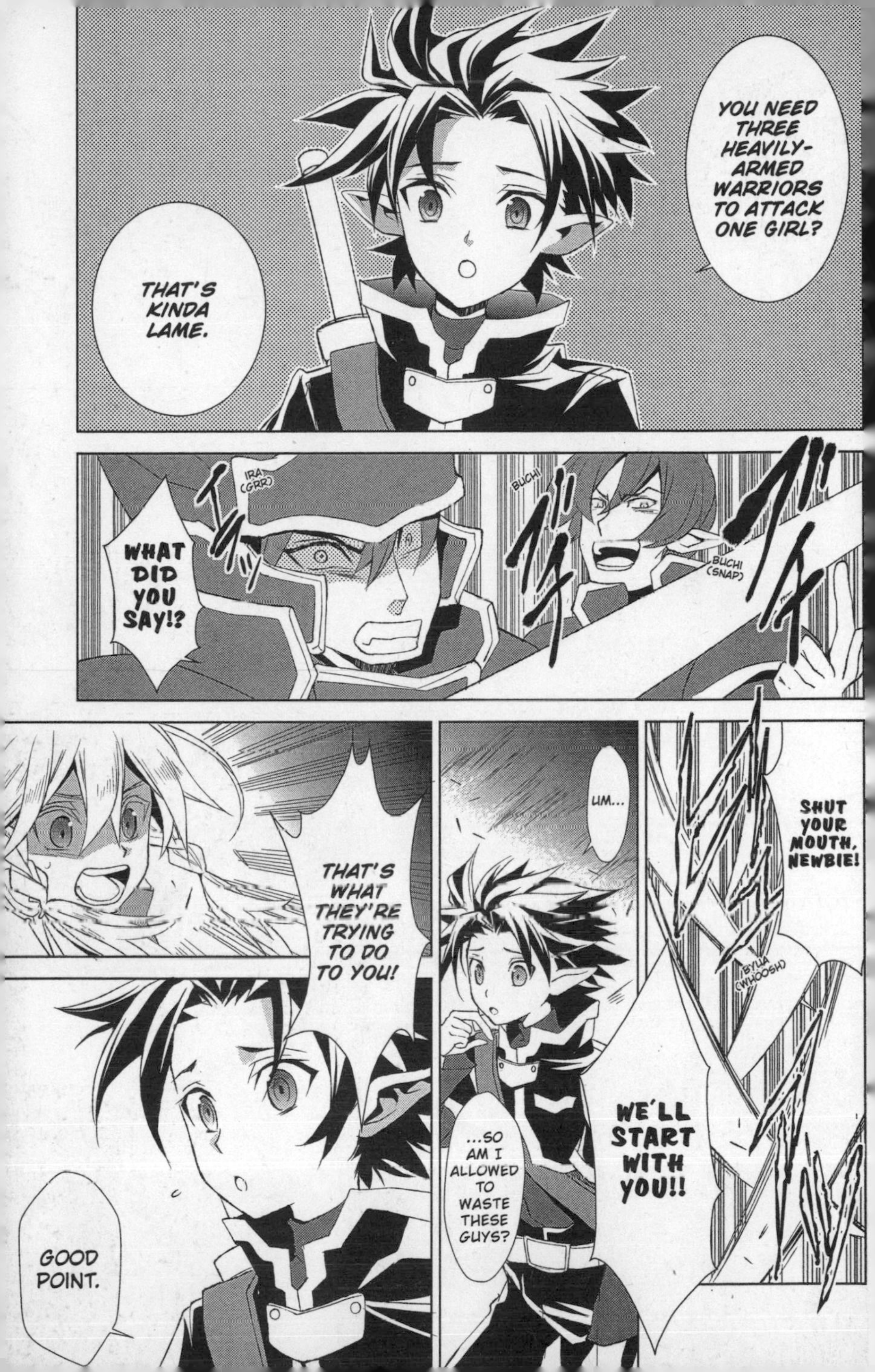
YOU NEED THREE HEAVILY-ARMED WARRIORS TO ATTACK ONE GIRL?
THAT'S KINDA LAME.
BUCHI
BUCHI (SNAP)
IRA (GRR)
WHAT DID YOU SAY!?
SHUT YOUR MOUTH, NEWBIE!
BYUA (WHOOSH)
WE'LL START WITH YOU!!
UM...
...SO AM I ALLOWED TO WASTE THESE GUYS?
THAT'S WHAT THEY'RE TRYING TO DO TO YOU!
GOOD POINT.

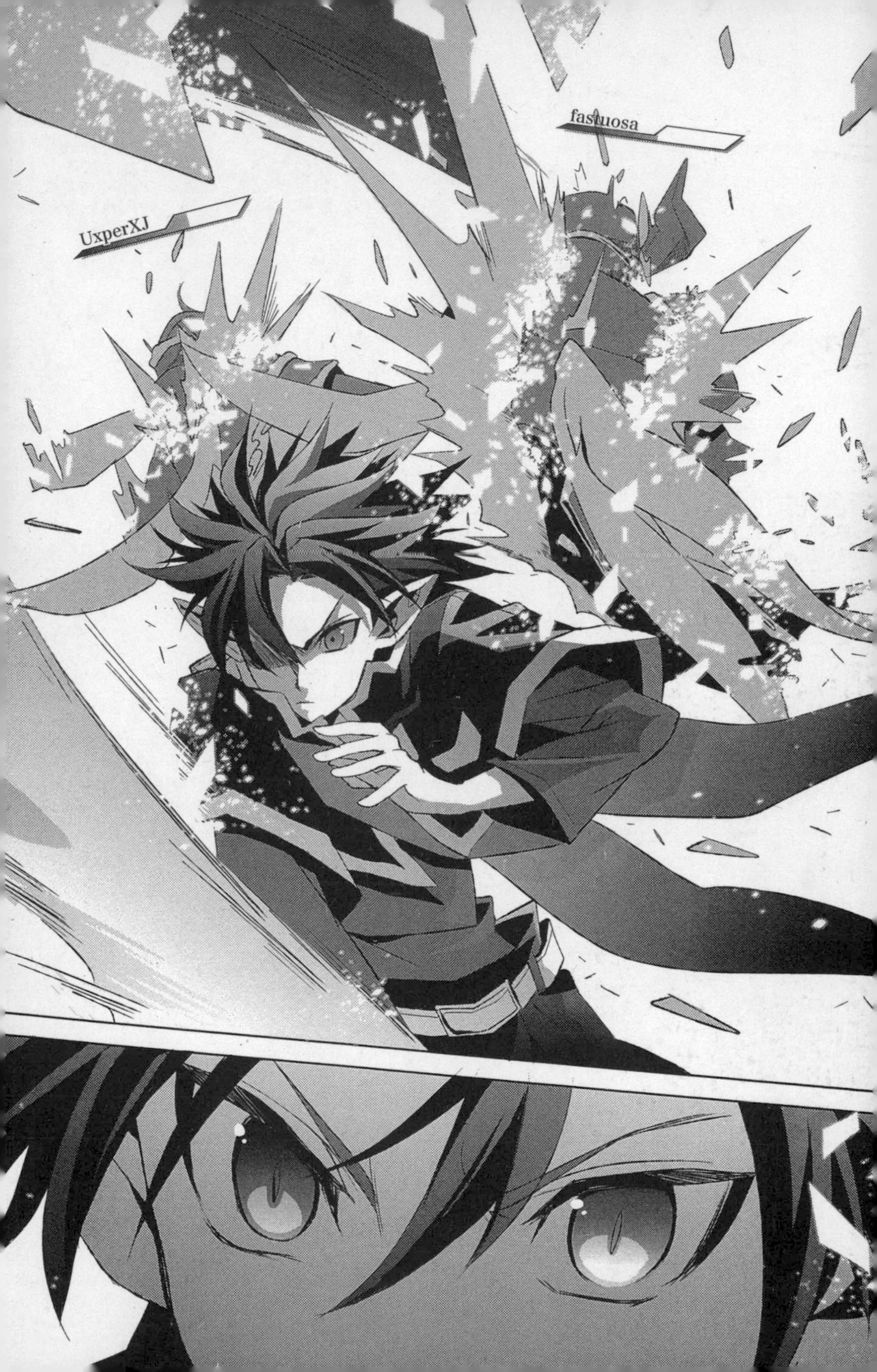
fastuosa
UxperXJ

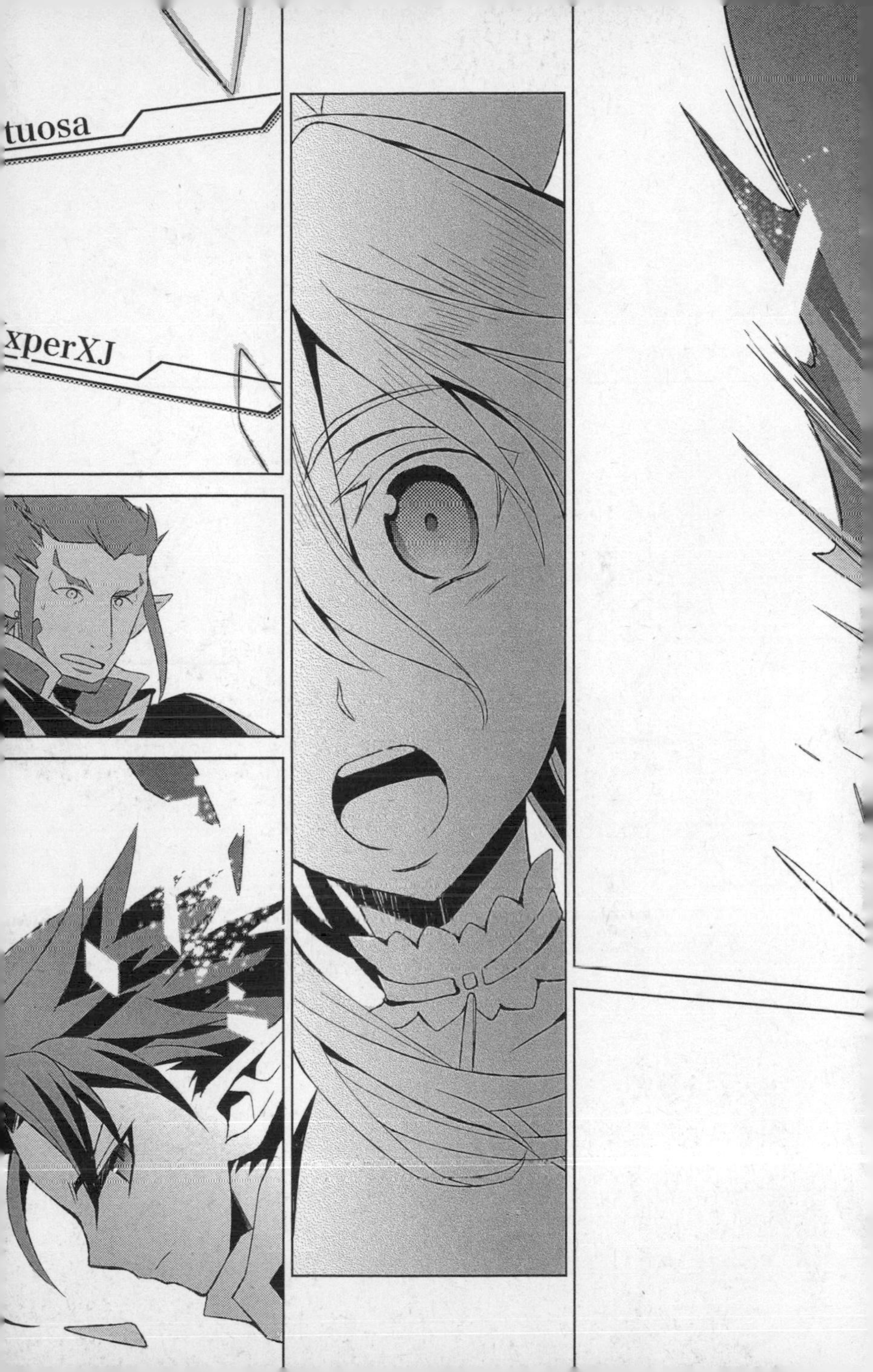
tuosa
xperXJ

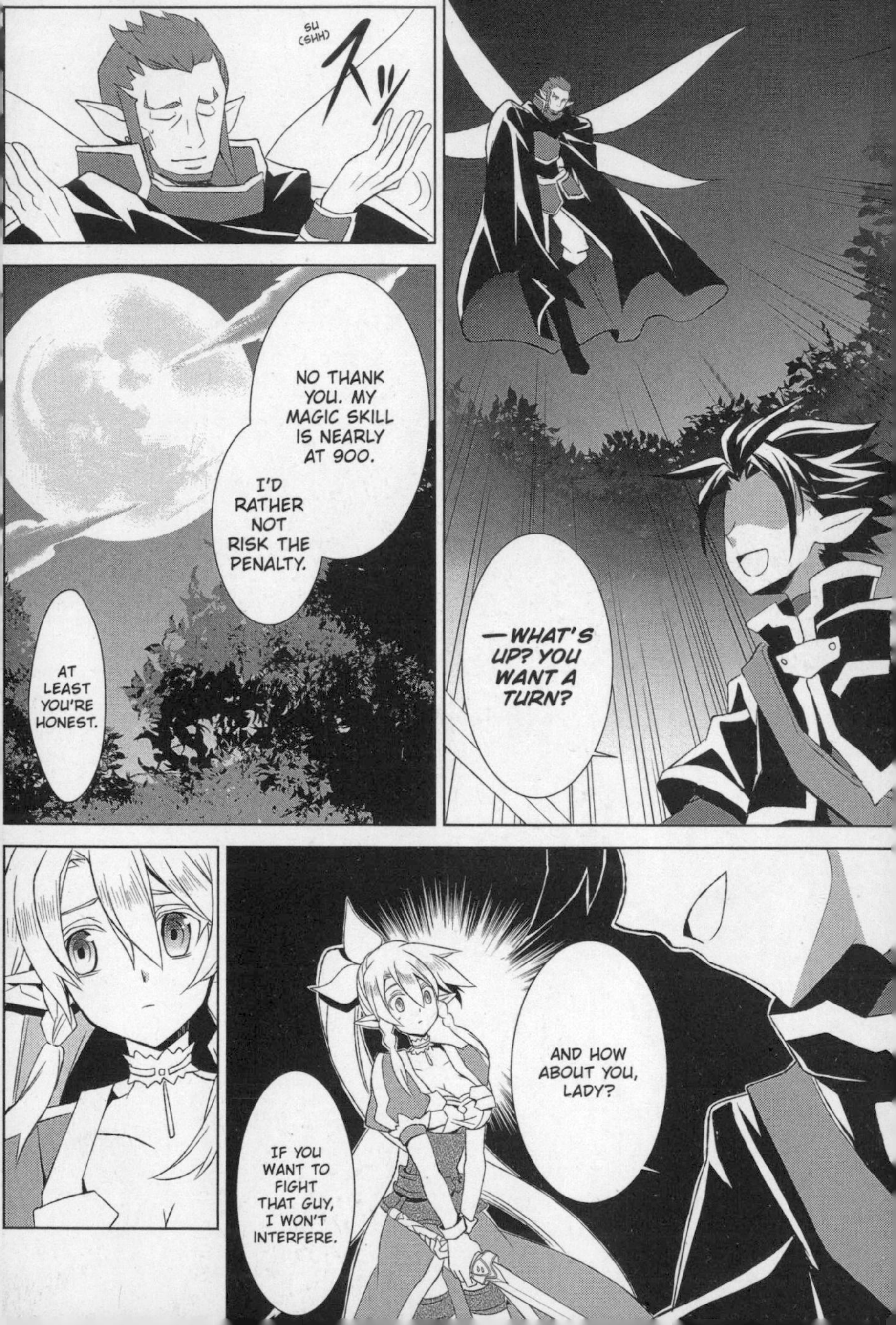
—WHAT'S UP? YOU WANT A TURN?
SU (SHH)
NO THANK YOU. MY MAGIC SKILL IS NEARLY AT 900.
I'D RATHER NOT RISK THE PENALTY.
AT LEAST YOU'RE HONEST.
AND HOW ABOUT YOU, LADY?
IF YOU WANT TO FIGHT THAT GUY, I WON'T INTERFERE.

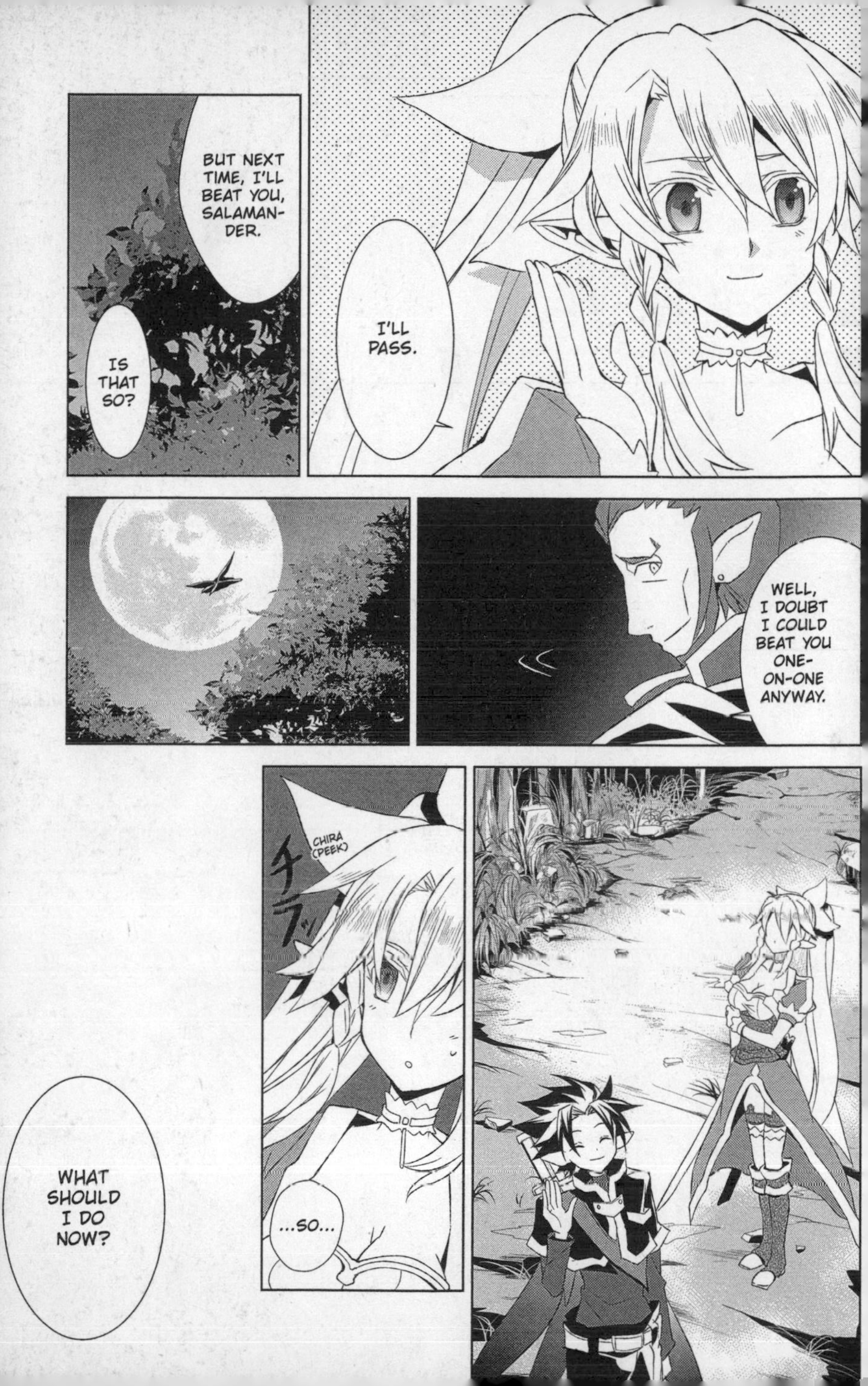
I'LL PASS.
BUT NEXT TIME, I'LL BEAT YOU, SALAMANDER.
IS THAT SO?
WELL, I DOUBT I COULD BEAT YOU ONE-ON-ONE ANYWAY.
CHIRA (PEEK)
...SO...
WHAT SHOULD I DO NOW?

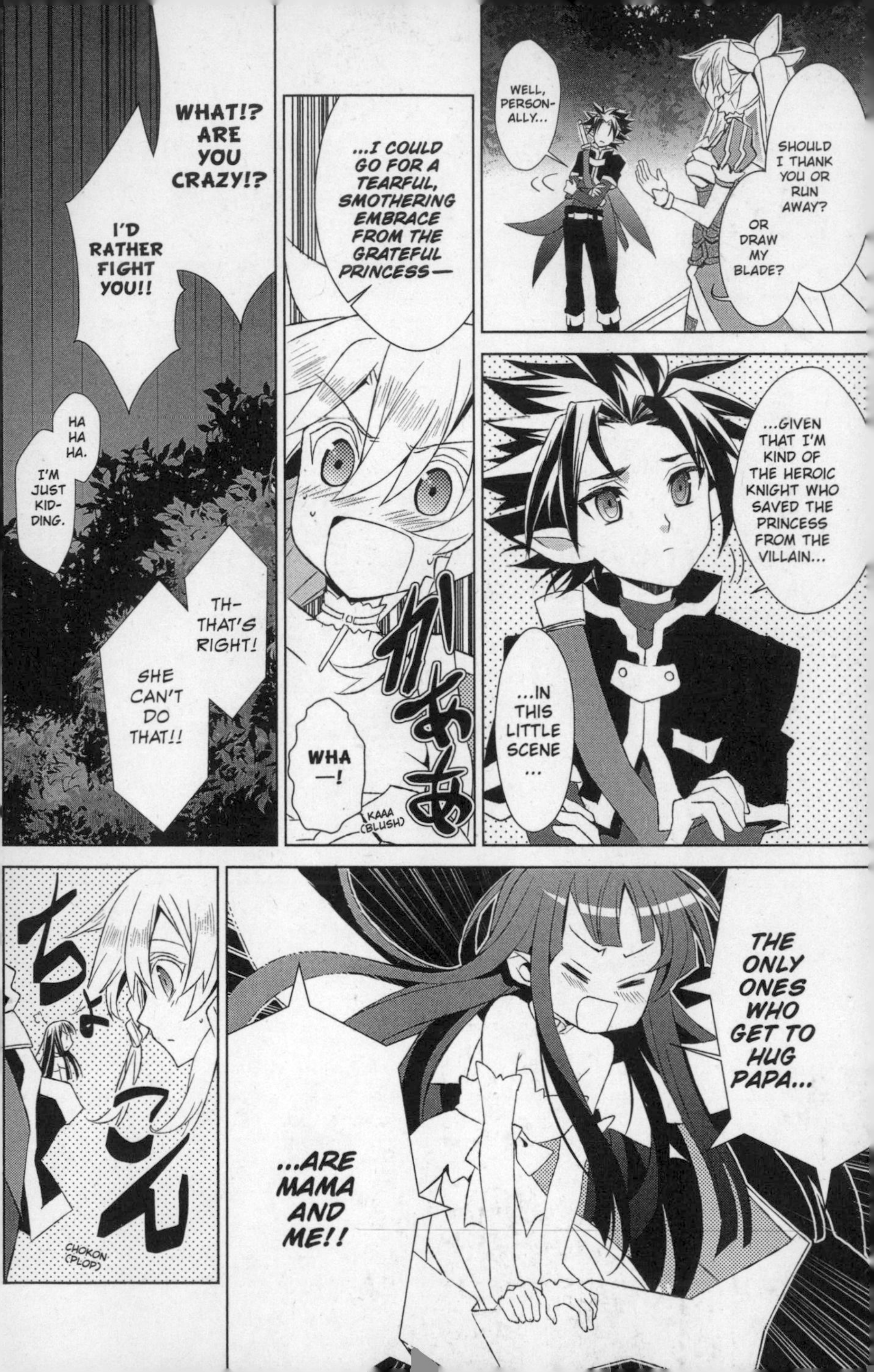
SHOULD I THANK YOU OR RUN AWAY?
OR DRAW MY BLADE?
WELL, PERSONALLY...
...GIVEN THAT I'M KIND OF THE HEROIC KNIGHT WHO SAVED THE PRINCESS FROM THE VILLAIN...
...IN THIS LITTLE SCENE...
...I COULD GO FOR A TEARFUL, SMOTHERING EMBRACE FROM THE GRATEFUL PRINCESS—
KAAA (BLUSH)
WHA—!
WHAT!? ARE YOU CRAZY!?
I'D RATHER FIGHT YOU!!
HA HA HA.
I'M JUST KID-DING.
TH-THAT'S RIGHT!
SHE CAN'T DO THAT!!
THE ONLY ONES WHO GET TO HUG PAPA...
...ARE MAMA AND ME!!
CHOKON (PLOP)

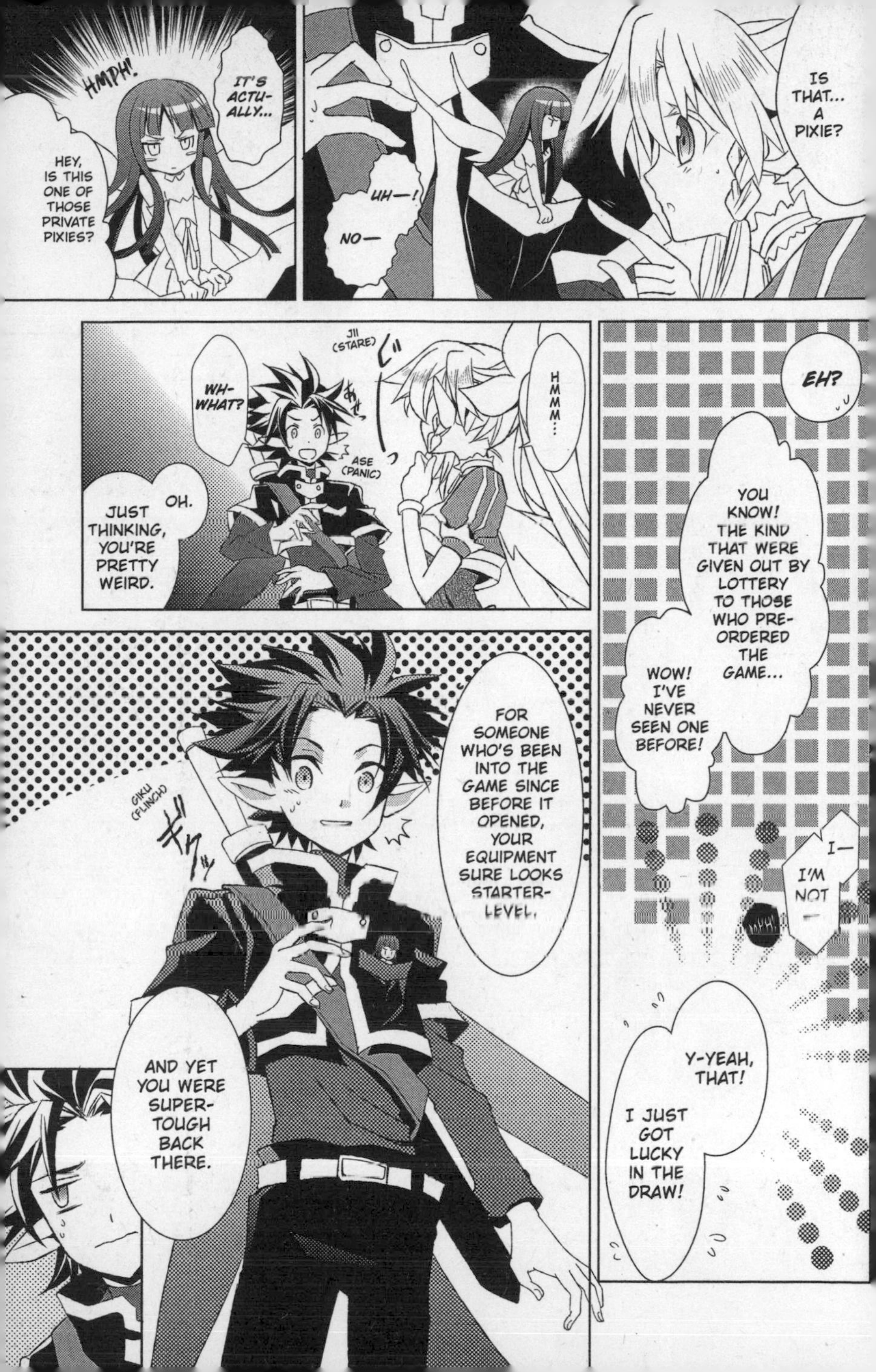
IS THAT... A PIXIE?
UH—!
NO—
IT'S ACTU-ALLY...
HMPH!
HEY, IS THIS ONE OF THOSE PRIVATE PIXIES?
EH?
YOU KNOW! THE KIND THAT WERE GIVEN OUT BY LOTTERY TO THOSE WHO PRE-ORDERED THE GAME...
WOW! I'VE NEVER SEEN ONE BEFORE!
I— I'M NOT —
Y-YEAH, THAT!
I JUST GOT LUCKY IN THE DRAW!
HMMM...
JII (STARE)
ASE (PANIC)
WH-WHAT?
OH.
JUST THINKING, YOU'RE PRETTY WEIRD.
FOR SOMEONE WHO'S BEEN INTO THE GAME SINCE BEFORE IT OPENED, YOUR EQUIPMENT SURE LOOKS STARTER-LEVEL.
GIKU (FLINCH)
AND YET YOU WERE SUPER-TOUGH BACK THERE.

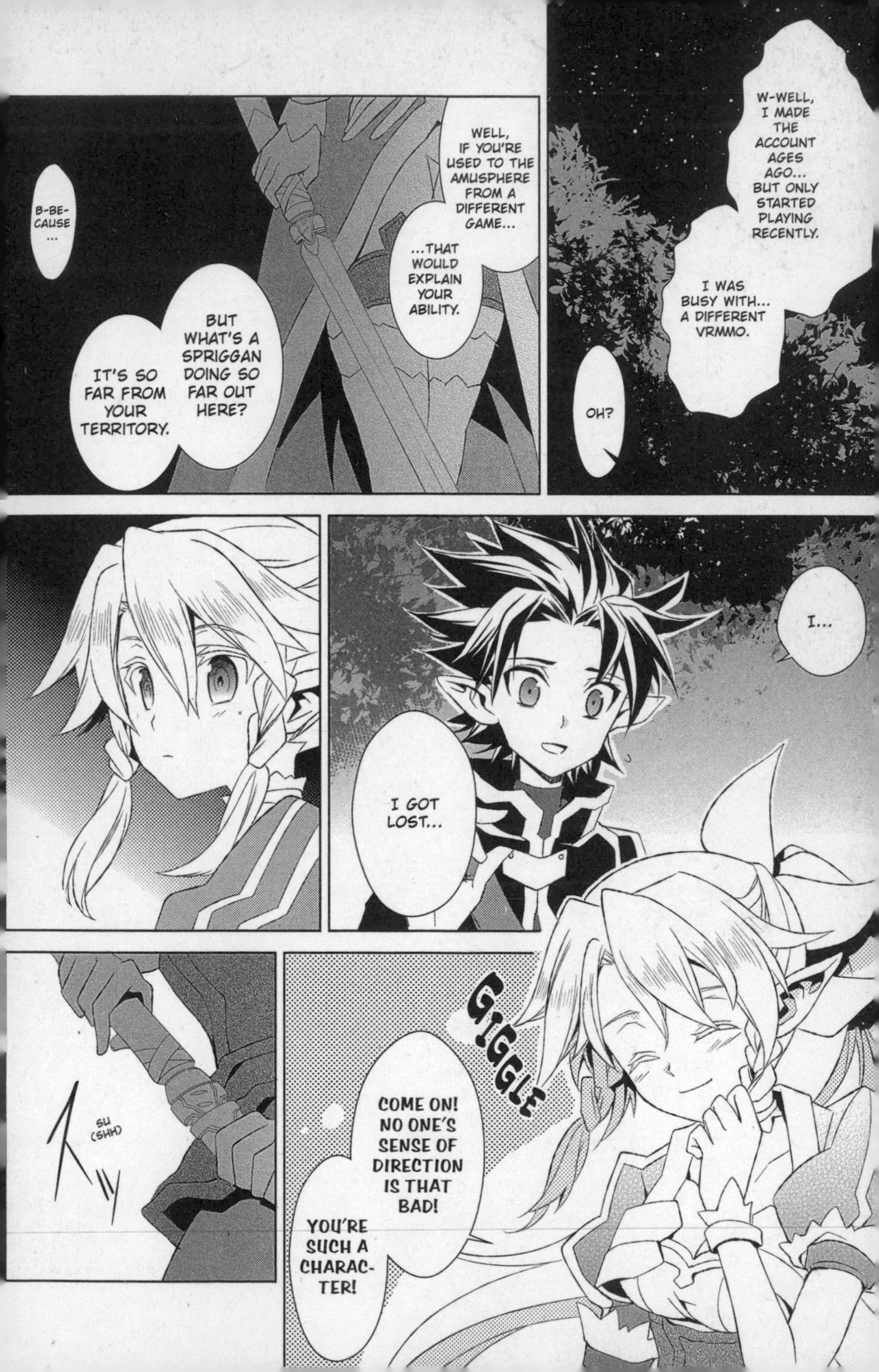
W-WELL, I MADE THE ACCOUNT AGES AGO... BUT ONLY STARTED PLAYING RECENTLY.
I WAS BUSY WITH... A DIFFERENT VRMMO.
OH?
WELL, IF YOU'RE USED TO THE AMUSPHERE FROM A DIFFERENT GAME...
...THAT WOULD EXPLAIN YOUR ABILITY.
B-BE-CAUSE ...
BUT WHAT'S A SPRIGGAN DOING SO FAR OUT HERE?
IT'S SO FAR FROM YOUR TERRITORY.
I...
I GOT LOST...
GIGGLE
COME ON! NO ONE'S SENSE OF DIRECTION IS THAT BAD!
YOU'RE SUCH A CHARAC-TER!
SU (SHH)

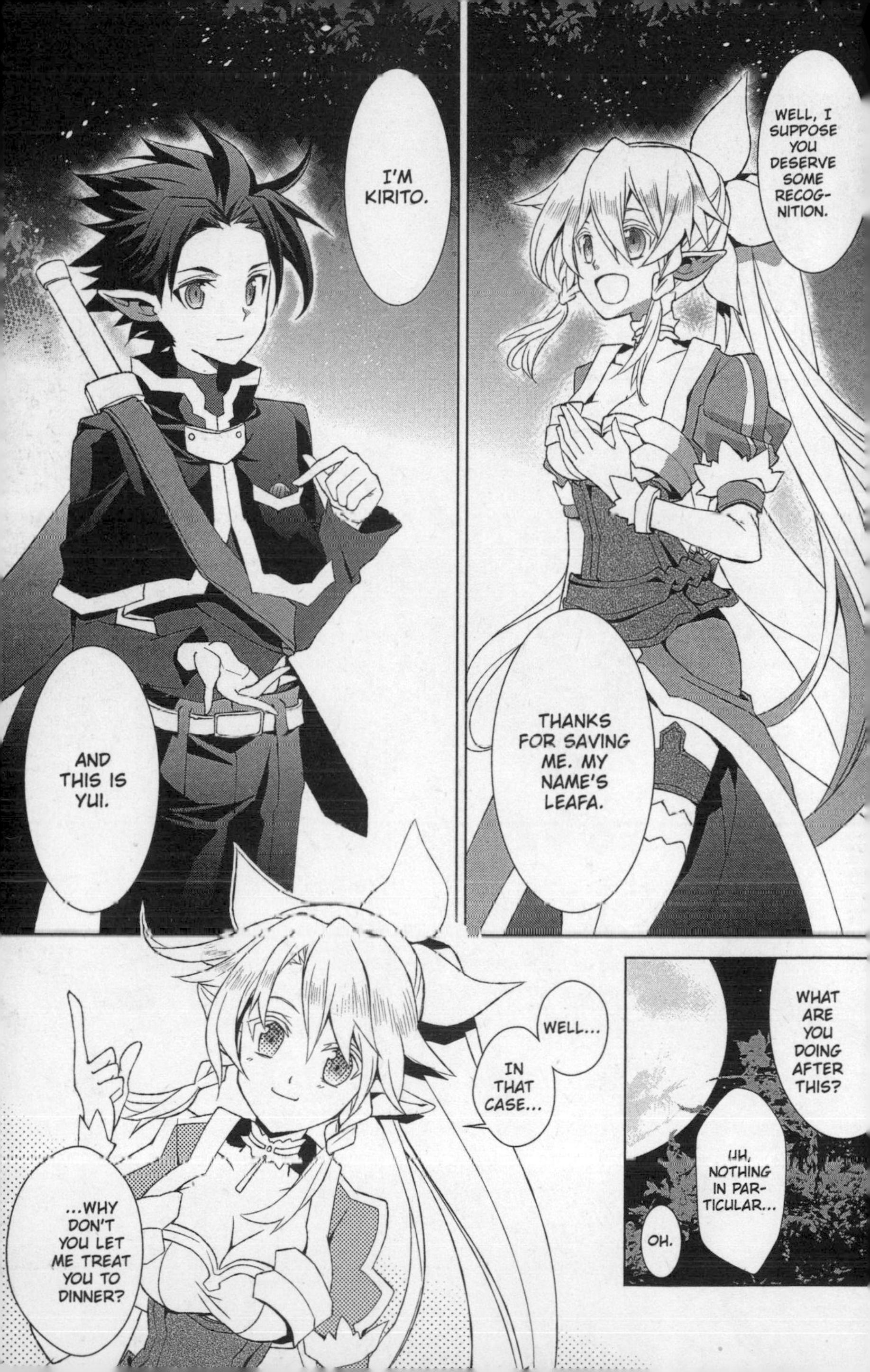
WELL, I SUPPOSE YOU DESERVE SOME RECOG-NITION.
THANKS FOR SAVING ME. MY NAME'S LEAFA.
I'M KIRITO.
AND THIS IS YUI.
WHAT ARE YOU DOING AFTER THIS?
UH, NOTHING IN PAR-TICULAR...
OH.
WELL...
IN THAT CASE...
...WHY DON'T YOU LET ME TREAT YOU TO DINNER?

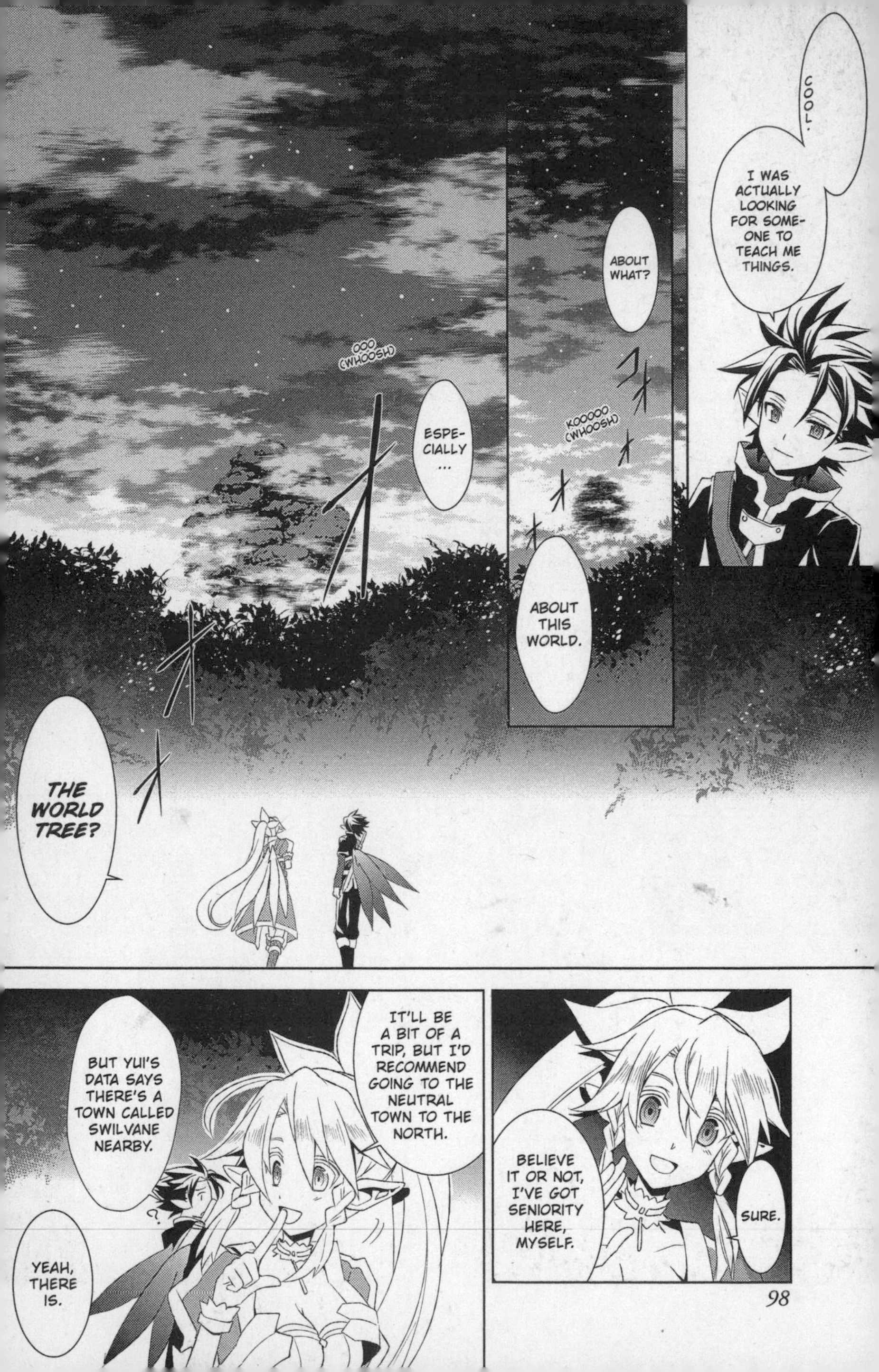
COOL.
I WAS ACTUALLY LOOKING FOR SOME-ONE TO TEACH ME THINGS.
ABOUT WHAT?
KOOOOO (WHOOSH)
ABOUT THIS WORLD.
OOO (WHOOSH)
ESPE-CIALLY ...
THE WORLD TREE?
SURE.
BELIEVE IT OR NOT, I'VE GOT SENIORITY HERE, MYSELF.
IT'LL BE A BIT OF A TRIP, BUT I'D RECOMMEND GOING TO THE NEUTRAL TOWN TO THE NORTH.
BUT YUI'S DATA SAYS THERE'S A TOWN CALLED SWILVANE NEARBY.
YEAH, THERE IS.

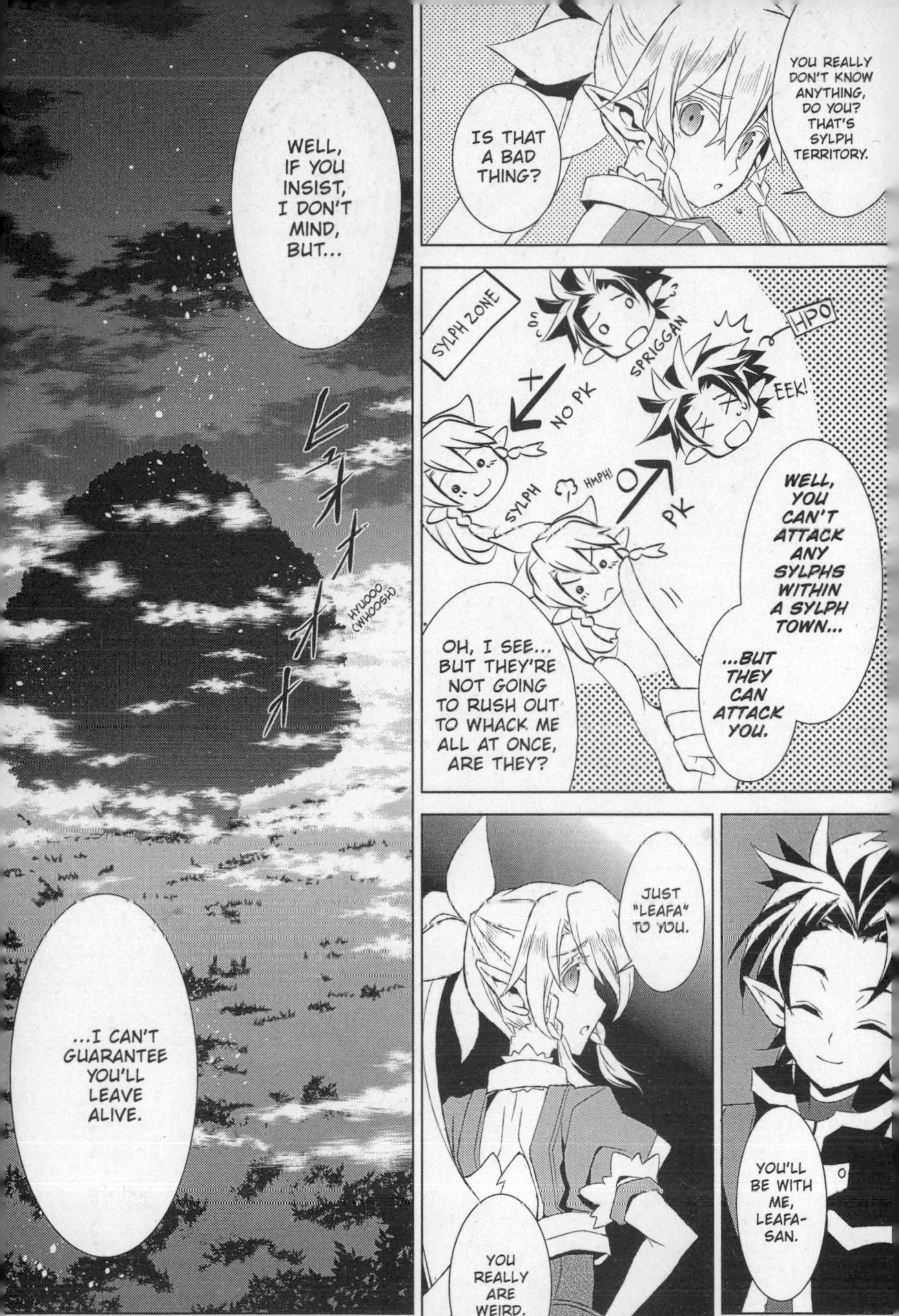
YOU REALLY DON'T KNOW ANYTHING, DO YOU? THAT'S SYLPH TERRITORY.
IS THAT A BAD THING?
SYLPH ZONE
SPRIGGAN
HP0
EEK!
NO PK
SYLPH
HMPH!
PK
WELL, YOU CAN'T ATTACK ANY SYLPHS WITHIN A SYLPH TOWN...
...BUT THEY CAN ATTACK YOU.
OH, I SEE... BUT THEY'RE NOT GOING TO RUSH OUT TO WHACK ME ALL AT ONCE, ARE THEY?
YOU'LL BE WITH ME, LEAFA-SAN.
JUST "LEAFA" TO YOU.
YOU REALLY ARE WEIRD.
WELL, IF YOU INSIST, I DON'T MIND, BUT...
HYUOOO (WHOOSH)
...I CAN'T GUARANTEE YOU'LL LEAVE ALIVE.

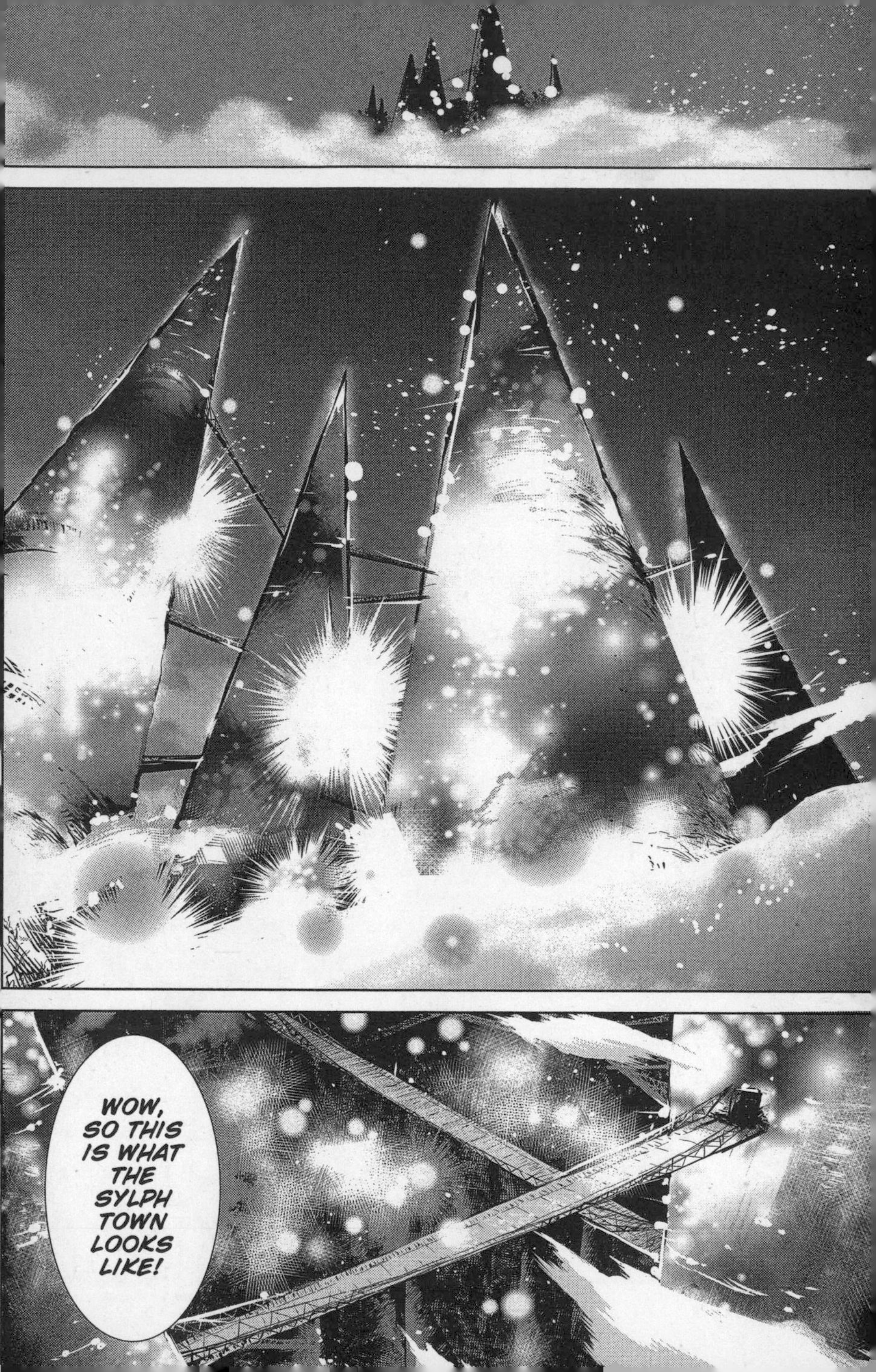
WOW, SO THIS IS WHAT THE SYLPH TOWN LOOKS LIKE!

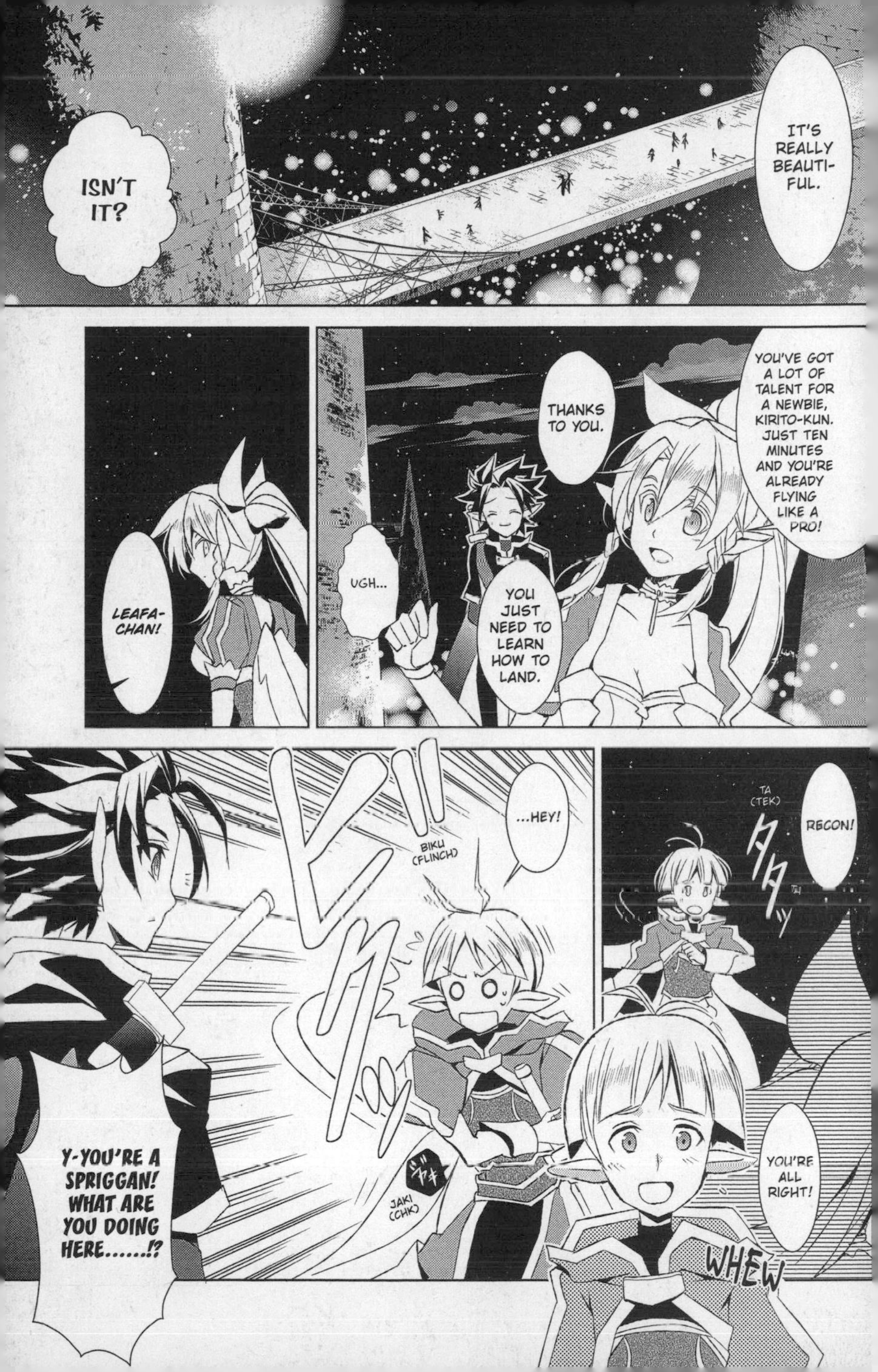
IT'S REALLY BEAUTIFUL.
ISN'T IT?
YOU'VE GOT A LOT OF TALENT FOR A NEWBIE, KIRITO-KUN. JUST TEN MINUTES AND YOU'RE ALREADY FLYING LIKE A PRO!
THANKS TO YOU.
YOU JUST NEED TO LEARN HOW TO LAND.
UGH...
LEAFA-CHAN!
TA (TEK)
RECON!
YOU'RE ALL RIGHT!
WHEW
...HEY!
BIKU (FLINCH)
JAKI (CHK)
Y-YOU'RE A SPRIGGAN! WHAT ARE YOU DOING HERE......!?

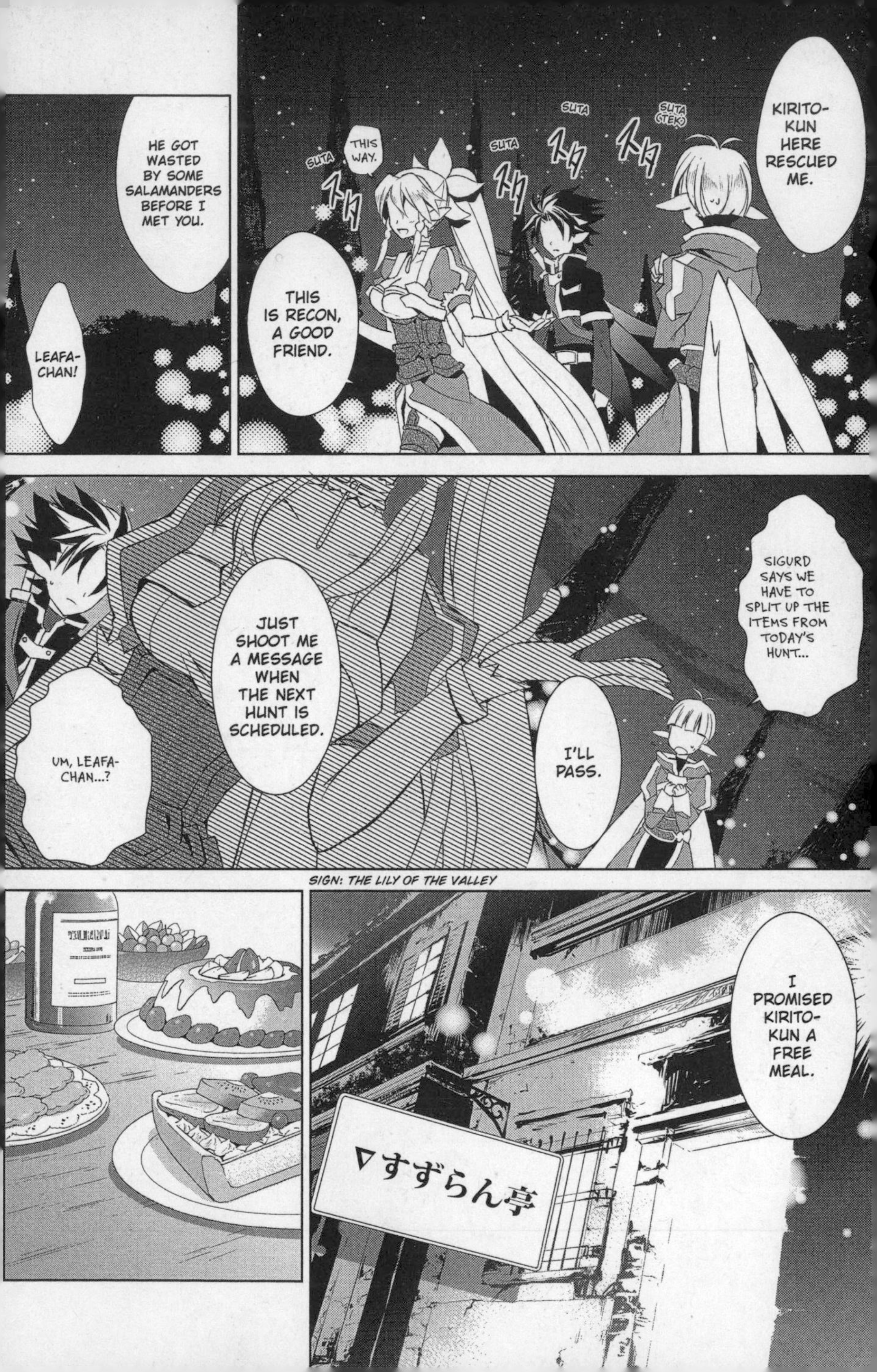
KIRITO-KUN HERE RESCUED ME.
SUTA (TEK)
SUTA
SUTA
THIS WAY.
SUTA
THIS IS RECON, A GOOD FRIEND.
HE GOT WASTED BY SOME SALAMANDERS BEFORE I MET YOU.
LEAFA-CHAN!
SIGURD SAYS WE HAVE TO SPLIT UP THE ITEMS FROM TODAY'S HUNT...
I'LL PASS.
JUST SHOOT ME A MESSAGE WHEN THE NEXT HUNT IS SCHEDULED.
UM, LEAFA-CHAN...?
SIGN: THE LILY OF THE VALLEY
I PROMISED KIRITO-KUN A FREE MEAL.
▽すずらん亭

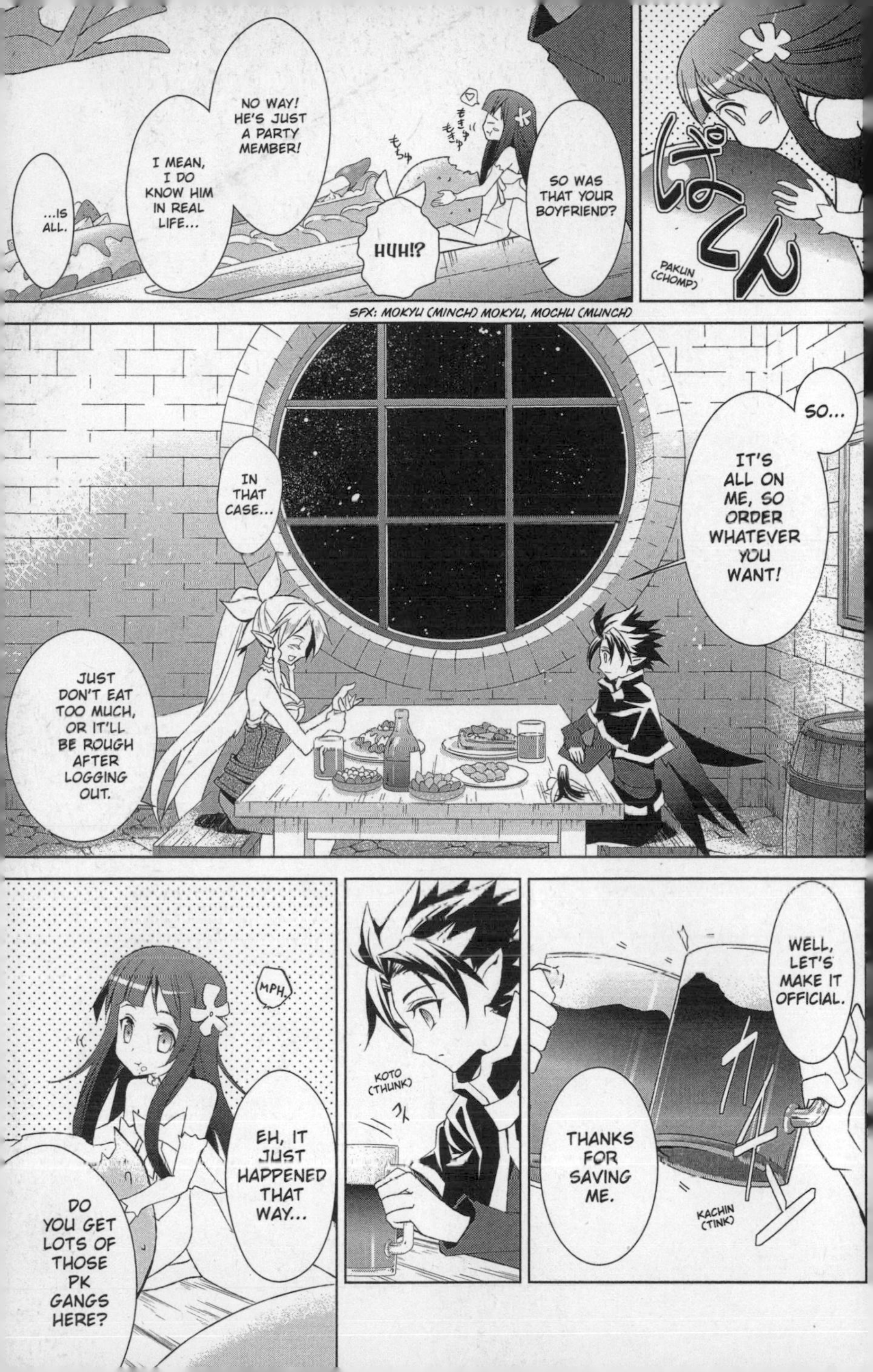
ぱくん
PAKUN (CHOMP)
SO WAS THAT YOUR BOYFRIEND?
HUH!?
NO WAY! HE'S JUST A PARTY MEMBER!
I MEAN, I DO KNOW HIM IN REAL LIFE...
...IS ALL.
SFX: MOKYU (MINCH) MOKYU, MOCHU (MUNCH)
SO...
IT'S ALL ON ME, SO ORDER WHATEVER YOU WANT!
IN THAT CASE...
JUST DON'T EAT TOO MUCH, OR IT'LL BE ROUGH AFTER LOGGING OUT.
WELL, LET'S MAKE IT OFFICIAL.
THANKS FOR SAVING ME.
KACHIN (TINK)
KOTO (THUNK)
EH, IT JUST HAPPENED THAT WAY...
MPH.
DO YOU GET LOTS OF THOSE PK GANGS HERE?

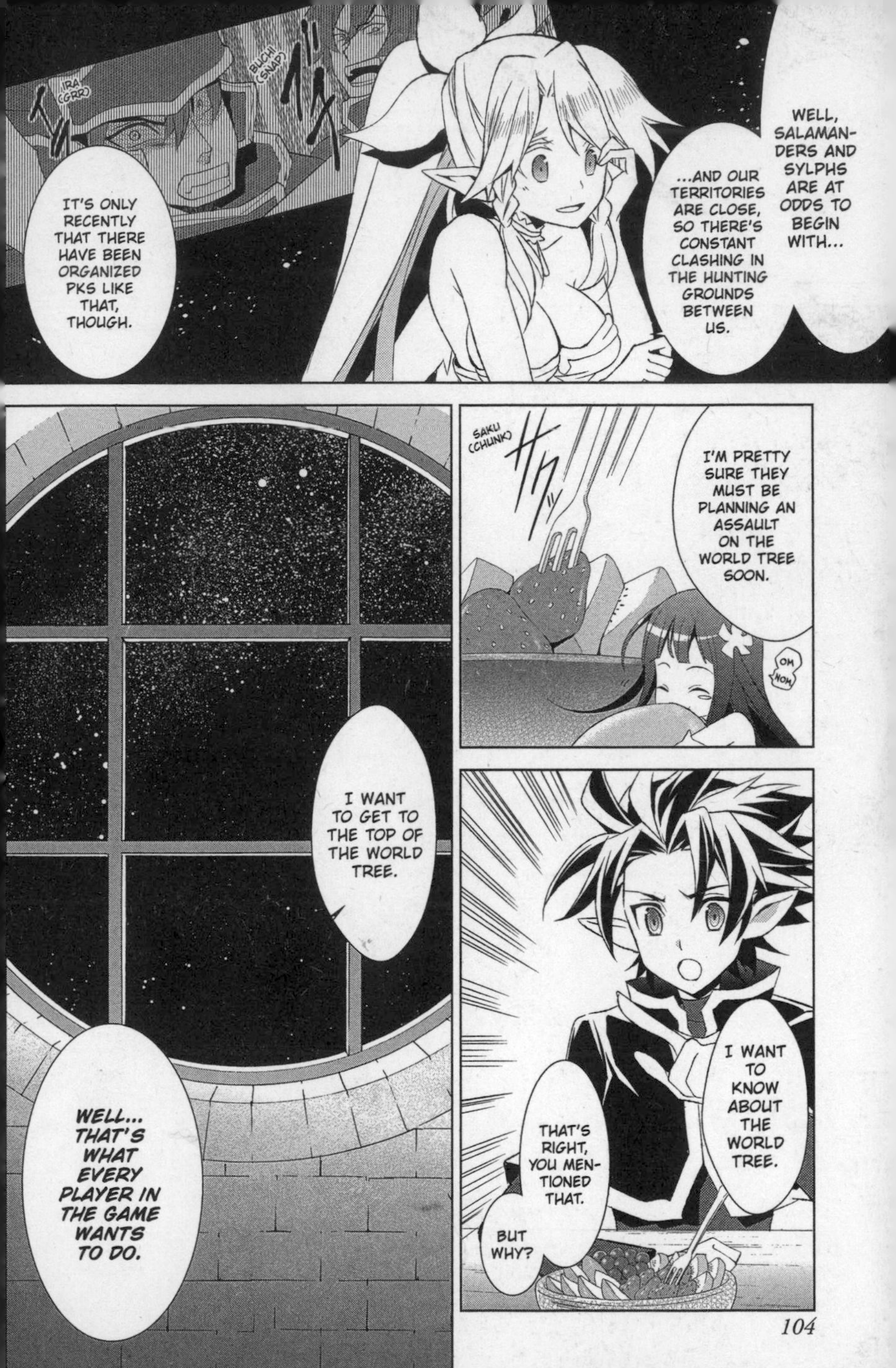
WELL, SALAMANDERS AND SYLPHS ARE AT ODDS TO BEGIN WITH...
...AND OUR TERRITORIES ARE CLOSE, SO THERE'S CONSTANT CLASHING IN THE HUNTING GROUNDS BETWEEN US.
BUCHI (SNAP)
IRA (GRR)
IT'S ONLY RECENTLY THAT THERE HAVE BEEN ORGANIZED PKS LIKE THAT, THOUGH.
I'M PRETTY SURE THEY MUST BE PLANNING AN ASSAULT ON THE WORLD TREE SOON.
SAKU (CHUNK)
OM NOM
I WANT TO KNOW ABOUT THE WORLD TREE.
THAT'S RIGHT, YOU MENTIONED THAT.
BUT WHY?
I WANT TO GET TO THE TOP OF THE WORLD TREE.
WELL... THAT'S WHAT EVERY PLAYER IN THE GAME WANTS TO DO.

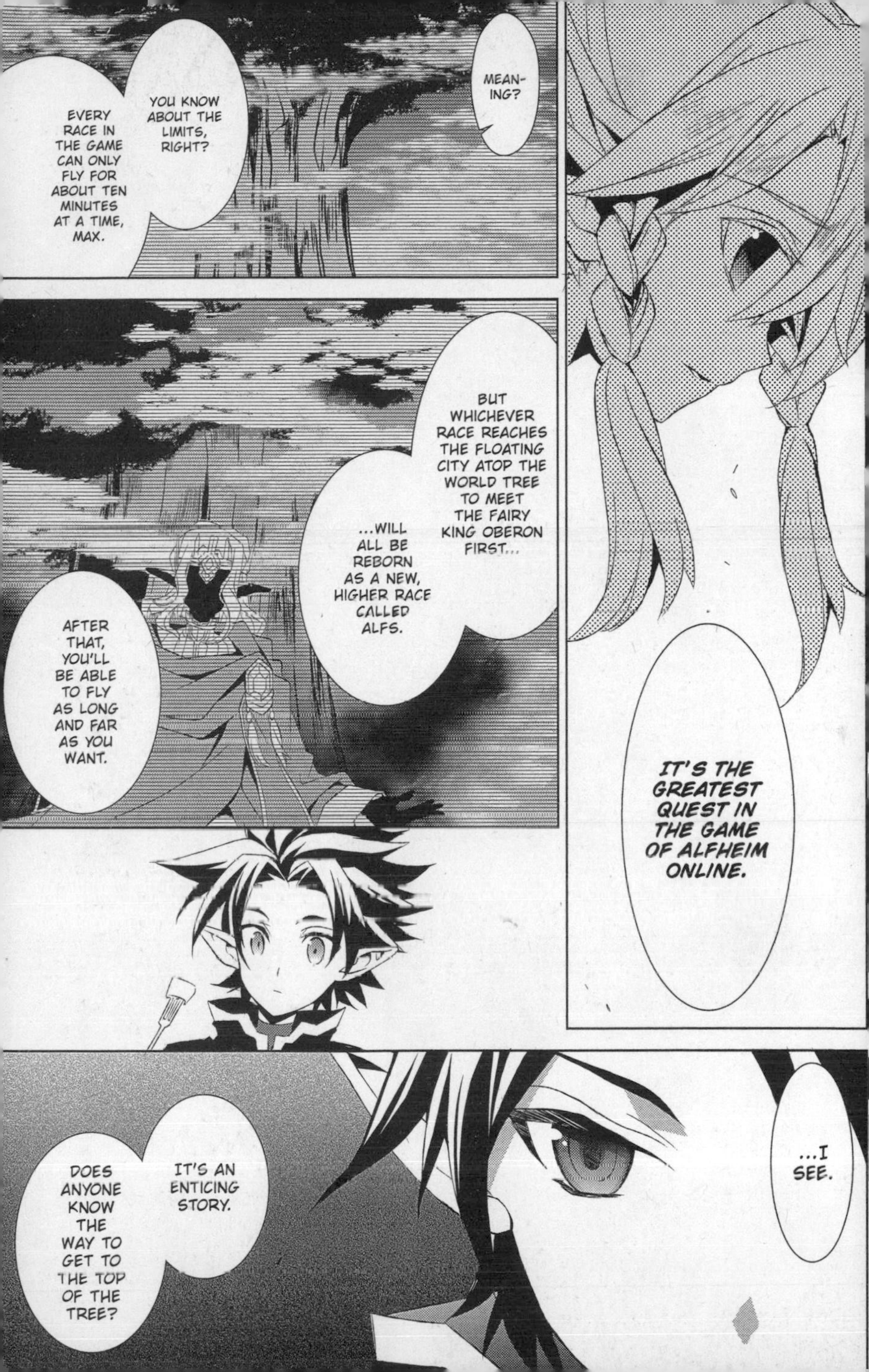
IT'S THE GREATEST QUEST IN THE GAME OF ALFHEIM ONLINE.
MEANING?
YOU KNOW ABOUT THE LIMITS, RIGHT?
EVERY RACE IN THE GAME CAN ONLY FLY FOR ABOUT TEN MINUTES AT A TIME, MAX.
BUT WHICHEVER RACE REACHES THE FLOATING CITY ATOP THE WORLD TREE TO MEET THE FAIRY KING OBERON FIRST...
...WILL ALL BE REBORN AS A NEW, HIGHER RACE CALLED ALFS.
AFTER THAT, YOU'LL BE ABLE TO FLY AS LONG AND FAR AS YOU WANT.
...I SEE.
IT'S AN ENTICING STORY.
DOES ANYONE KNOW THE WAY TO GET TO THE TOP OF THE TREE?

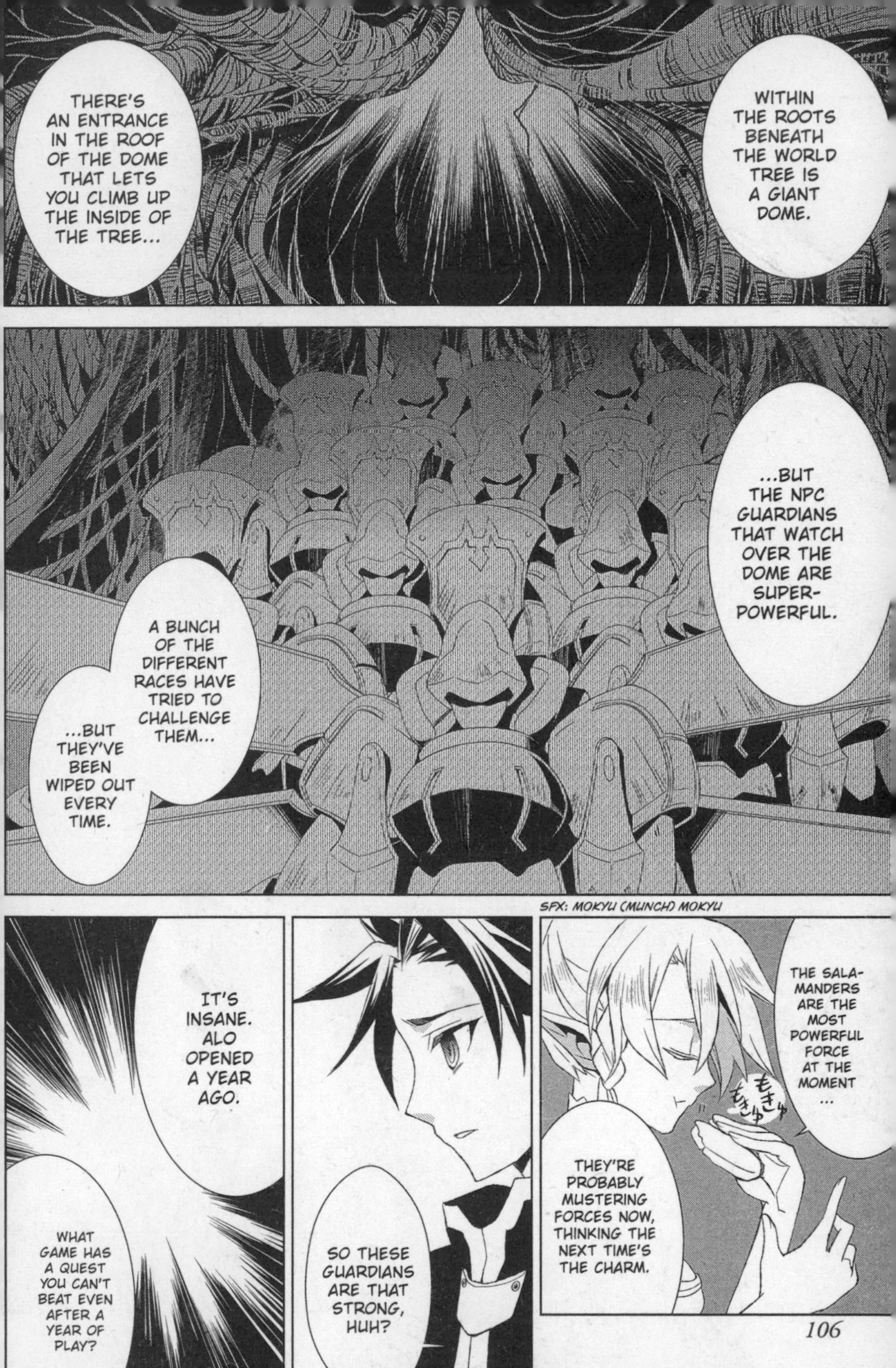
WITHIN THE ROOTS BENEATH THE WORLD TREE IS A GIANT DOME.
THERE'S AN ENTRANCE IN THE ROOF OF THE DOME THAT LETS YOU CLIMB UP THE INSIDE OF THE TREE...
...BUT THE NPC GUARDIANS THAT WATCH OVER THE DOME ARE SUPER-POWERFUL.
A BUNCH OF THE DIFFERENT RACES HAVE TRIED TO CHALLENGE THEM...
...BUT THEY'VE BEEN WIPED OUT EVERY TIME.
SFX: MOKYU (MUNCH) MOKYU
THE SALAMANDERS ARE THE MOST POWERFUL FORCE AT THE MOMENT...
もきゅもきゅ
THEY'RE PROBABLY MUSTERING FORCES NOW, THINKING THE NEXT TIME'S THE CHARM.
SO THESE GUARDIANS ARE THAT STRONG, HUH?
IT'S INSANE. ALO OPENED A YEAR AGO.
WHAT GAME HAS A QUEST YOU CAN'T BEAT EVEN AFTER A YEAR OF PLAY?

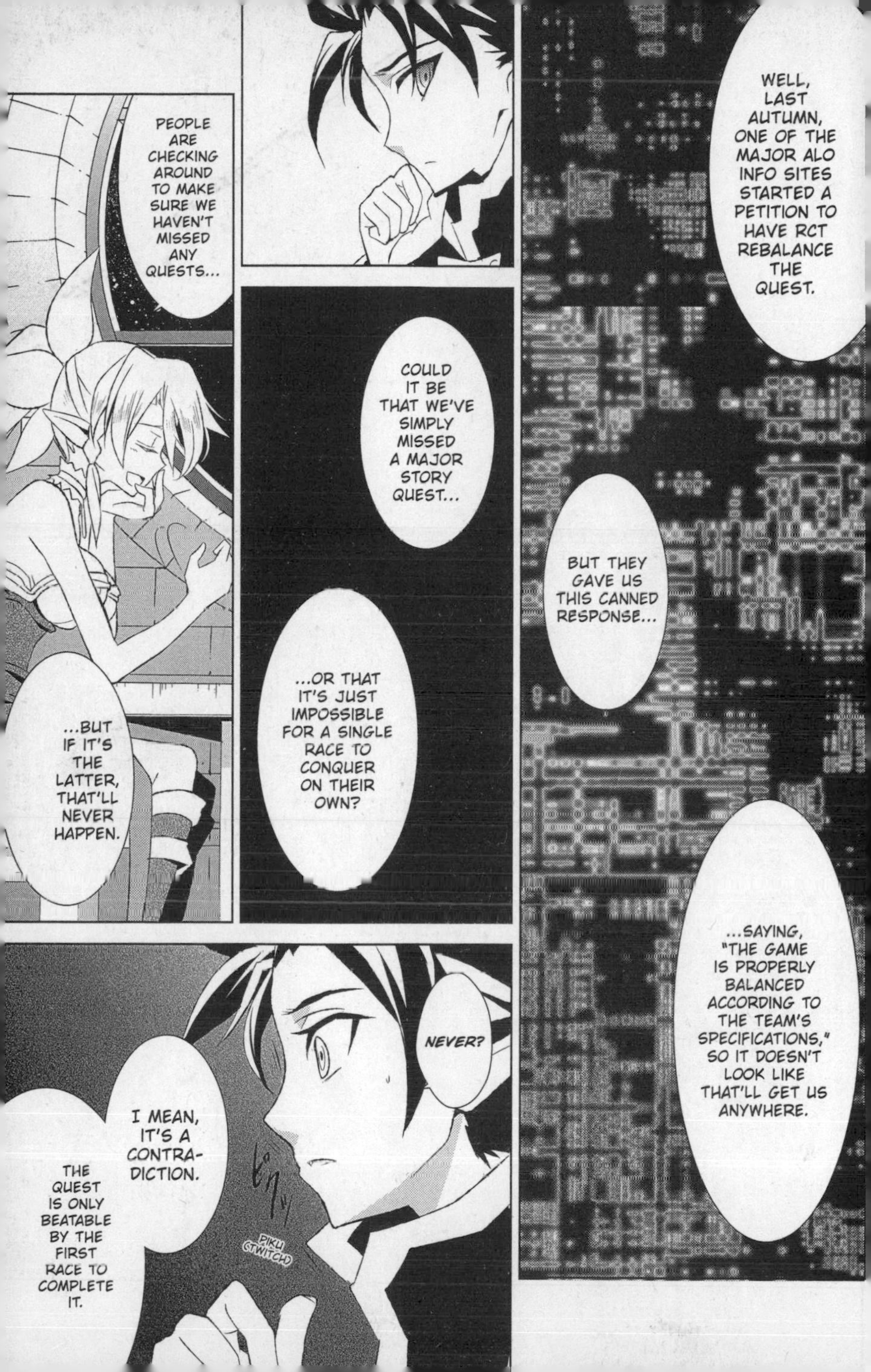
WELL, LAST AUTUMN, ONE OF THE MAJOR ALO INFO SITES STARTED A PETITION TO HAVE RCT REBALANCE THE QUEST.
BUT THEY GAVE US THIS CANNED RESPONSE...
...SAYING, "THE GAME IS PROPERLY BALANCED ACCORDING TO THE TEAM'S SPECIFICATIONS," SO IT DOESN'T LOOK LIKE THAT'LL GET US ANYWHERE.
COULD IT BE THAT WE'VE SIMPLY MISSED A MAJOR STORY QUEST...
...OR THAT IT'S JUST IMPOSSIBLE FOR A SINGLE RACE TO CONQUER ON THEIR OWN?
PEOPLE ARE CHECKING AROUND TO MAKE SURE WE HAVEN'T MISSED ANY QUESTS...
...BUT IF IT'S THE LATTER, THAT'LL NEVER HAPPEN.
NEVER?
PIKU (TWITCH)
I MEAN, IT'S A CONTRA-DICTION.
THE QUEST IS ONLY BEATABLE BY THE FIRST RACE TO COMPLETE IT.

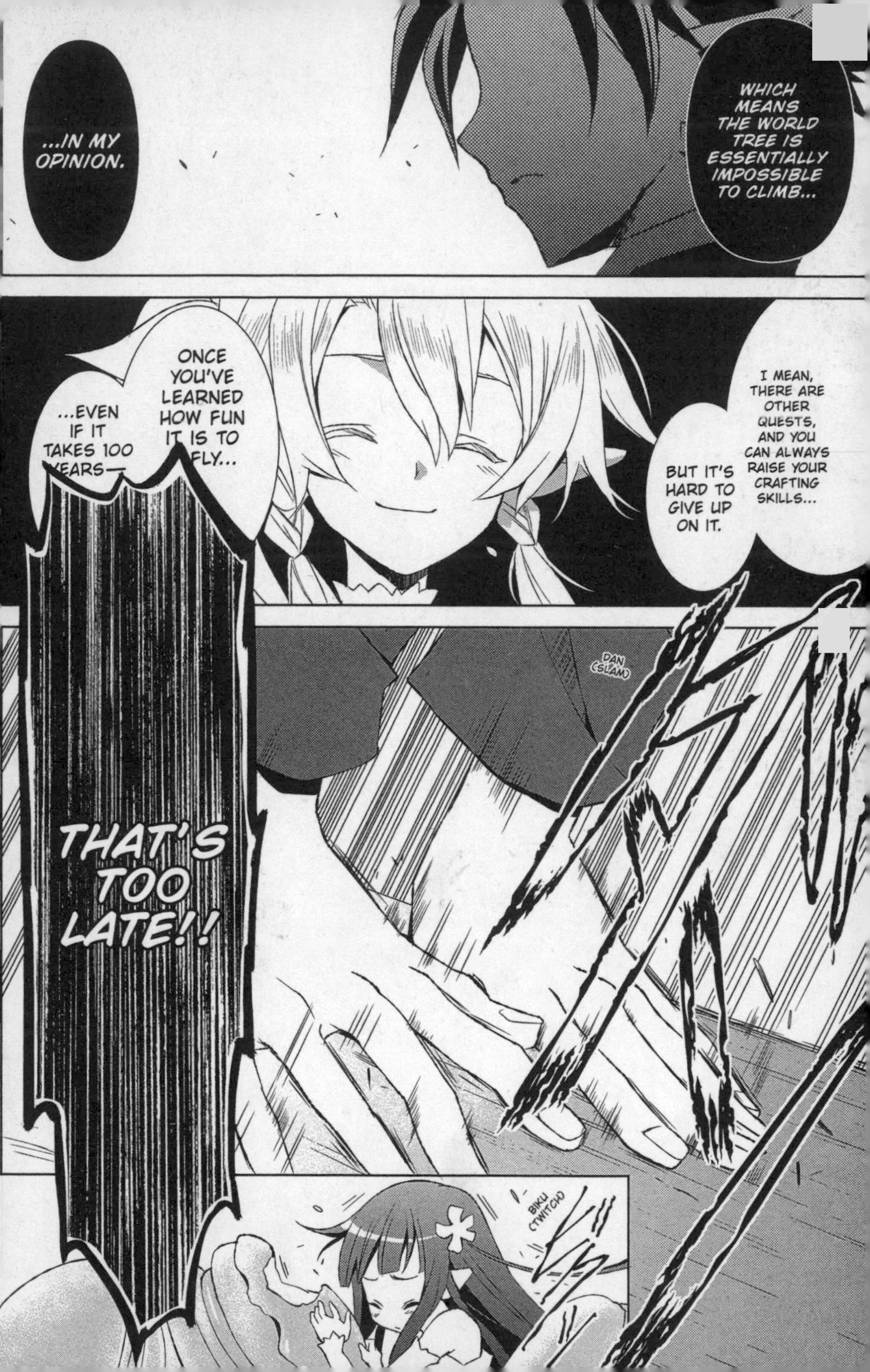
WHICH MEANS THE WORLD TREE IS ESSENTIALLY IMPOSSIBLE TO CLIMB...
...IN MY OPINION.
I MEAN, THERE ARE OTHER QUESTS, AND YOU CAN ALWAYS RAISE YOUR CRAFTING SKILLS...
BUT IT'S HARD TO GIVE UP ON IT.
ONCE YOU'VE LEARNED HOW FUN IT IS TO FLY...
...EVEN IF IT TAKES 100 YEARS—
DAN (SLAM)
THAT'S TOO LATE!!
BIKU (TWITCH)

PAPA
...?

WHAT DO YOU MEAN?

I'M SORRY TO STARTLE YOU.

I'M... LOOKING FOR SOMEONE.

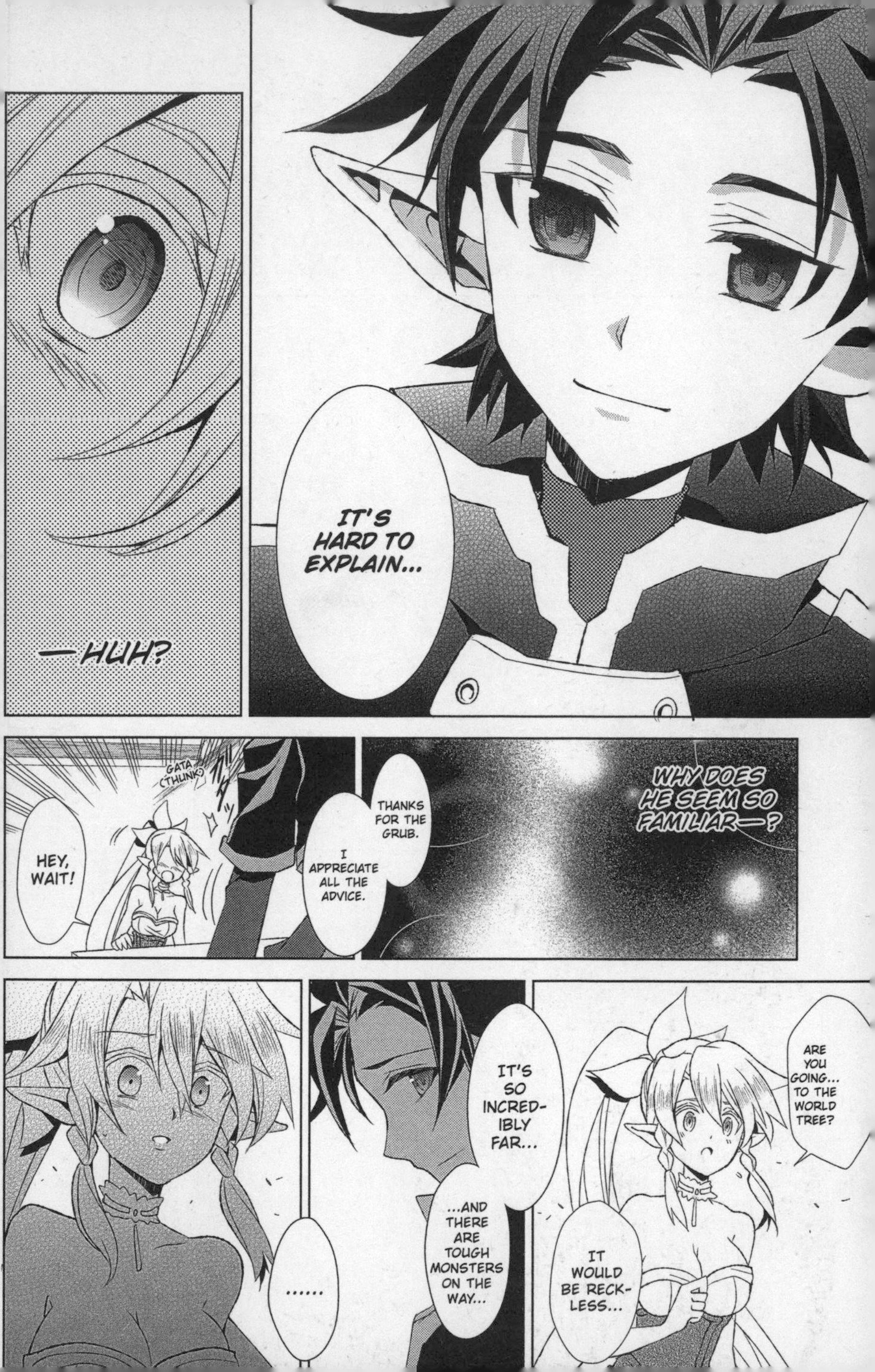
IT'S HARD TO EXPLAIN...
—HUH?
WHY DOES HE SEEM SO FAMILIAR—?
THANKS FOR THE GRUB.
I APPRECIATE ALL THE ADVICE.
GATA (THUNK)
HEY, WAIT!
ARE YOU GOING... TO THE WORLD TREE?
IT WOULD BE RECK-LESS...
IT'S SO INCRED-IBLY FAR...
...AND THERE ARE TOUGH MONSTERS ON THE WAY...
......

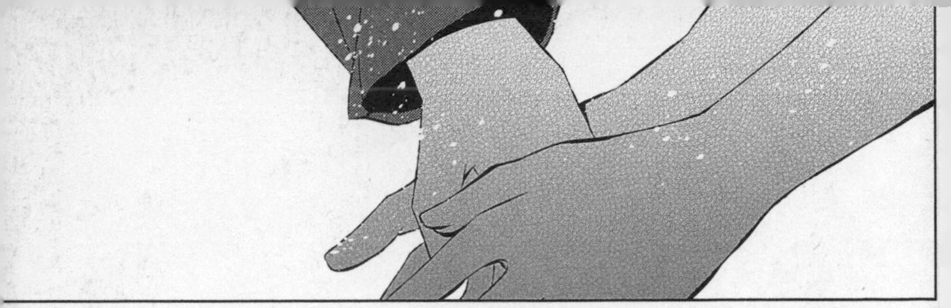
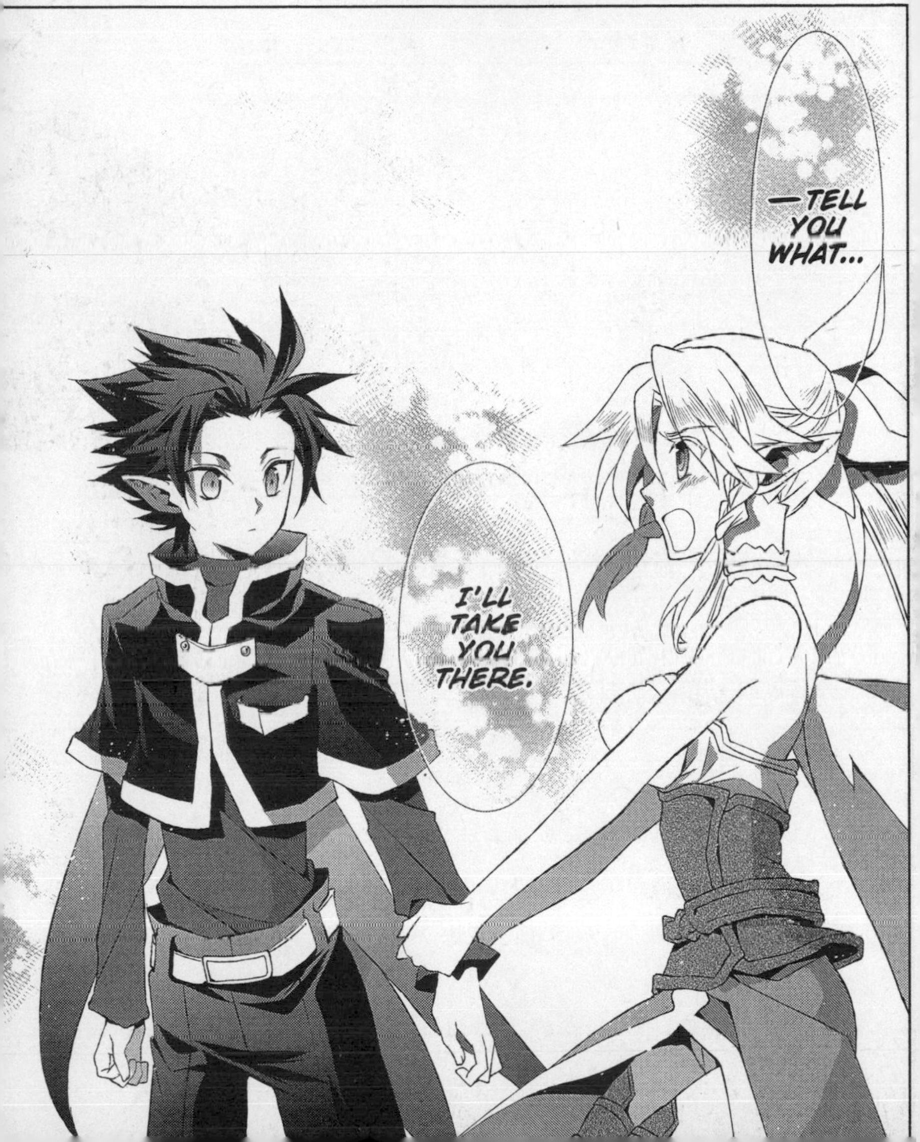
—TELL YOU WHAT...
I'LL TAKE YOU THERE.

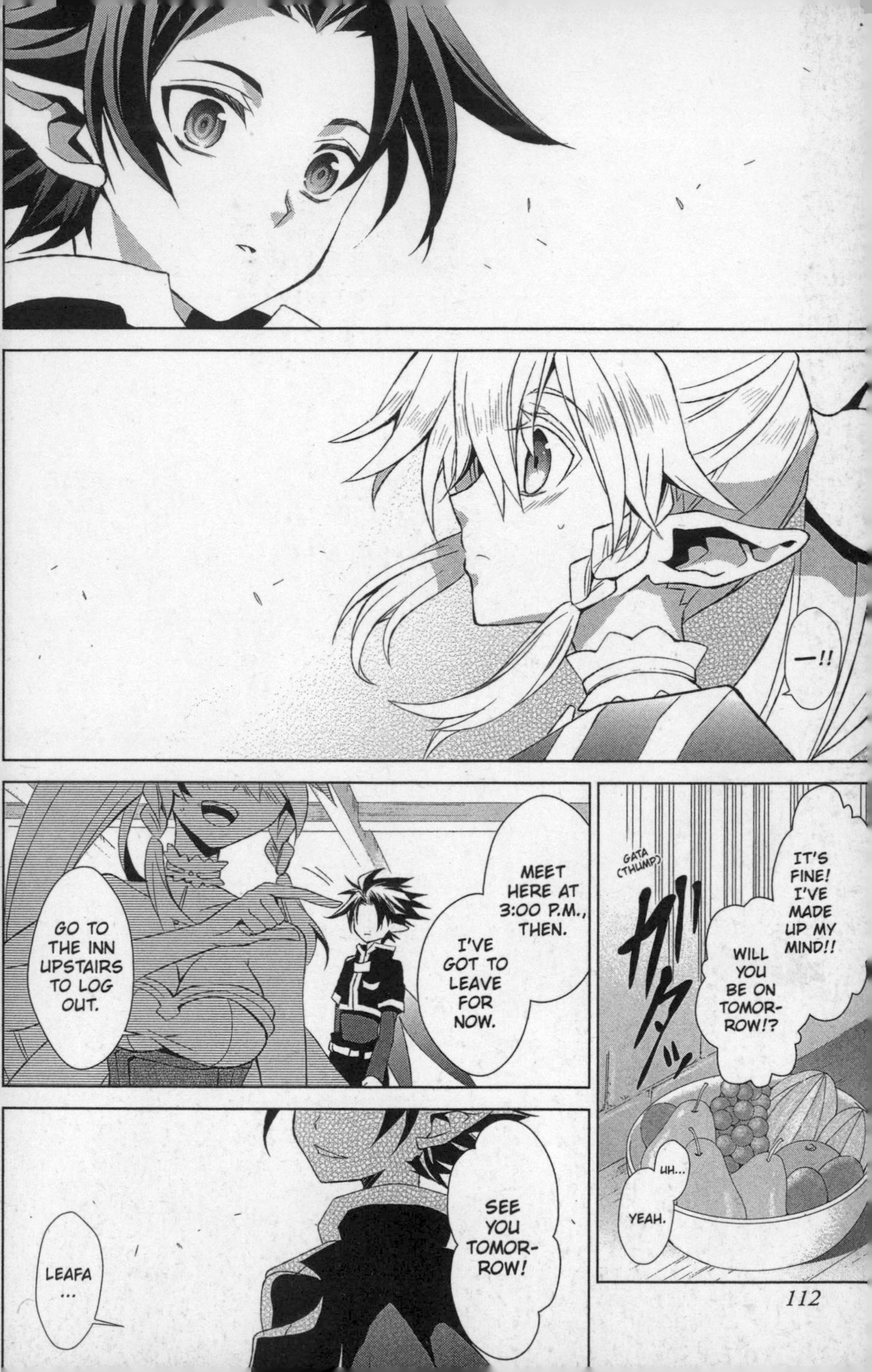
—!!
IT'S FINE! I'VE MADE UP MY MIND!!
GATA (THUMP)
WILL YOU BE ON TOMORROW!?
UH...
YEAH.
MEET HERE AT 3:00 P.M., THEN.
I'VE GOT TO LEAVE FOR NOW.
GO TO THE INN UPSTAIRS TO LOG OUT.
SEE YOU TOMORROW!
LEAFA...

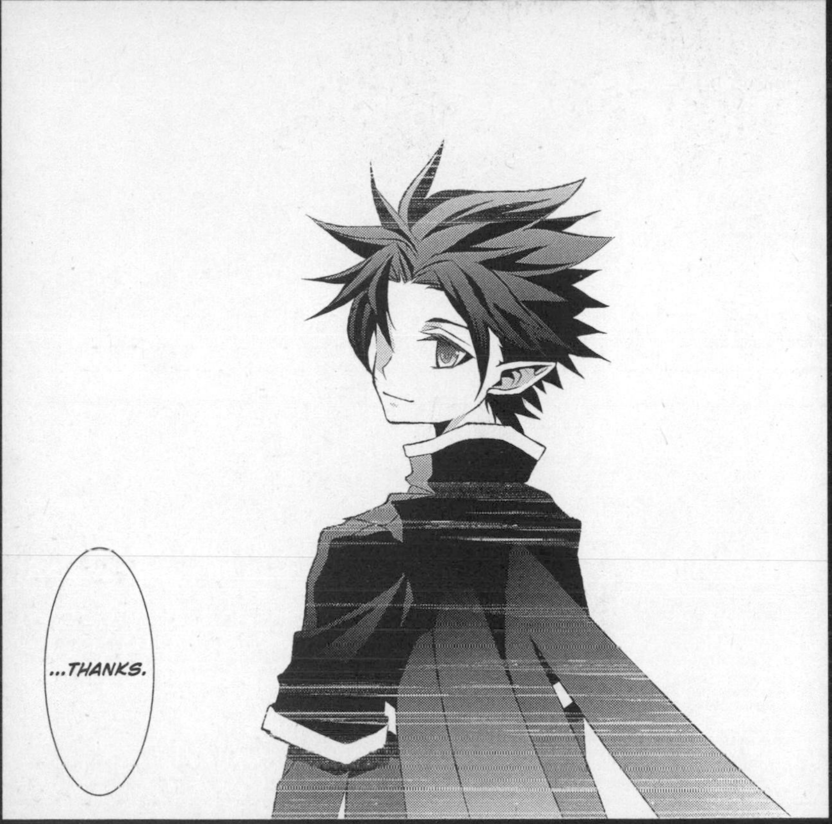
...THANKS.
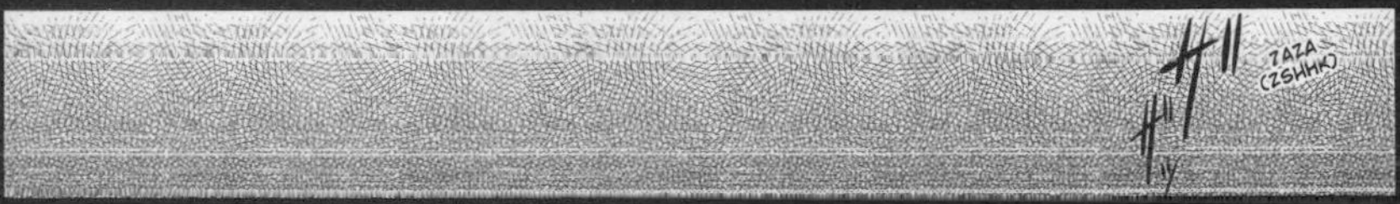
ZAZA
(ZSHHK)

LOG OUT

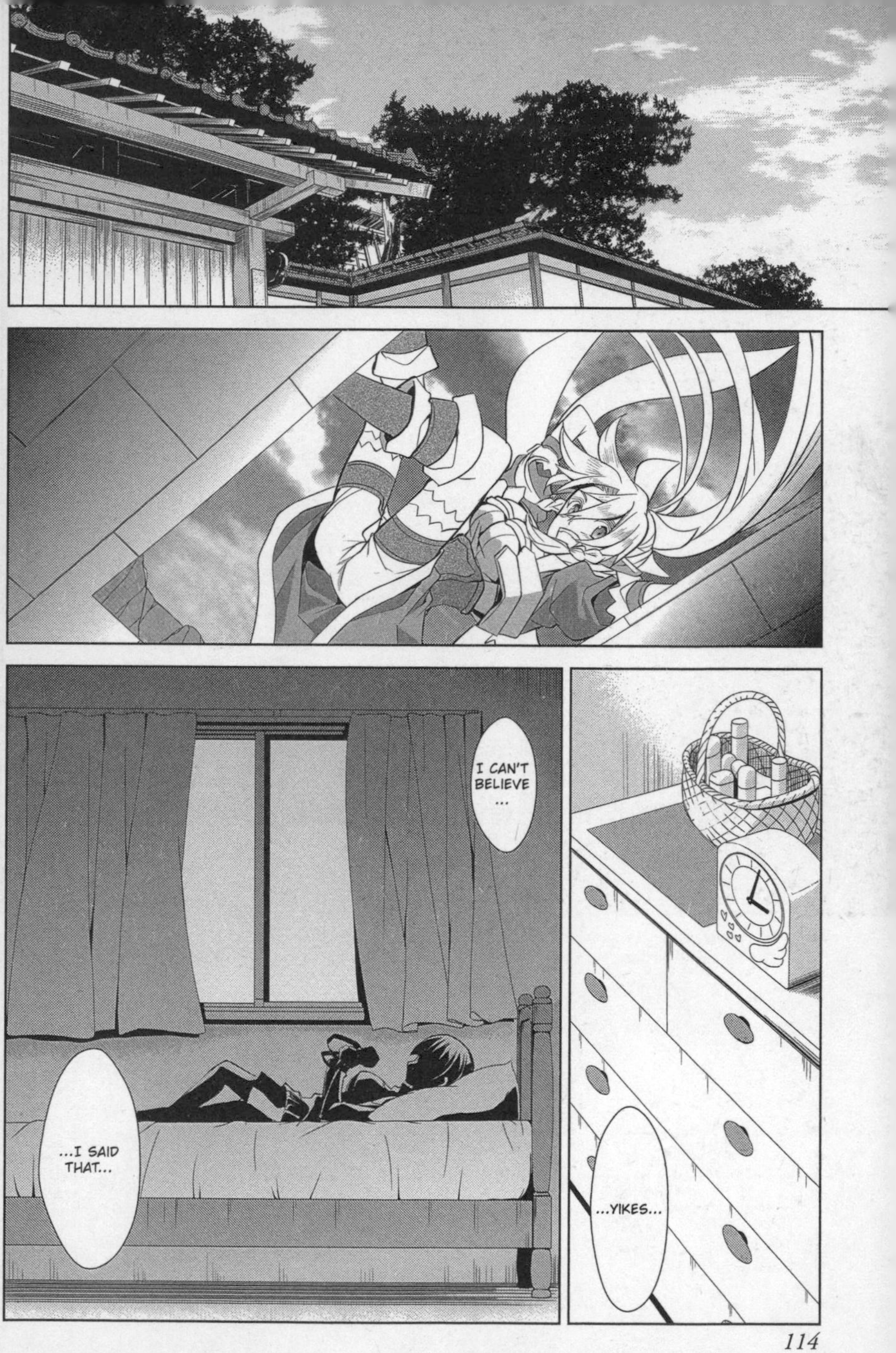
...YIKES...
I CAN'T BELIEVE ...
...I SAID THAT...

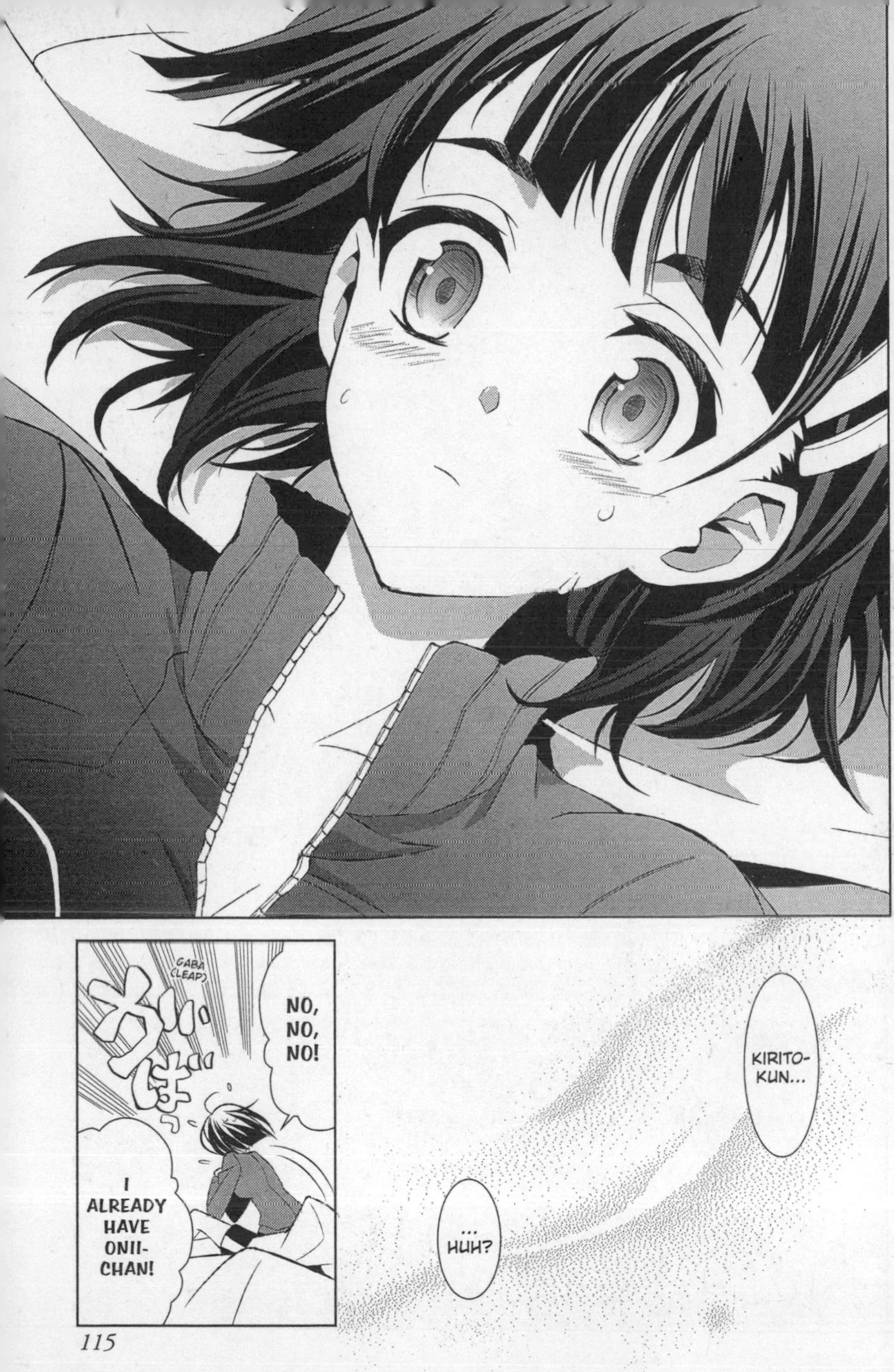
KIRITO-KUN...
...HUH?
GABA (LEAP)
NO, NO, NO!
I ALREADY HAVE ONII-CHAN!

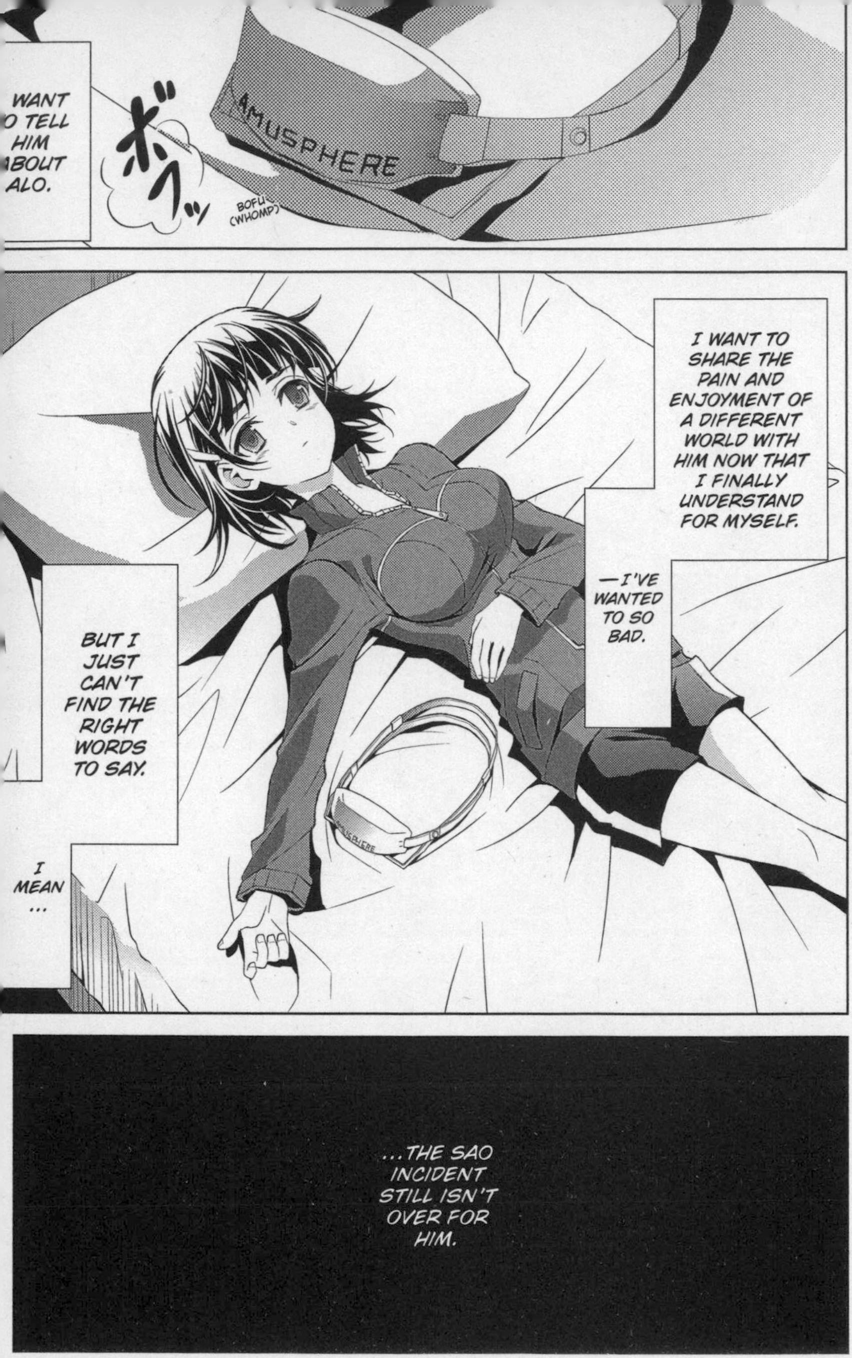
WANT O TELL HIM ABOUT ALO.
ボフッ
BOFU (WHOMP)
I WANT TO SHARE THE PAIN AND ENJOYMENT OF A DIFFERENT WORLD WITH HIM NOW THAT I FINALLY UNDERSTAND FOR MYSELF.
—I'VE WANTED TO SO BAD.
BUT I JUST CAN'T FIND THE RIGHT WORDS TO SAY.
I MEAN ...
...THE SAO INCIDENT STILL ISN'T OVER FOR HIM.

SWORD ART ONLINE
fairy dance

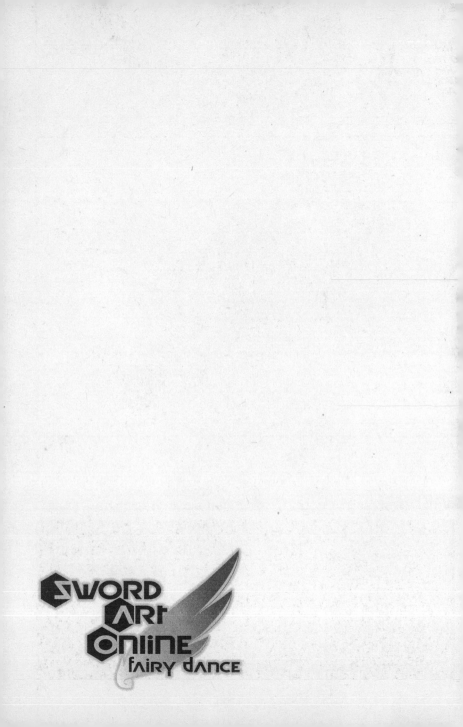

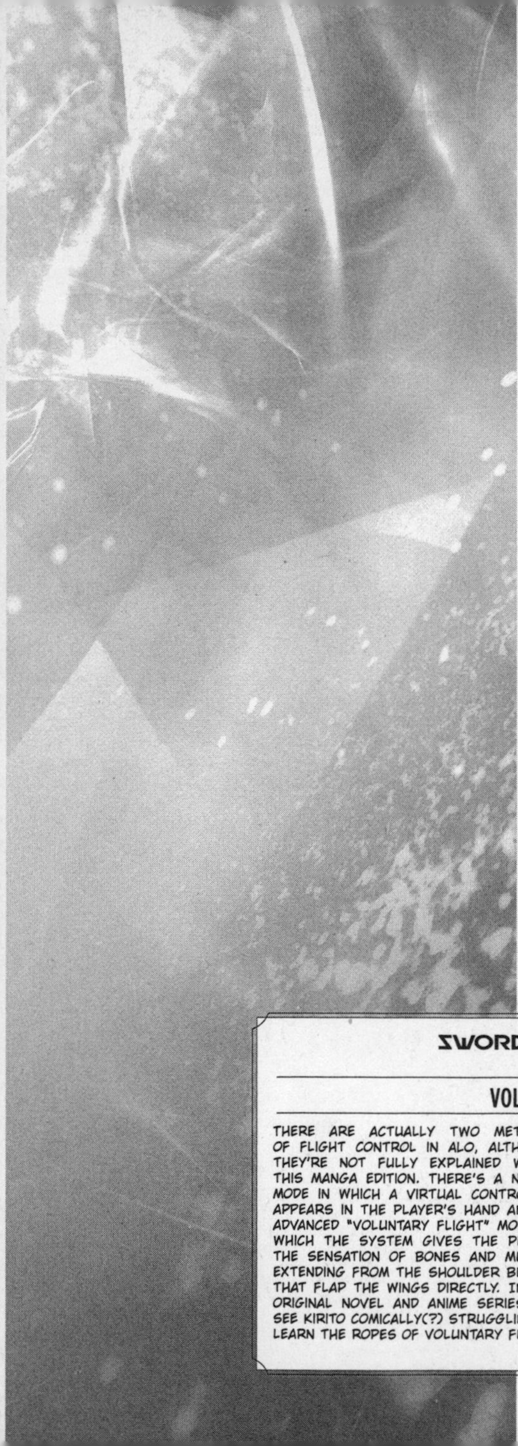

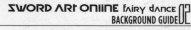

SWORD ART ONLINE fairy dance BACKGROUND GUIDE 02

VOLUNTARY FLIGHT AND CONTROLLERS

THERE ARE ACTUALLY TWO METHODS OF FLIGHT CONTROL IN ALO, ALTHOUGH THEY'RE NOT FULLY EXPLAINED WITHIN THIS MANGA EDITION. THERE'S A NOVICE MODE IN WHICH A VIRTUAL CONTROLLER APPEARS IN THE PLAYER'S HAND AND AN ADVANCED "VOLUNTARY FLIGHT" MODE, IN WHICH THE SYSTEM GIVES THE PLAYER THE SENSATION OF BONES AND MUSCLE EXTENDING FROM THE SHOULDER BLADES THAT FLAP THE WINGS DIRECTLY. IN THE ORIGINAL NOVEL AND ANIME SERIES, WE SEE KIRITO COMICALLY(?) STRUGGLING TO LEARN THE ROPES OF VOLUNTARY FLIGHT.

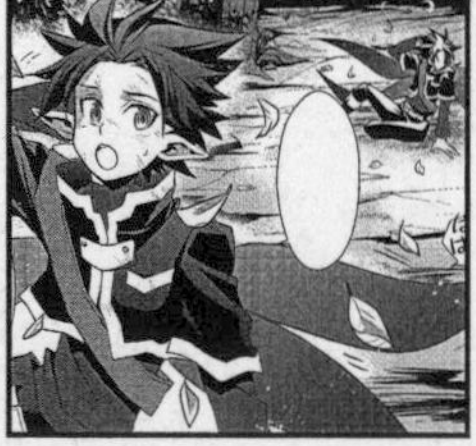

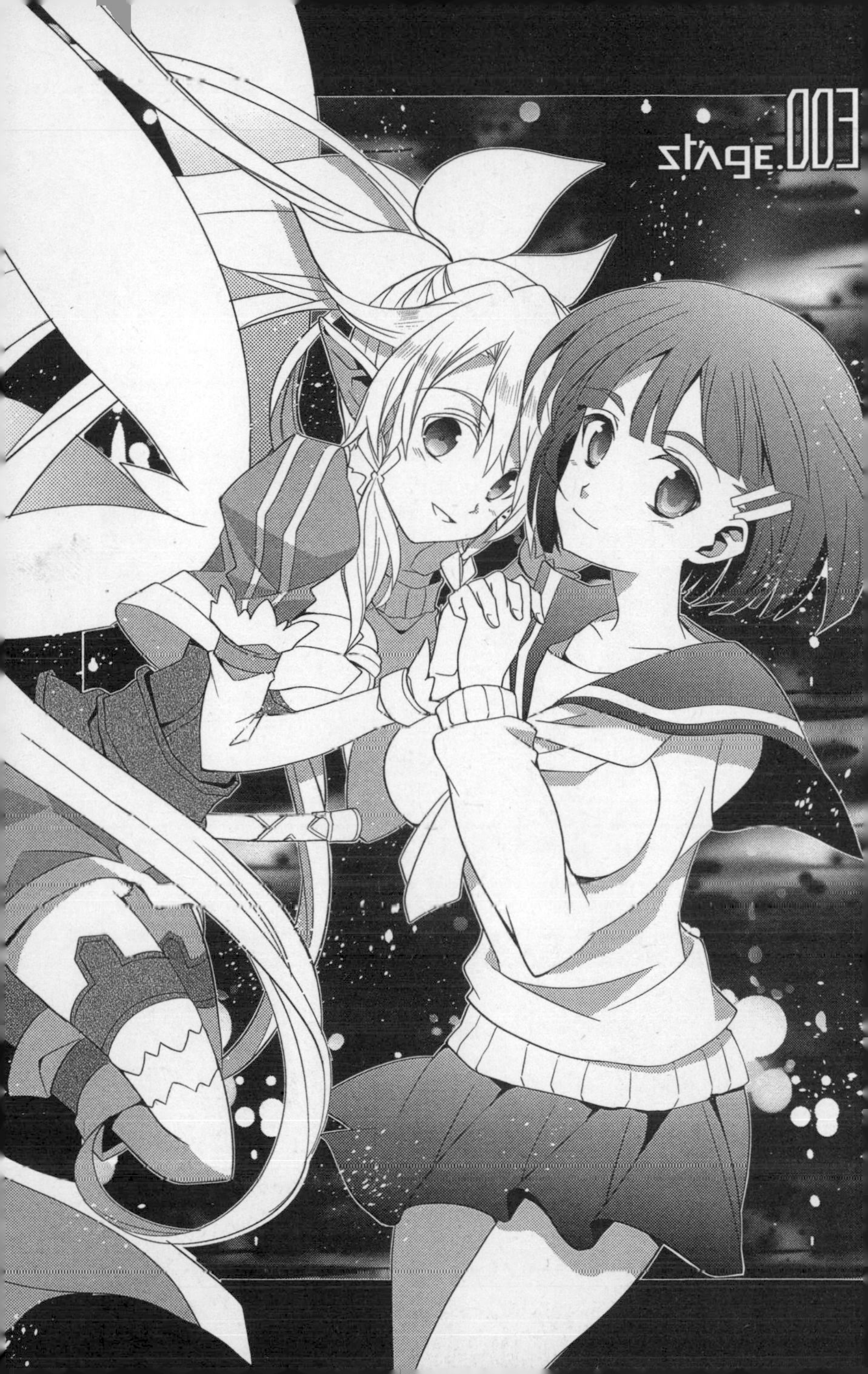
stage.003

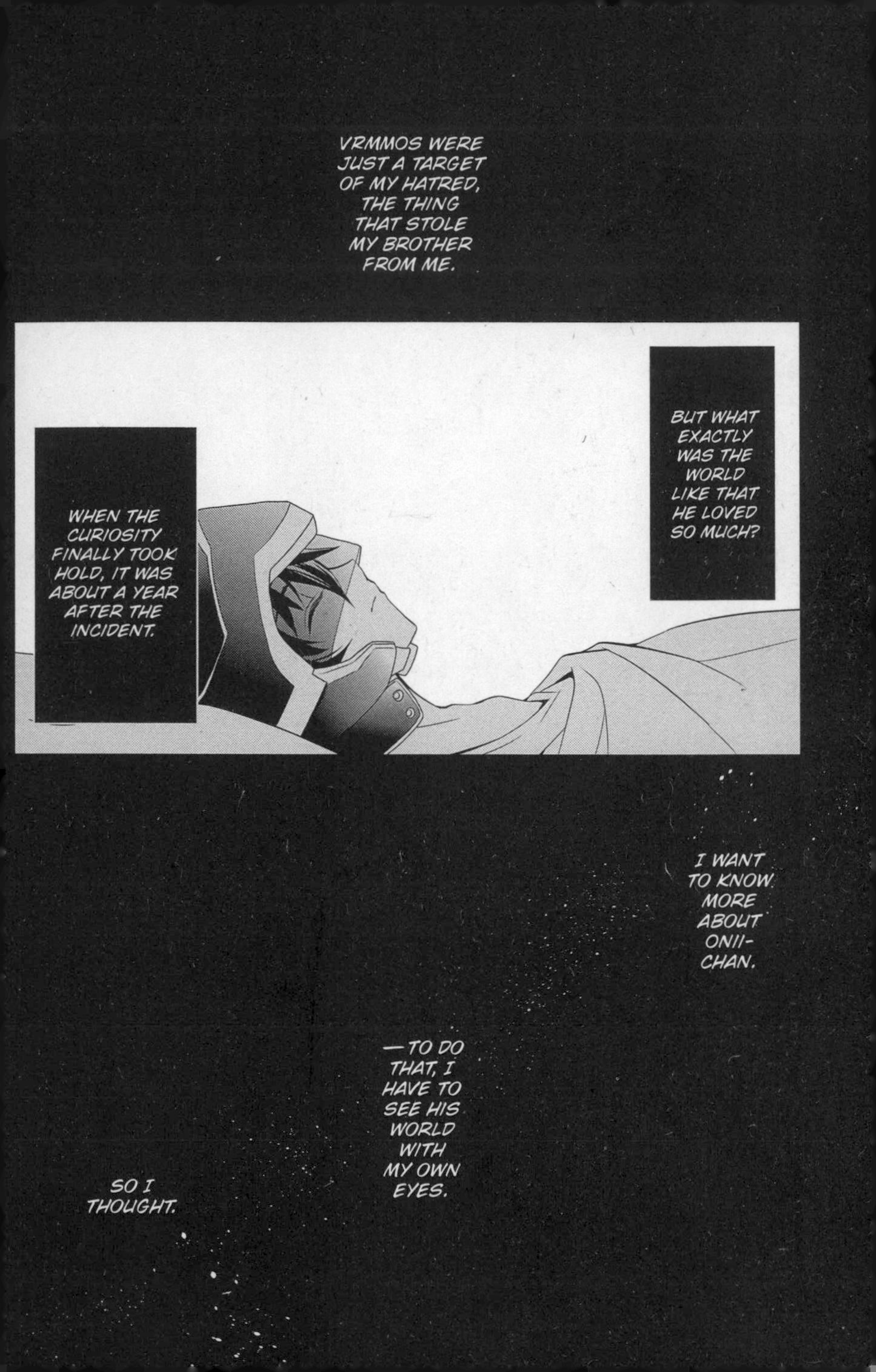
VRMMOS WERE JUST A TARGET OF MY HATRED, THE THING THAT STOLE MY BROTHER FROM ME.
BUT WHAT EXACTLY WAS THE WORLD LIKE THAT HE LOVED SO MUCH?
WHEN THE CURIOSITY FINALLY TOOK HOLD, IT WAS ABOUT A YEAR AFTER THE INCIDENT.
I WANT TO KNOW MORE ABOUT ONII-CHAN.
—TO DO THAT, I HAVE TO SEE HIS WORLD WITH MY OWN EYES.
SO I THOUGHT.

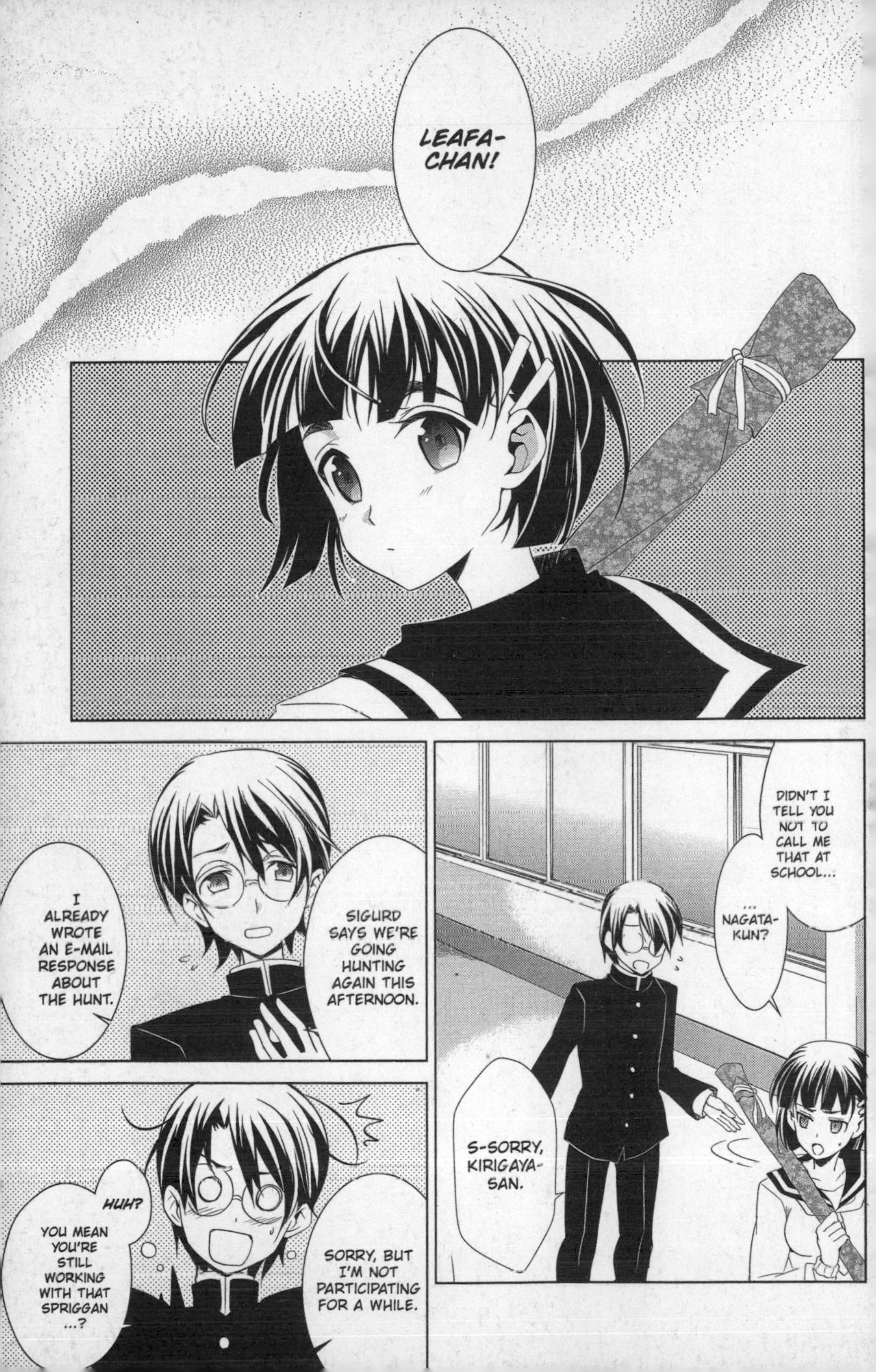
LEAFA-CHAN!
DIDN'T I TELL YOU NOT TO CALL ME THAT AT SCHOOL...
...NAGATA-KUN?
S-SORRY, KIRIGAYA-SAN.
SIGURD SAYS WE'RE GOING HUNTING AGAIN THIS AFTERNOON.
I ALREADY WROTE AN E-MAIL RESPONSE ABOUT THE HUNT.
SORRY, BUT I'M NOT PARTICIPATING FOR A WHILE.
HUH?
YOU MEAN YOU'RE STILL WORKING WITH THAT SPRIGGAN...?

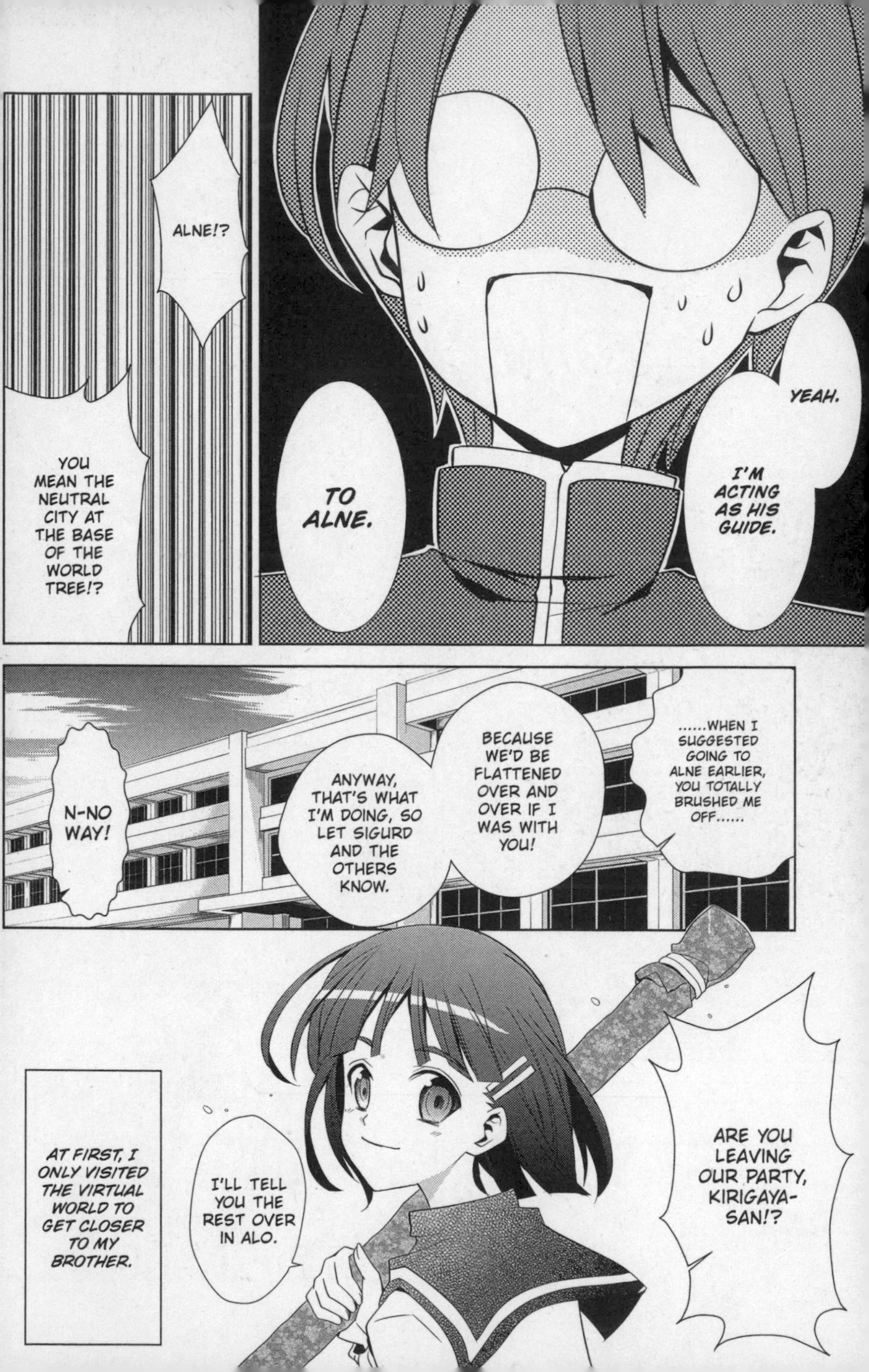
YEAH.
I'M ACTING AS HIS GUIDE.
TO ALNE.
ALNE!?
YOU MEAN THE NEUTRAL CITY AT THE BASE OF THE WORLD TREE!?
......WHEN I SUGGESTED GOING TO ALNE EARLIER, YOU TOTALLY BRUSHED ME OFF......
BECAUSE WE'D BE FLATTENED OVER AND OVER IF I WAS WITH YOU!
ANYWAY, THAT'S WHAT I'M DOING, SO LET SIGURD AND THE OTHERS KNOW.
N-NO WAY!
ARE YOU LEAVING OUR PARTY, KIRIGAYA-SAN!?
I'LL TELL YOU THE REST OVER IN ALO.
AT FIRST, I ONLY VISITED THE VIRTUAL WORLD TO GET CLOSER TO MY BROTHER.

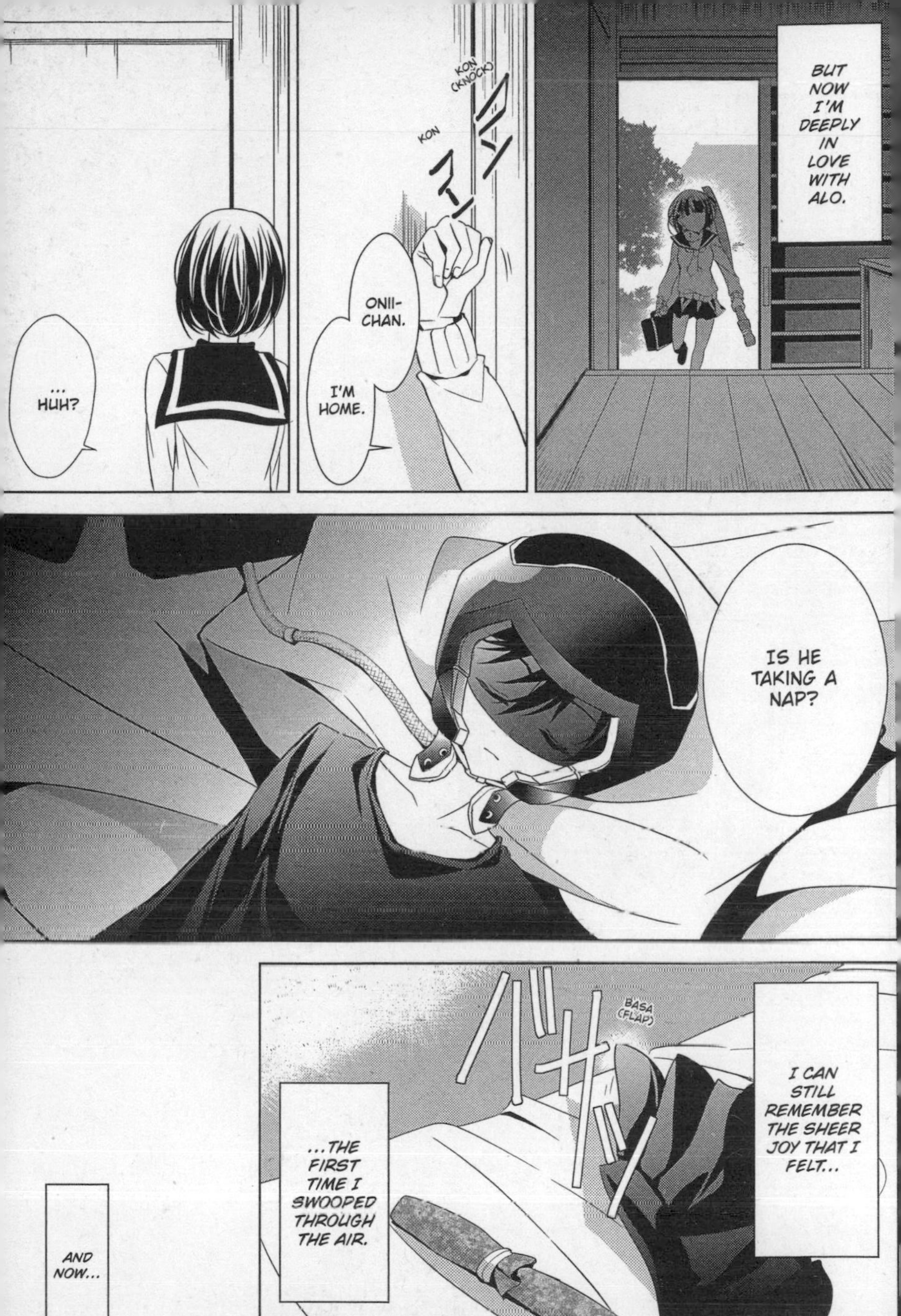
BUT NOW I'M DEEPLY IN LOVE WITH ALO.
KON (KNOCK)
KON
ONII-CHAN.
I'M HOME.
...HUH?
IS HE TAKING A NAP?
BASA (FLAP)
I CAN STILL REMEMBER THE SHEER JOY THAT I FELT...
...THE FIRST TIME I SWOOPED THROUGH THE AIR.
AND NOW...

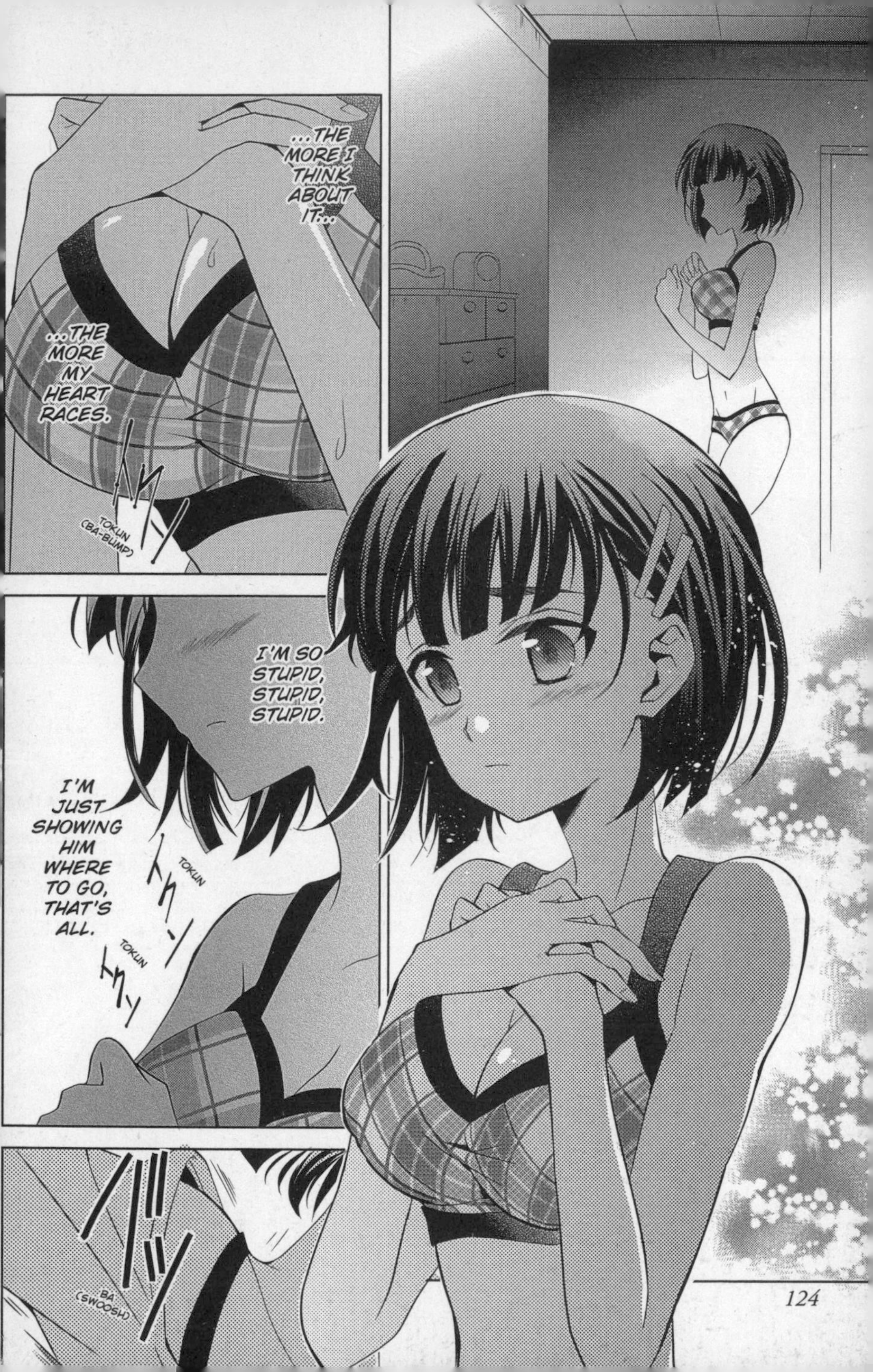
...THE MORE I THINK ABOUT IT...
...THE MORE MY HEART RACES.
TOKUN (BA-BUMP)
I'M SO STUPID, STUPID, STUPID.
I'M JUST SHOWING HIM WHERE TO GO, THAT'S ALL.
TOKUN
TOKUN
BA (SWOOSH)

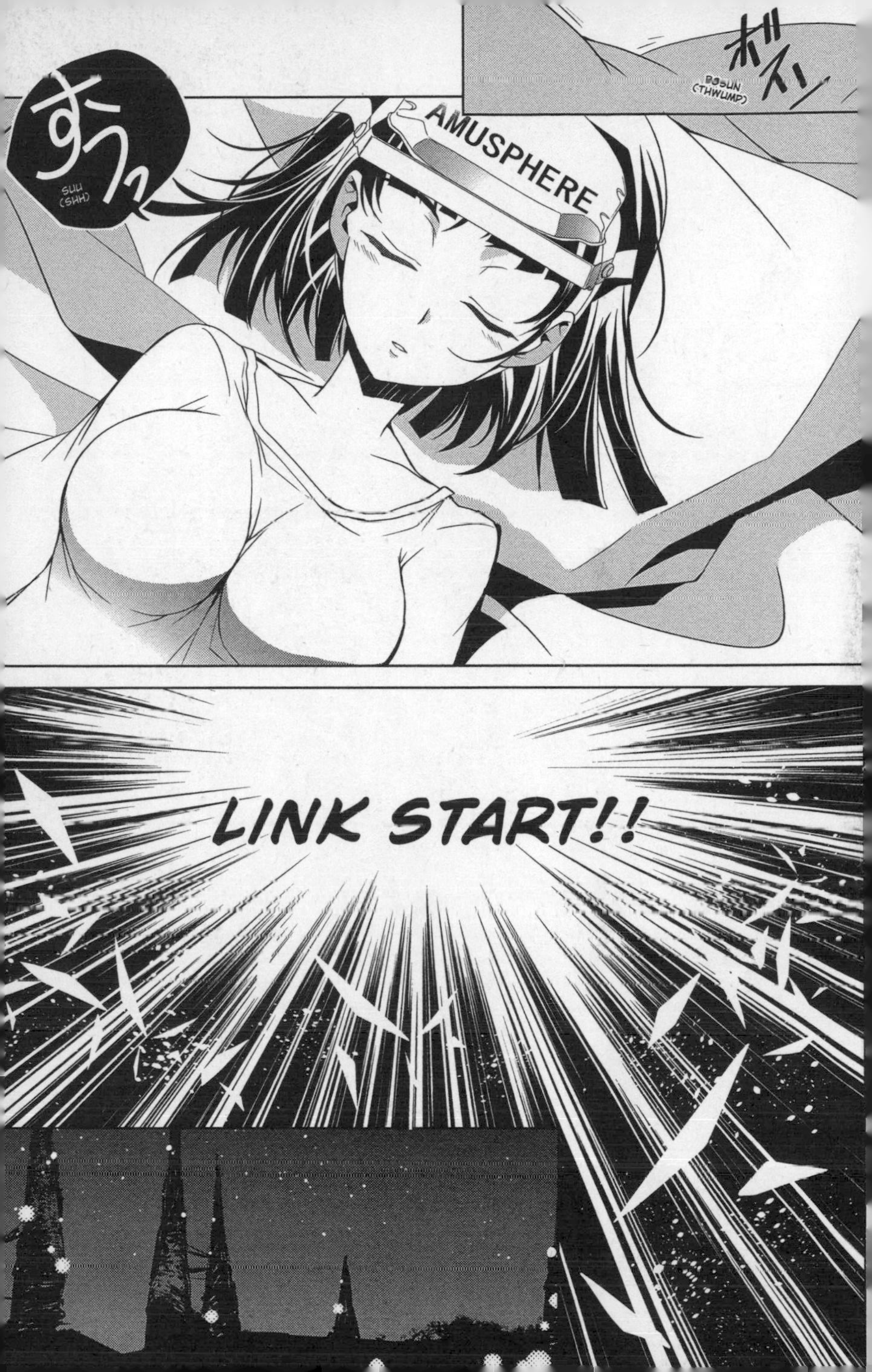
ボスン
BOSUN (THWUMP)
すぅっ
SUU (SHH)
AMUSPHERE
LINK START!!

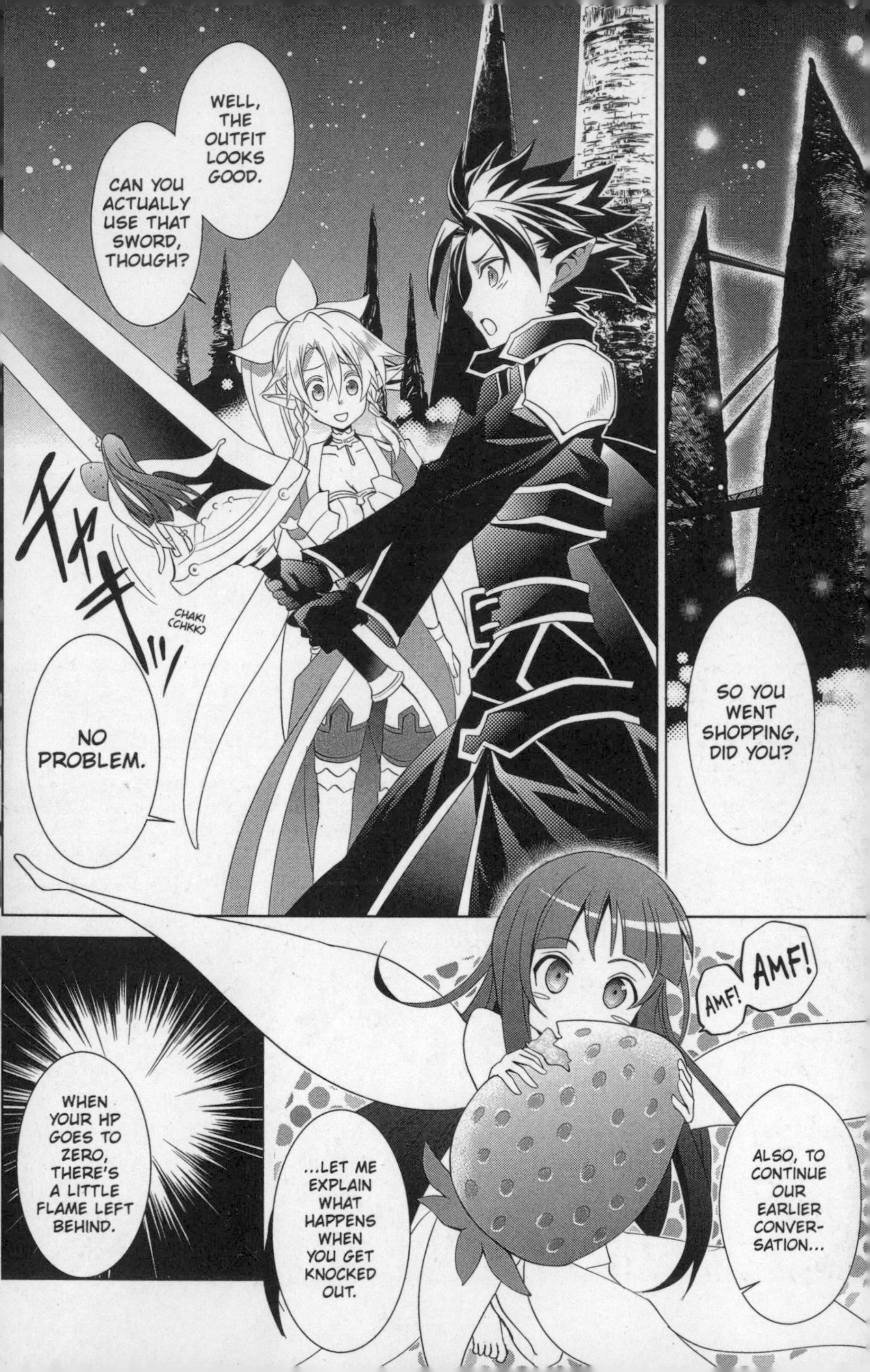
SO YOU WENT SHOPPING, DID YOU?
WELL, THE OUTFIT LOOKS GOOD.
CAN YOU ACTUALLY USE THAT SWORD, THOUGH?
CHAKI (CHKK)
NO PROBLEM.
AMF!
AMF!
ALSO, TO CONTINUE OUR EARLIER CONVERSATION...
...LET ME EXPLAIN WHAT HAPPENS WHEN YOU GET KNOCKED OUT.
WHEN YOUR HP GOES TO ZERO, THERE'S A LITTLE FLAME LEFT BEHIND.

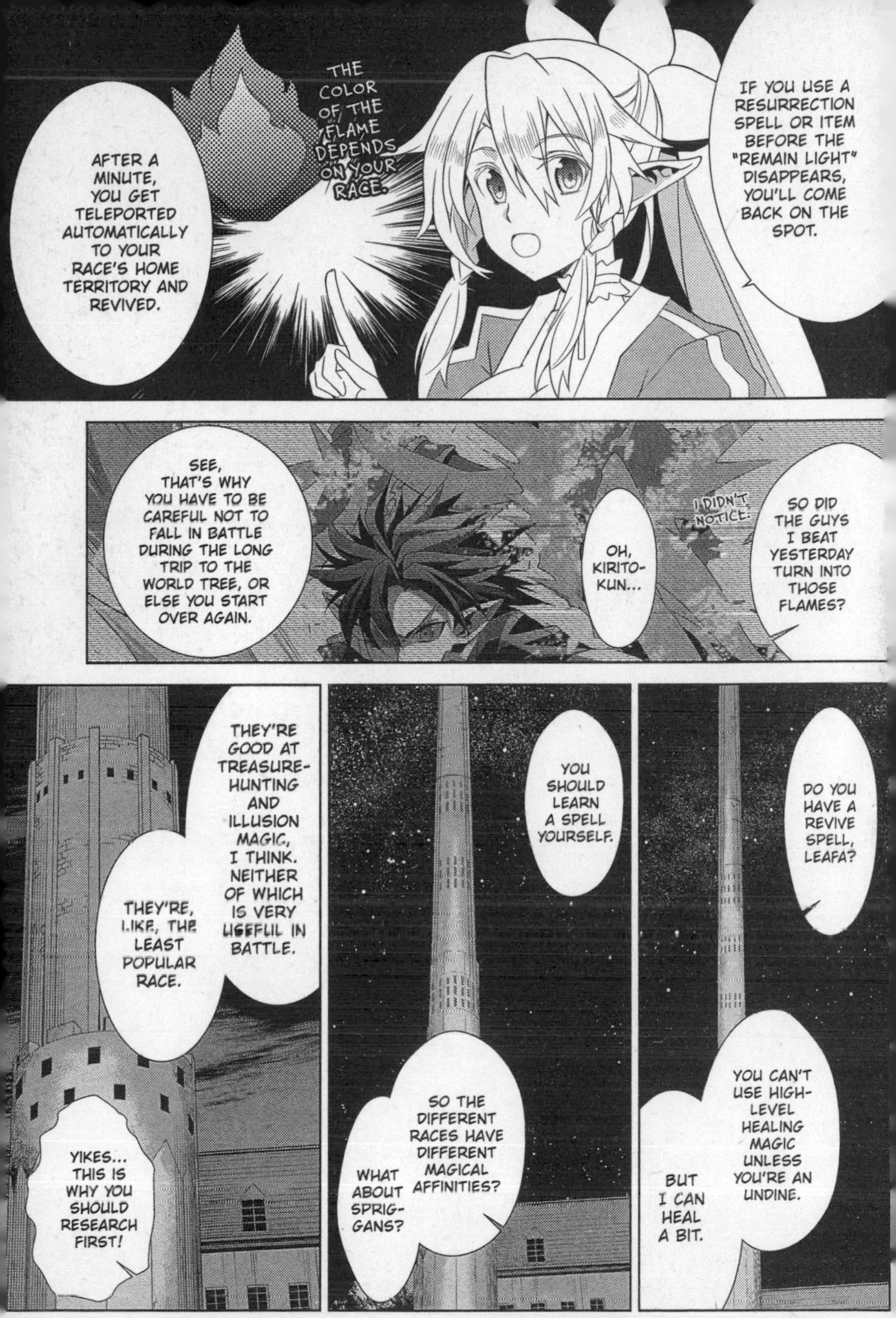
IF YOU USE A RESURRECTION SPELL OR ITEM BEFORE THE "REMAIN LIGHT" DISAPPEARS, YOU'LL COME BACK ON THE SPOT.
THE COLOR OF THE FLAME DEPENDS ON YOUR RACE.
AFTER A MINUTE, YOU GET TELEPORTED AUTOMATICALLY TO YOUR RACE'S HOME TERRITORY AND REVIVED.
SO DID THE GUYS I BEAT YESTERDAY TURN INTO THOSE FLAMES?
I DIDN'T NOTICE.
OH, KIRITO-KUN...
SEE, THAT'S WHY YOU HAVE TO BE CAREFUL NOT TO FALL IN BATTLE DURING THE LONG TRIP TO THE WORLD TREE, OR ELSE YOU START OVER AGAIN.
DO YOU HAVE A REVIVE SPELL, LEAFA?
YOU CAN'T USE HIGH-LEVEL HEALING MAGIC UNLESS YOU'RE AN UNDINE.
BUT I CAN HEAL A BIT.
YOU SHOULD LEARN A SPELL YOURSELF.
SO THE DIFFERENT RACES HAVE DIFFERENT MAGICAL AFFINITIES?
WHAT ABOUT SPRIGGANS?
THEY'RE GOOD AT TREASURE-HUNTING AND ILLUSION MAGIC, I THINK. NEITHER OF WHICH IS VERY USEFUL IN BATTLE.
THEY'RE, LIKE, THE LEAST POPULAR RACE.
YIKES... THIS IS WHY YOU SHOULD RESEARCH FIRST!

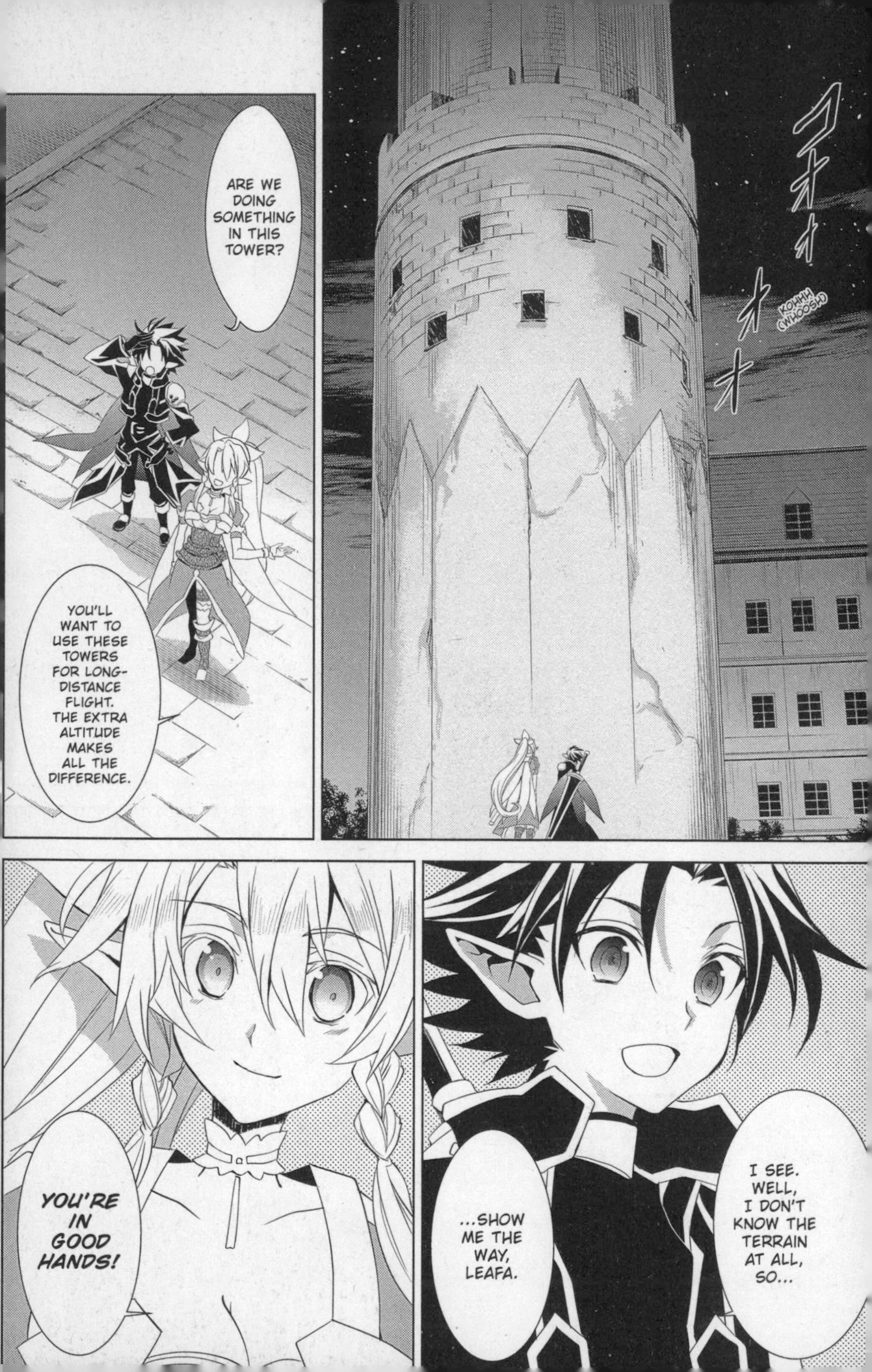
KOHHH (WHOOSH)
ARE WE DOING SOMETHING IN THIS TOWER?
YOU'LL WANT TO USE THESE TOWERS FOR LONG-DISTANCE FLIGHT. THE EXTRA ALTITUDE MAKES ALL THE DIFFERENCE.
I SEE. WELL, I DON'T KNOW THE TERRAIN AT ALL, SO...
...SHOW ME THE WAY, LEAFA.
YOU'RE IN GOOD HANDS!

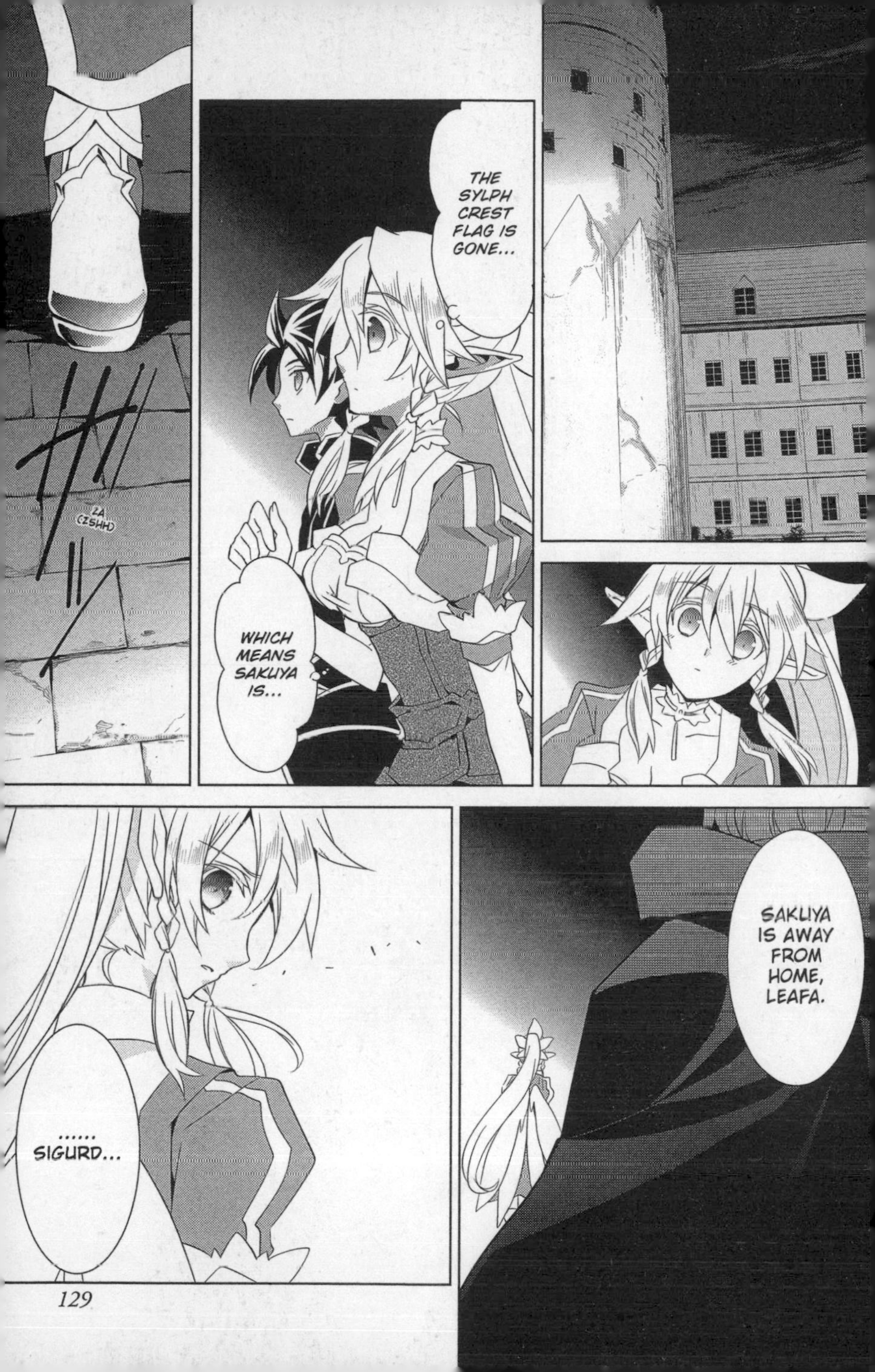
THE SYLPH CREST FLAG IS GONE...
WHICH MEANS SAKUYA IS...
ZA (ZSHH)
SAKUYA IS AWAY FROM HOME, LEAFA.
...... SIGURD...

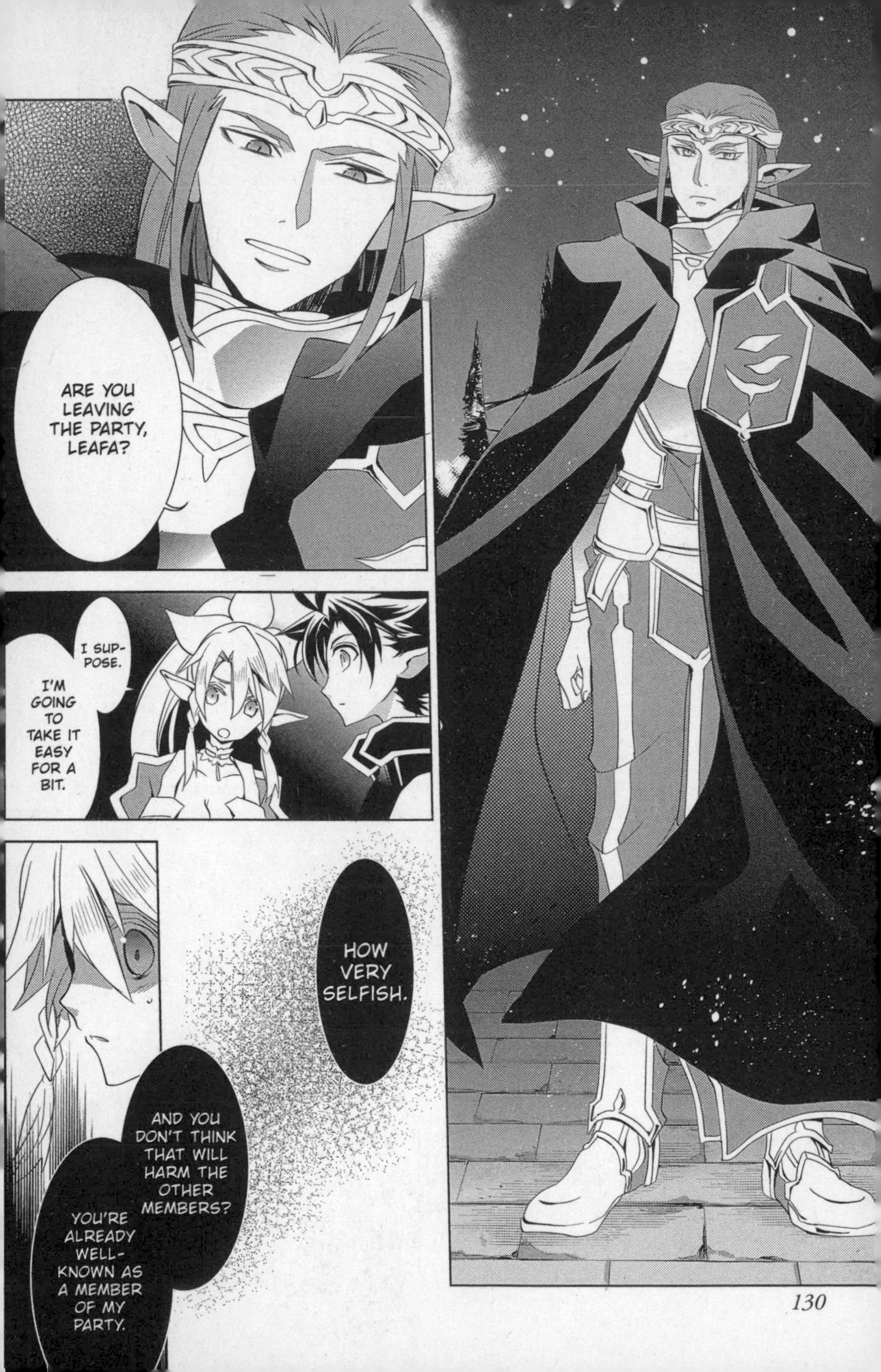
ARE YOU LEAVING THE PARTY, LEAFA?
I SUP-POSE.
I'M GOING TO TAKE IT EASY FOR A BIT.
HOW VERY SELFISH.
AND YOU DON'T THINK THAT WILL HARM THE OTHER MEMBERS?
YOU'RE ALREADY WELL-KNOWN AS A MEMBER OF MY PARTY.

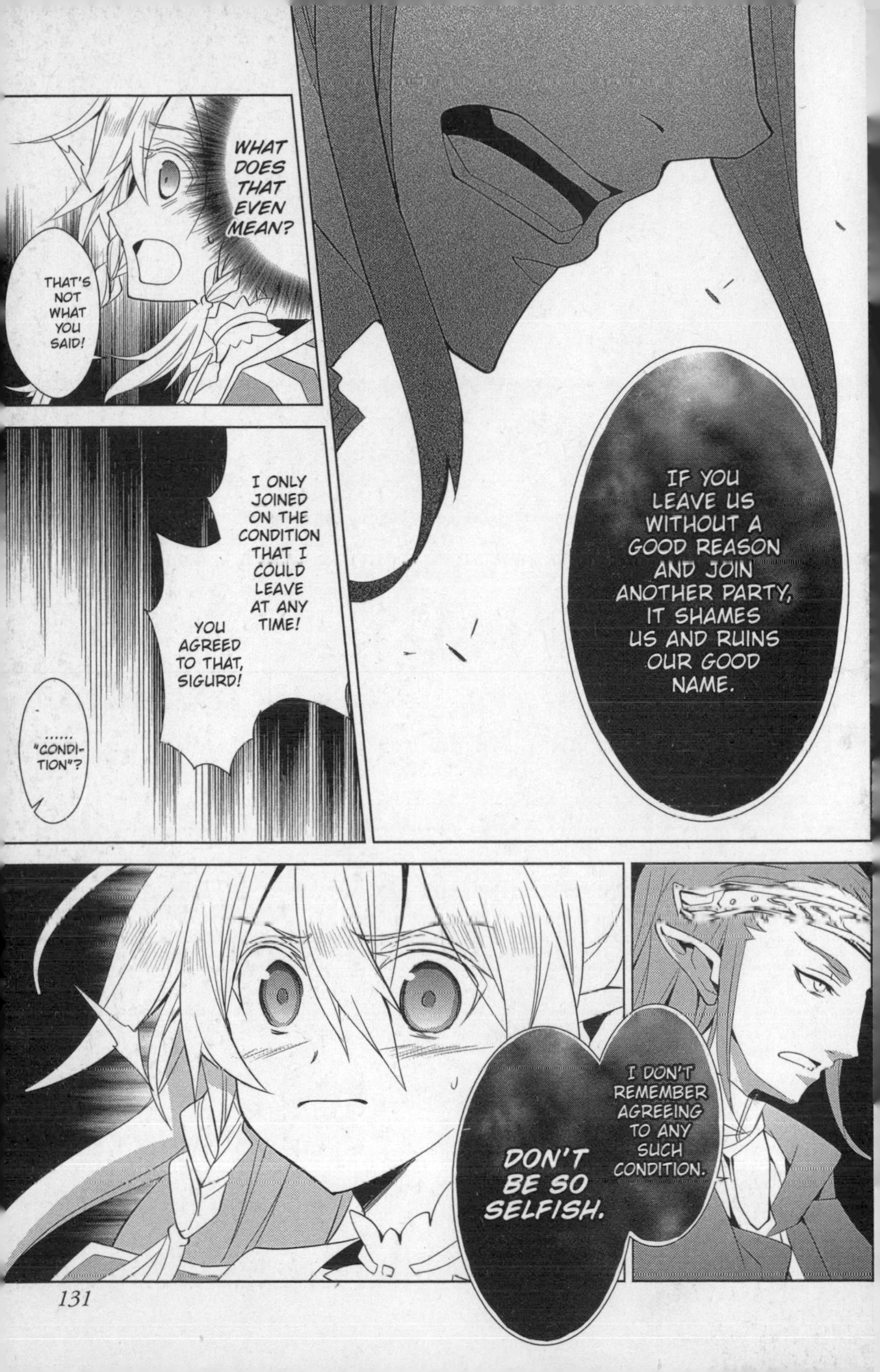
IF YOU LEAVE US WITHOUT A GOOD REASON AND JOIN ANOTHER PARTY, IT SHAMES US AND RUINS OUR GOOD NAME.
WHAT DOES THAT EVEN MEAN?
THAT'S NOT WHAT YOU SAID!
I ONLY JOINED ON THE CONDITION THAT I COULD LEAVE AT ANY TIME!
YOU AGREED TO THAT, SIGURD!
......"CONDITION"?
I DON'T REMEMBER AGREEING TO ANY SUCH CONDITION.
DON'T BE SO SELFISH.

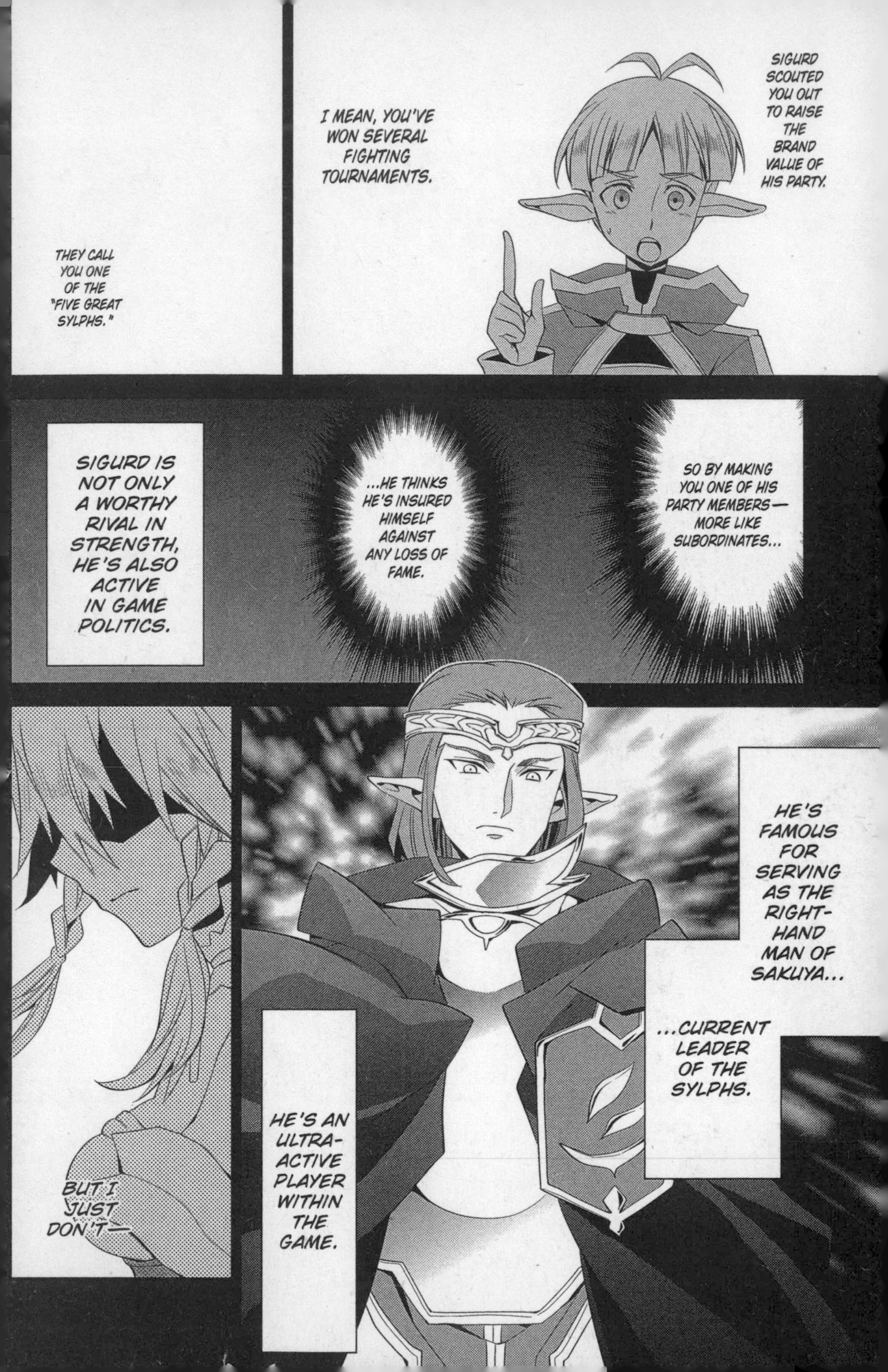
SIGURD SCOUTED YOU OUT TO RAISE THE BRAND VALUE OF HIS PARTY.
I MEAN, YOU'VE WON SEVERAL FIGHTING TOURNAMENTS.
THEY CALL YOU ONE OF THE "FIVE GREAT SYLPHS."
SO BY MAKING YOU ONE OF HIS PARTY MEMBERS—MORE LIKE SUBORDINATES...
...HE THINKS HE'S INSURED HIMSELF AGAINST ANY LOSS OF FAME.
SIGURD IS NOT ONLY A WORTHY RIVAL IN STRENGTH, HE'S ALSO ACTIVE IN GAME POLITICS.
HE'S FAMOUS FOR SERVING AS THE RIGHT-HAND MAN OF SAKUYA...
...CURRENT LEADER OF THE SYLPHS.
HE'S AN ULTRA-ACTIVE PLAYER WITHIN THE GAME.
BUT I JUST DON'T—

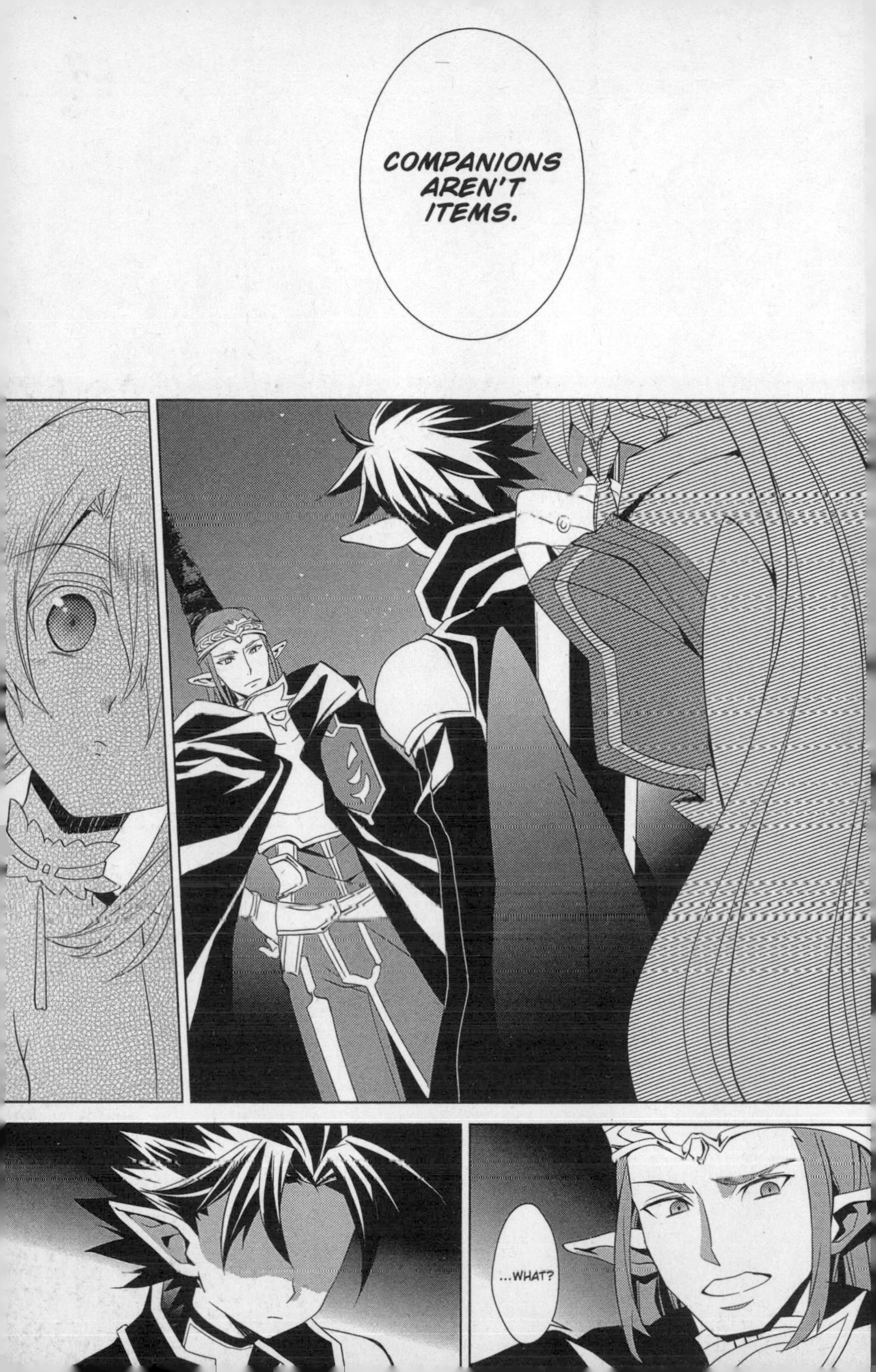
COMPANIONS AREN'T ITEMS.
...WHAT?

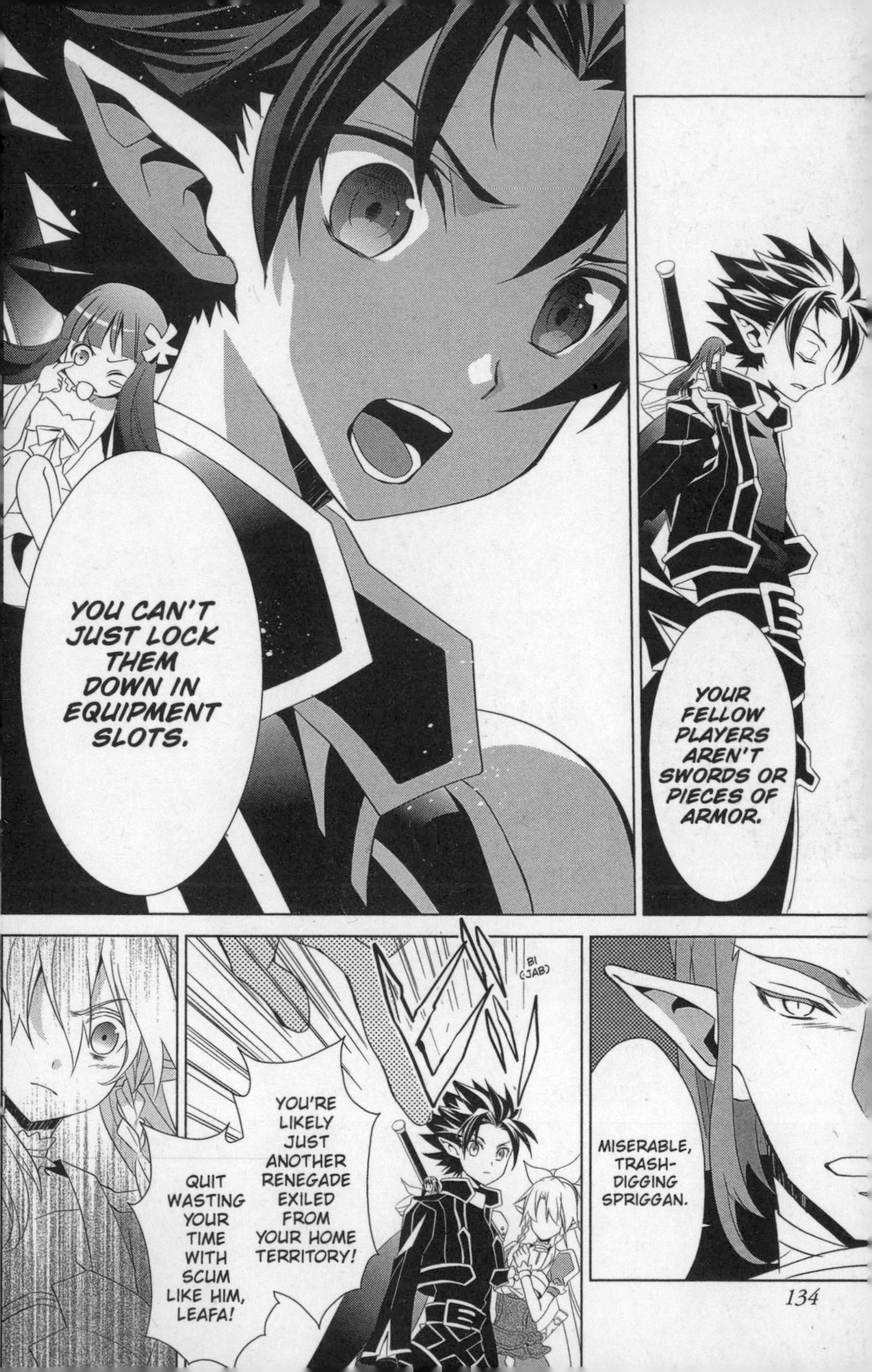
YOUR FELLOW PLAYERS AREN'T SWORDS OR PIECES OF ARMOR.
YOU CAN'T JUST LOCK THEM DOWN IN EQUIPMENT SLOTS.
MISERABLE, TRASH-DIGGING SPRIGGAN.
BI (JAB)
YOU'RE LIKELY JUST ANOTHER RENEGADE EXILED FROM YOUR HOME TERRITORY!
QUIT WASTING YOUR TIME WITH SCUM LIKE HIM, LEAFA!

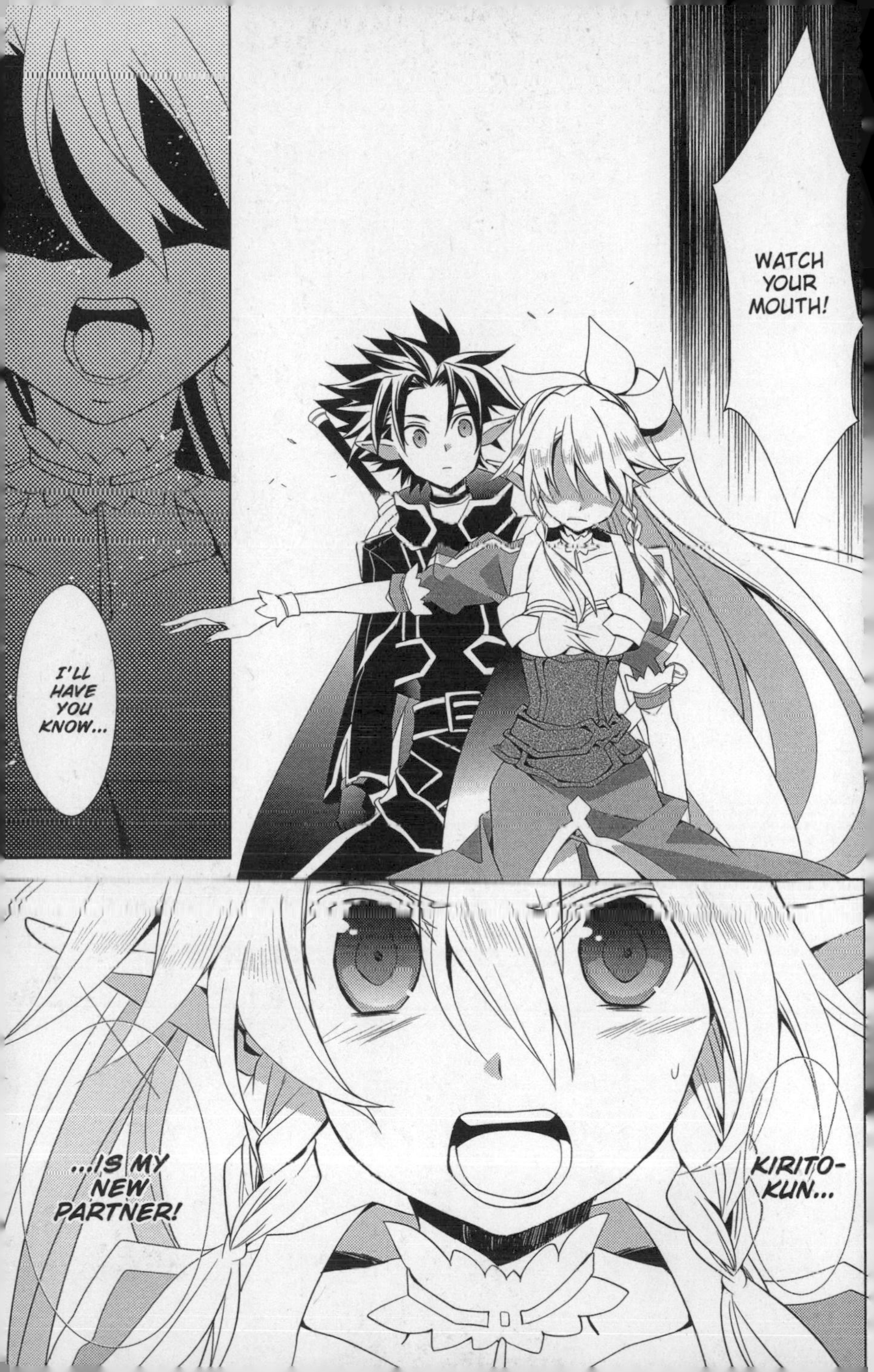
WATCH YOUR MOUTH!
I'LL HAVE YOU KNOW...
KIRITO-KUN...
...IS MY NEW PARTNER!

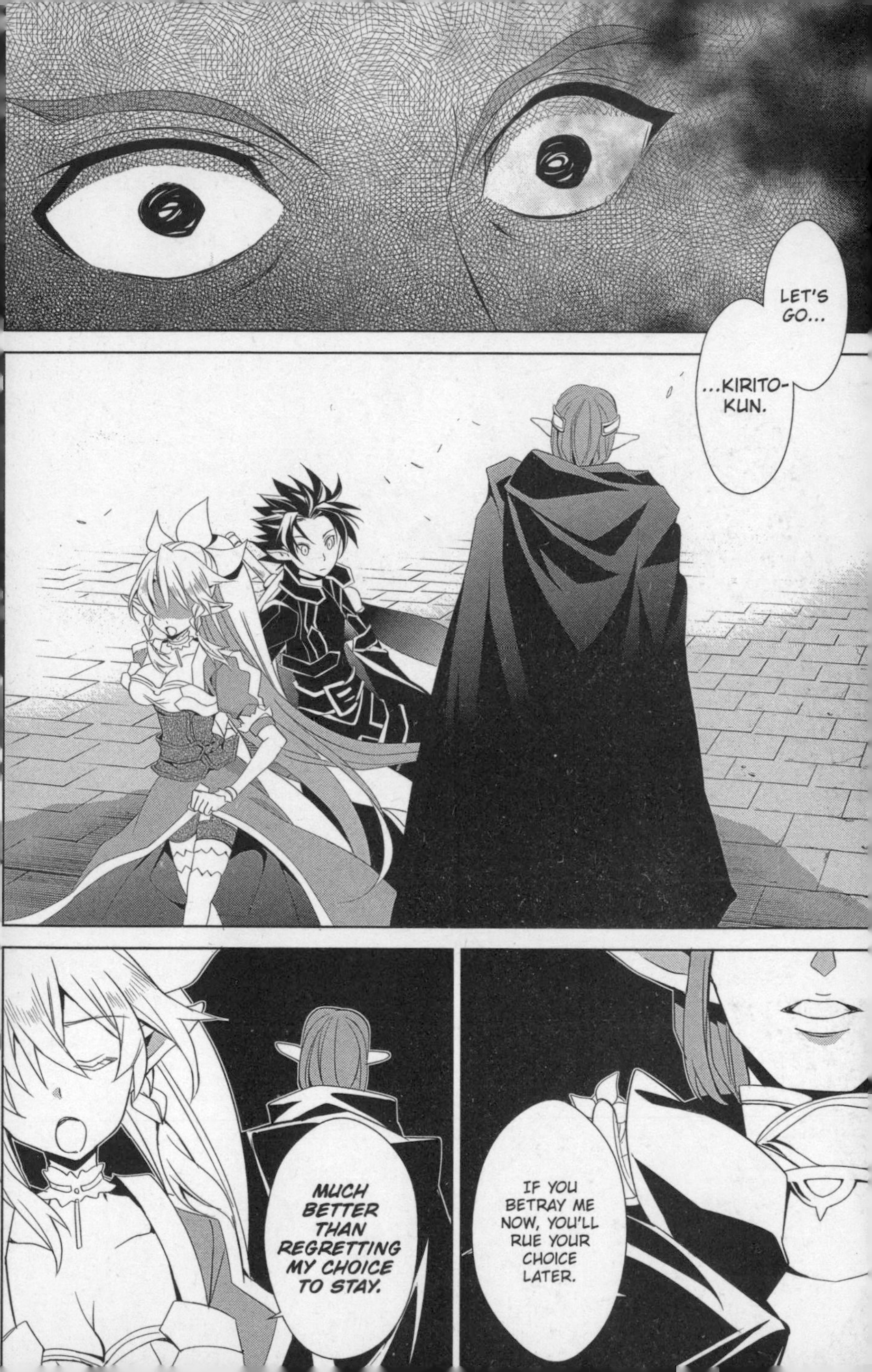
LET'S GO...
...KIRITO-KUN.
IF YOU BETRAY ME NOW, YOU'LL RUE YOUR CHOICE LATER.
MUCH BETTER THAN REGRETTING MY CHOICE TO STAY.

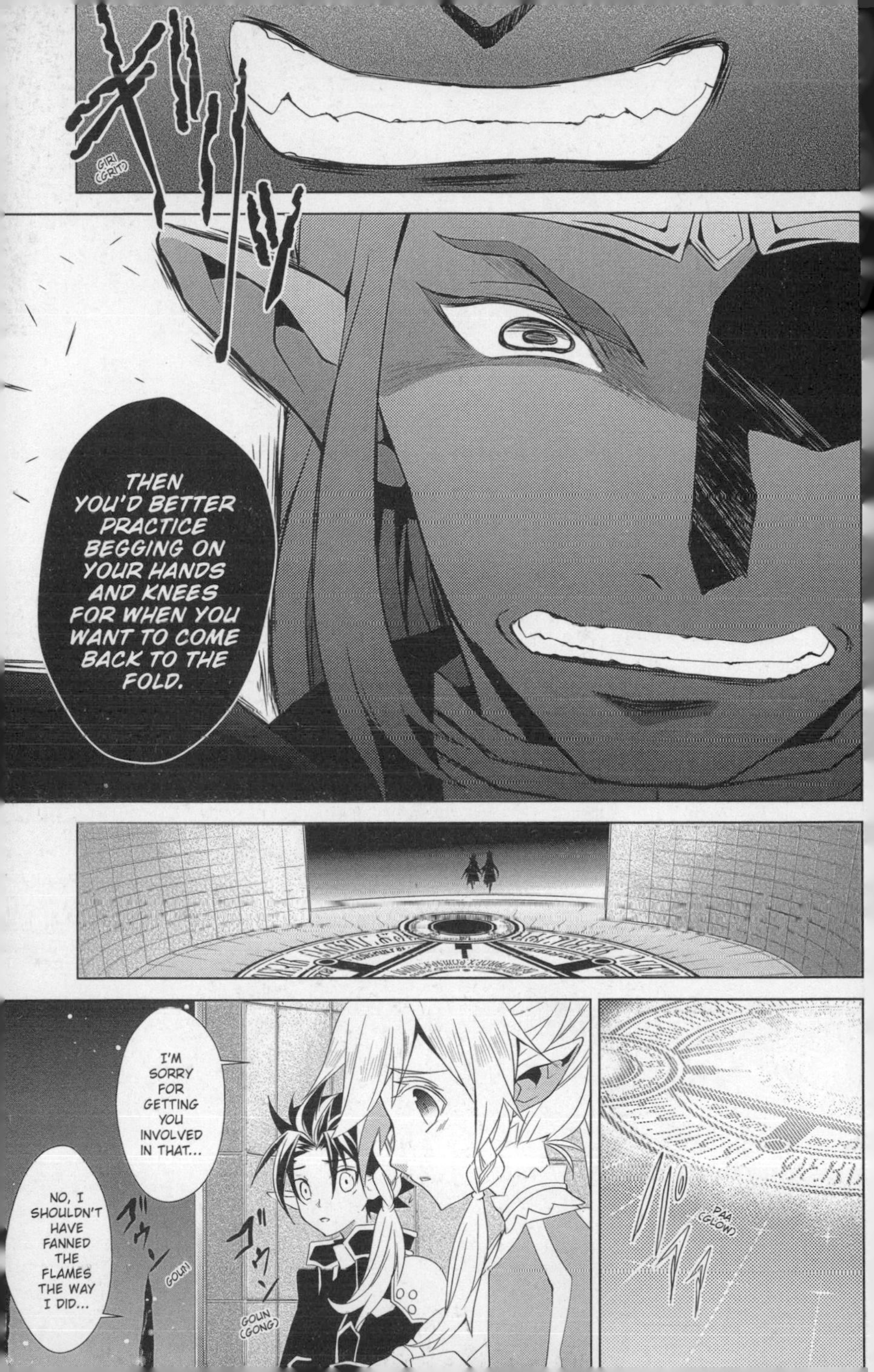
GIRI (GRIT)
THEN YOU'D BETTER PRACTICE BEGGING ON YOUR HANDS AND KNEES FOR WHEN YOU WANT TO COME BACK TO THE FOLD.
PAA (GLOW)
I'M SORRY FOR GETTING YOU INVOLVED IN THAT...
NO, I SHOULDN'T HAVE FANNED THE FLAMES THE WAY I DID...
GOUN (GONG)
GOUN

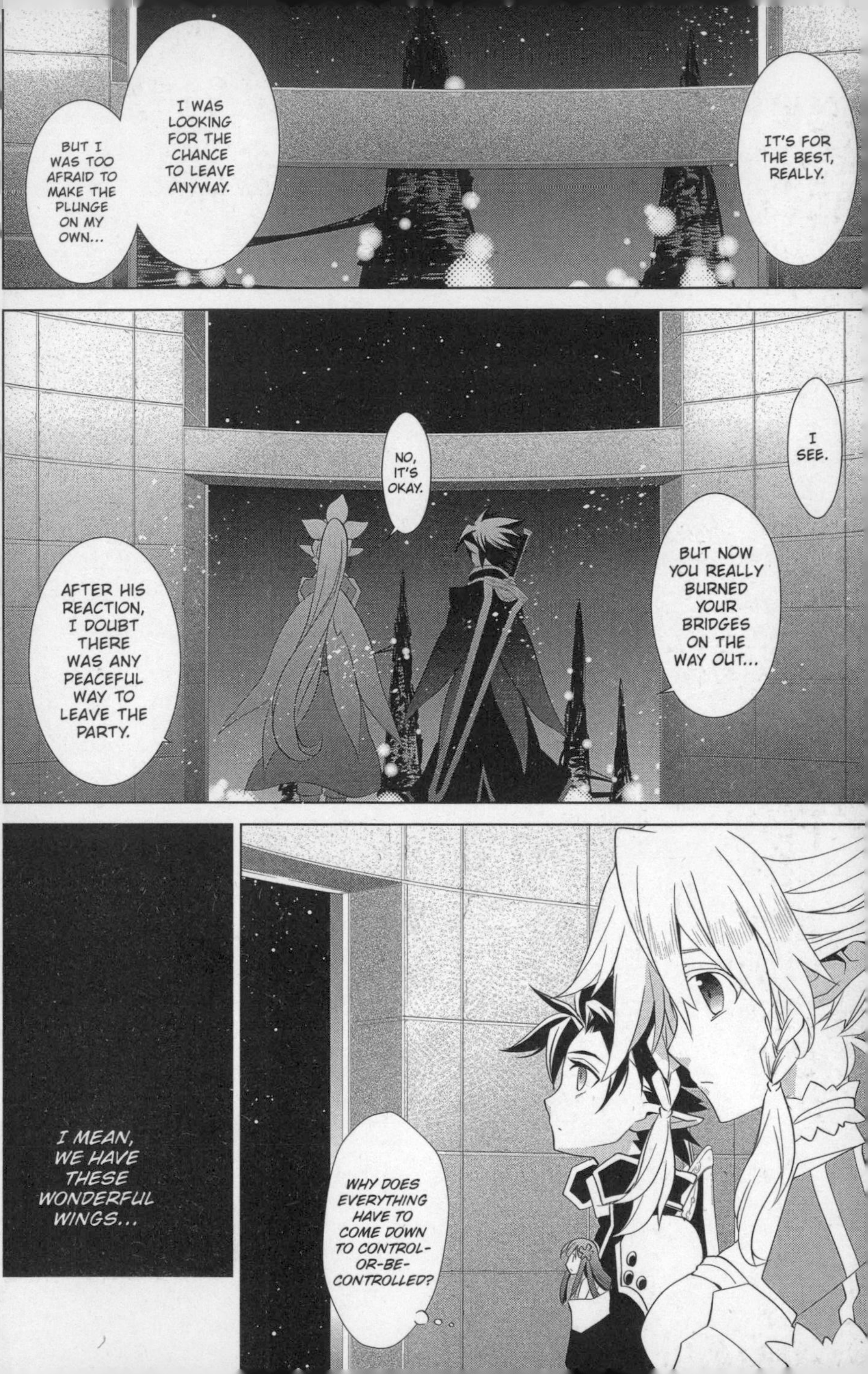
IT'S FOR THE BEST, REALLY.
I WAS LOOKING FOR THE CHANCE TO LEAVE ANYWAY.
BUT I WAS TOO AFRAID TO MAKE THE PLUNGE ON MY OWN...
I SEE.
BUT NOW YOU REALLY BURNED YOUR BRIDGES ON THE WAY OUT...
NO, IT'S OKAY.
AFTER HIS REACTION, I DOUBT THERE WAS ANY PEACEFUL WAY TO LEAVE THE PARTY.
WHY DOES EVERYTHING HAVE TO COME DOWN TO CONTROL-OR-BE-CONTROLLED?
I MEAN, WE HAVE THESE WONDERFUL WINGS...

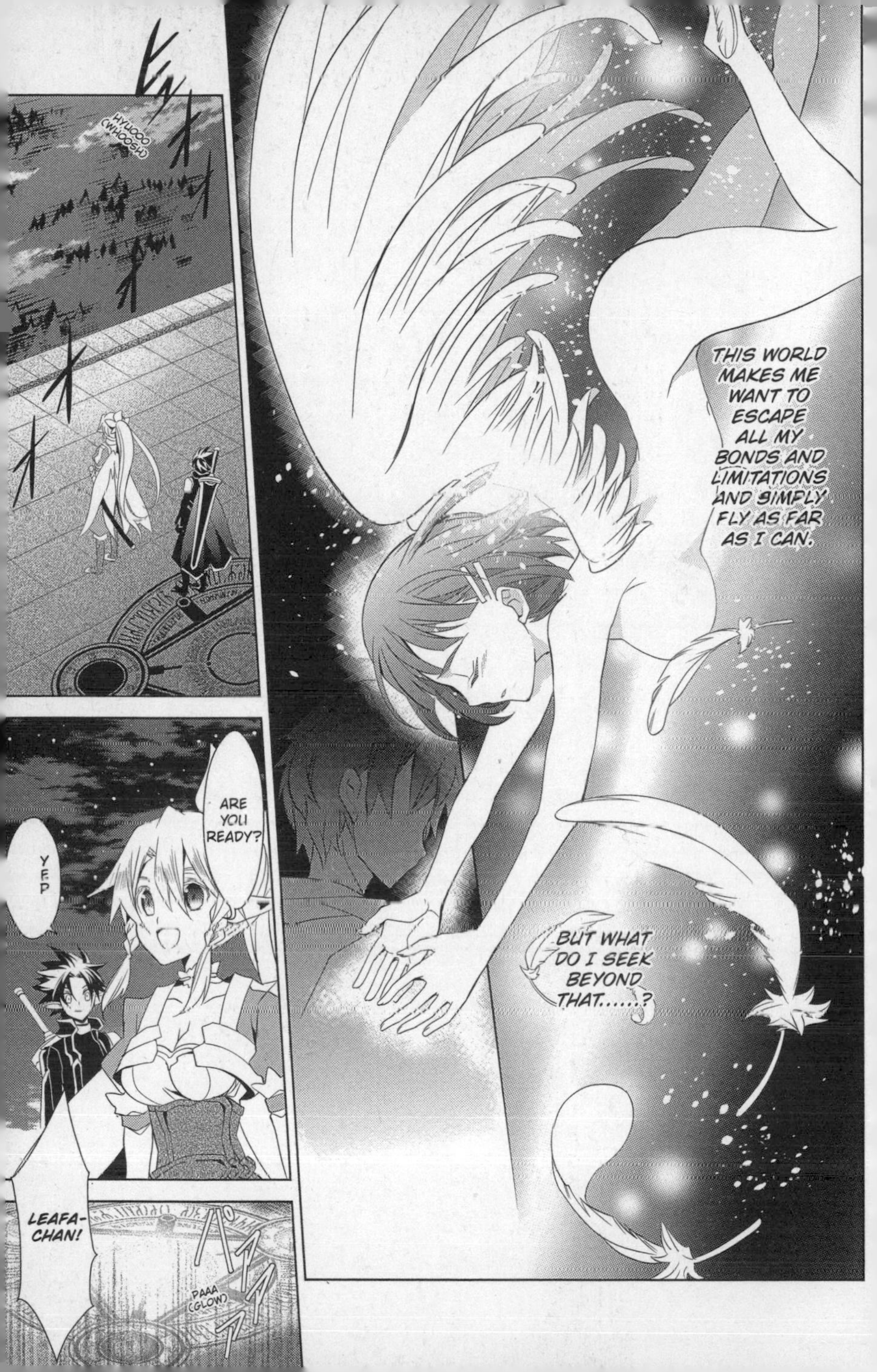
THIS WORLD MAKES ME WANT TO ESCAPE ALL MY BONDS AND LIMITATIONS AND SIMPLY FLY AS FAR AS I CAN.
BUT WHAT DO I SEEK BEYOND THAT......?
HYUOOO (WHOOSH)
ARE YOU READY?
YEP
LEAFA-CHAN!
PAAA (GLOW)

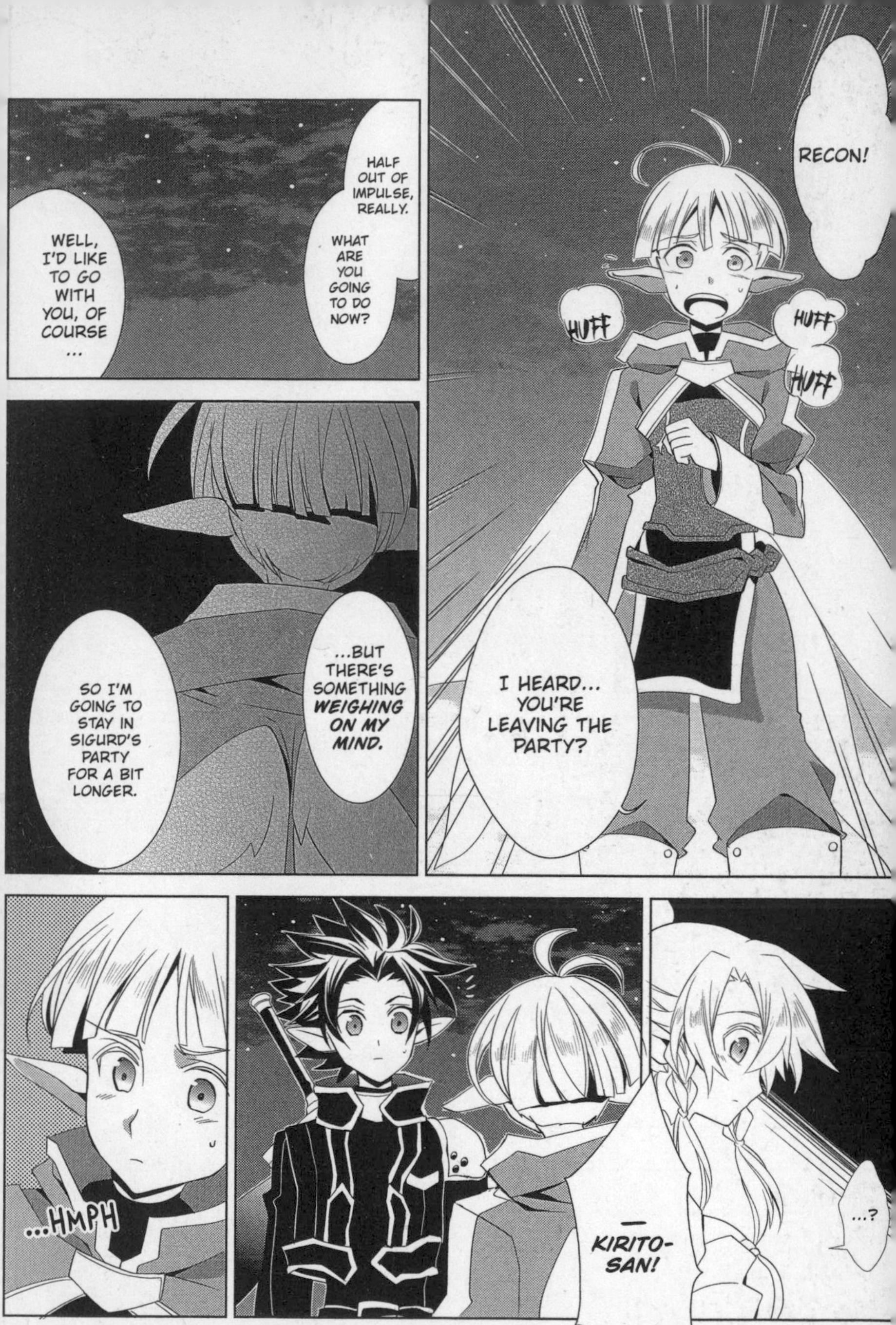
RECON!
HUFF
HUFF
HUFF
I HEARD... YOU'RE LEAVING THE PARTY?
HALF OUT OF IMPULSE, REALLY.
WHAT ARE YOU GOING TO DO NOW?
WELL, I'D LIKE TO GO WITH YOU, OF COURSE ...
...BUT THERE'S SOMETHING *WEIGHING ON MY MIND.*
SO I'M GOING TO STAY IN SIGURD'S PARTY FOR A BIT LONGER.
...?
—KIRITO-SAN!
...HMPH

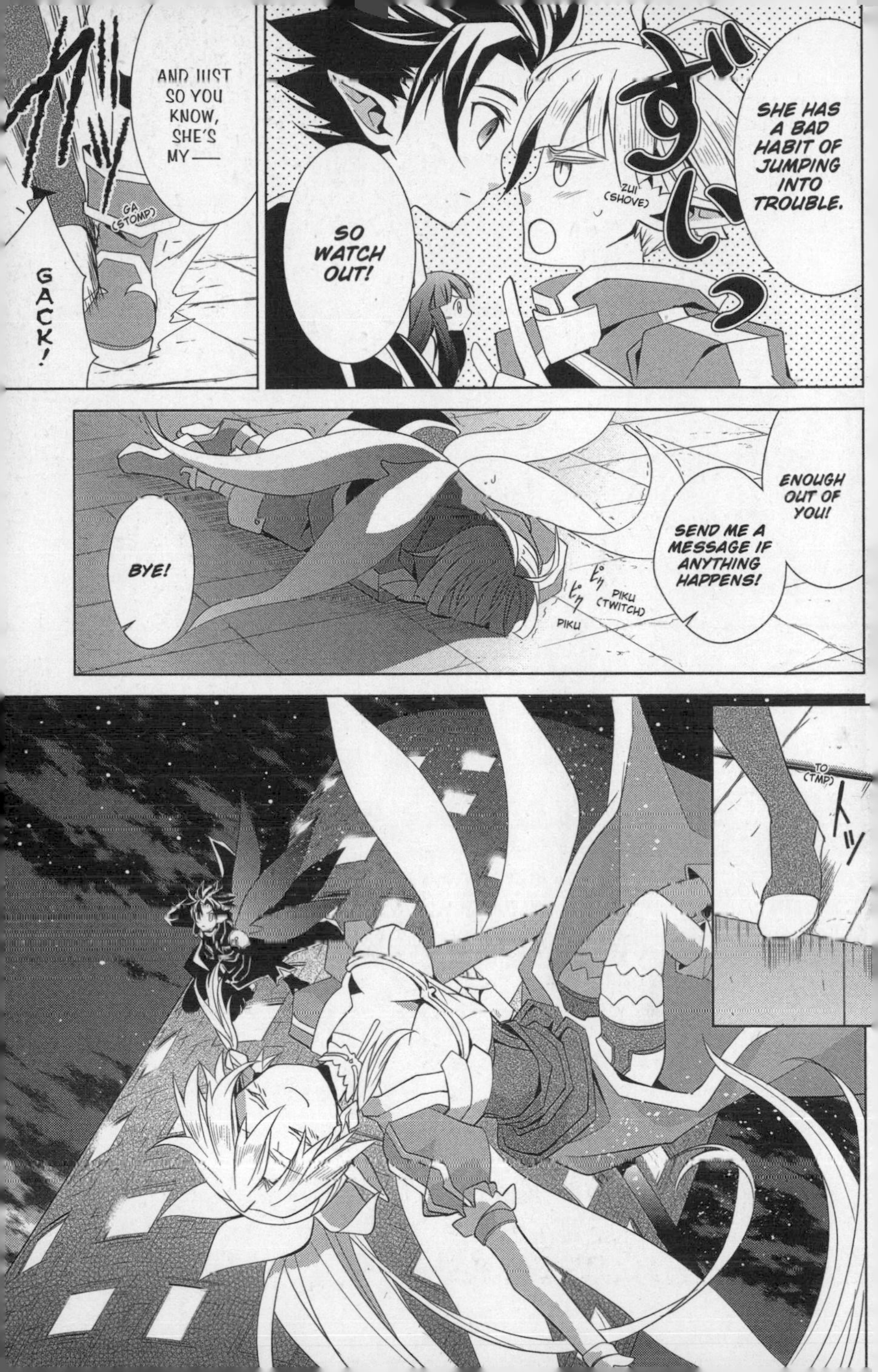
SHE HAS A BAD HABIT OF JUMPING INTO TROUBLE.
ZUI (SHOVE)
SO WATCH OUT!
AND JUST SO YOU KNOW, SHE'S MY——
GA (STOMP)
GACK!
ENOUGH OUT OF YOU!
SEND ME A MESSAGE IF ANYTHING HAPPENS!
PIKU (TWITCH)
PIKU
BYE!
TO (TMP)

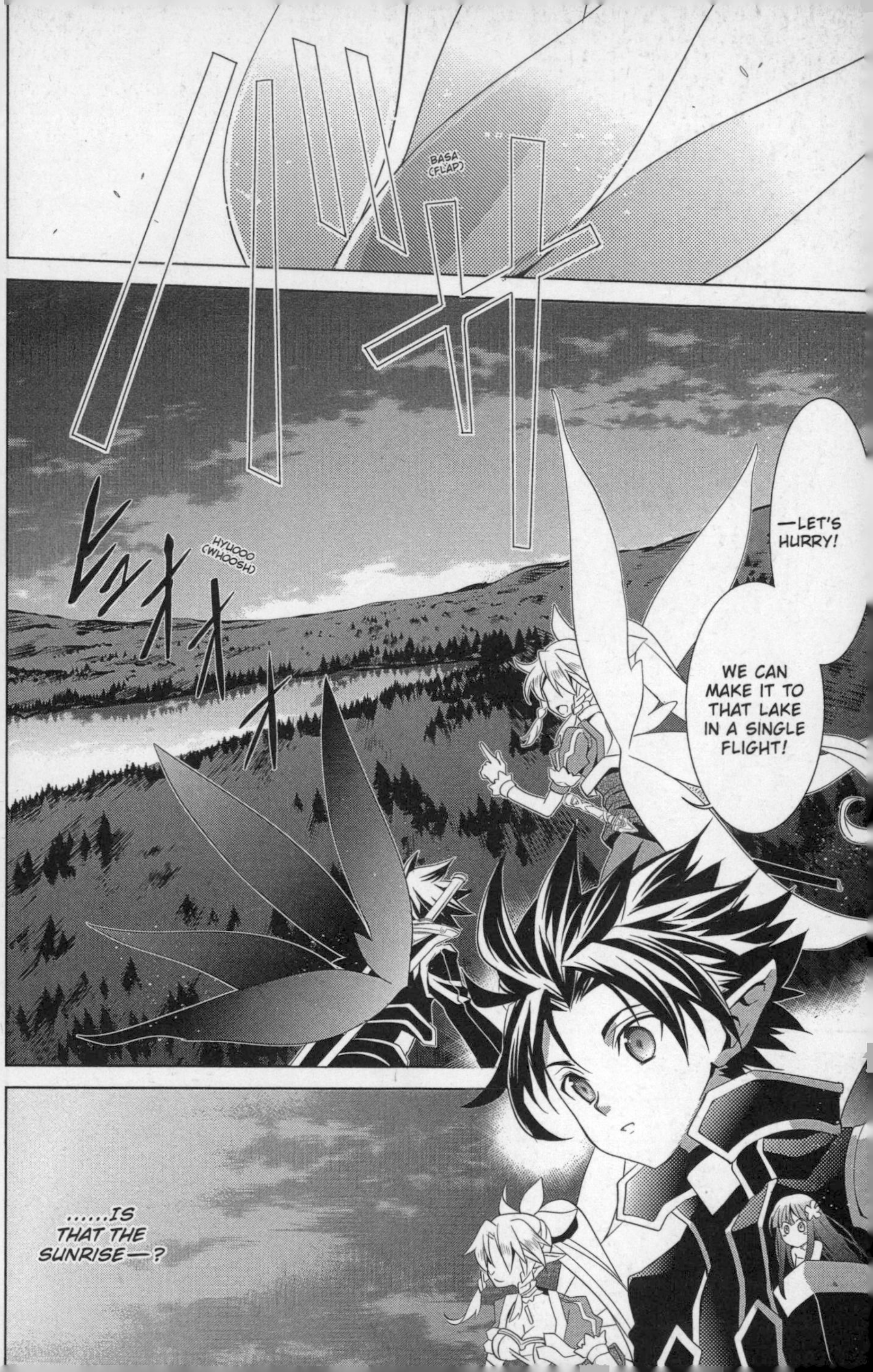
BASA (FLAP)
—LET'S HURRY!
WE CAN MAKE IT TO THAT LAKE IN A SINGLE FLIGHT!
HYUOOO (WHOOSH)
......IS THAT THE SUNRISE—?

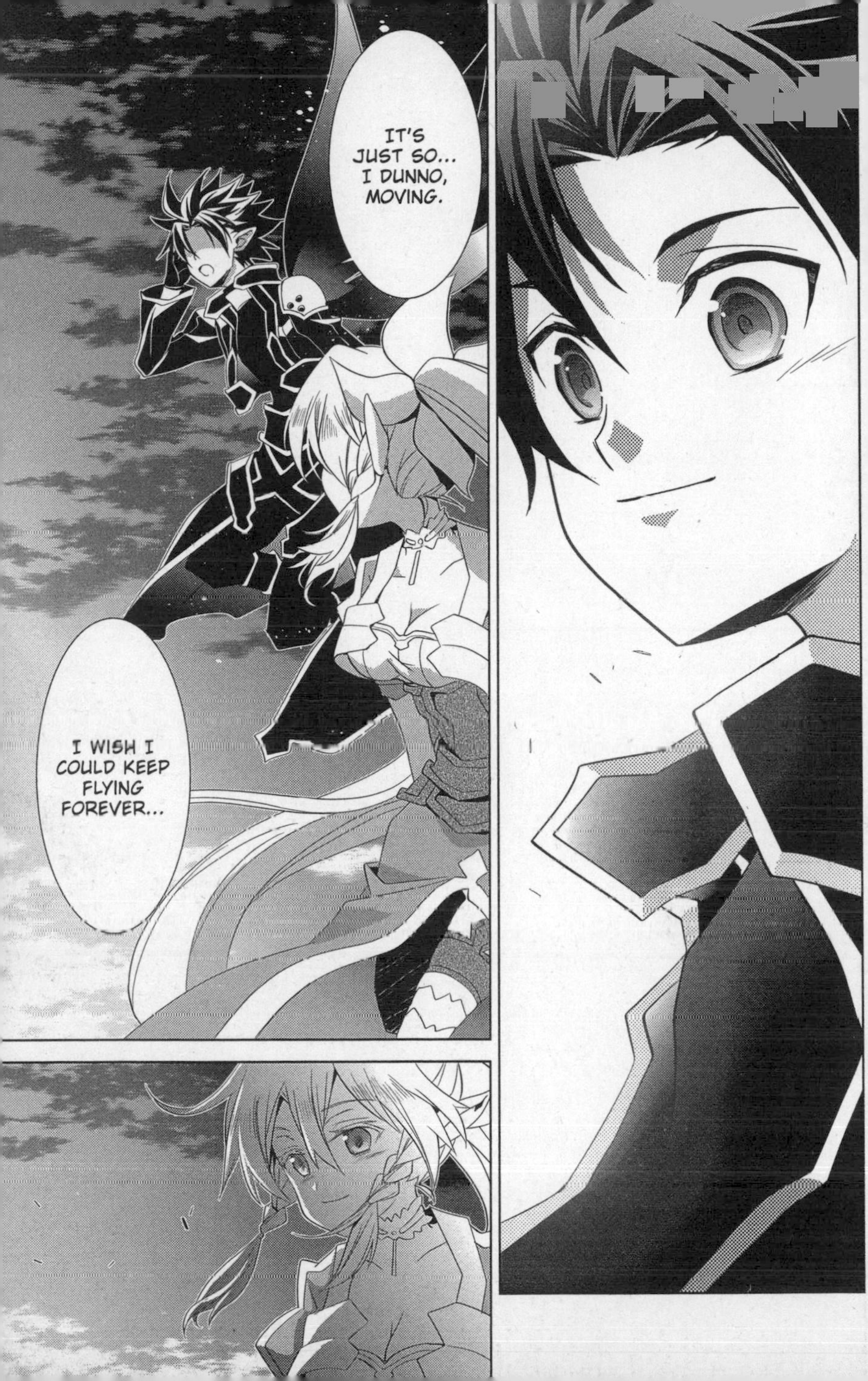
IT'S JUST SO... I DUNNO, MOVING.
I WISH I COULD KEEP FLYING FOREVER...

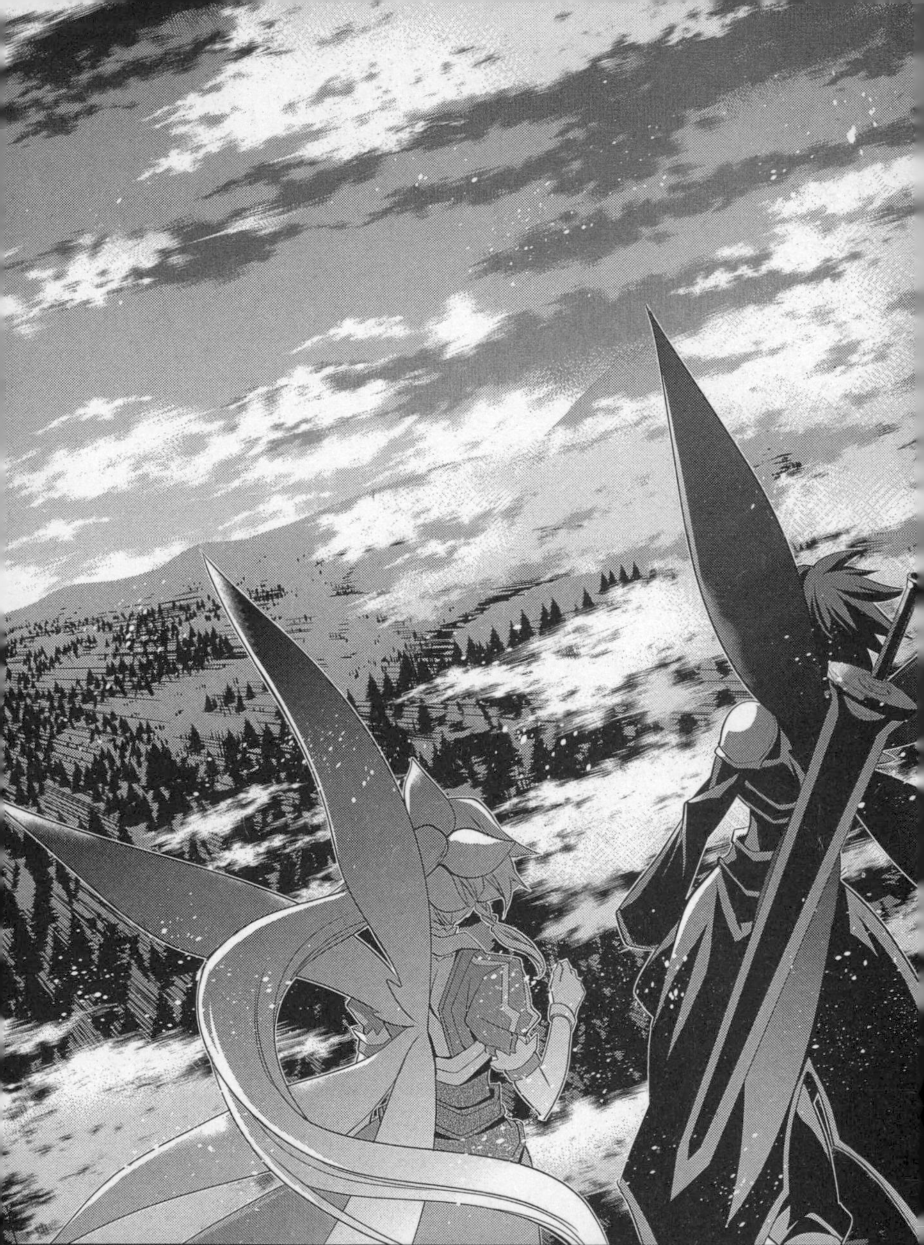

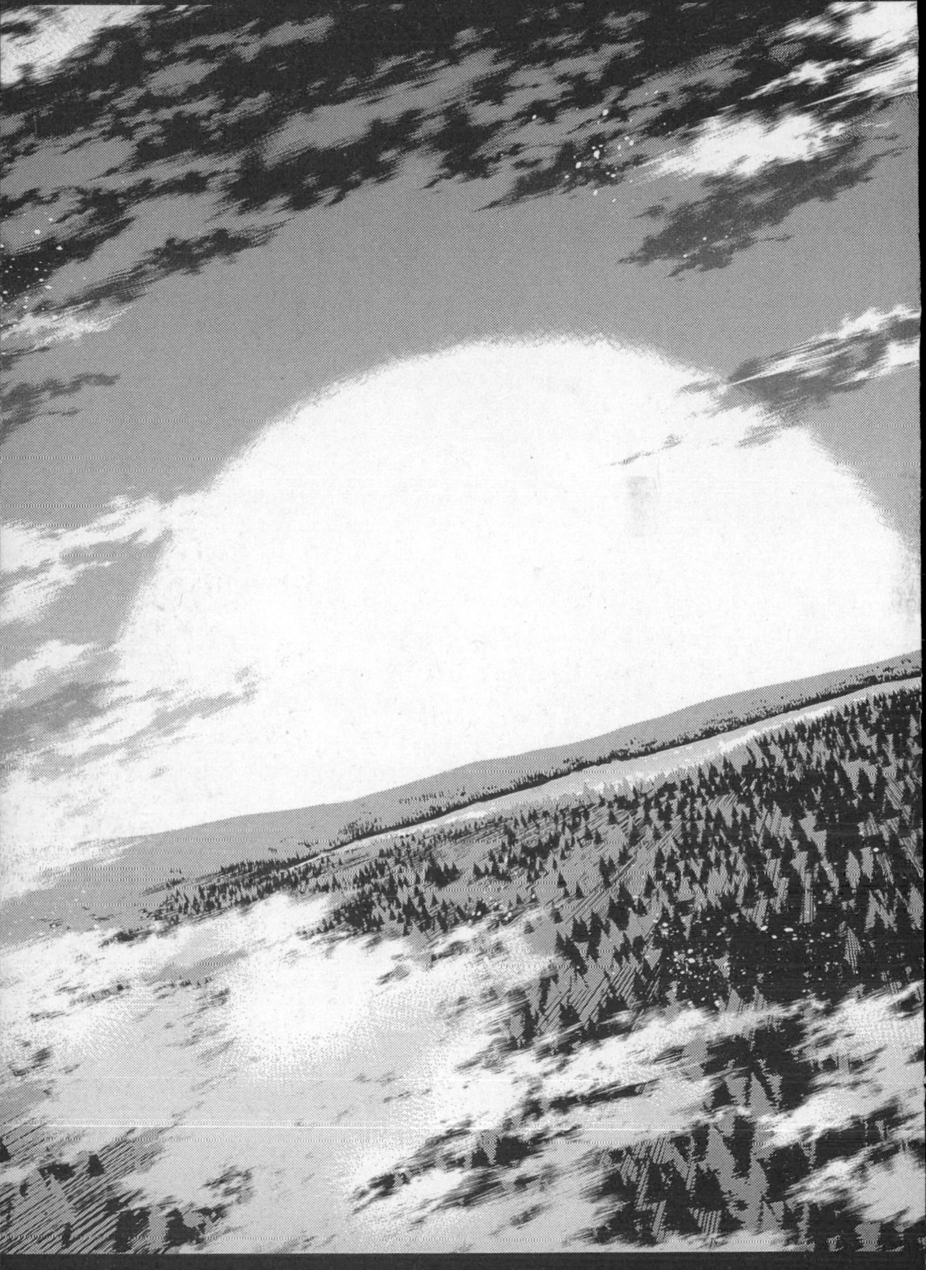

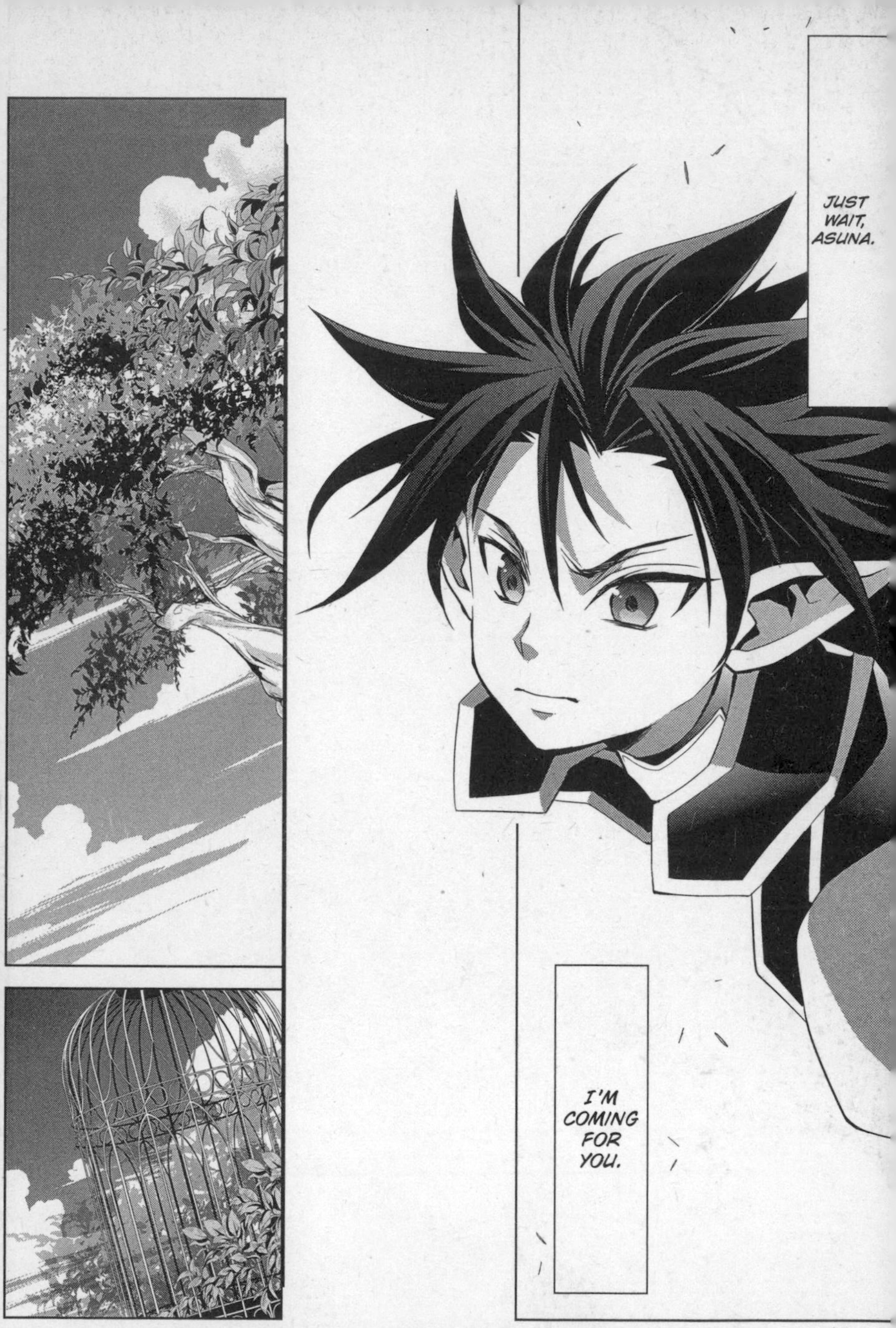
JUST WAIT, ASUNA.
I'M COMING FOR YOU.

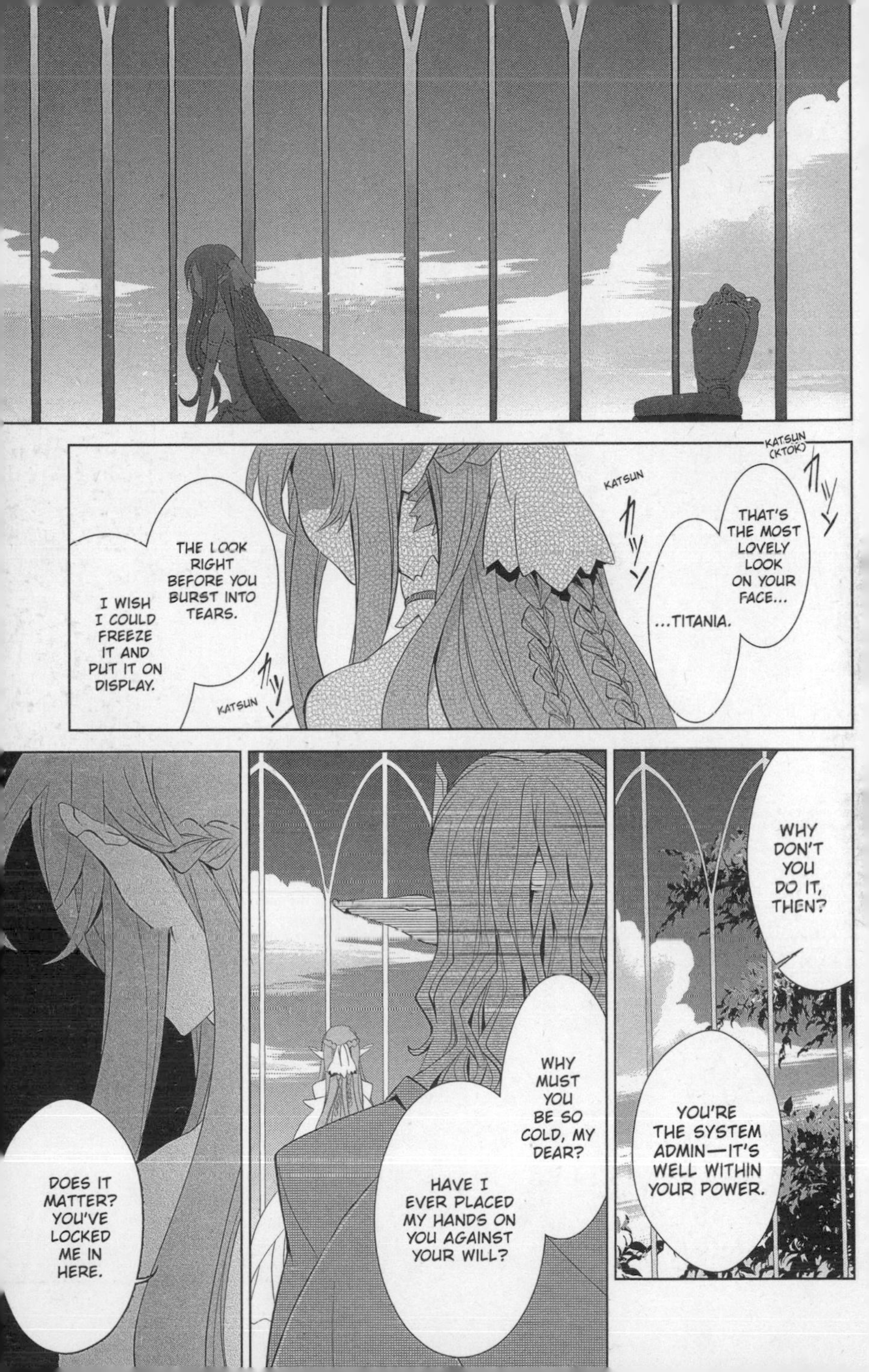
KATSUN (KTOK)
THAT'S THE MOST LOVELY LOOK ON YOUR FACE...
...TITANIA.
KATSUN
THE LOOK RIGHT BEFORE YOU BURST INTO TEARS.
I WISH I COULD FREEZE IT AND PUT IT ON DISPLAY.
KATSUN
WHY DON'T YOU DO IT, THEN?
YOU'RE THE SYSTEM ADMIN—IT'S WELL WITHIN YOUR POWER.
WHY MUST YOU BE SO COLD, MY DEAR?
HAVE I EVER PLACED MY HANDS ON YOU AGAINST YOUR WILL?
DOES IT MATTER? YOU'VE LOCKED ME IN HERE.

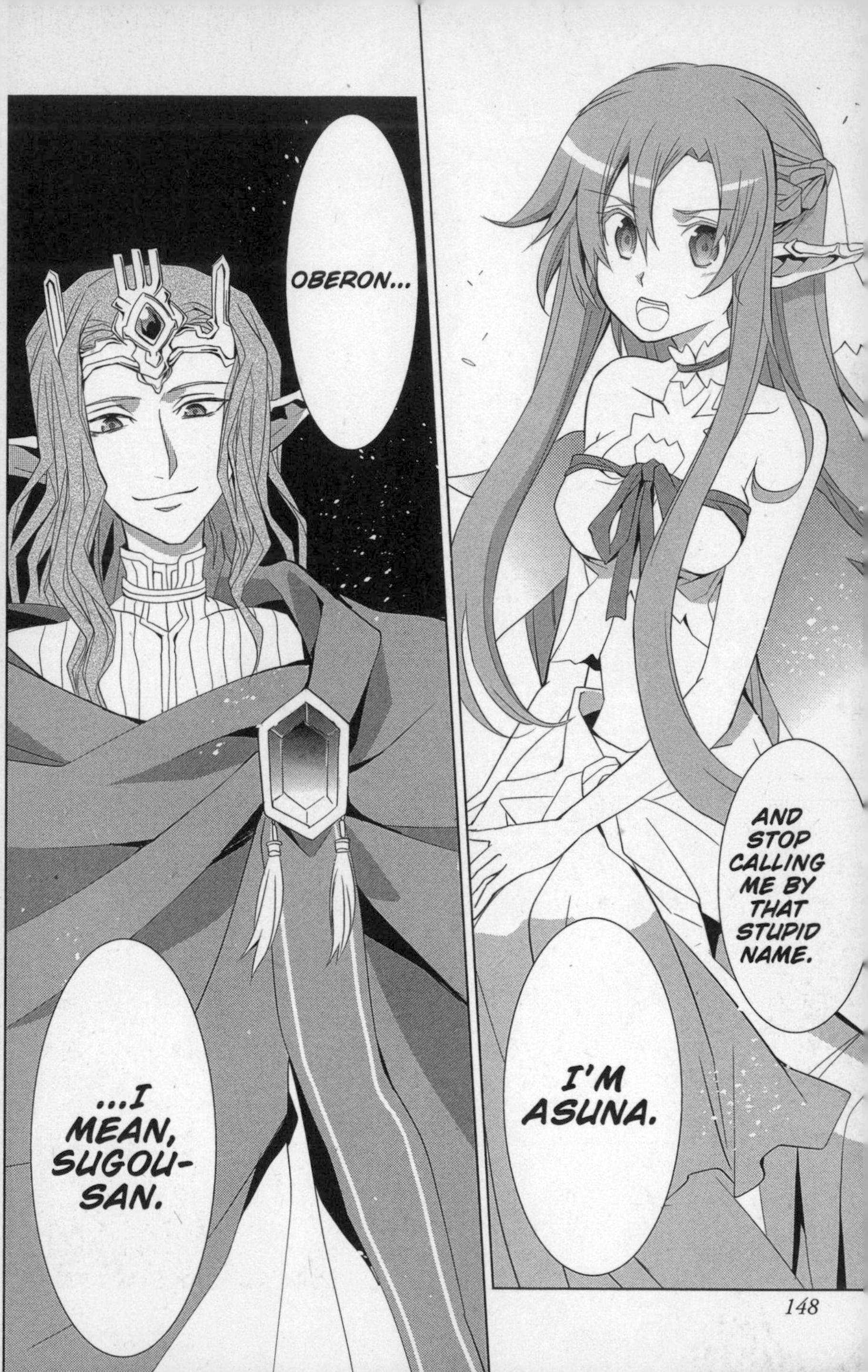
OBERON...
...I MEAN, SUGOU-SAN.
AND STOP CALLING ME BY THAT STUPID NAME.
I'M ASUNA.

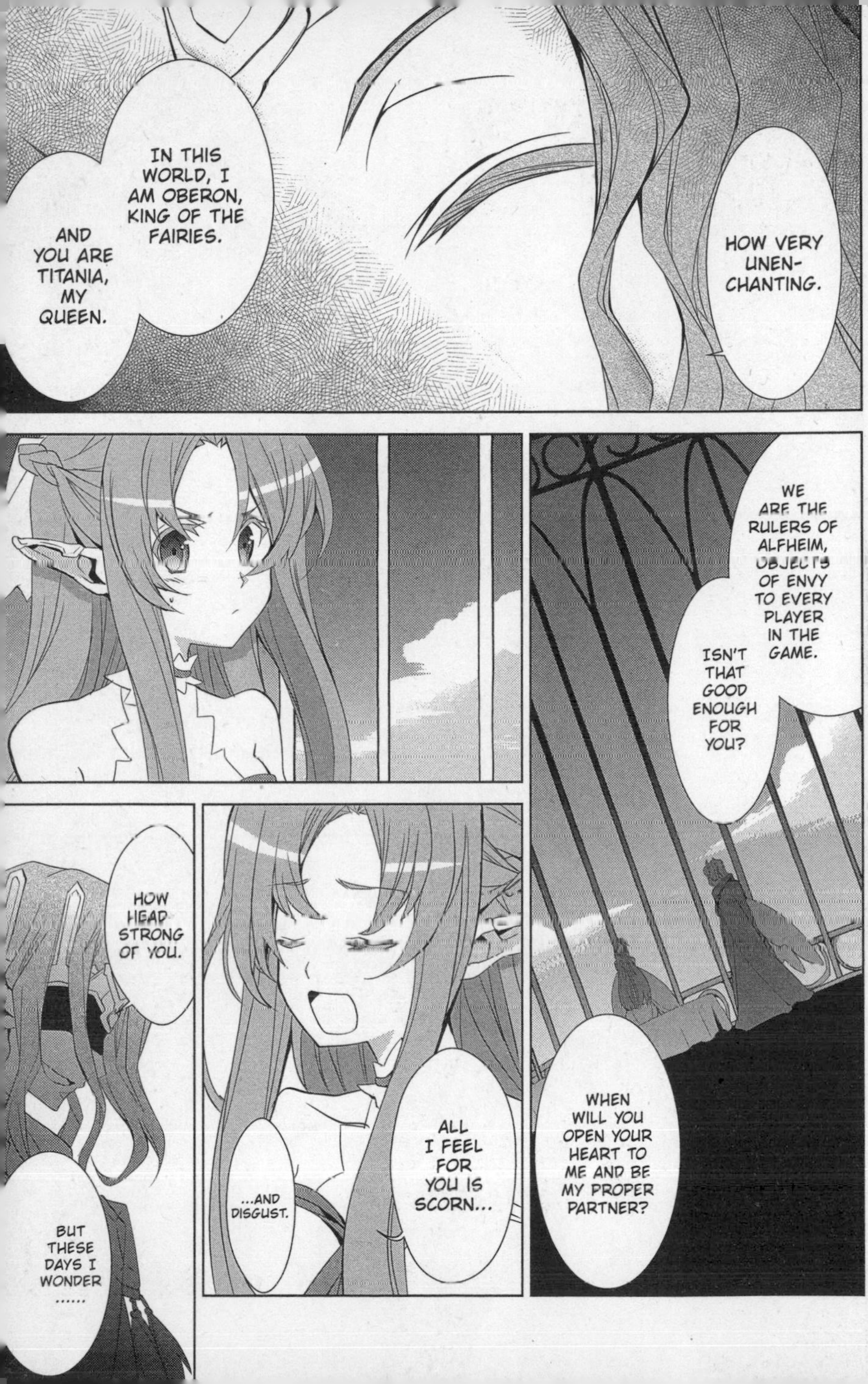
HOW VERY UNEN-CHANTING.
IN THIS WORLD, I AM OBERON, KING OF THE FAIRIES.
AND YOU ARE TITANIA, MY QUEEN.
WE ARE THE RULERS OF ALFHEIM, OBJECTS OF ENVY TO EVERY PLAYER IN THE GAME.
ISN'T THAT GOOD ENOUGH FOR YOU?
WHEN WILL YOU OPEN YOUR HEART TO ME AND BE MY PROPER PARTNER?
ALL I FEEL FOR YOU IS SCORN...
...AND DISGUST.
HOW HEAD-STRONG OF YOU.
BUT THESE DAYS I WONDER ......

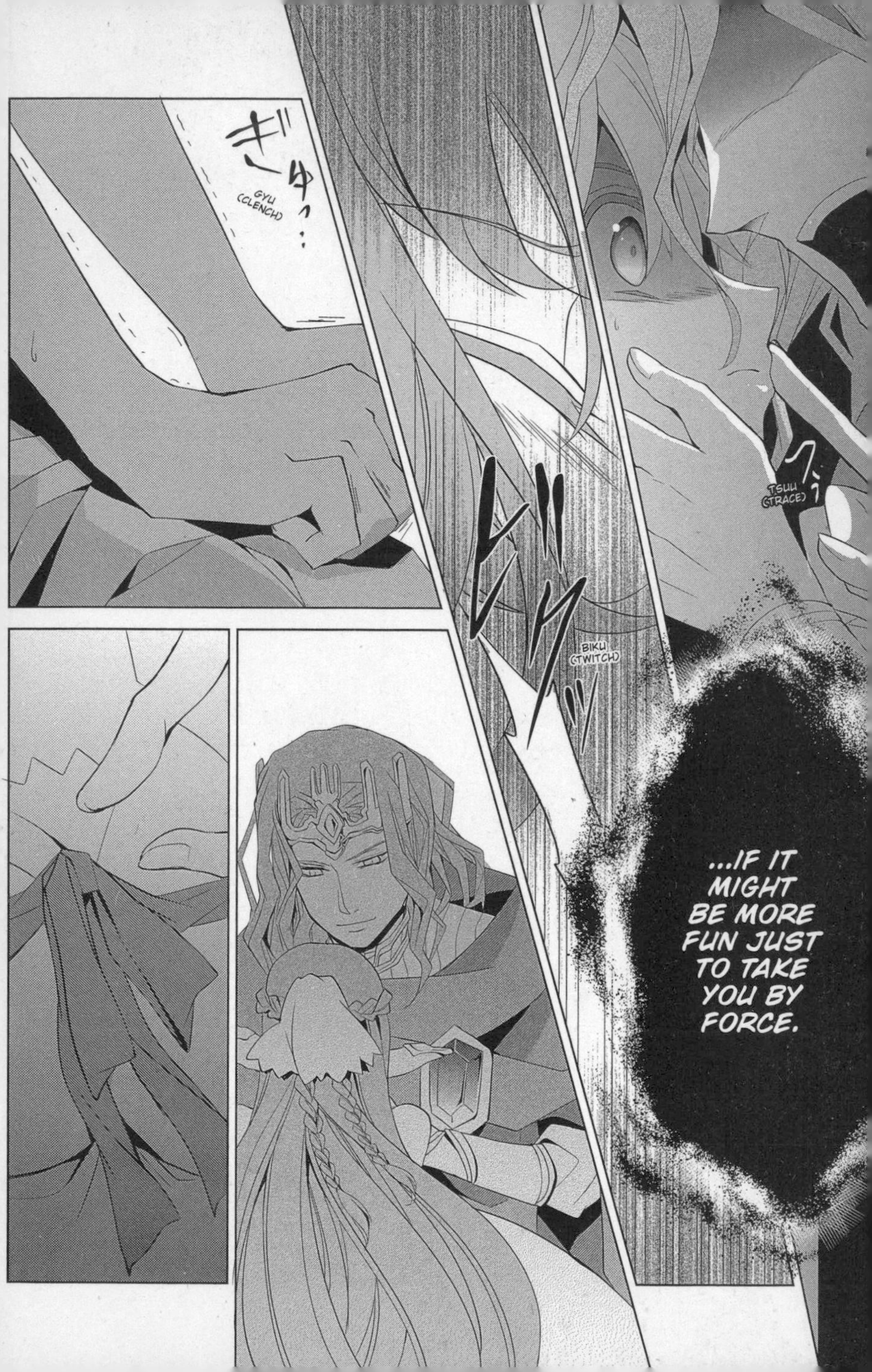
TSUU (TRACE)
...IF IT MIGHT BE MORE FUN JUST TO TAKE YOU BY FORCE.
ビクッ
BIKU (TWITCH)
ぎゅっ
GYU (CLENCH)

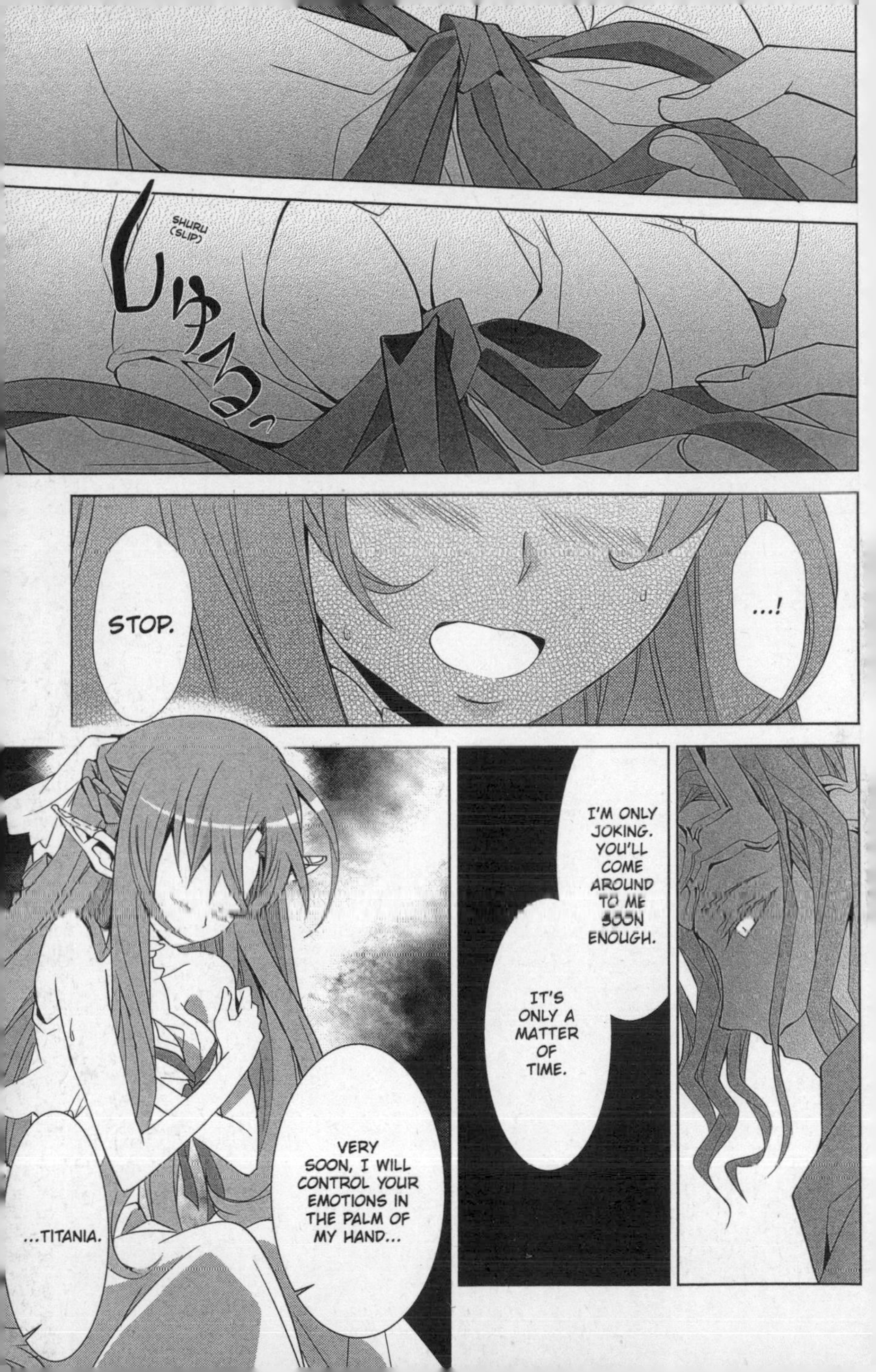
SHURU (SLIP)
...!
STOP.
I'M ONLY JOKING. YOU'LL COME AROUND TO ME SOON ENOUGH.
IT'S ONLY A MATTER OF TIME.
VERY SOON, I WILL CONTROL YOUR EMOTIONS IN THE PALM OF MY HAND...
...TITANIA.

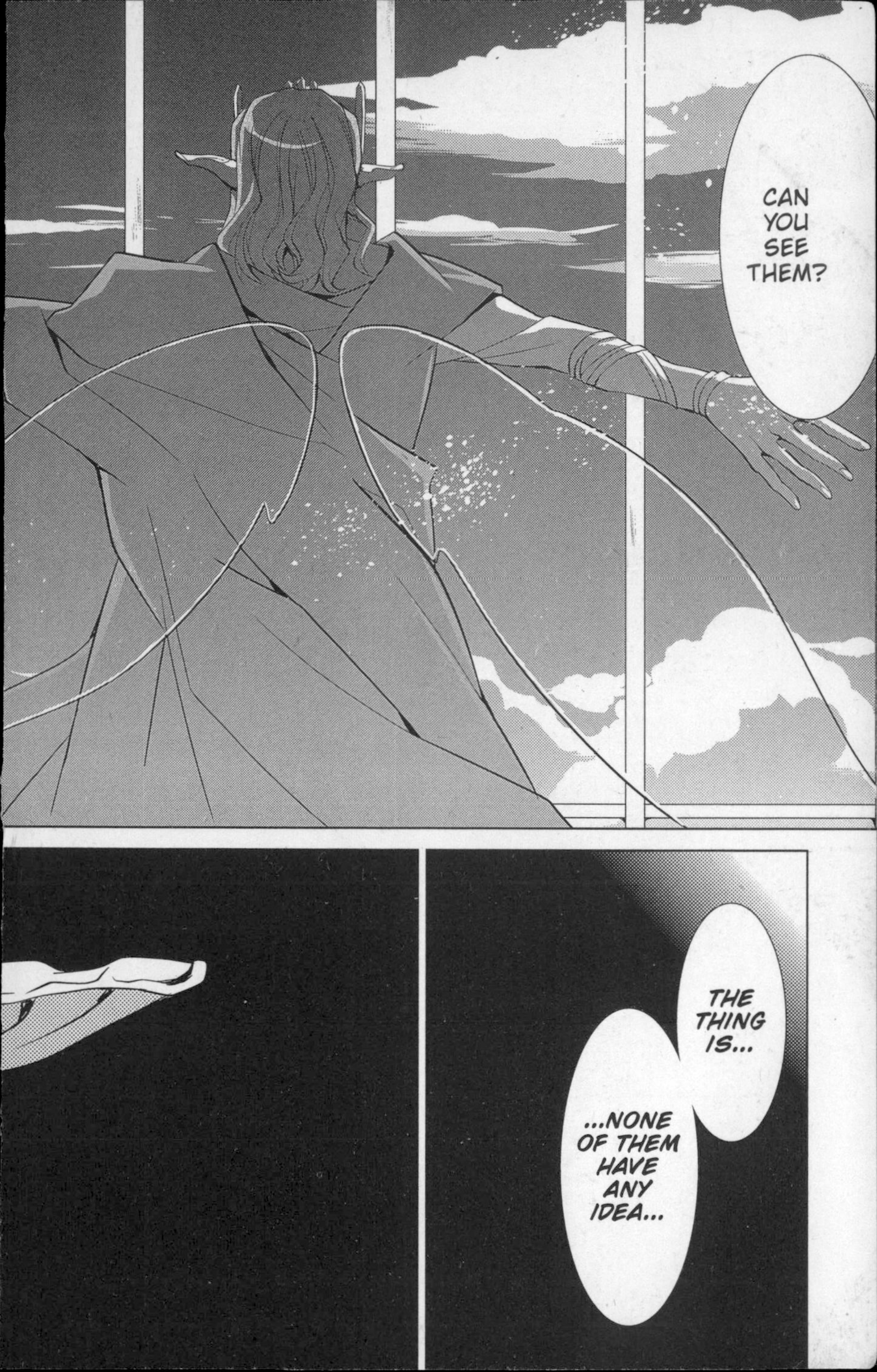
CAN YOU SEE THEM?
THE THING IS...
...NONE OF THEM HAVE ANY IDEA...

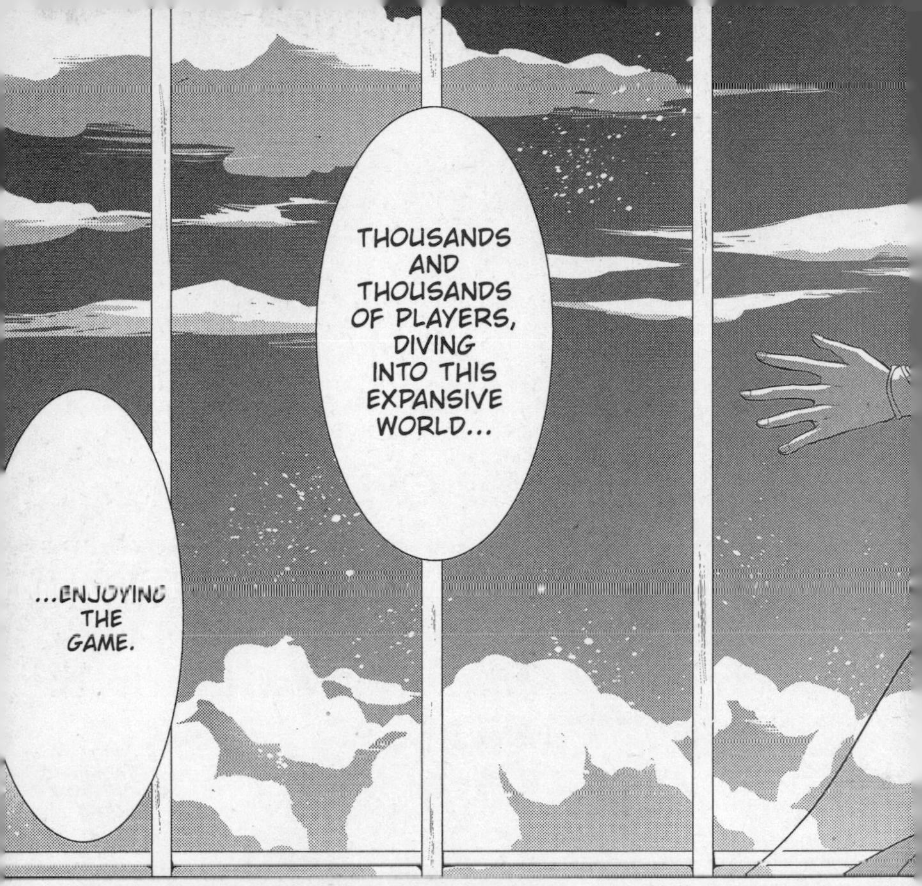
THOUSANDS AND THOUSANDS OF PLAYERS, DIVING INTO THIS EXPANSIVE WORLD...
...ENJOYING THE GAME.

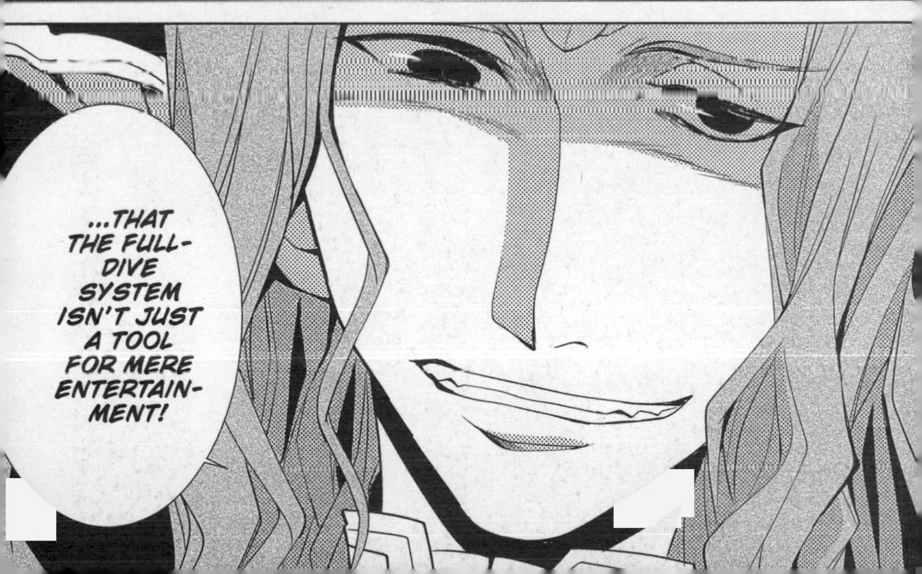
...THAT THE FULL-DIVE SYSTEM ISN'T JUST A TOOL FOR MERE ENTERTAIN-MENT!

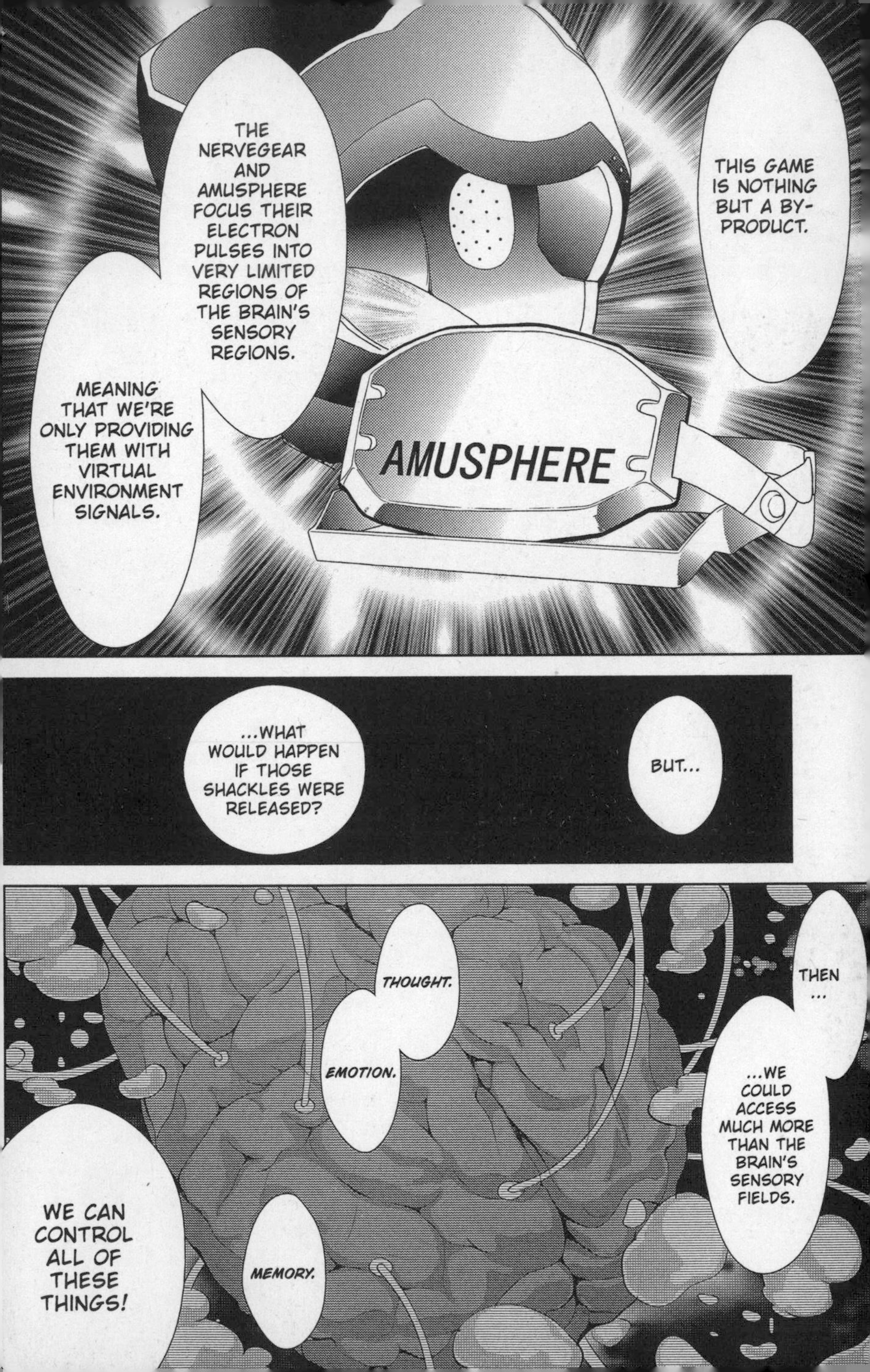
THIS GAME IS NOTHING BUT A BY-PRODUCT.
THE NERVEGEAR AND AMUSPHERE FOCUS THEIR ELECTRON PULSES INTO VERY LIMITED REGIONS OF THE BRAIN'S SENSORY REGIONS.
AMUSPHERE
MEANING THAT WE'RE ONLY PROVIDING THEM WITH VIRTUAL ENVIRONMENT SIGNALS.
BUT...
...WHAT WOULD HAPPEN IF THOSE SHACKLES WERE RELEASED?
THEN ...
...WE COULD ACCESS MUCH MORE THAN THE BRAIN'S SENSORY FIELDS.
THOUGHT.
EMOTION.
MEMORY.
WE CAN CONTROL ALL OF THESE THINGS!

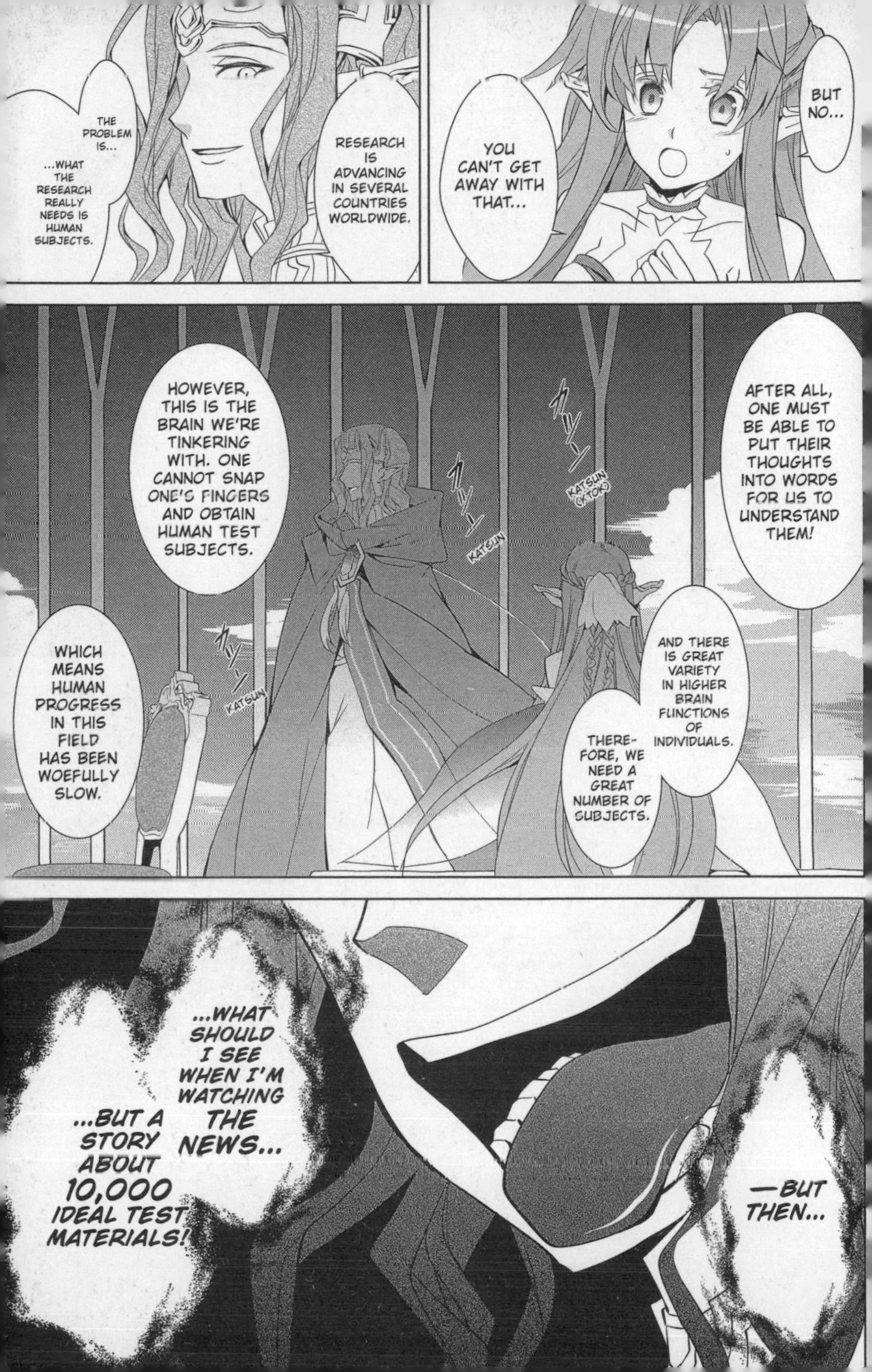
BUT NO...
YOU CAN'T GET AWAY WITH THAT...
RESEARCH IS ADVANCING IN SEVERAL COUNTRIES WORLDWIDE.
THE PROBLEM IS...
...WHAT THE RESEARCH REALLY NEEDS IS HUMAN SUBJECTS.
AFTER ALL, ONE MUST BE ABLE TO PUT THEIR THOUGHTS INTO WORDS FOR US TO UNDERSTAND THEM!
AND THERE IS GREAT VARIETY IN HIGHER BRAIN FUNCTIONS OF INDIVIDUALS.
THEREFORE, WE NEED A GREAT NUMBER OF SUBJECTS.
KATSUN (KTOK)
KATSUN
HOWEVER, THIS IS THE BRAIN WE'RE TINKERING WITH. ONE CANNOT SNAP ONE'S FINGERS AND OBTAIN HUMAN TEST SUBJECTS.
KATSUN
WHICH MEANS HUMAN PROGRESS IN THIS FIELD HAS BEEN WOEFULLY SLOW.
—BUT THEN...
...WHAT SHOULD I SEE WHEN I'M WATCHING THE NEWS...
...BUT A STORY ABOUT 10,000 IDEAL TEST MATERIALS!

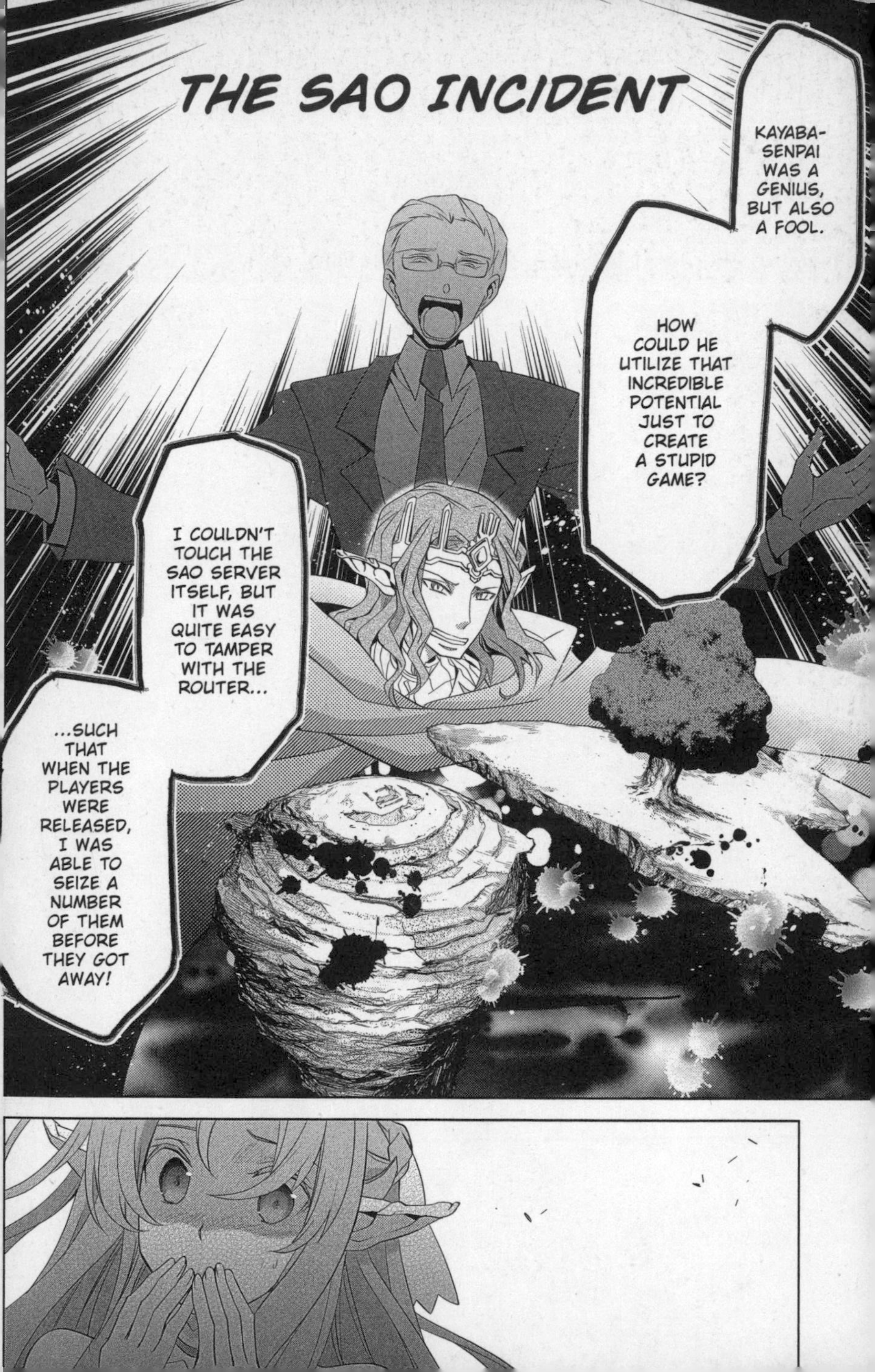
KAYABA-SENPAI WAS A GENIUS, BUT ALSO A FOOL.
THE SAO INCIDENT
HOW COULD HE UTILIZE THAT INCREDIBLE POTENTIAL JUST TO CREATE A STUPID GAME?
I COULDN'T TOUCH THE SAO SERVER ITSELF, BUT IT WAS QUITE EASY TO TAMPER WITH THE ROUTER...
...SUCH THAT WHEN THE PLAYERS WERE RELEASED, I WAS ABLE TO SEIZE A NUMBER OF THEM BEFORE THEY GOT AWAY!

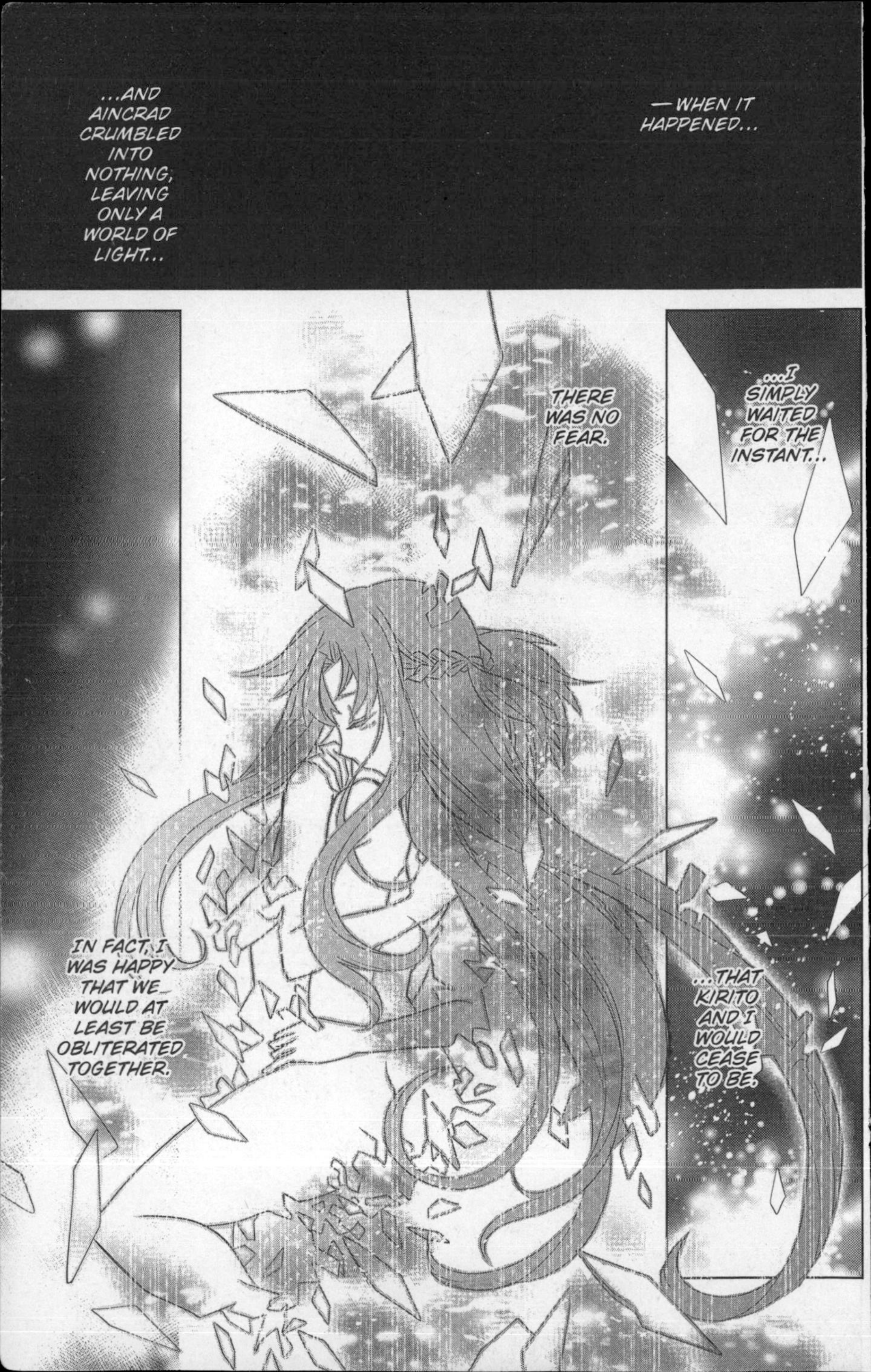
—WHEN IT HAPPENED...
...AND AINCRAD CRUMBLED INTO NOTHING, LEAVING ONLY A WORLD OF LIGHT...
...I SIMPLY WAITED FOR THE INSTANT...
...THAT KIRITO AND I WOULD CEASE TO BE.
THERE WAS NO FEAR.
IN FACT, I WAS HAPPY THAT WE WOULD AT LEAST BE OBLITERATED TOGETHER.

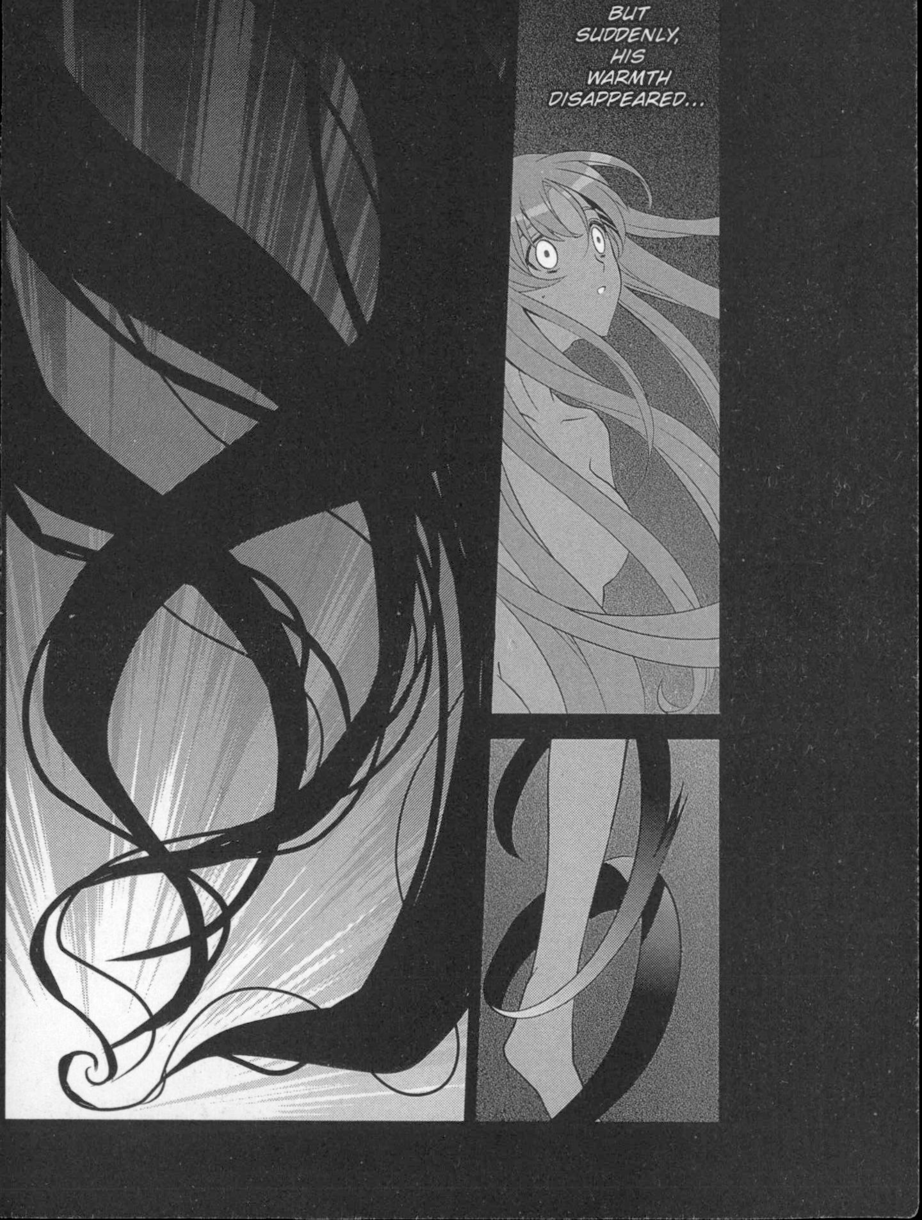
BUT SUDDENLY, HIS WARMTH DISAPPEARED...

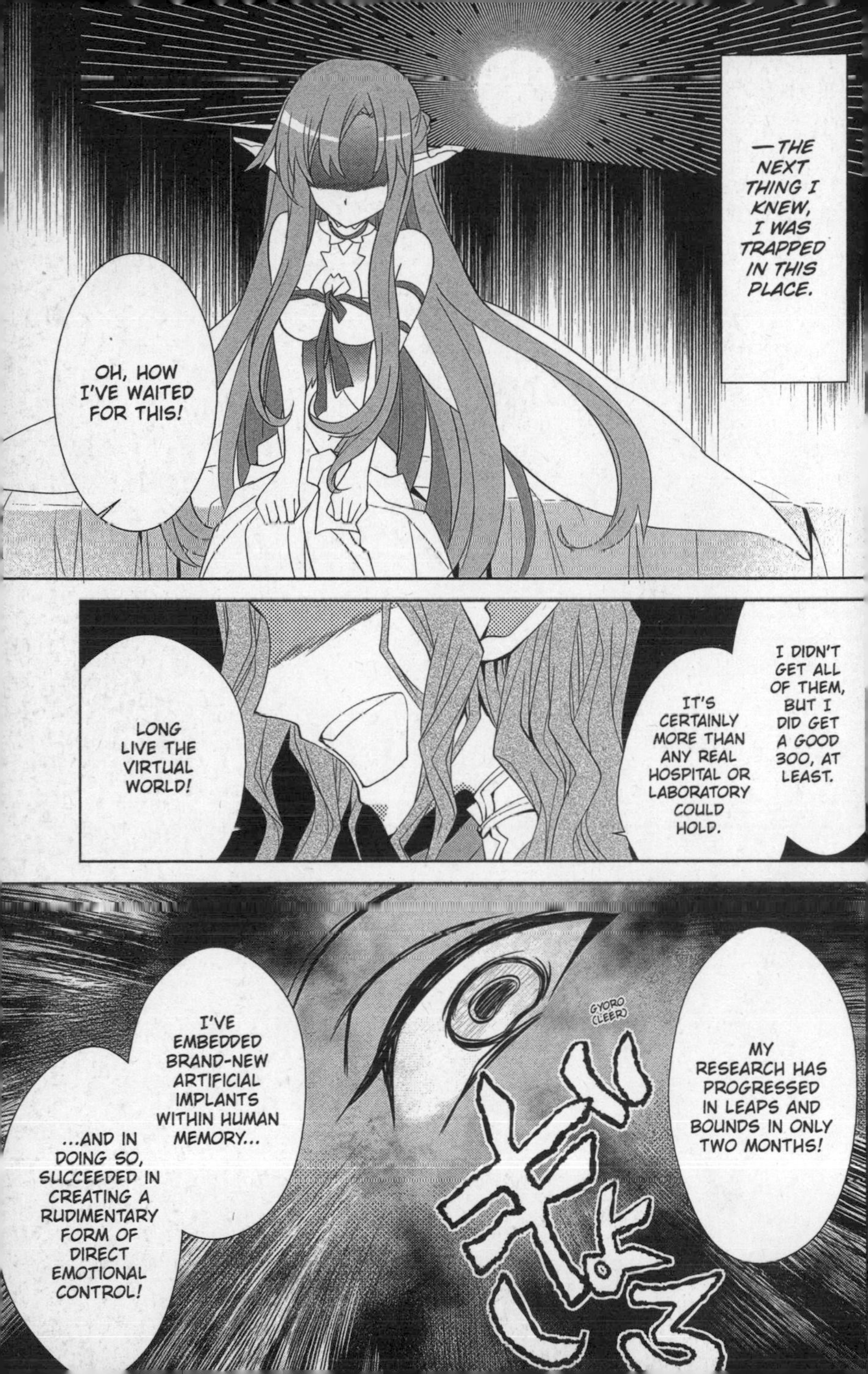
—THE NEXT THING I KNEW, I WAS TRAPPED IN THIS PLACE.
OH, HOW I'VE WAITED FOR THIS!
I DIDN'T GET ALL OF THEM, BUT I DID GET A GOOD 300, AT LEAST.
IT'S CERTAINLY MORE THAN ANY REAL HOSPITAL OR LABORATORY COULD HOLD.
LONG LIVE THE VIRTUAL WORLD!
MY RESEARCH HAS PROGRESSED IN LEAPS AND BOUNDS IN ONLY TWO MONTHS!
GYORO (LEER)
I'VE EMBEDDED BRAND-NEW ARTIFICIAL IMPLANTS WITHIN HUMAN MEMORY...
...AND IN DOING SO, SUCCEEDED IN CREATING A RUDIMENTARY FORM OF DIRECT EMOTIONAL CONTROL!

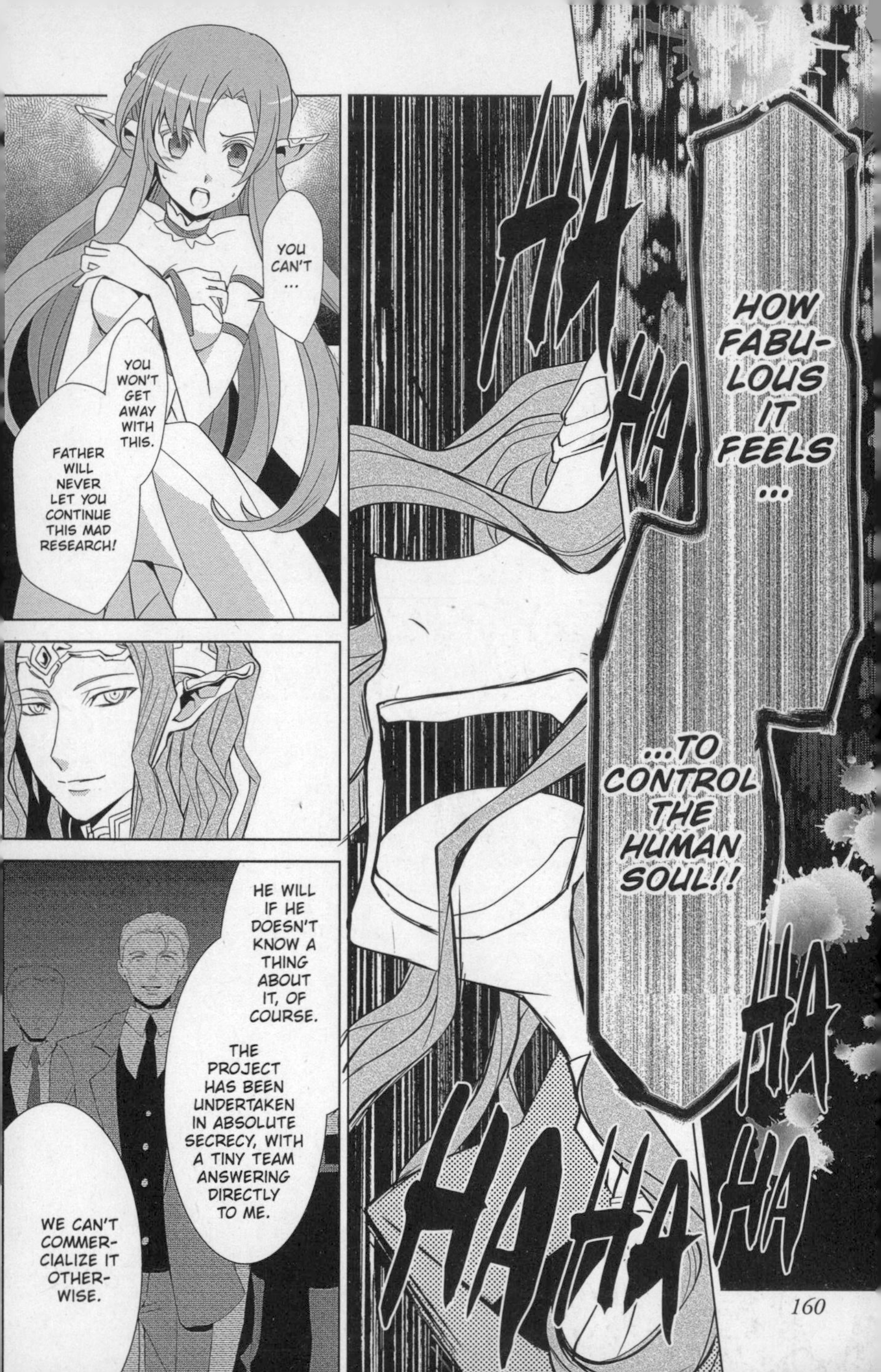

HA
HA
HOW FABULOUS IT FEELS...
...TO CONTROL THE HUMAN SOUL!!
HA
HA
HA
HA
HA
YOU CAN'T...
YOU WON'T GET AWAY WITH THIS.
FATHER WILL NEVER LET YOU CONTINUE THIS MAD RESEARCH!
HE WILL IF HE DOESN'T KNOW A THING ABOUT IT, OF COURSE.
THE PROJECT HAS BEEN UNDERTAKEN IN ABSOLUTE SECRECY, WITH A TINY TEAM ANSWERING DIRECTLY TO ME.
WE CAN'T COMMERCIALIZE IT OTHERWISE.

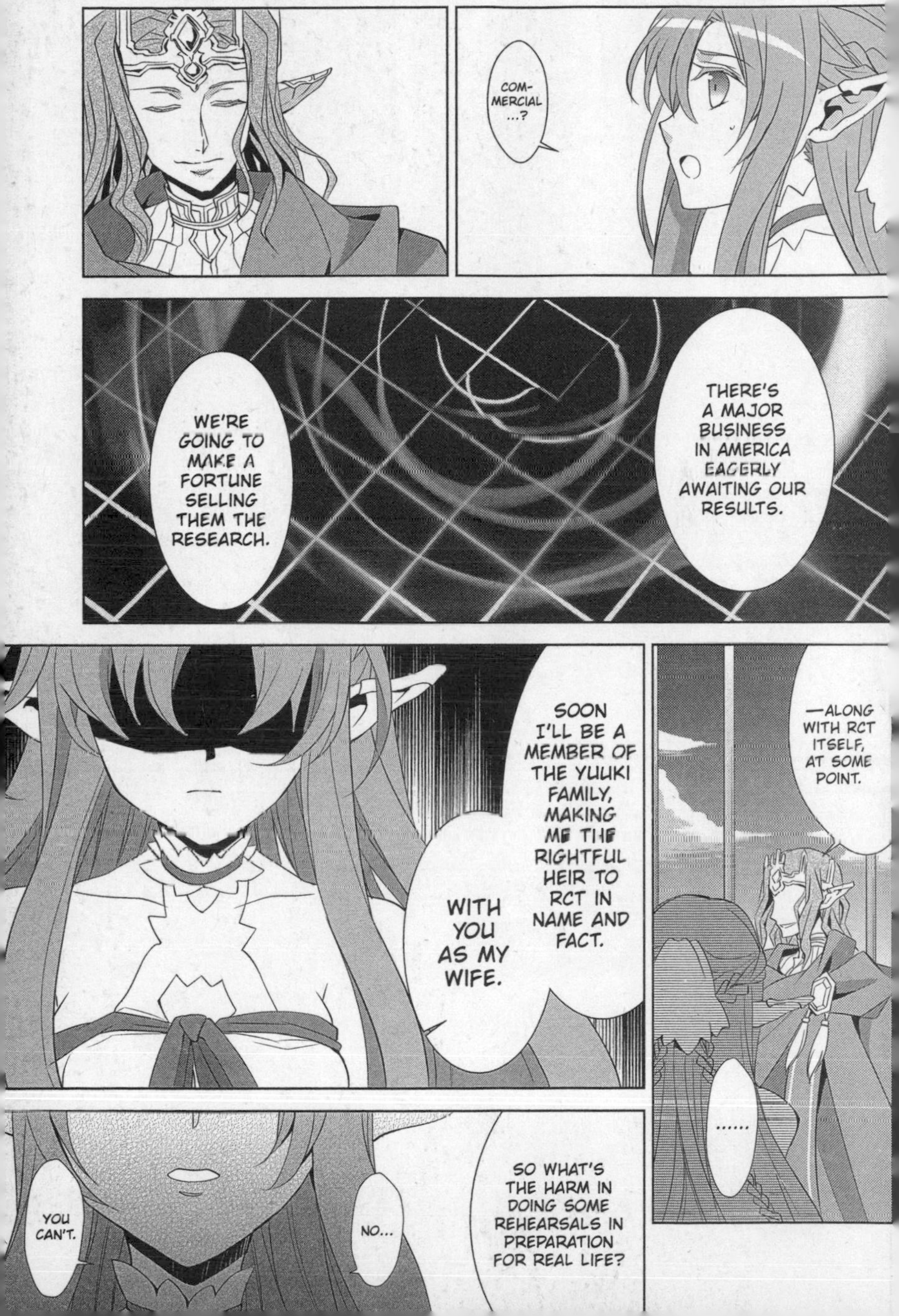
COM-MERCIAL ...?
THERE'S A MAJOR BUSINESS IN AMERICA EAGERLY AWAITING OUR RESULTS.
WE'RE GOING TO MAKE A FORTUNE SELLING THEM THE RESEARCH.
—ALONG WITH RCT ITSELF, AT SOME POINT.
......
SOON I'LL BE A MEMBER OF THE YUUKI FAMILY, MAKING ME THE RIGHTFUL HEIR TO RCT IN NAME AND FACT.
WITH YOU AS MY WIFE.
SO WHAT'S THE HARM IN DOING SOME REHEARSALS IN PREPARATION FOR REAL LIFE?
NO...
YOU CAN'T.

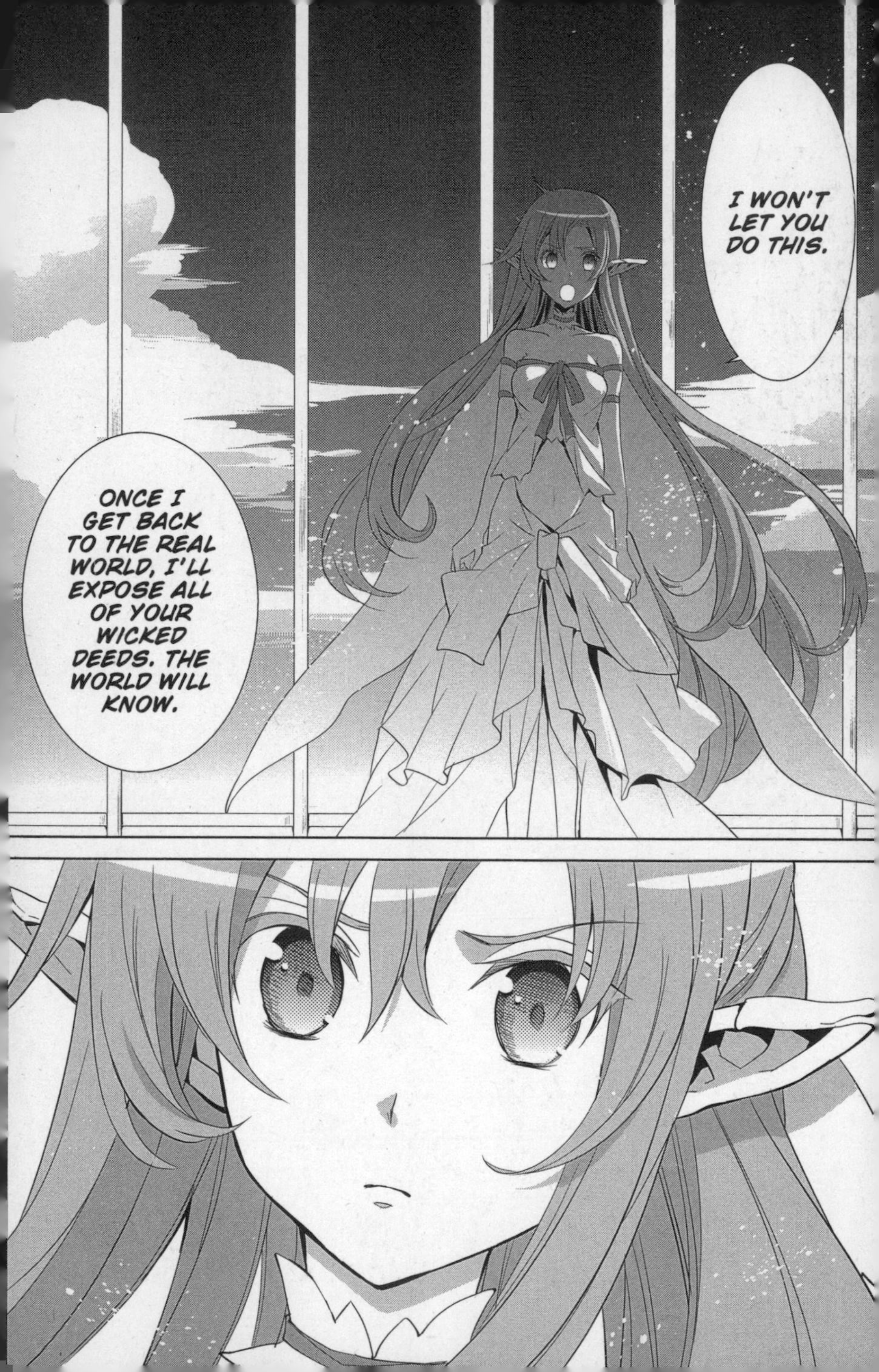
I WON'T LET YOU DO THIS.
ONCE I GET BACK TO THE REAL WORLD, I'LL EXPOSE ALL OF YOUR WICKED DEEDS. THE WORLD WILL KNOW.

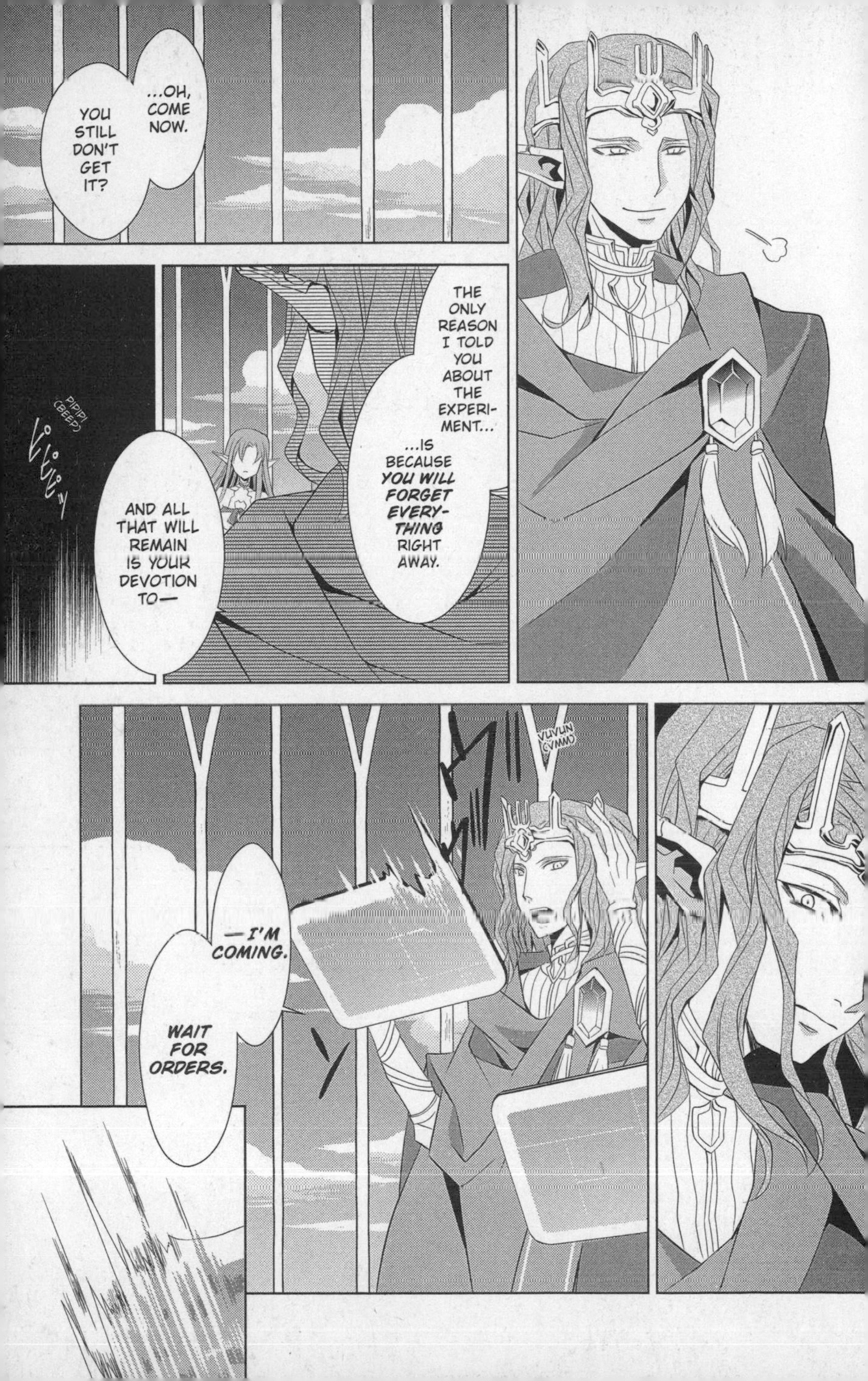
...OH, COME NOW.
YOU STILL DON'T GET IT?
THE ONLY REASON I TOLD YOU ABOUT THE EXPERIMENT...
...IS BECAUSE *YOU WILL FORGET EVERYTHING* RIGHT AWAY.
AND ALL THAT WILL REMAIN IS YOUR DEVOTION TO—
PIPIPI (BEEP)
VUVUN (VMM)
—I'M COMING.
WAIT FOR ORDERS.

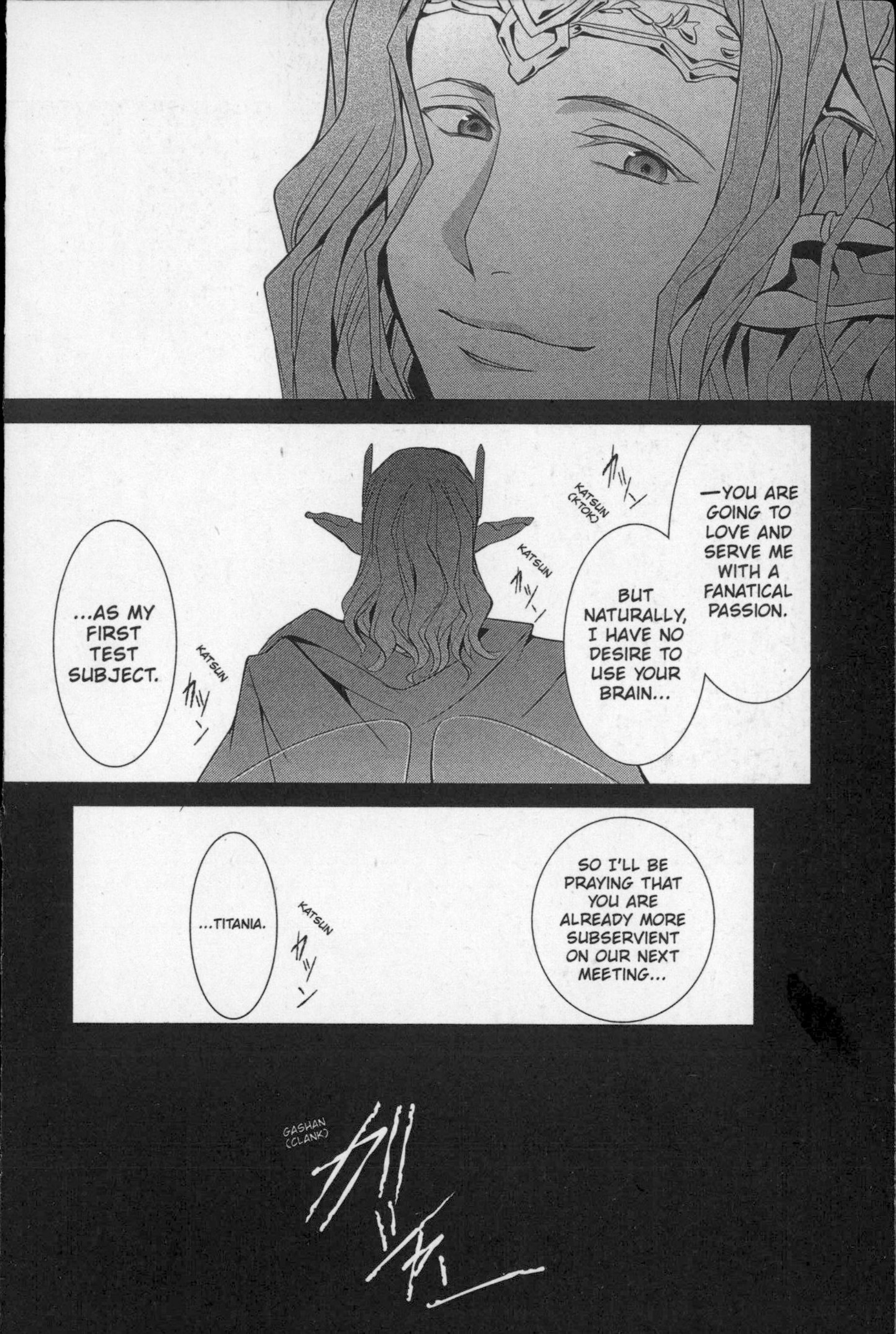
—YOU ARE GOING TO LOVE AND SERVE ME WITH A FANATICAL PASSION.
KATSUN (KTOK)
BUT NATURALLY, I HAVE NO DESIRE TO USE YOUR BRAIN...
KATSUN
KATSUN
...AS MY FIRST TEST SUBJECT.
SO I'LL BE PRAYING THAT YOU ARE ALREADY MORE SUBSERVIENT ON OUR NEXT MEETING...
KATSUN
...TITANIA.
GASHAN (CLANK)

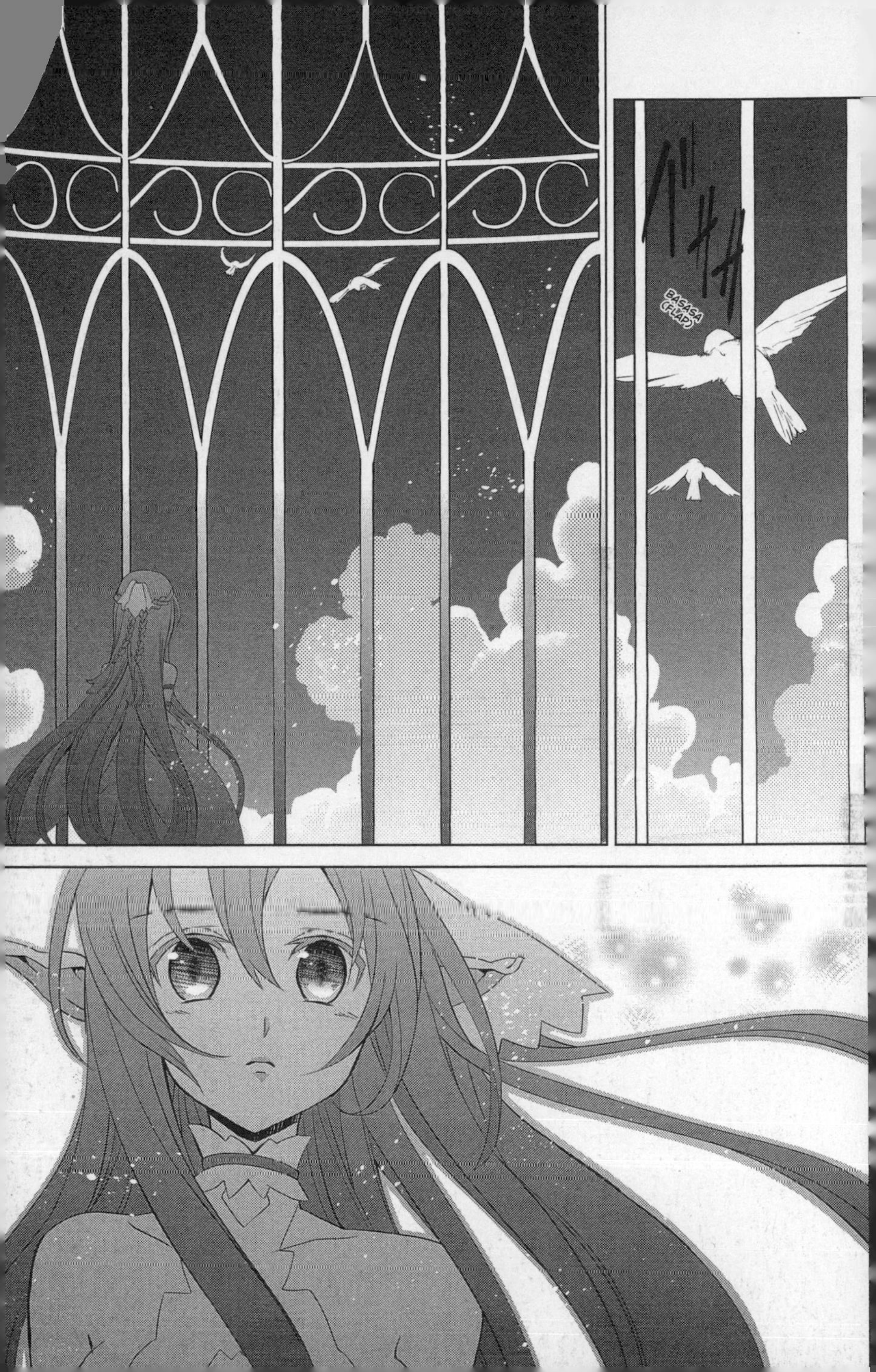
バササ
BASASA (FLAP)

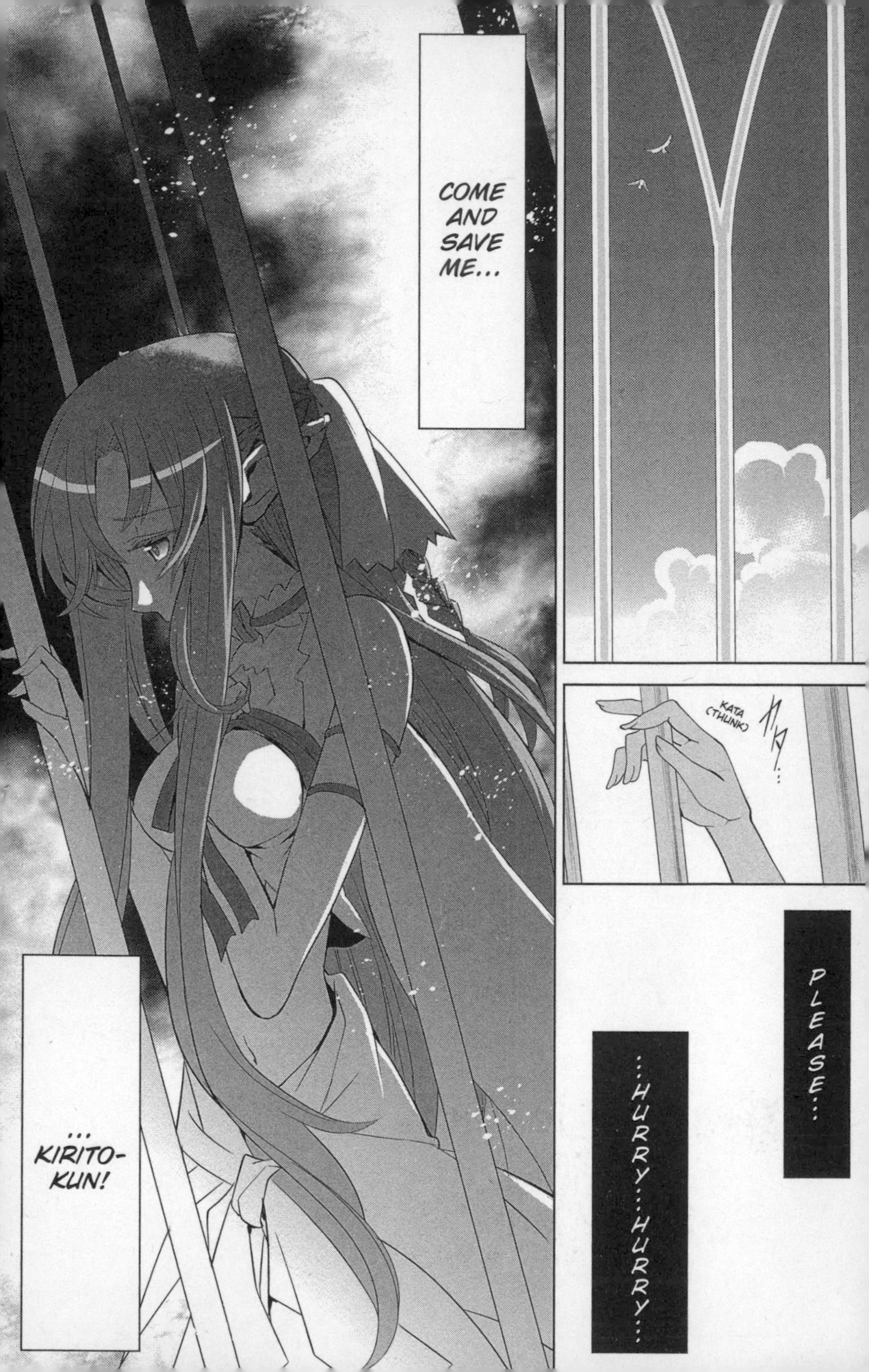
KATA (THUNK)
PLEASE...
...HURRY...HURRY...
COME AND SAVE ME...
... KIRITO-KUN!

SWORD ART ONLINE
fairy dance

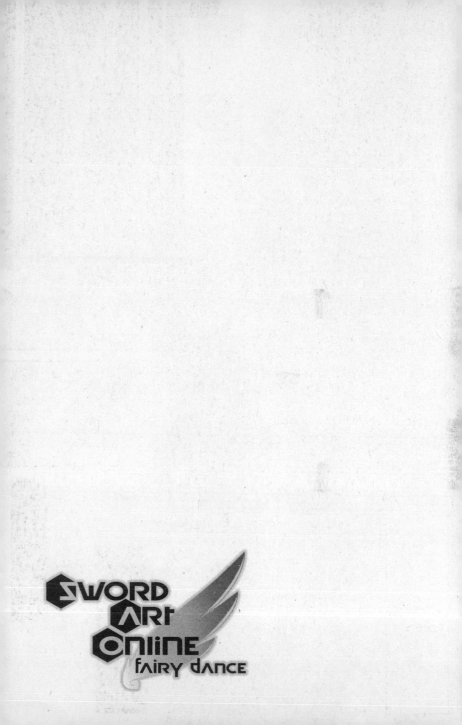

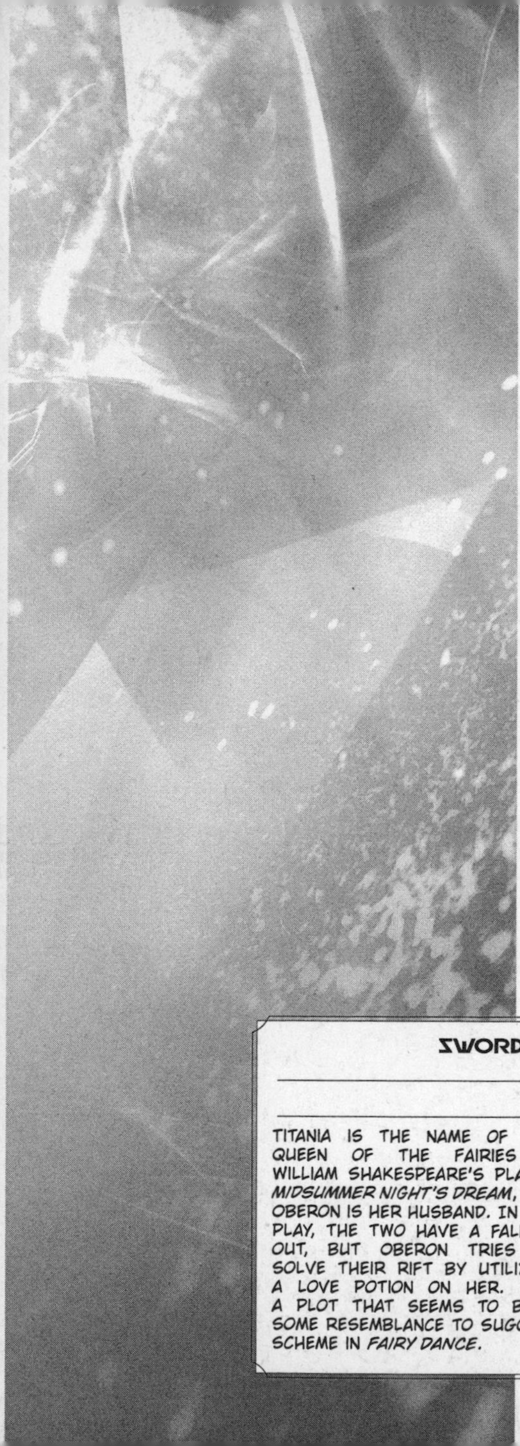

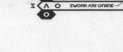

SWORD ART ONLINE fairy dance 03
BACKGROUND GUIDE

TITANIA AND OBERON

TITANIA IS THE NAME OF THE QUEEN OF THE FAIRIES IN WILLIAM SHAKESPEARE'S PLAY *A MIDSUMMER NIGHT'S DREAM*, AND OBERON IS HER HUSBAND. IN THE PLAY, THE TWO HAVE A FALLING OUT, BUT OBERON TRIES TO SOLVE THEIR RIFT BY UTILIZING A LOVE POTION ON HER. IT'S A PLOT THAT SEEMS TO BEAR SOME RESEMBLANCE TO SUGOU'S SCHEME IN *FAIRY DANCE*.

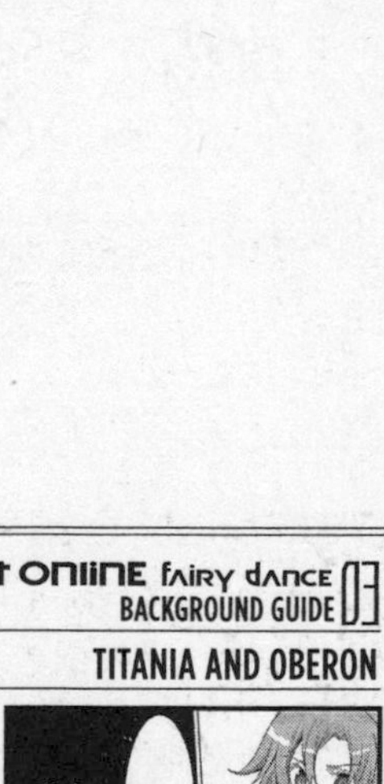

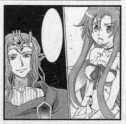

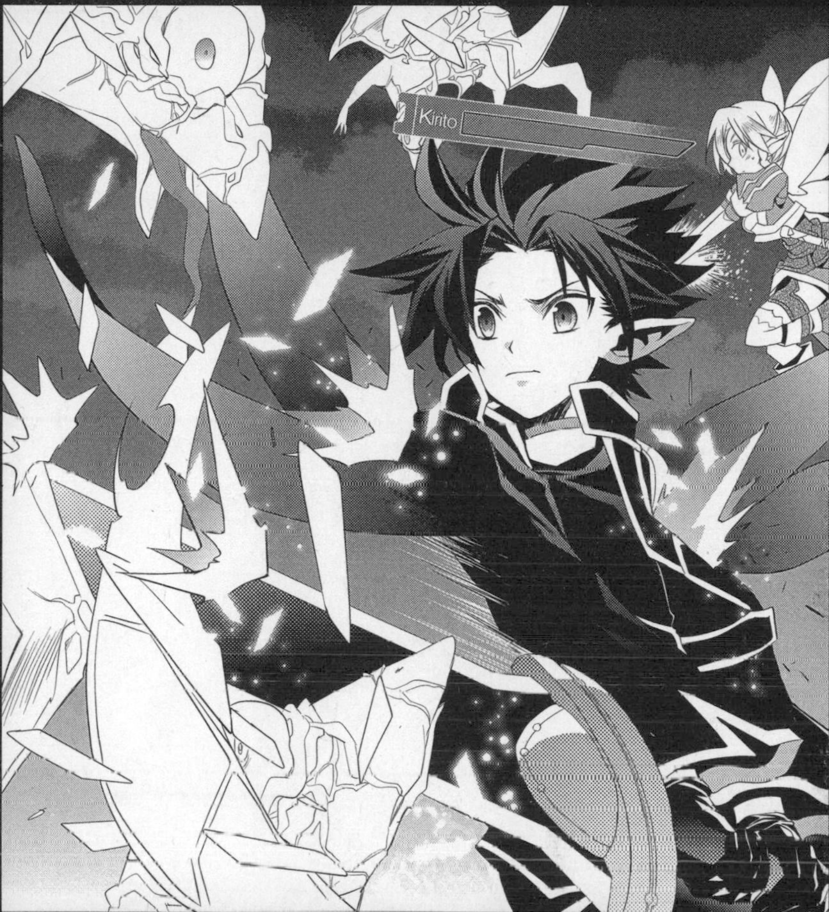
Kirito

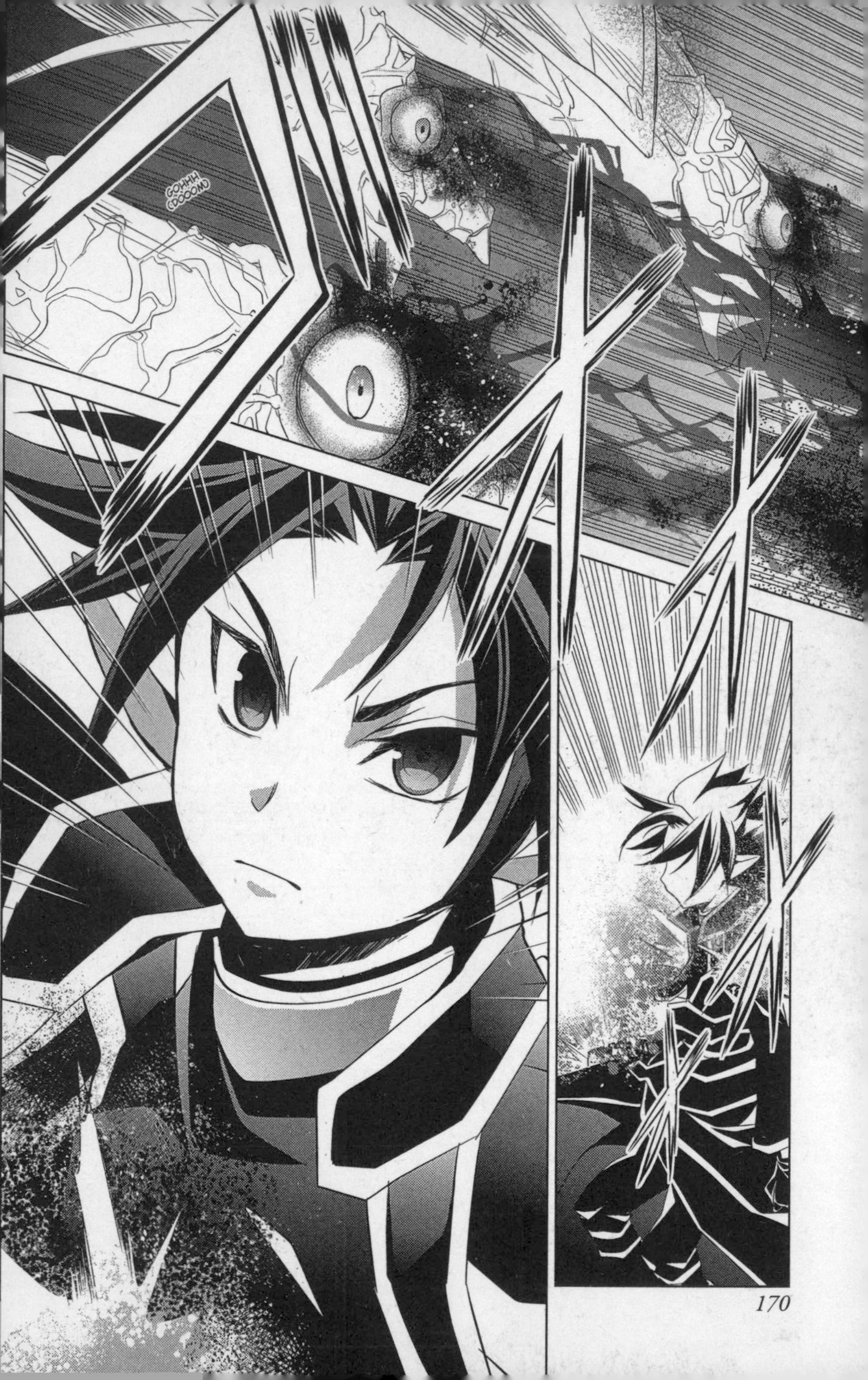
GOHHH
(DOOOM)

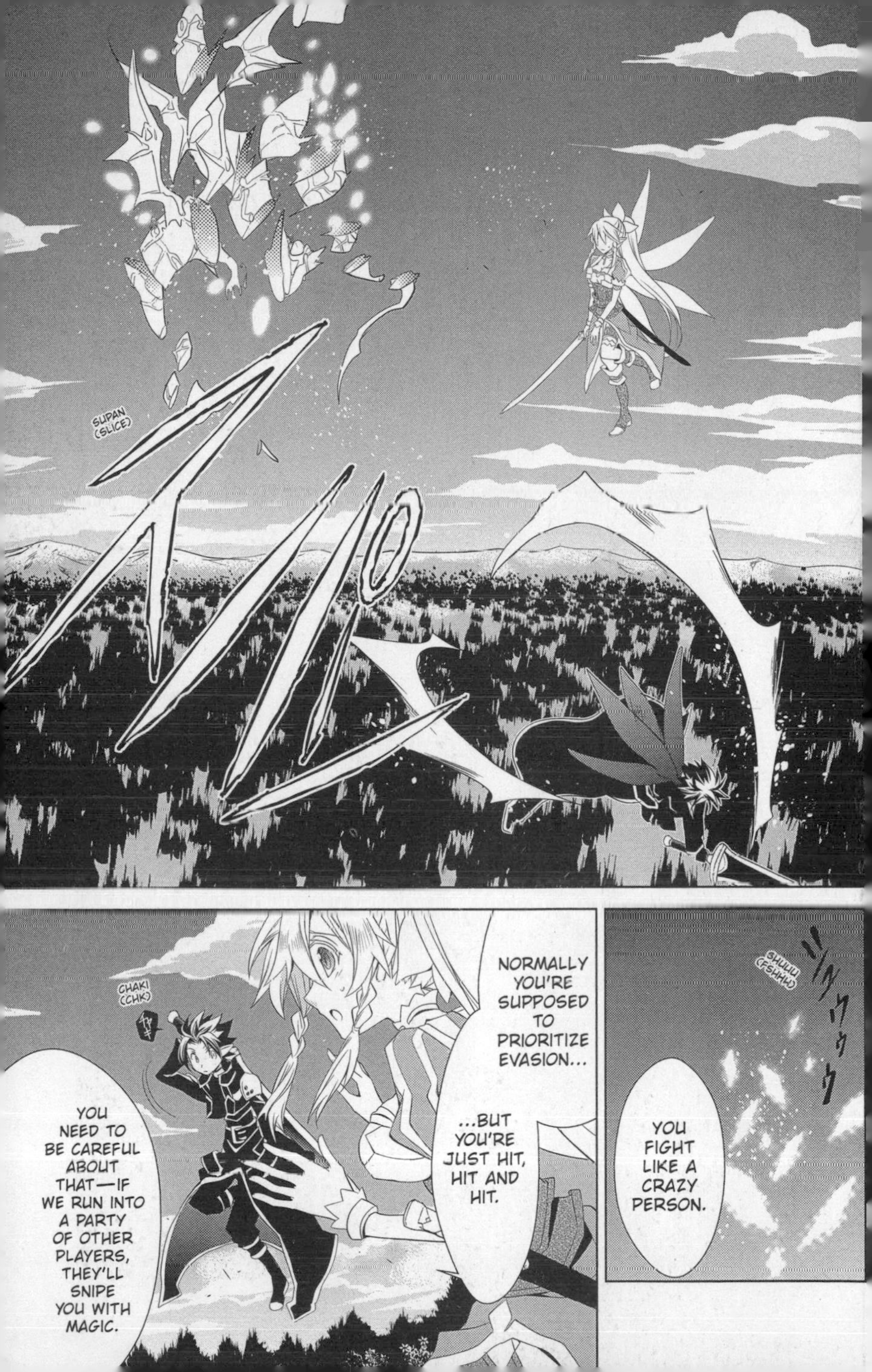
SUPAN (SLICE)
SHUUU (FSHHH)
YOU FIGHT LIKE A CRAZY PERSON.
NORMALLY YOU'RE SUPPOSED TO PRIORITIZE EVASION...
...BUT YOU'RE JUST HIT, HIT AND HIT.
CHAKI (CHK)
YOU NEED TO BE CAREFUL ABOUT THAT—IF WE RUN INTO A PARTY OF OTHER PLAYERS, THEY'LL SNIPE YOU WITH MAGIC.

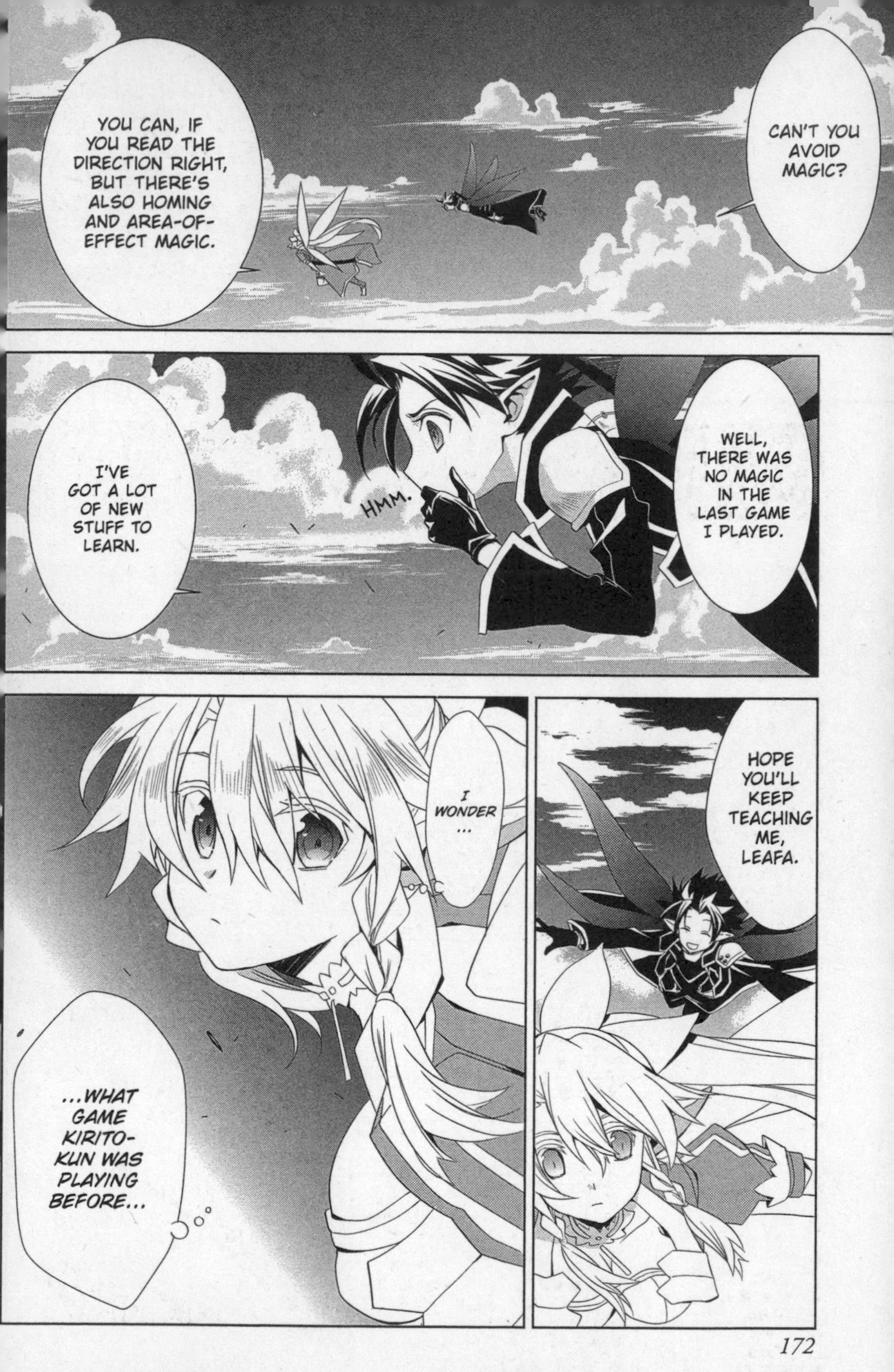
CAN'T YOU AVOID MAGIC?
YOU CAN, IF YOU READ THE DIRECTION RIGHT, BUT THERE'S ALSO HOMING AND AREA-OF-EFFECT MAGIC.
WELL, THERE WAS NO MAGIC IN THE LAST GAME I PLAYED.
HMM.
I'VE GOT A LOT OF NEW STUFF TO LEARN.
HOPE YOU'LL KEEP TEACHING ME, LEAFA.
I WONDER...
...WHAT GAME KIRITO-KUN WAS PLAYING BEFORE...

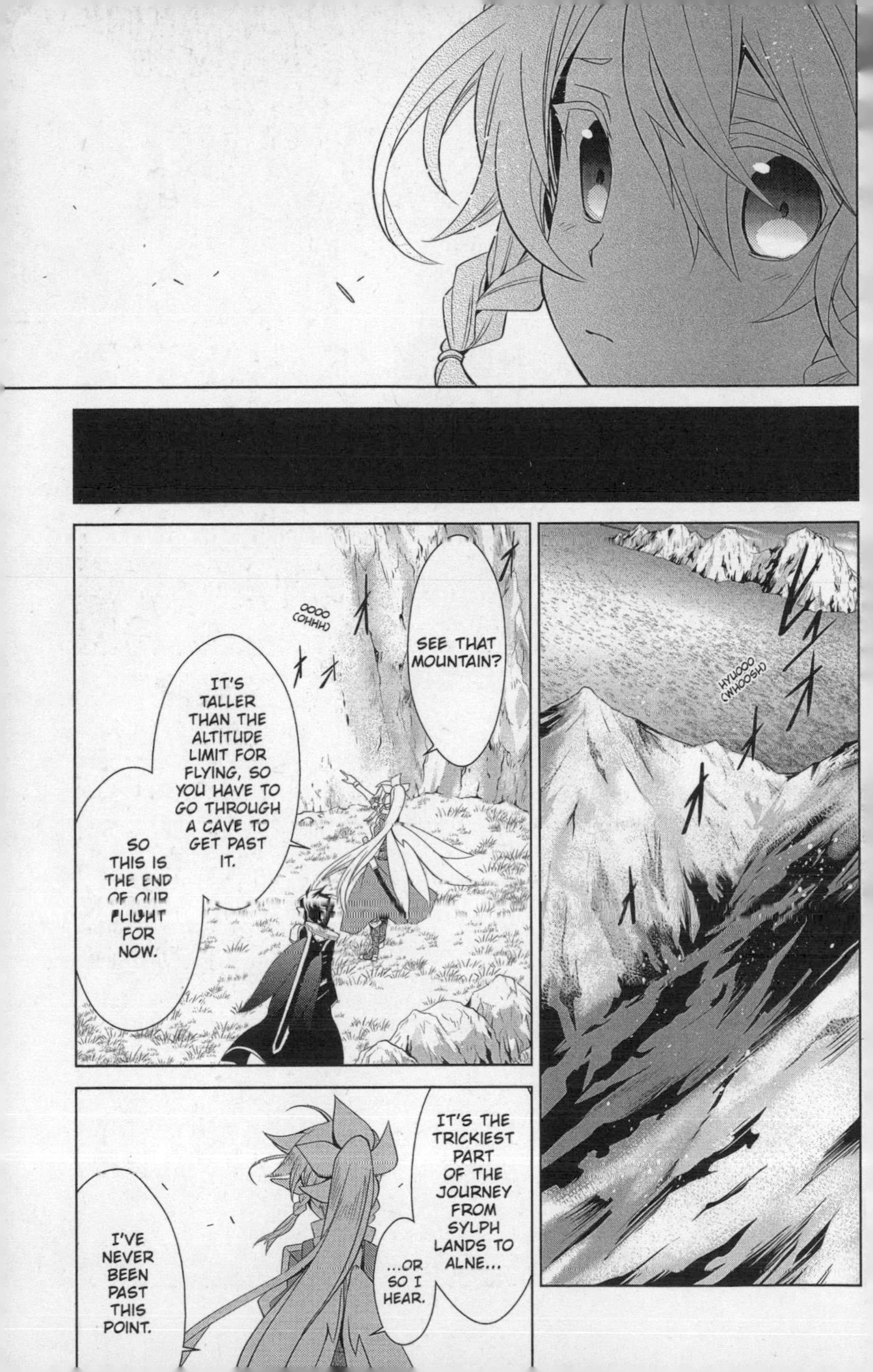
HYUOOO (WHOOSH)
SEE THAT MOUNTAIN?
OOOO (OHHH)
IT'S TALLER THAN THE ALTITUDE LIMIT FOR FLYING, SO YOU HAVE TO GO THROUGH A CAVE TO GET PAST IT.
SO THIS IS THE END OF OUR FLIGHT FOR NOW.
IT'S THE TRICKIEST PART OF THE JOURNEY FROM SYLPH LANDS TO ALNE...
...OR SO I HEAR.
I'VE NEVER BEEN PAST THIS POINT.

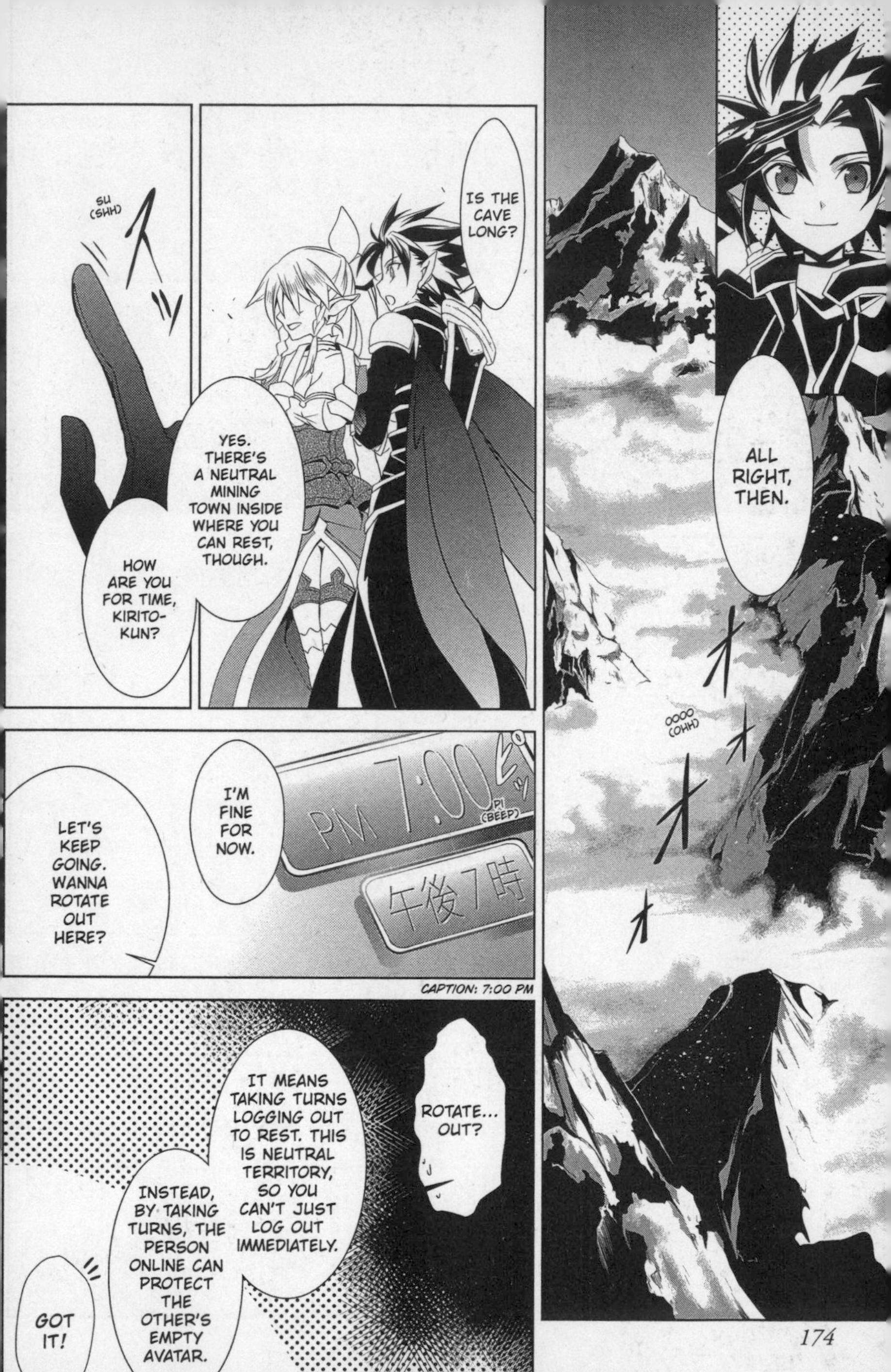
ALL RIGHT, THEN.
OOOO (OHH)
IS THE CAVE LONG?
YES. THERE'S A NEUTRAL MINING TOWN INSIDE WHERE YOU CAN REST, THOUGH.
HOW ARE YOU FOR TIME, KIRITO-KUN?
SU (SHH)
PI (BEEP)
PM 7:00
午後7時
I'M FINE FOR NOW.
LET'S KEEP GOING. WANNA ROTATE OUT HERE?
CAPTION: 7:00 PM
ROTATE... OUT?
IT MEANS TAKING TURNS LOGGING OUT TO REST. THIS IS NEUTRAL TERRITORY, SO YOU CAN'T JUST LOG OUT IMMEDIATELY.
INSTEAD, BY TAKING TURNS, THE PERSON ONLINE CAN PROTECT THE OTHER'S EMPTY AVATAR.
GOT IT!

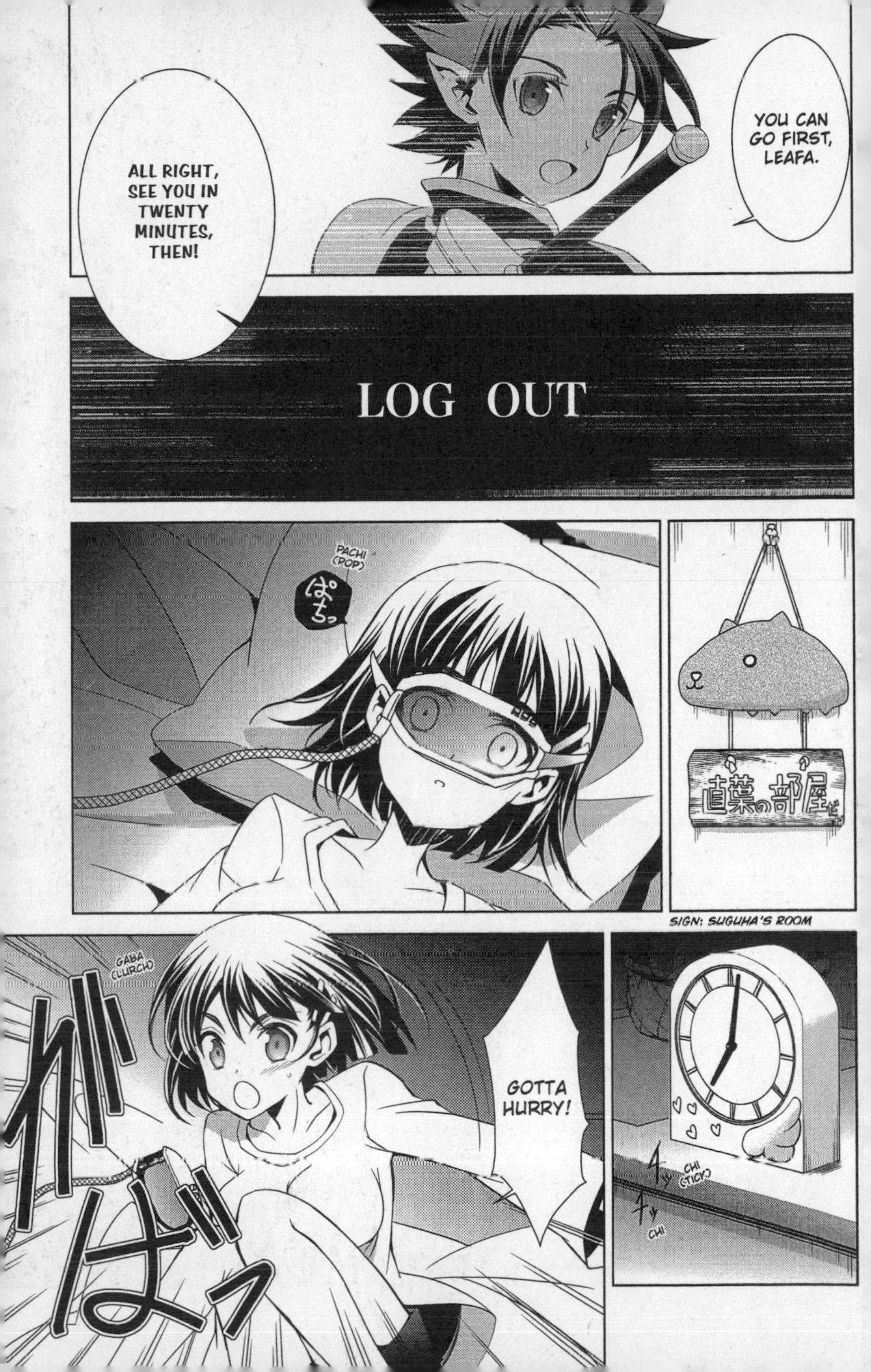
YOU CAN GO FIRST, LEAFA.
ALL RIGHT, SEE YOU IN TWENTY MINUTES, THEN!
LOG OUT
直葉の部屋
SIGN: SUGUHA'S ROOM
PACHI (POP)
ぱちっ
CHI (TICK)
CHI
GABA (LURCH)
がばっ
GOTTA HURRY!

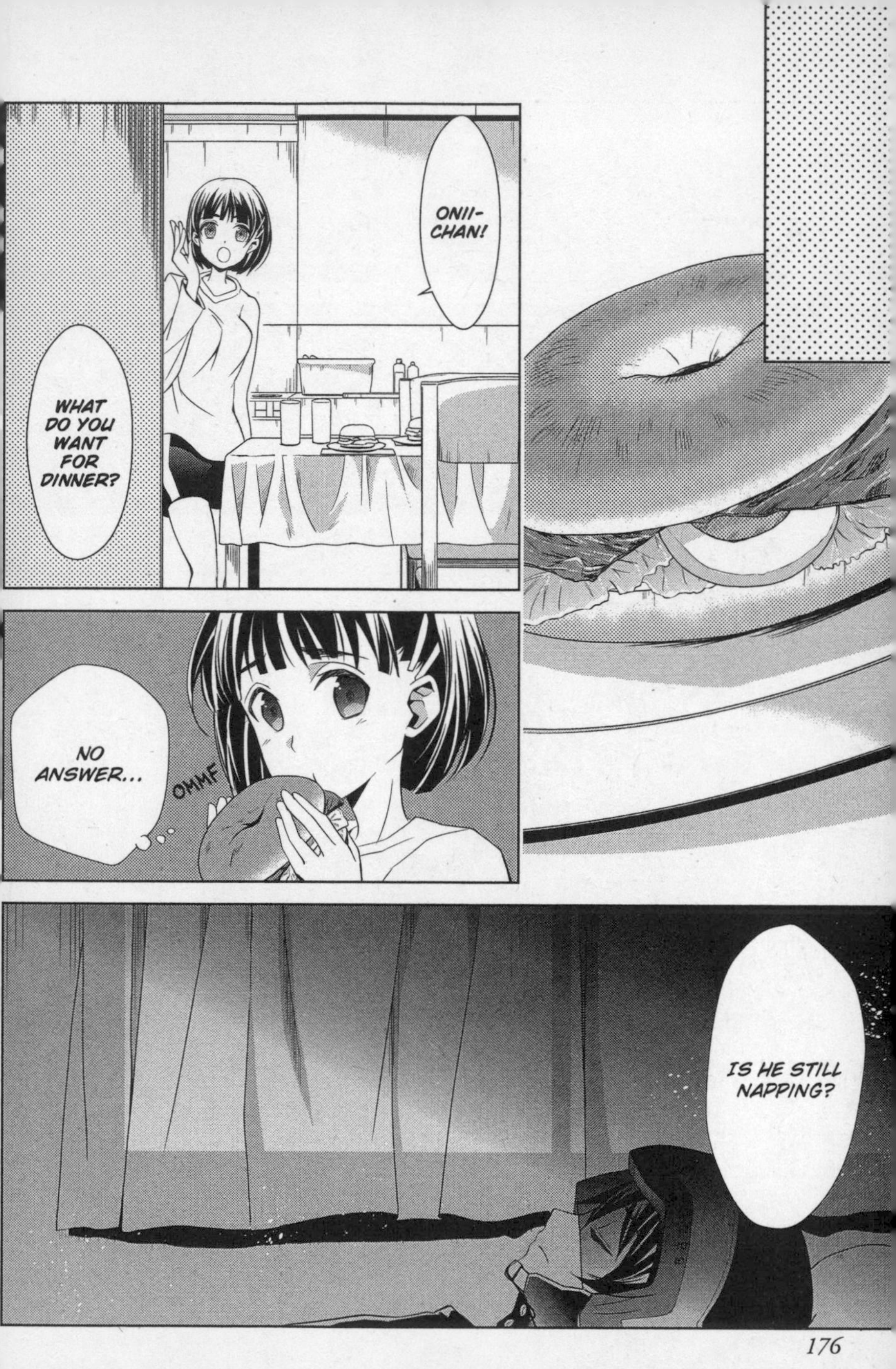
ONII-CHAN!
WHAT DO YOU WANT FOR DINNER?
OMMF
NO ANSWER...
IS HE STILL NAPPING?

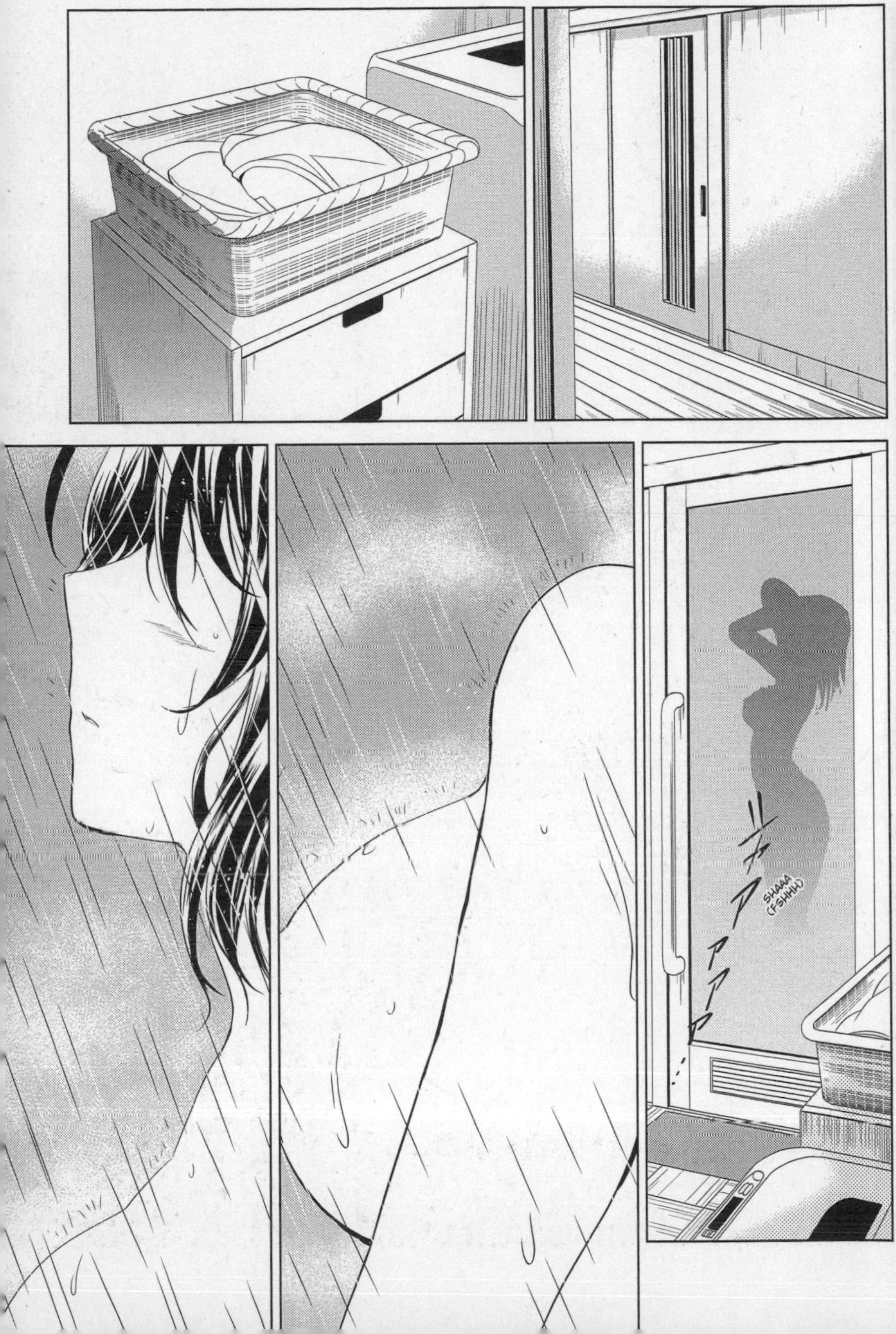
SHAAA (FSHHH)

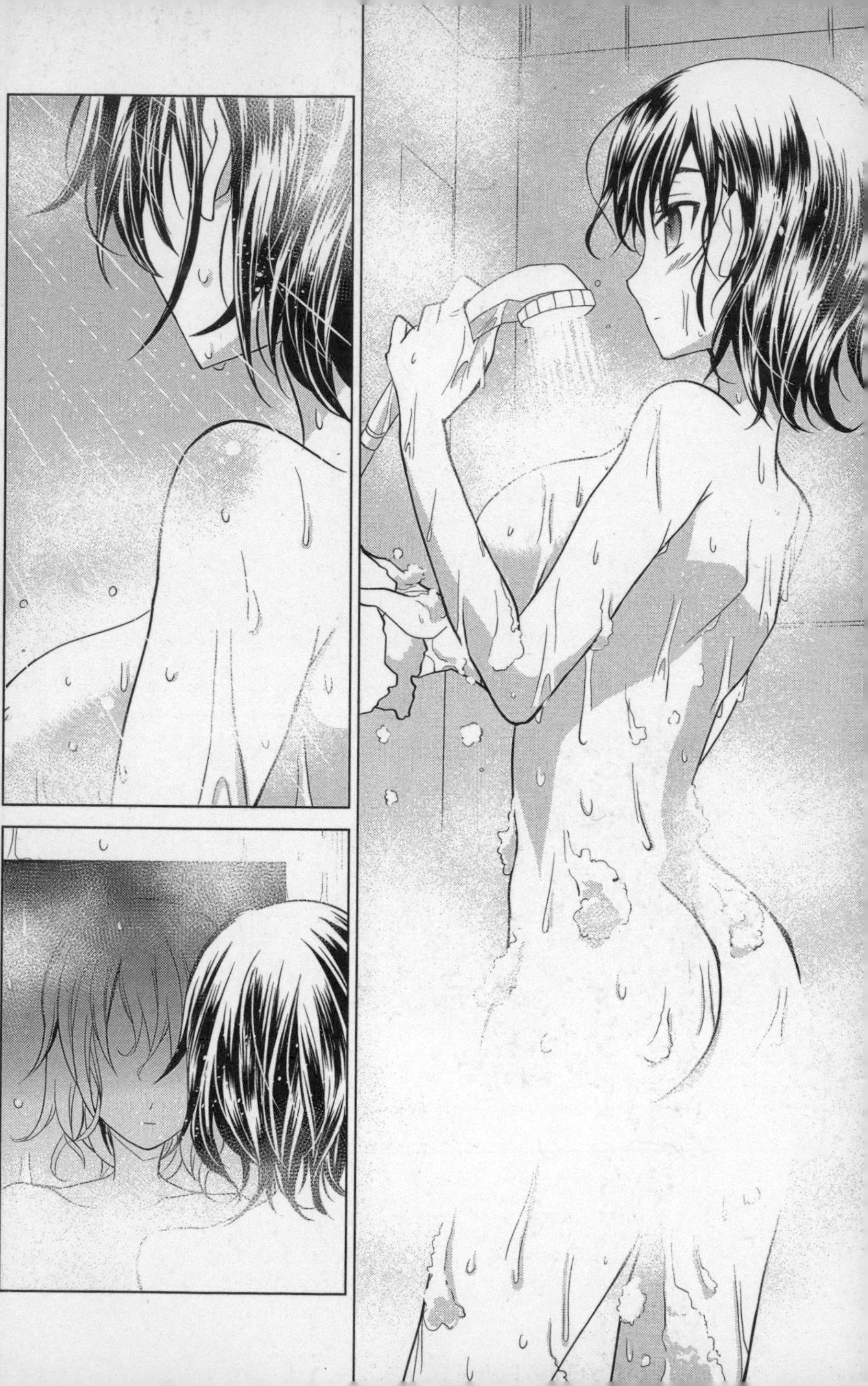

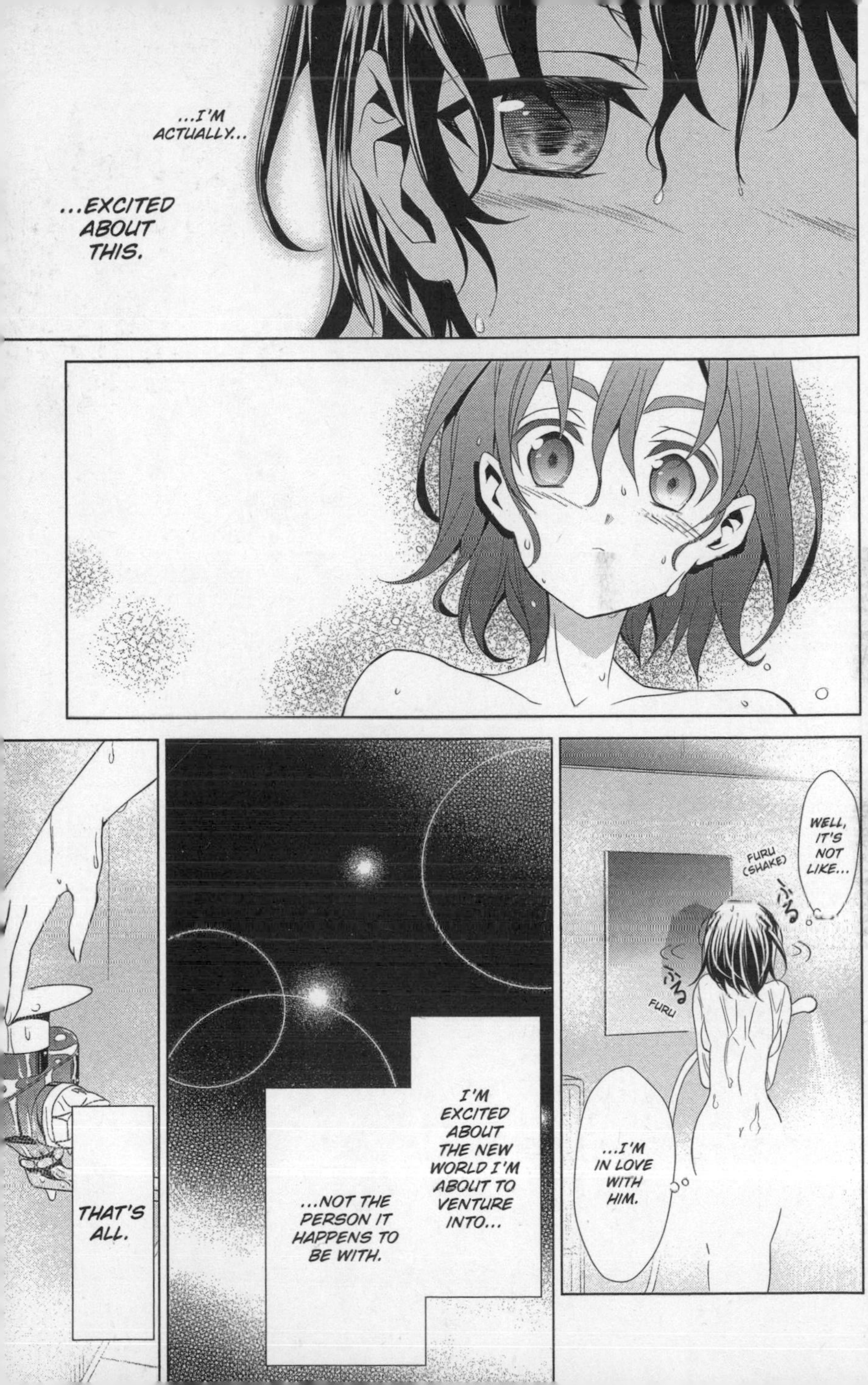
...I'M ACTUALLY...
...EXCITED ABOUT THIS.
WELL, IT'S NOT LIKE...
ふる
FURU (SHAKE)
ふる
FURU
...I'M IN LOVE WITH HIM.
I'M EXCITED ABOUT THE NEW WORLD I'M ABOUT TO VENTURE INTO...
...NOT THE PERSON IT HAPPENS TO BE WITH.
THAT'S ALL.

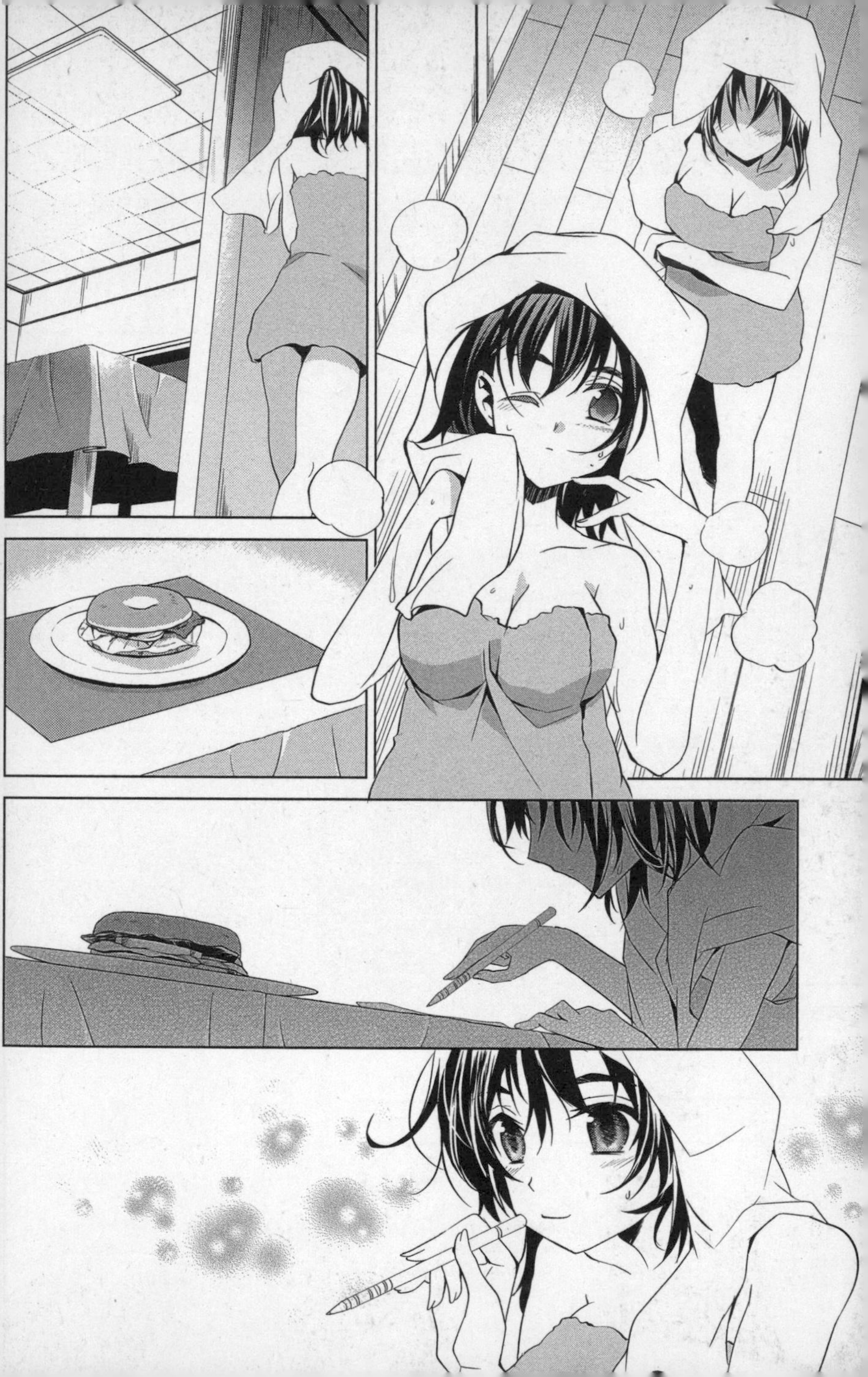

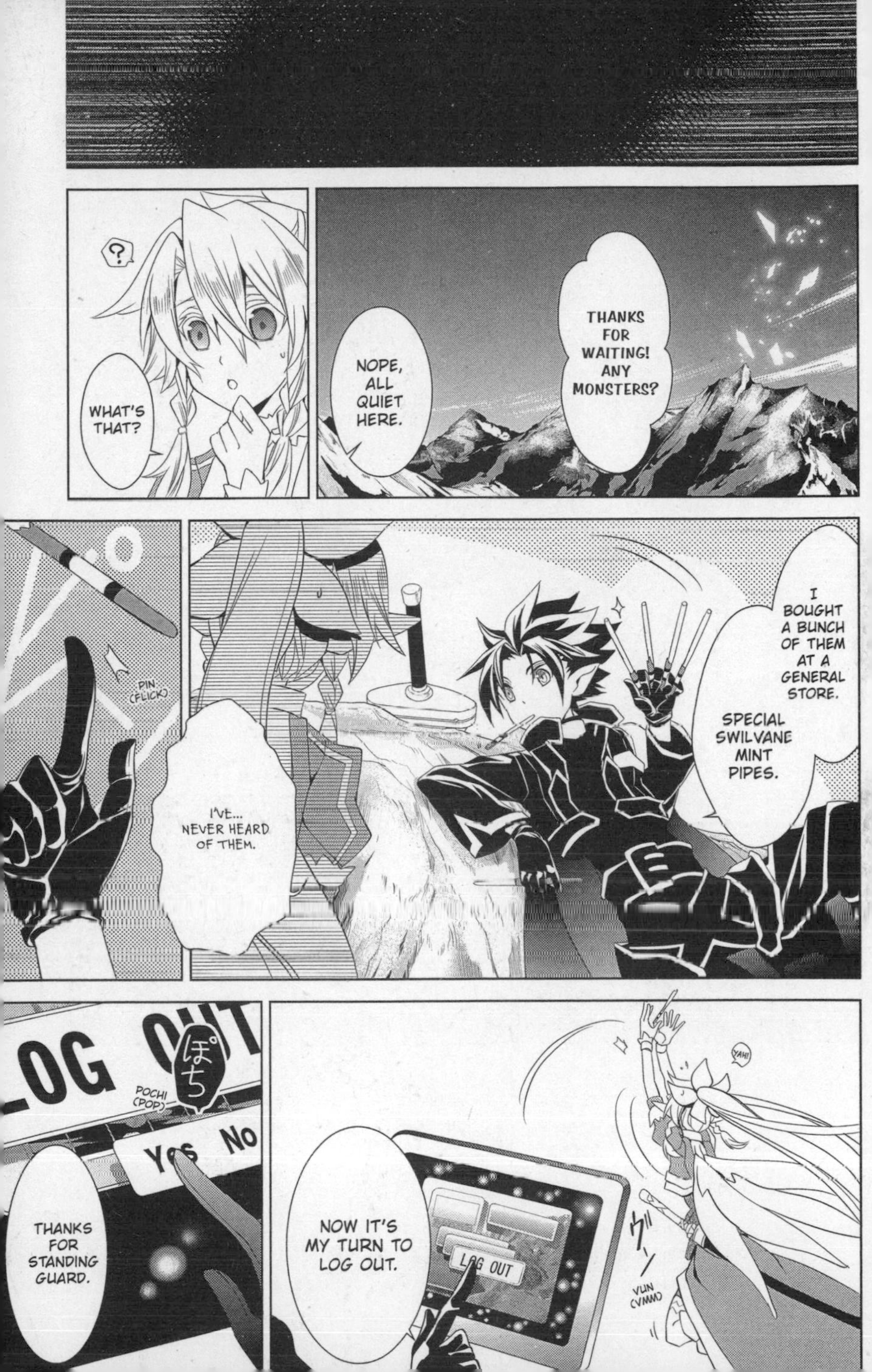
THANKS FOR WAITING! ANY MONSTERS?
NOPE, ALL QUIET HERE.
?
WHAT'S THAT?
I BOUGHT A BUNCH OF THEM AT A GENERAL STORE.
SPECIAL SWILVANE MINT PIPES.
I'VE... NEVER HEARD OF THEM.
PIN (FLICK)
YAH!
NOW IT'S MY TURN TO LOG OUT.
LOG OUT
ヴン
VUN (VMM)
LOG OUT
ぽち
POCHI (POP)
Yes No
THANKS FOR STANDING GUARD.

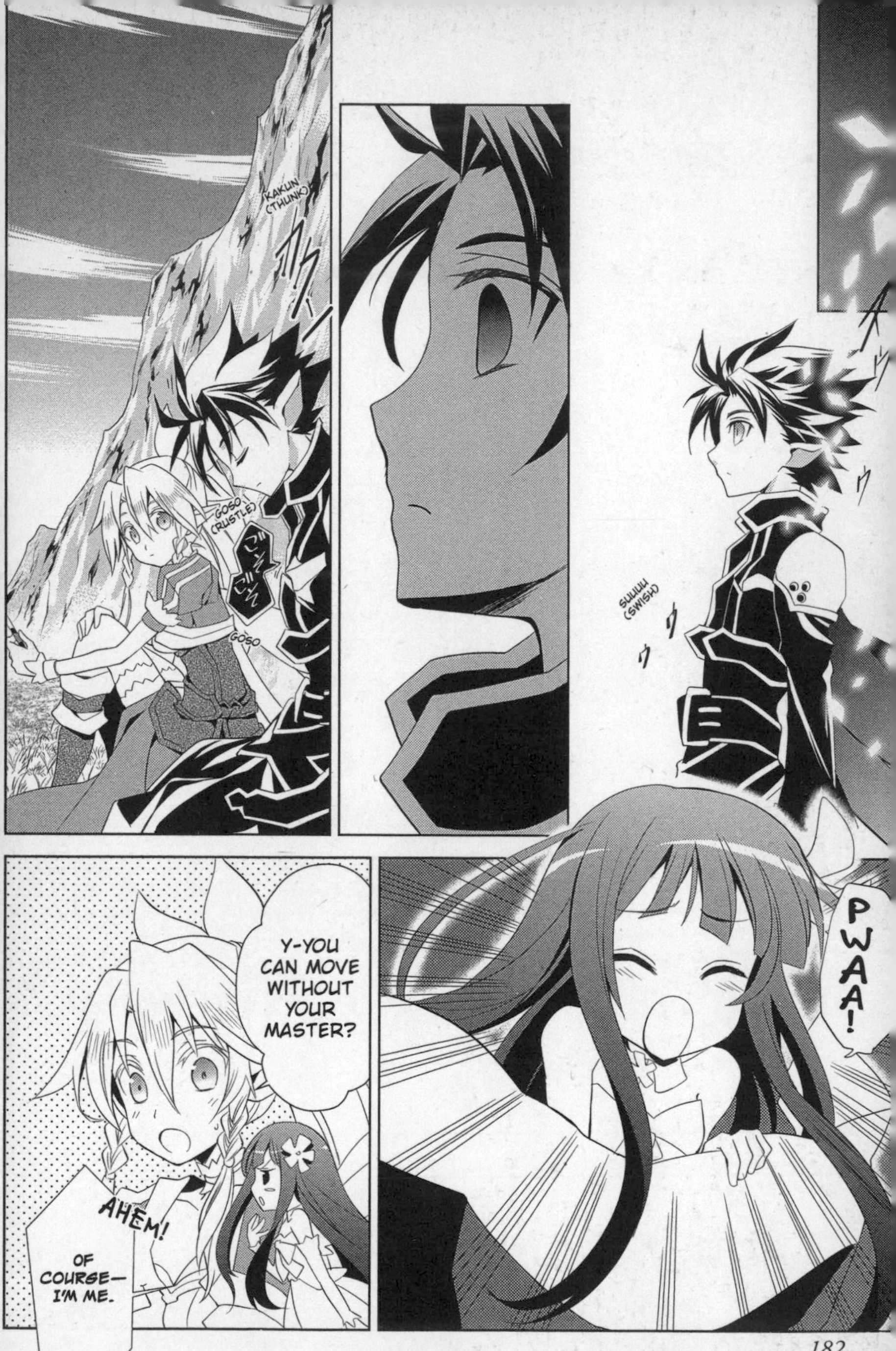
SUUUU (SWISH)
KAKUN (THUNK)
GOSO (RUSTLE)
GOSO
PWAA!
Y-YOU CAN MOVE WITHOUT YOUR MASTER?
AHEM!
OF COURSE— I'M ME.

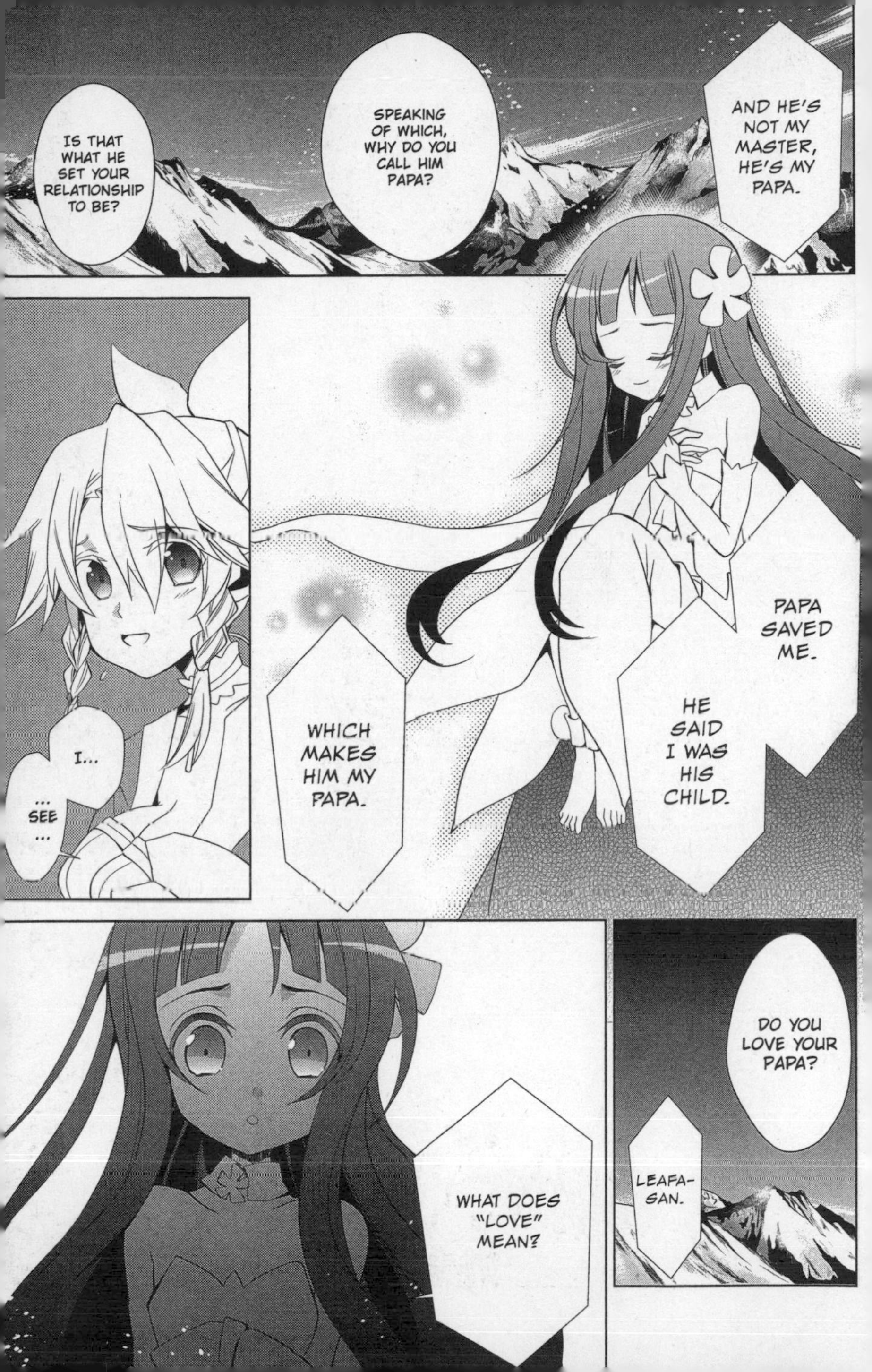
AND HE'S NOT MY MASTER, HE'S MY PAPA.
SPEAKING OF WHICH, WHY DO YOU CALL HIM PAPA?
IS THAT WHAT HE SET YOUR RELATIONSHIP TO BE?
PAPA SAVED ME.
HE SAID I WAS HIS CHILD.
WHICH MAKES HIM MY PAPA.
I... ...SEE...
DO YOU LOVE YOUR PAPA?
LEAFA-SAN.
WHAT DOES "LOVE" MEAN?

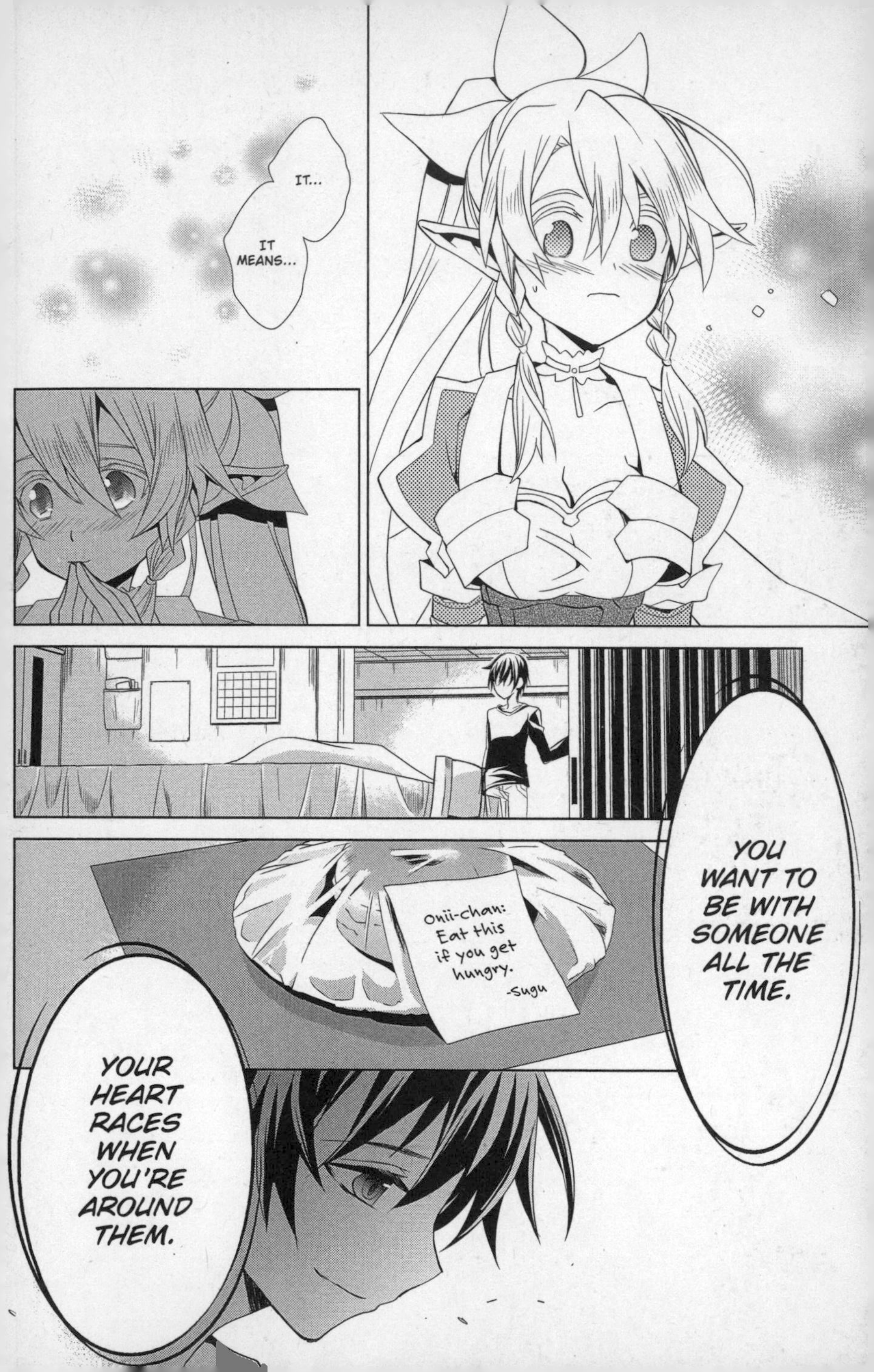
IT...
IT MEANS...
YOU WANT TO BE WITH SOMEONE ALL THE TIME.
Onii-chan: Eat this if you get hungry. -Sugu
YOUR HEART RACES WHEN YOU'RE AROUND THEM.

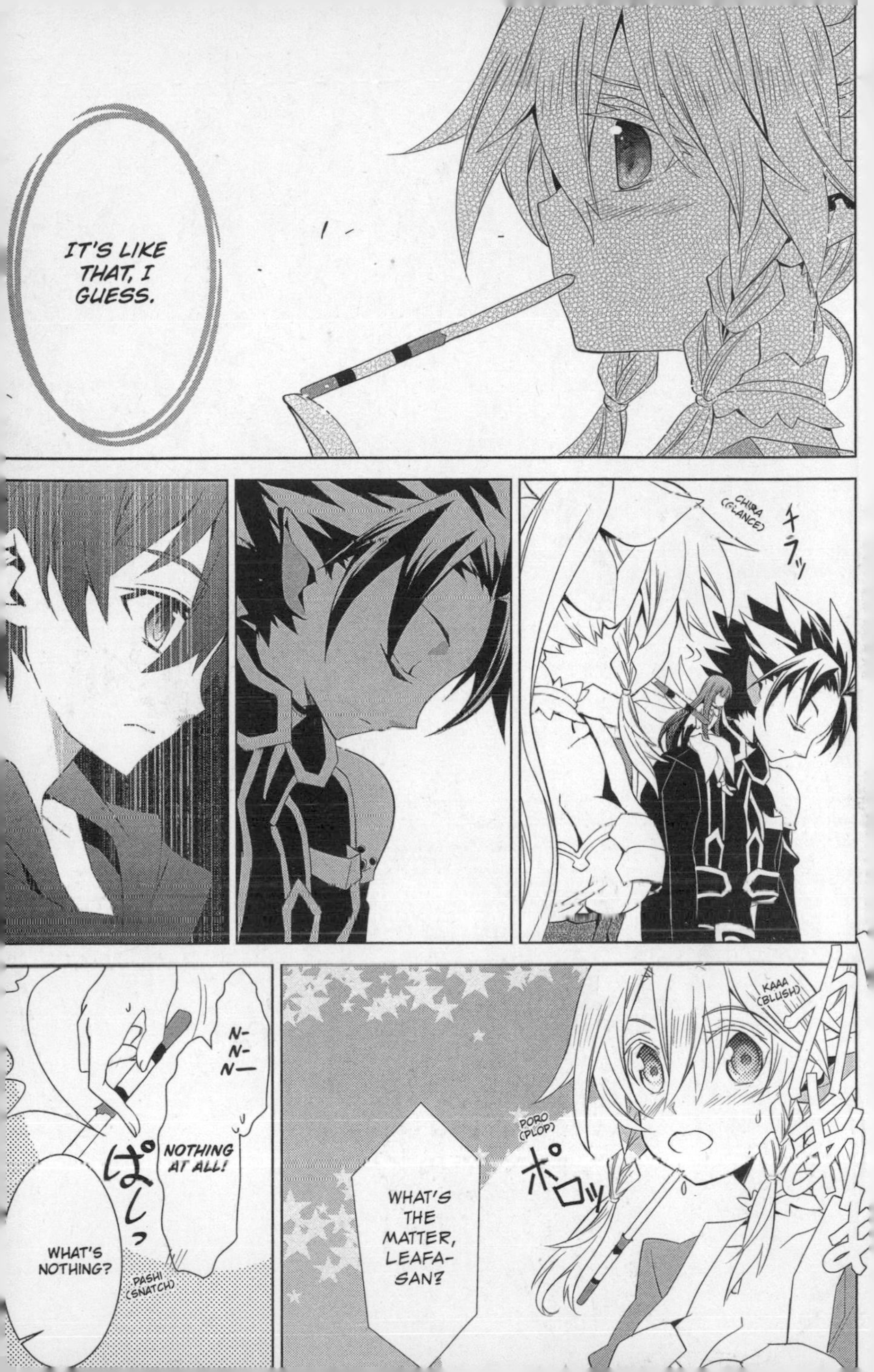
IT'S LIKE THAT, I GUESS.
CHIRA (GLANCE)
チラッ
KAAA (BLUSH)
PORO (PLOP)
ポロッ
WHAT'S THE MATTER, LEAFA-SAN?
N-N-N—
NOTHING AT ALL!
ぱしっ
PASHI (SNATCH)
WHAT'S NOTHING?

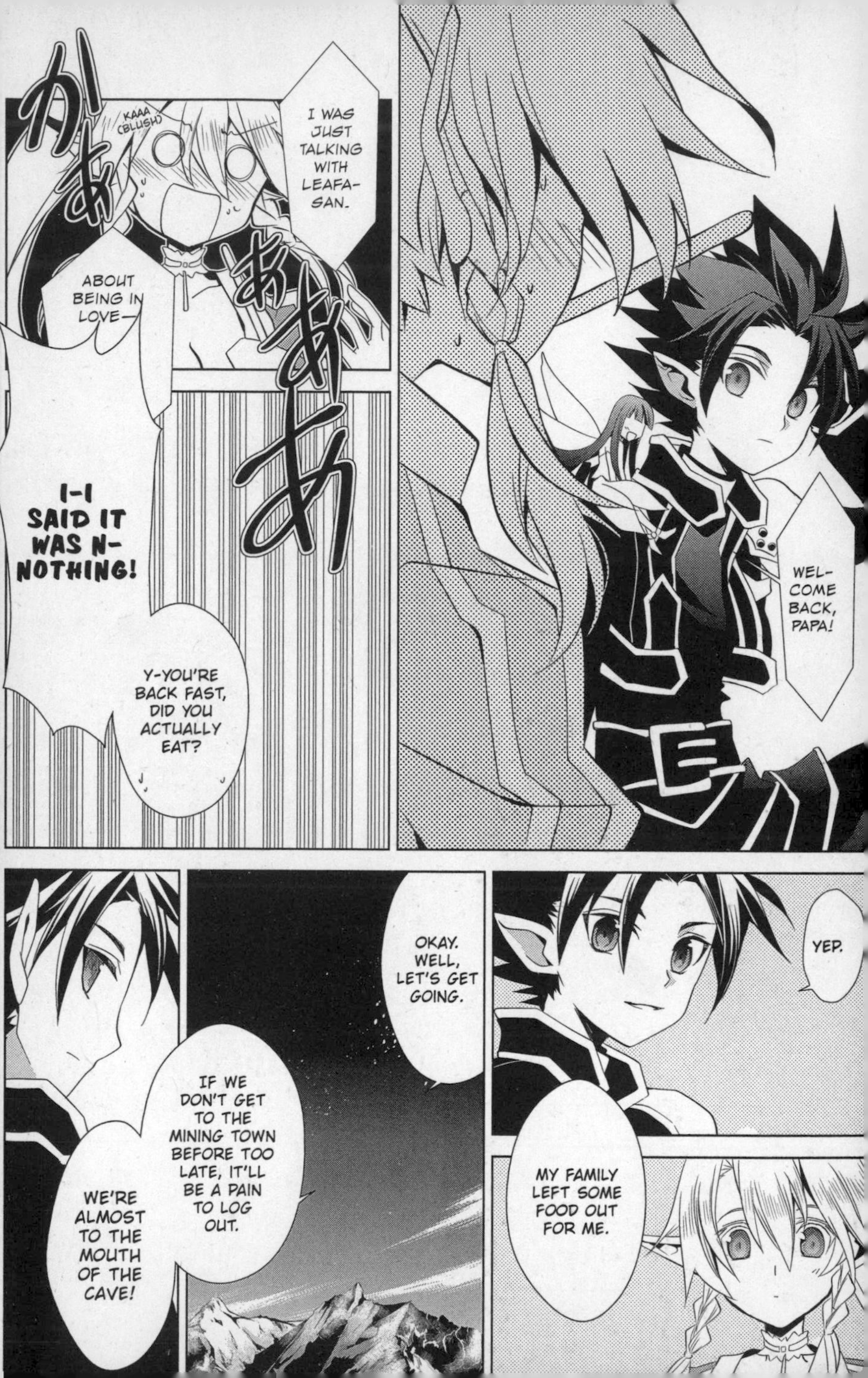
WEL-COME BACK, PAPA!
I WAS JUST TALKING WITH LEAFA-SAN.
KAAA (BLUSH)
ABOUT BEING IN LOVE—
I-I SAID IT WAS N-NOTHING!
Y-YOU'RE BACK FAST, DID YOU ACTUALLY EAT?
YEP.
MY FAMILY LEFT SOME FOOD OUT FOR ME.
OKAY. WELL, LET'S GET GOING.
IF WE DON'T GET TO THE MINING TOWN BEFORE TOO LATE, IT'LL BE A PAIN TO LOG OUT.
WE'RE ALMOST TO THE MOUTH OF THE CAVE!

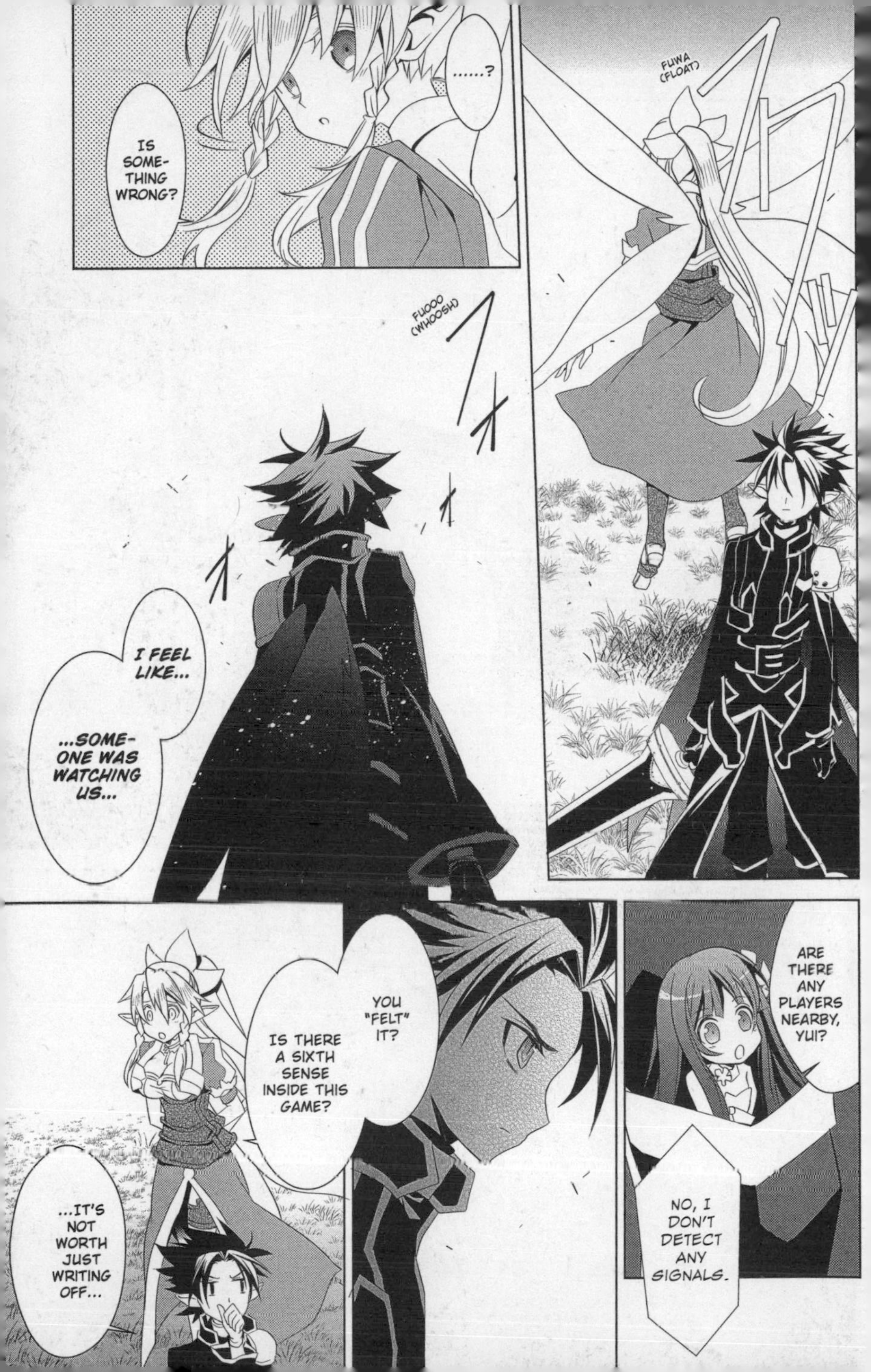

FUWA (FLOAT)
......?
IS SOMETHING WRONG?
FUOOO (WHOOSH)
I FEEL LIKE...
...SOMEONE WAS WATCHING US...
ARE THERE ANY PLAYERS NEARBY, YUI?
NO, I DON'T DETECT ANY SIGNALS.
YOU "FELT" IT?
IS THERE A SIXTH SENSE INSIDE THIS GAME?
...IT'S NOT WORTH JUST WRITING OFF...

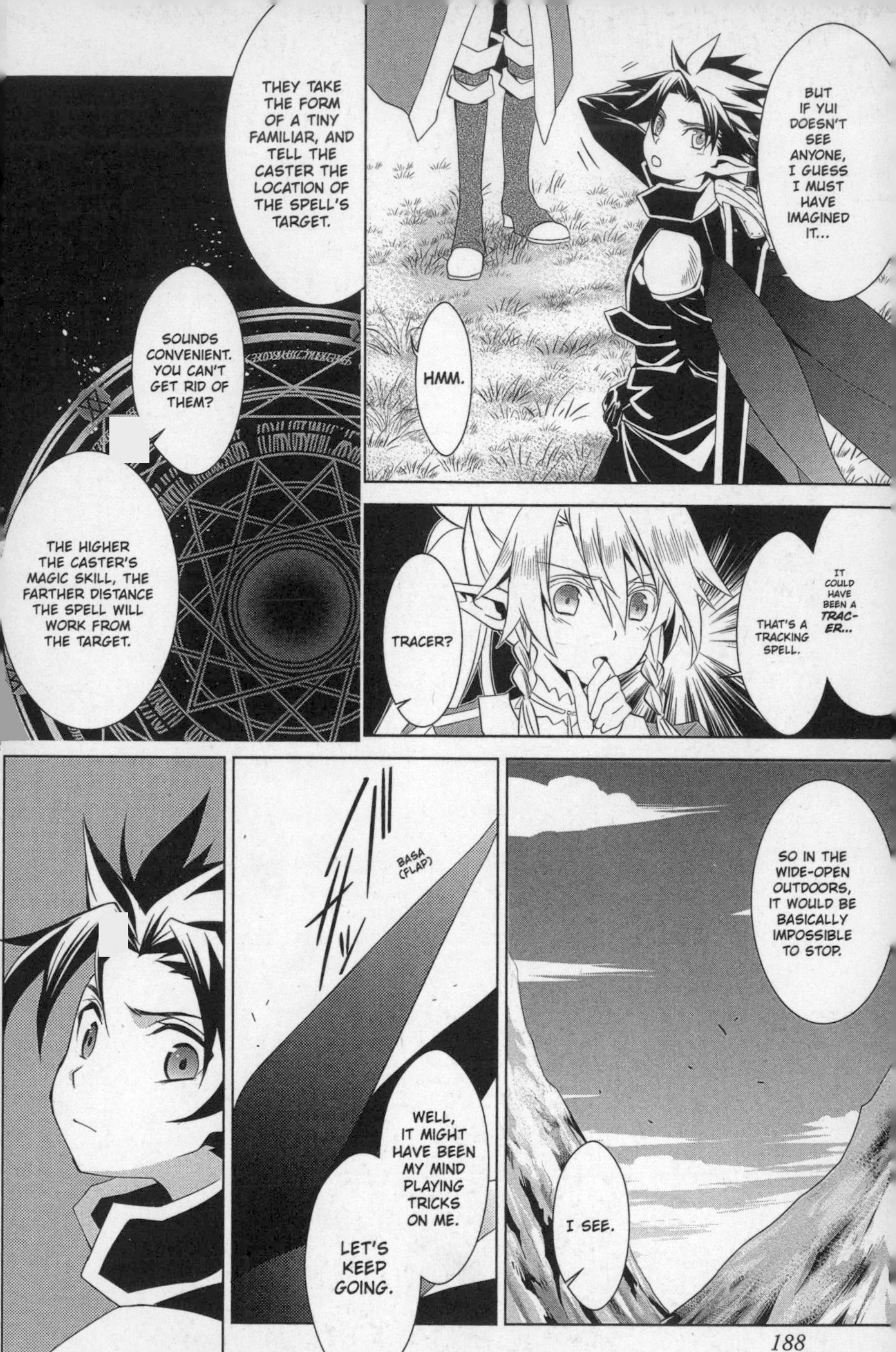
BUT IF YUI DOESN'T SEE ANYONE, I GUESS I MUST HAVE IMAGINED IT...
HMM.
IT COULD HAVE BEEN A TRACER...
THAT'S A TRACKING SPELL.
TRACER?
THEY TAKE THE FORM OF A TINY FAMILIAR, AND TELL THE CASTER THE LOCATION OF THE SPELL'S TARGET.
SOUNDS CONVENIENT. YOU CAN'T GET RID OF THEM?
THE HIGHER THE CASTER'S MAGIC SKILL, THE FARTHER DISTANCE THE SPELL WILL WORK FROM THE TARGET.
SO IN THE WIDE-OPEN OUTDOORS, IT WOULD BE BASICALLY IMPOSSIBLE TO STOP.
I SEE.
BASA (FLAP)
WELL, IT MIGHT HAVE BEEN MY MIND PLAYING TRICKS ON ME.
LET'S KEEP GOING.

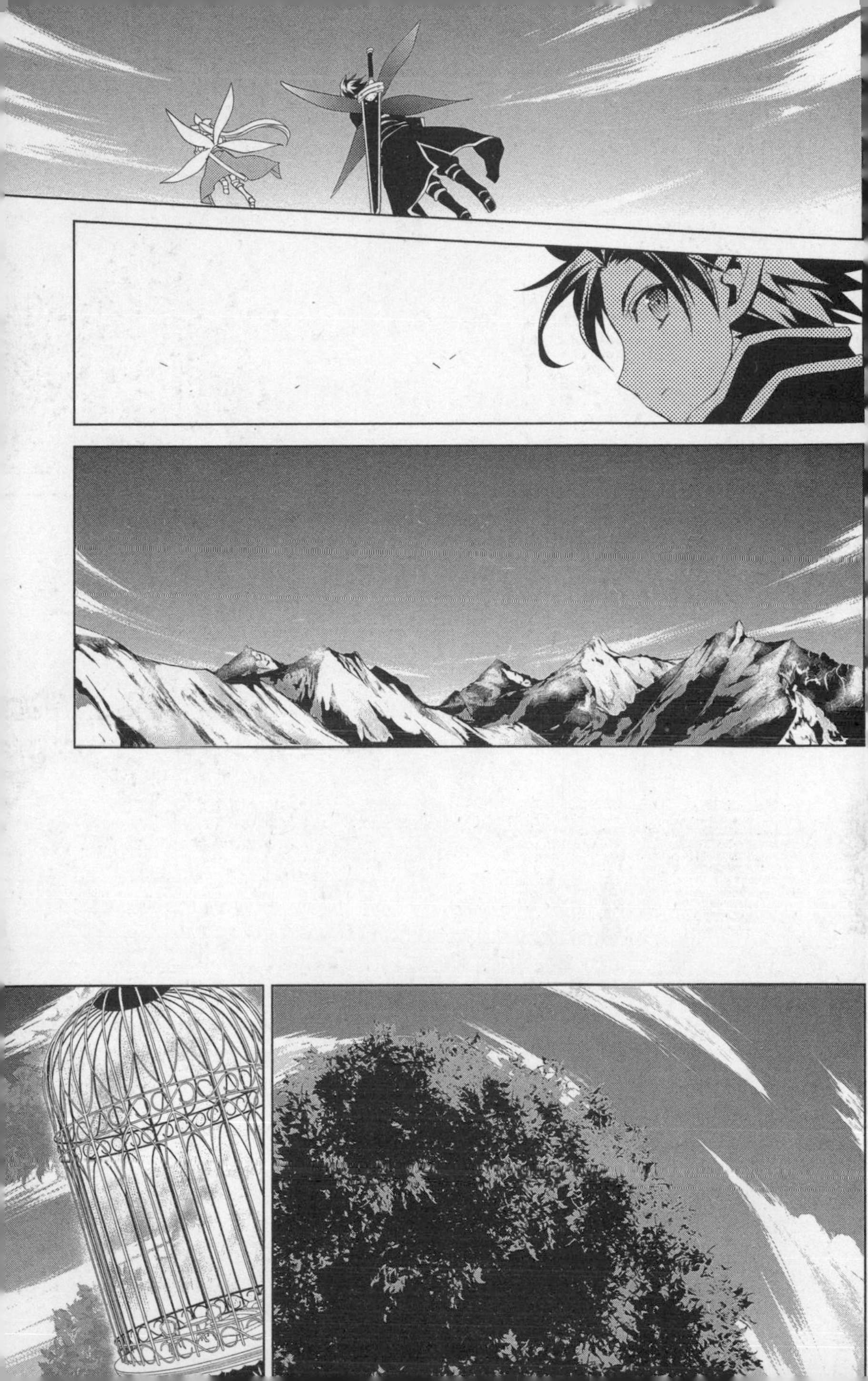

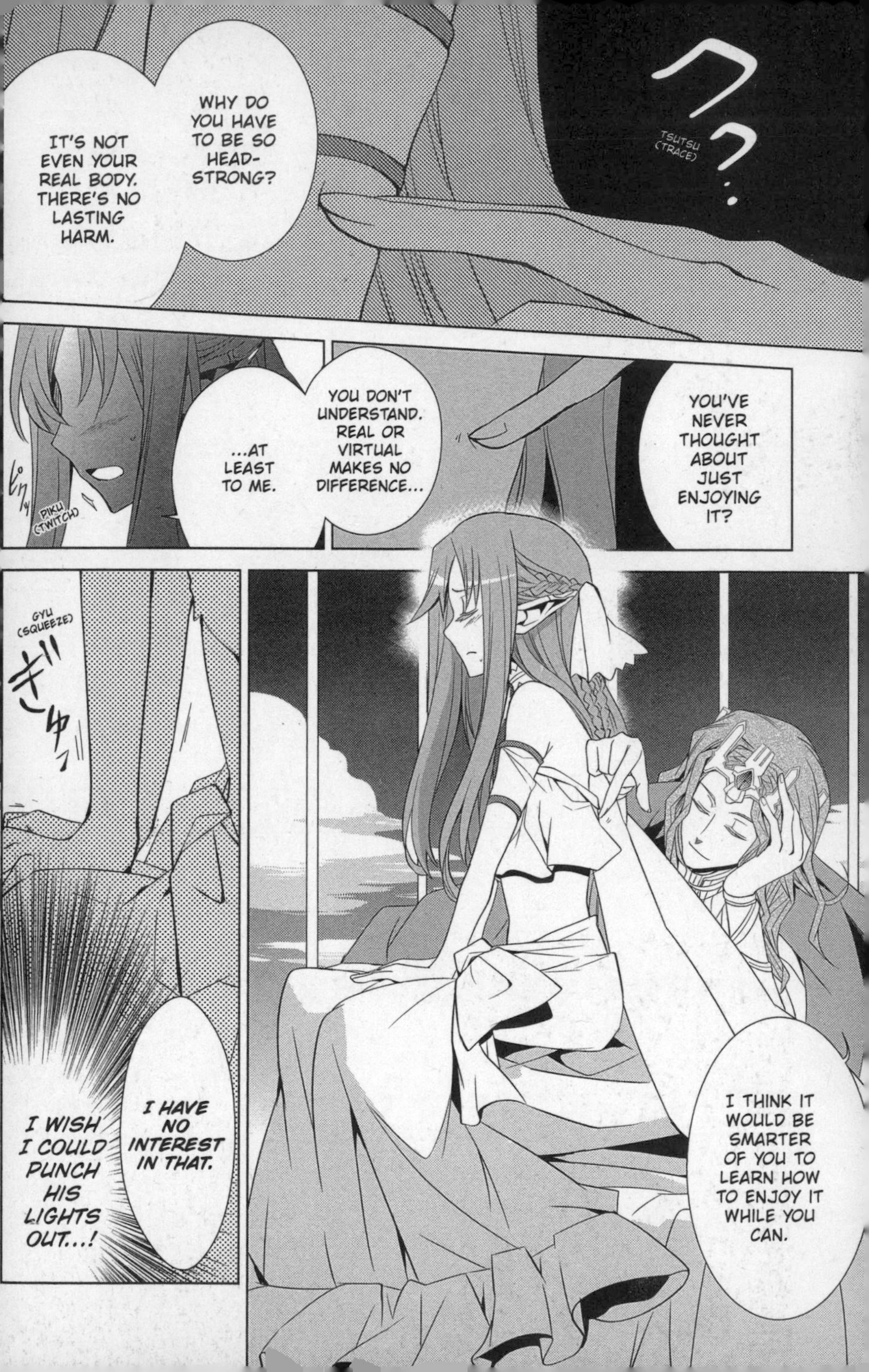
TSUTSU (TRACE)
WHY DO YOU HAVE TO BE SO HEAD-STRONG?
IT'S NOT EVEN YOUR REAL BODY. THERE'S NO LASTING HARM.
YOU'VE NEVER THOUGHT ABOUT JUST ENJOYING IT?
YOU DON'T UNDERSTAND. REAL OR VIRTUAL MAKES NO DIFFERENCE...
...AT LEAST TO ME.
PIKU (TWITCH)
I THINK IT WOULD BE SMARTER OF YOU TO LEARN HOW TO ENJOY IT WHILE YOU CAN.
GYU (SQUEEZE)
I HAVE NO INTEREST IN THAT.
I WISH I COULD PUNCH HIS LIGHTS OUT...!

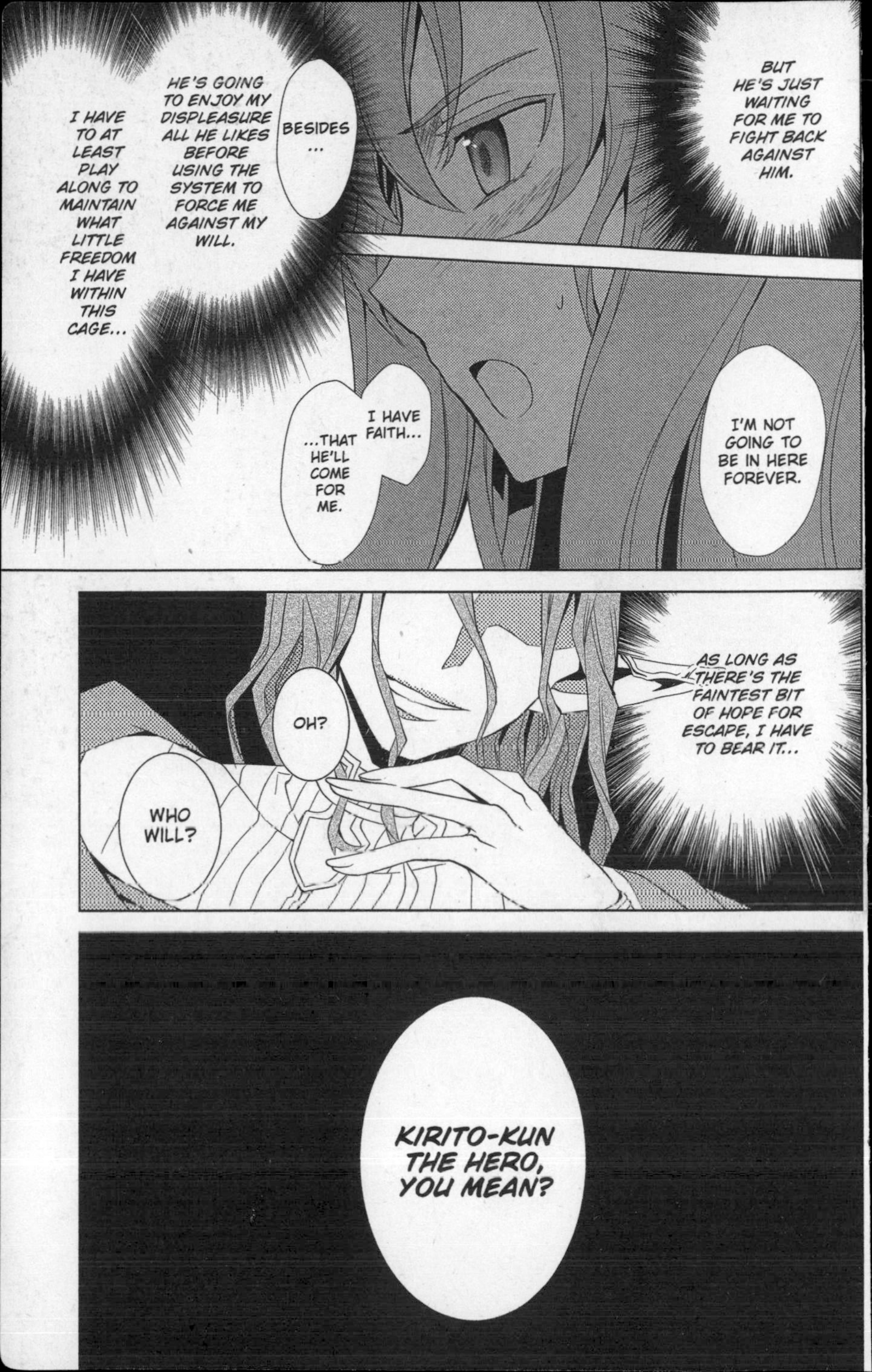
BUT HE'S JUST WAITING FOR ME TO FIGHT BACK AGAINST HIM.
BESIDES...
HE'S GOING TO ENJOY MY DISPLEASURE ALL HE LIKES BEFORE USING THE SYSTEM TO FORCE ME AGAINST MY WILL.
I HAVE TO AT LEAST PLAY ALONG TO MAINTAIN WHAT LITTLE FREEDOM I HAVE WITHIN THIS CAGE...
I'M NOT GOING TO BE IN HERE FOREVER.
I HAVE FAITH...
...THAT HE'LL COME FOR ME.
AS LONG AS THERE'S THE FAINTEST BIT OF HOPE FOR ESCAPE, I HAVE TO BEAR IT...
OH?
WHO WILL?
KIRITO-KUN THE HERO, YOU MEAN?

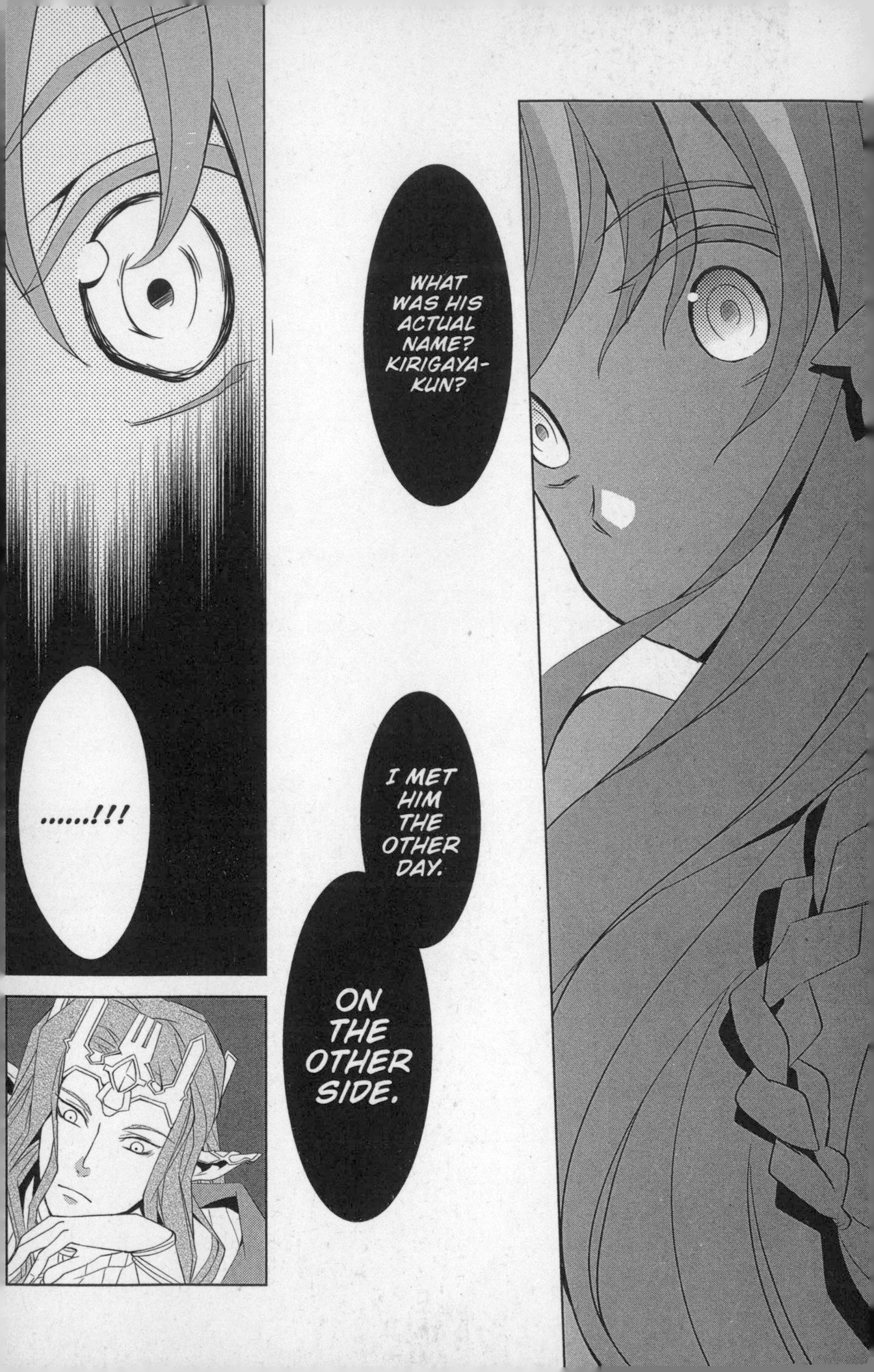
WHAT WAS HIS ACTUAL NAME? KIRIGAYA-KUN?
I MET HIM THE OTHER DAY.
ON THE OTHER SIDE.
......!!!

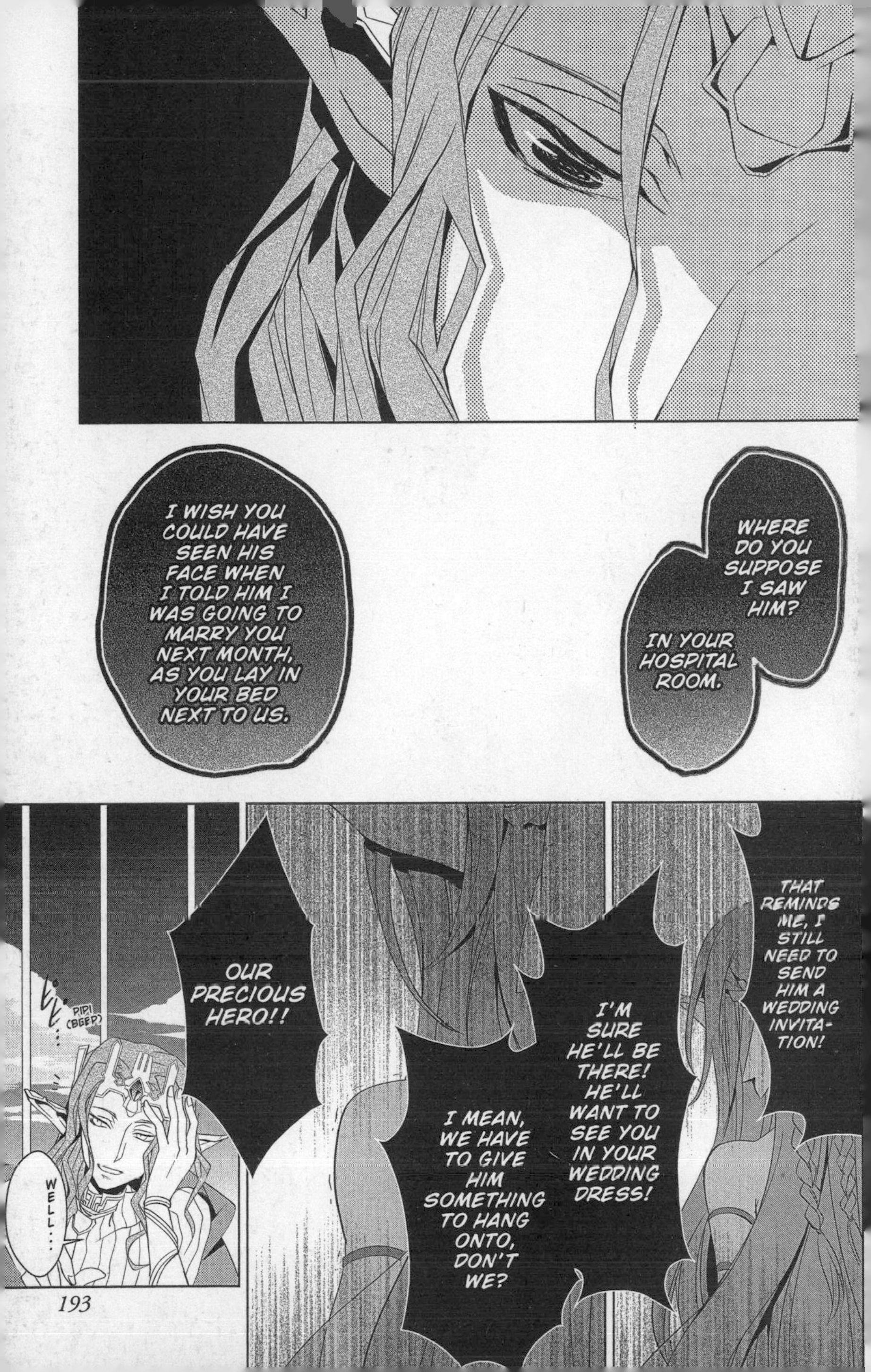
WHERE DO YOU SUPPOSE I SAW HIM?
IN YOUR HOSPITAL ROOM.
I WISH YOU COULD HAVE SEEN HIS FACE WHEN I TOLD HIM I WAS GOING TO MARRY YOU NEXT MONTH, AS YOU LAY IN YOUR BED NEXT TO US.
THAT REMINDS ME, I STILL NEED TO SEND HIM A WEDDING INVITATION!
I'M SURE HE'LL BE THERE! HE'LL WANT TO SEE YOU IN YOUR WEDDING DRESS!
I MEAN, WE HAVE TO GIVE HIM SOMETHING TO HANG ONTO, DON'T WE?
OUR PRECIOUS HERO!!
PIPI (BEEP)
WELL...

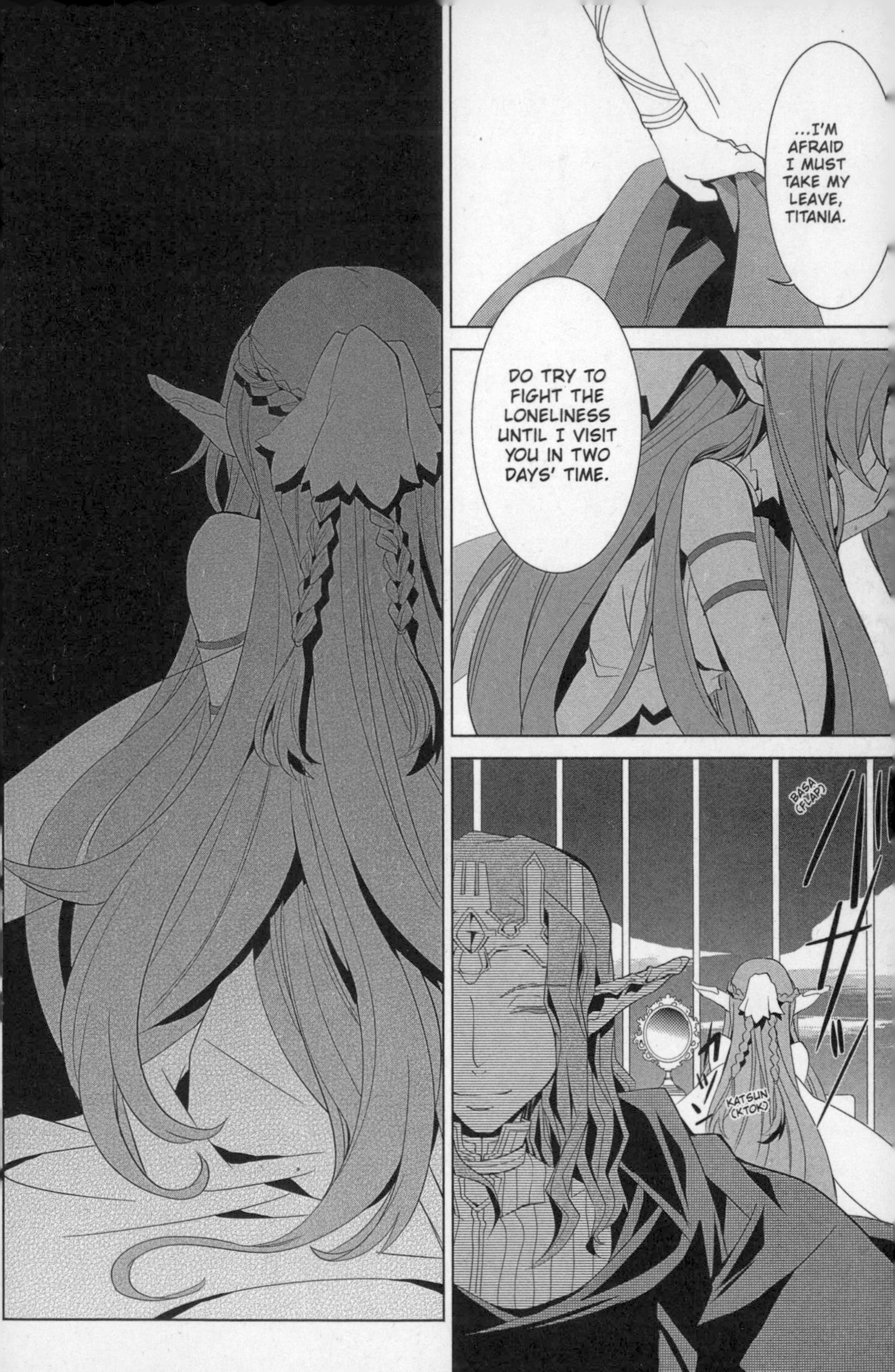
...I'M AFRAID I MUST TAKE MY LEAVE, TITANIA.
DO TRY TO FIGHT THE LONELINESS UNTIL I VISIT YOU IN TWO DAYS' TIME.
BASA (FLAP)
KATSUN (KTOK)

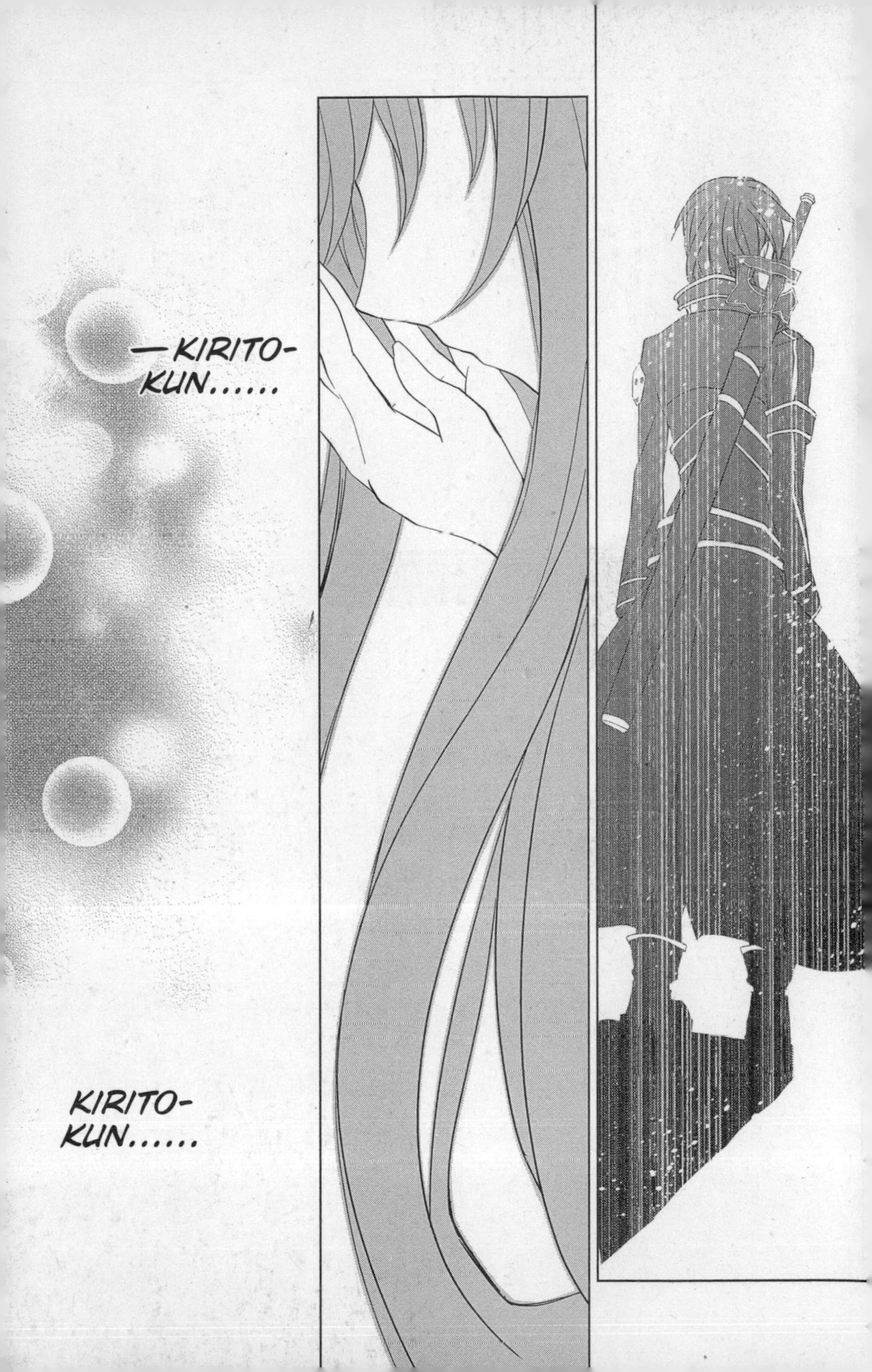
—KIRITO-KUN......
KIRITO-KUN......

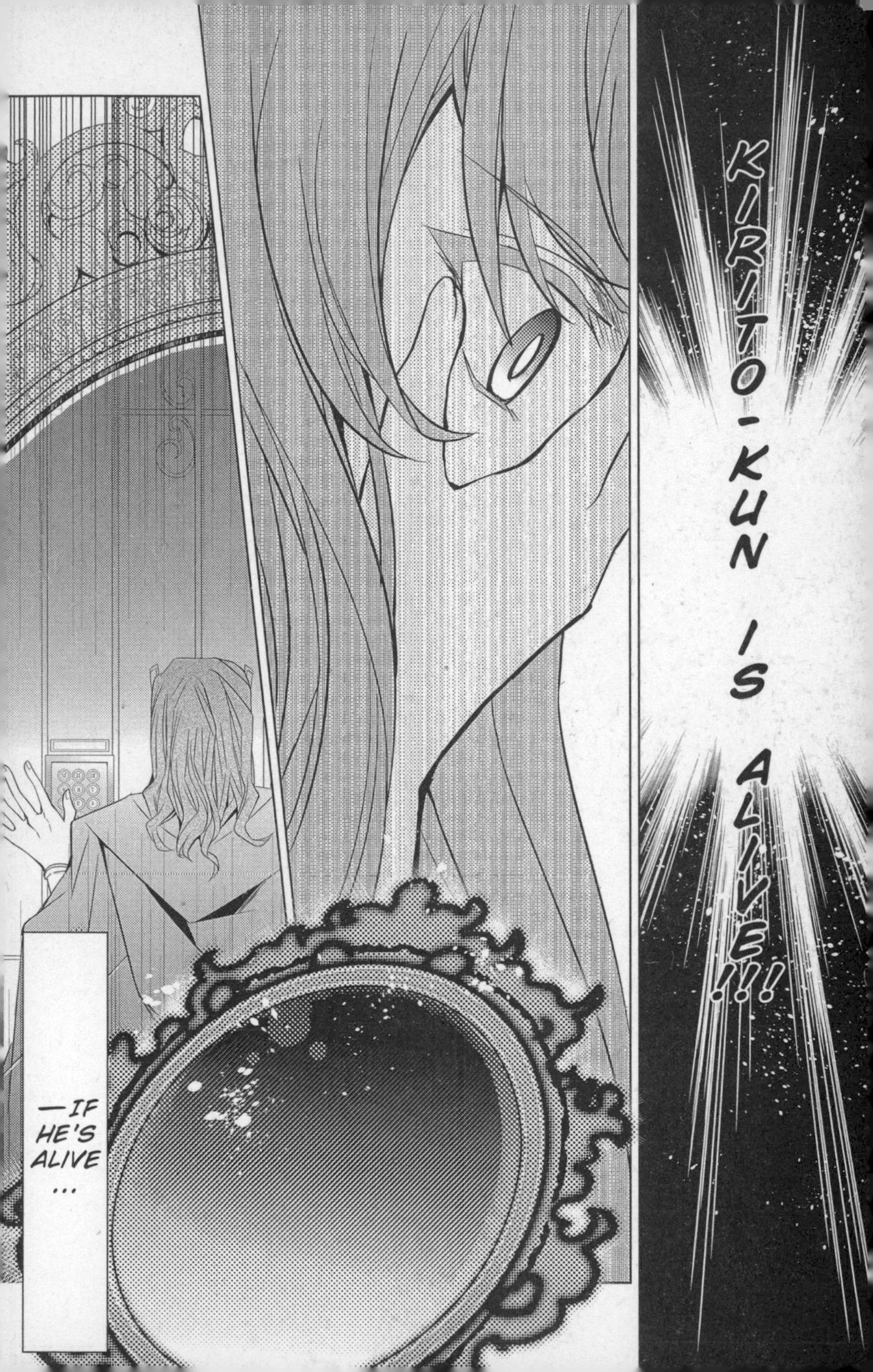
KIRITO-KUN IS ALIVE!!!
—IF HE'S ALIVE ...

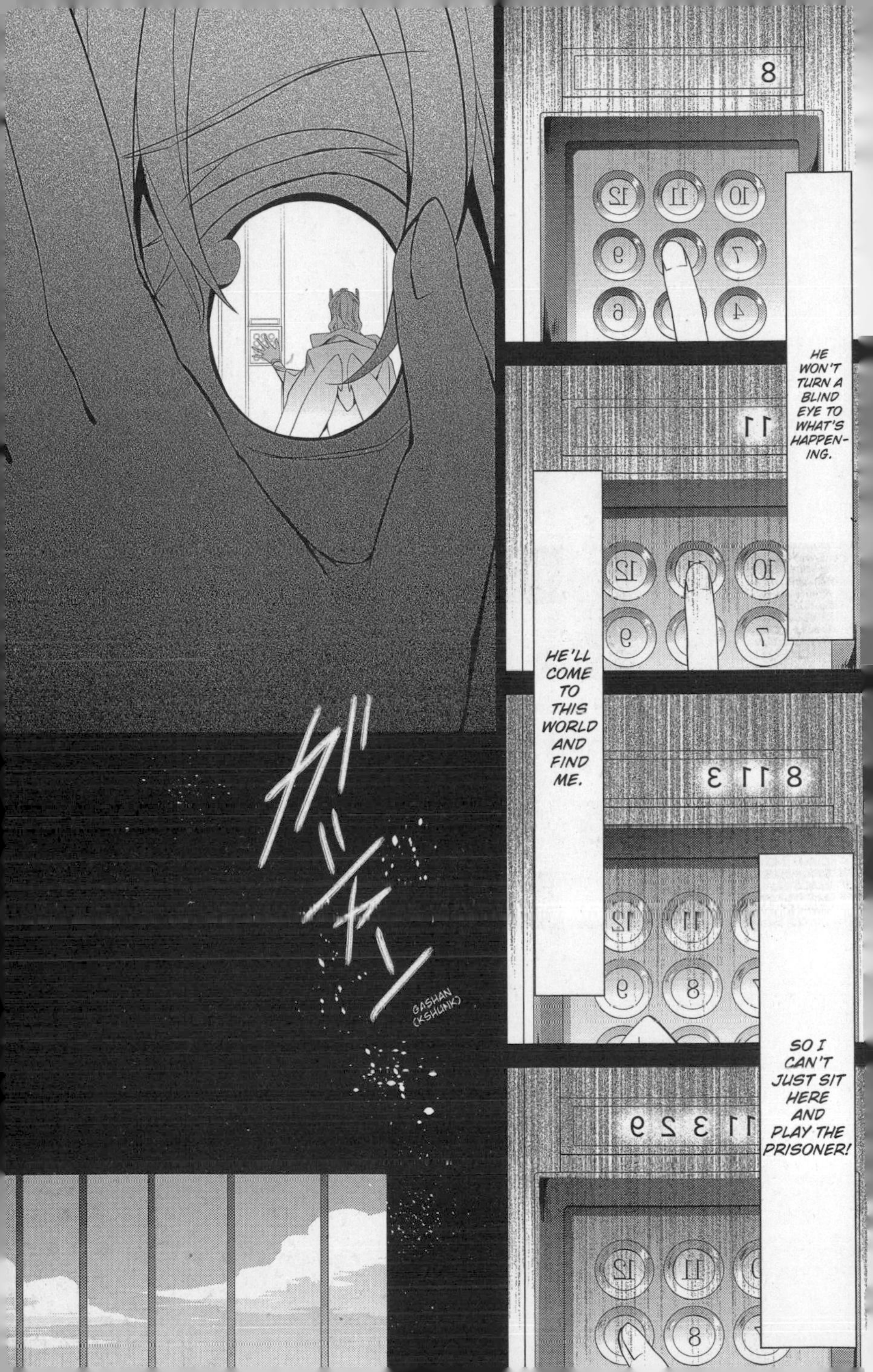
HE WON'T TURN A BLIND EYE TO WHAT'S HAPPEN-ING.
HE'LL COME TO THIS WORLD AND FIND ME.
SO I CAN'T JUST SIT HERE AND PLAY THE PRISONER!
GASHAN (KSHUNK)

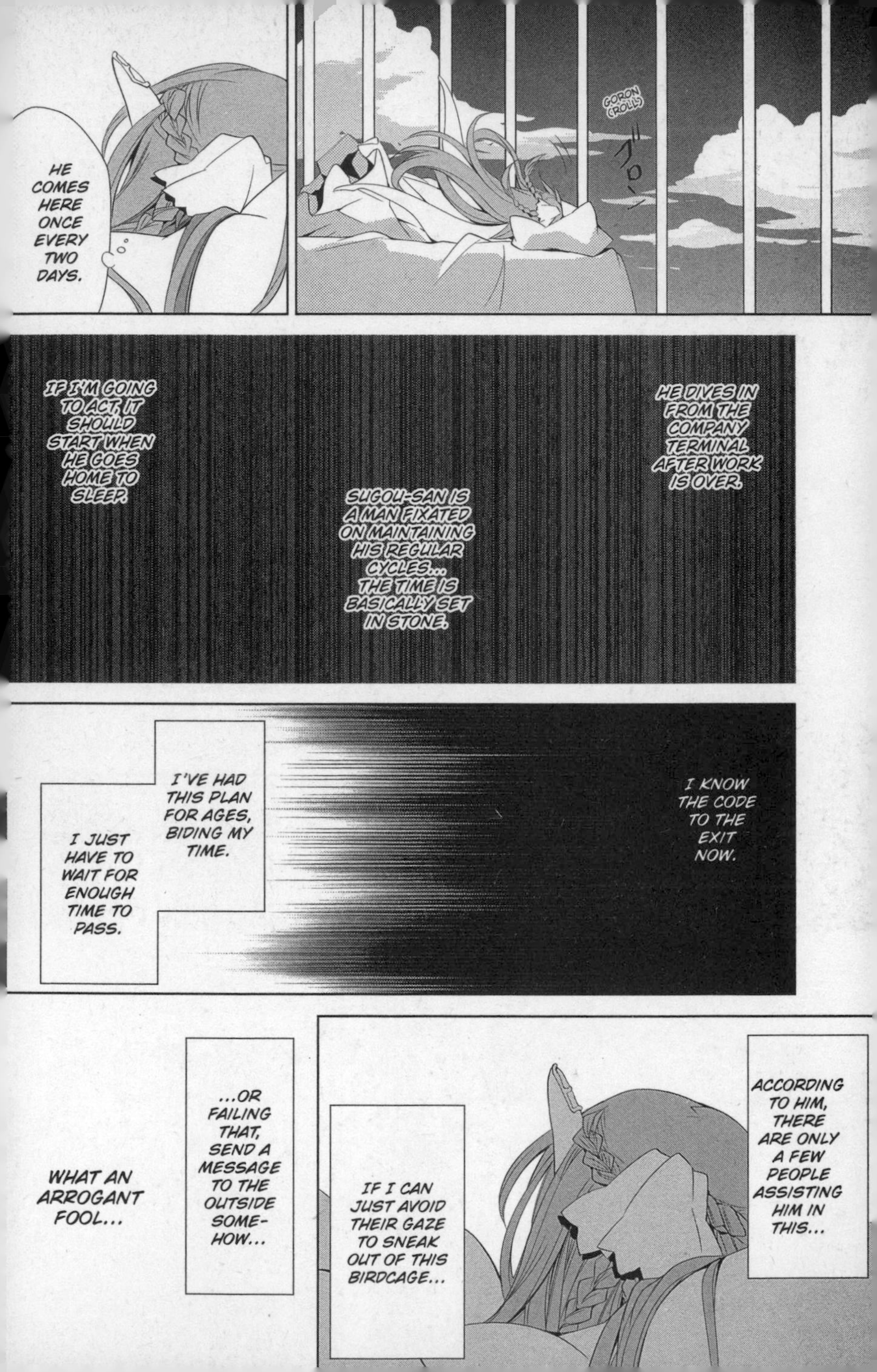
GORON (ROLL)
HE COMES HERE ONCE EVERY TWO DAYS.
HE DIVES IN FROM THE COMPANY TERMINAL AFTER WORK IS OVER.
SUGOU-SAN IS A MAN FIXATED ON MAINTAINING HIS REGULAR CYCLES... THE TIME IS BASICALLY SET IN STONE.
IF I'M GOING TO ACT, IT SHOULD START WHEN HE GOES HOME TO SLEEP.
I KNOW THE CODE TO THE EXIT NOW.
I'VE HAD THIS PLAN FOR AGES, BIDING MY TIME.
I JUST HAVE TO WAIT FOR ENOUGH TIME TO PASS.
ACCORDING TO HIM, THERE ARE ONLY A FEW PEOPLE ASSISTING HIM IN THIS...
IF I CAN JUST AVOID THEIR GAZE TO SNEAK OUT OF THIS BIRDCAGE...
...OR FAILING THAT, SEND A MESSAGE TO THE OUTSIDE SOME-HOW...
WHAT AN ARROGANT FOOL...

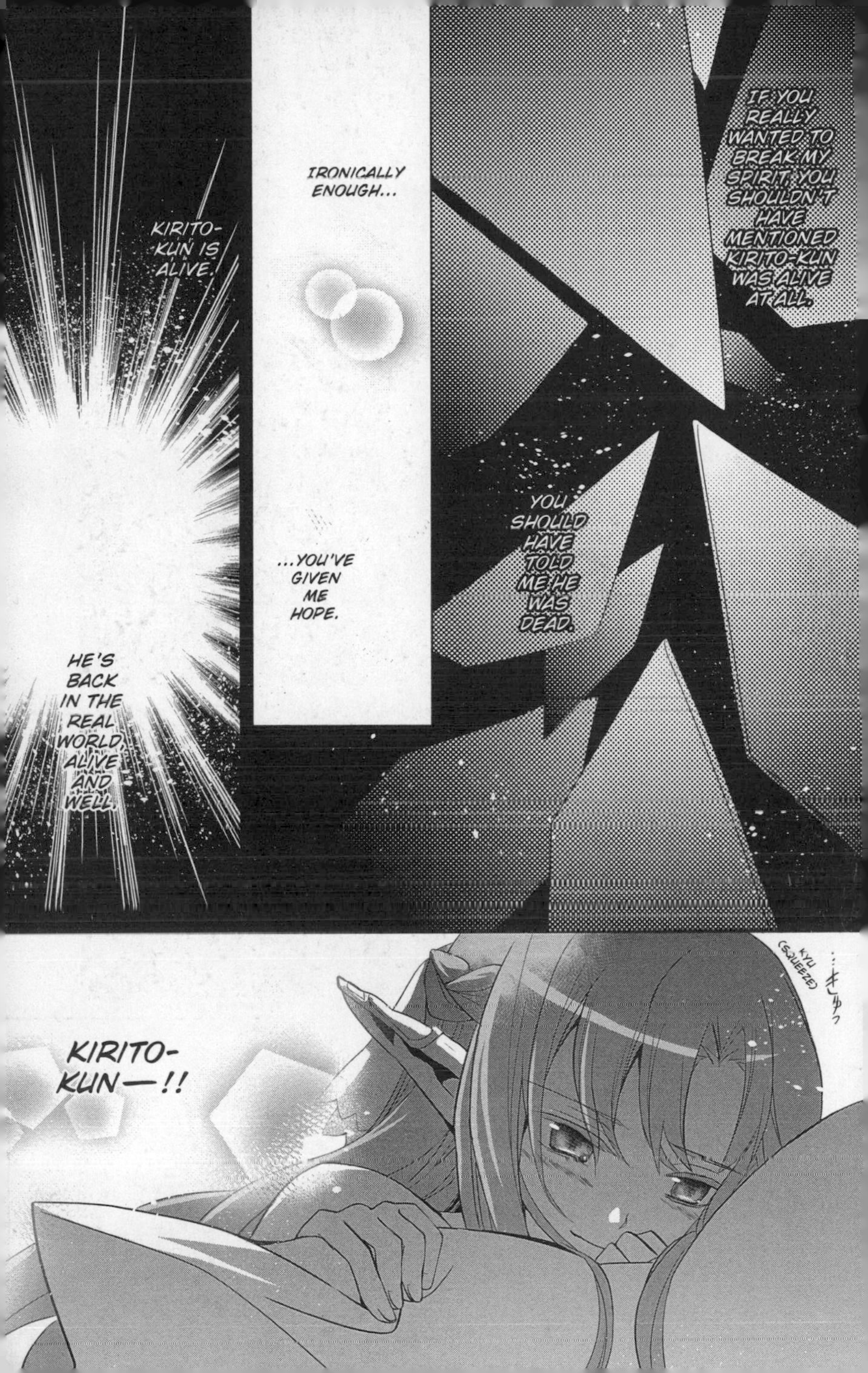
IF YOU REALLY WANTED TO BREAK MY SPIRIT, YOU SHOULDN'T HAVE MENTIONED KIRITO-KUN WAS ALIVE AT ALL.
YOU SHOULD HAVE TOLD ME HE WAS DEAD.
IRONICALLY ENOUGH...
...YOU'VE GIVEN ME HOPE.
KIRITO-KUN IS ALIVE.
HE'S BACK IN THE REAL WORLD, ALIVE AND WELL.
...キュッ
KYU (SQUEEZE)
KIRITO-KUN—!!

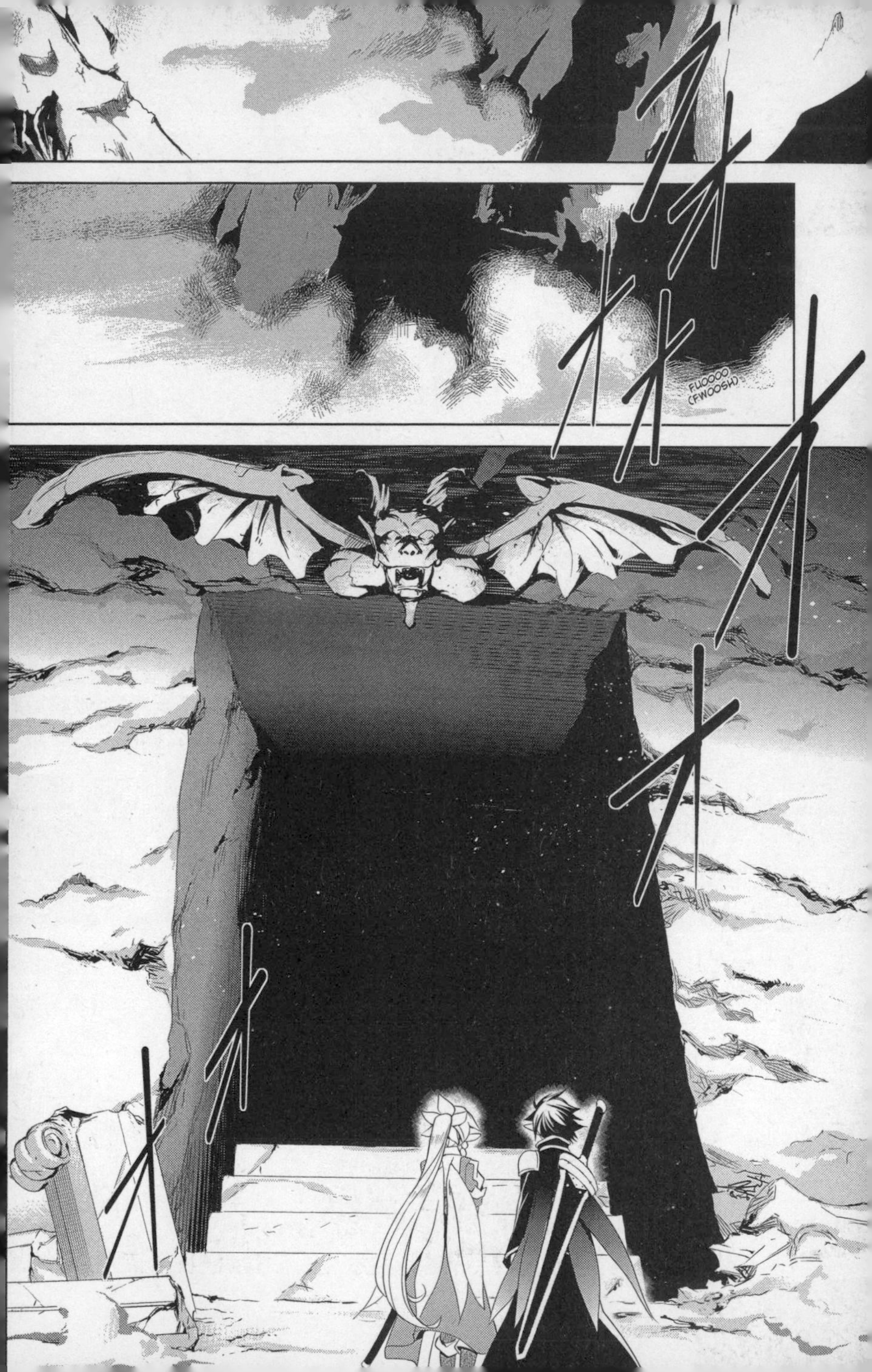
FUOOOO
(FWOOSH)

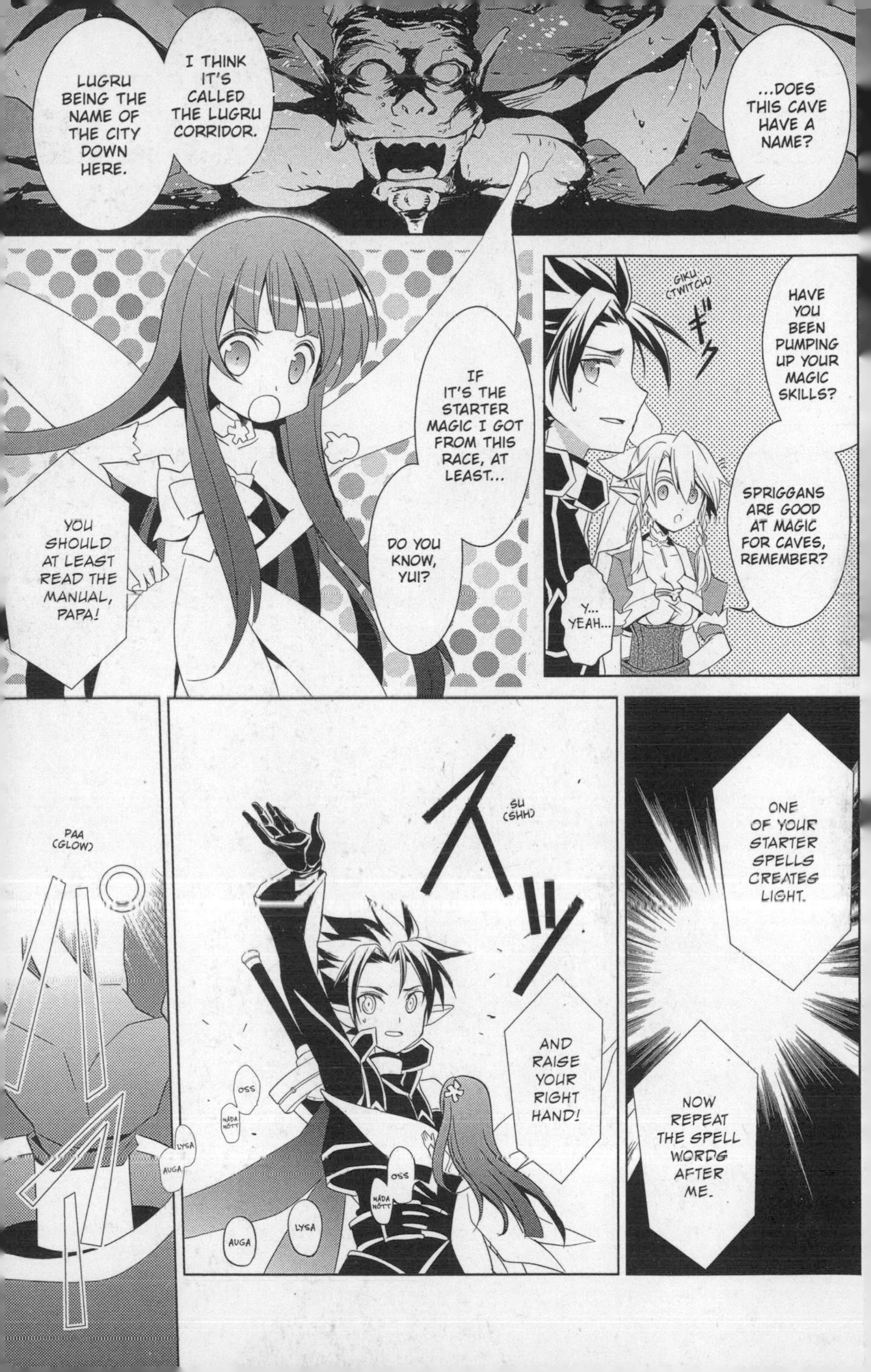
...DOES THIS CAVE HAVE A NAME?
I THINK IT'S CALLED THE LUGRU CORRIDOR.
LUGRU BEING THE NAME OF THE CITY DOWN HERE.
GIKU (TWITCH)
HAVE YOU BEEN PUMPING UP YOUR MAGIC SKILLS?
SPRIGGANS ARE GOOD AT MAGIC FOR CAVES, REMEMBER?
Y... YEAH...
IF IT'S THE STARTER MAGIC I GOT FROM THIS RACE, AT LEAST...
DO YOU KNOW, YUI?
YOU SHOULD AT LEAST READ THE MANUAL, PAPA!
ONE OF YOUR STARTER SPELLS CREATES LIGHT.
NOW REPEAT THE SPELL WORDS AFTER ME.
SU (SHH)
AND RAISE YOUR RIGHT HAND!
OSS
NÁDA NÓTT
LYSA
AUGA
OSS
NÁDA NÓTT
LYSA
AUGA
PAA (GLOW)

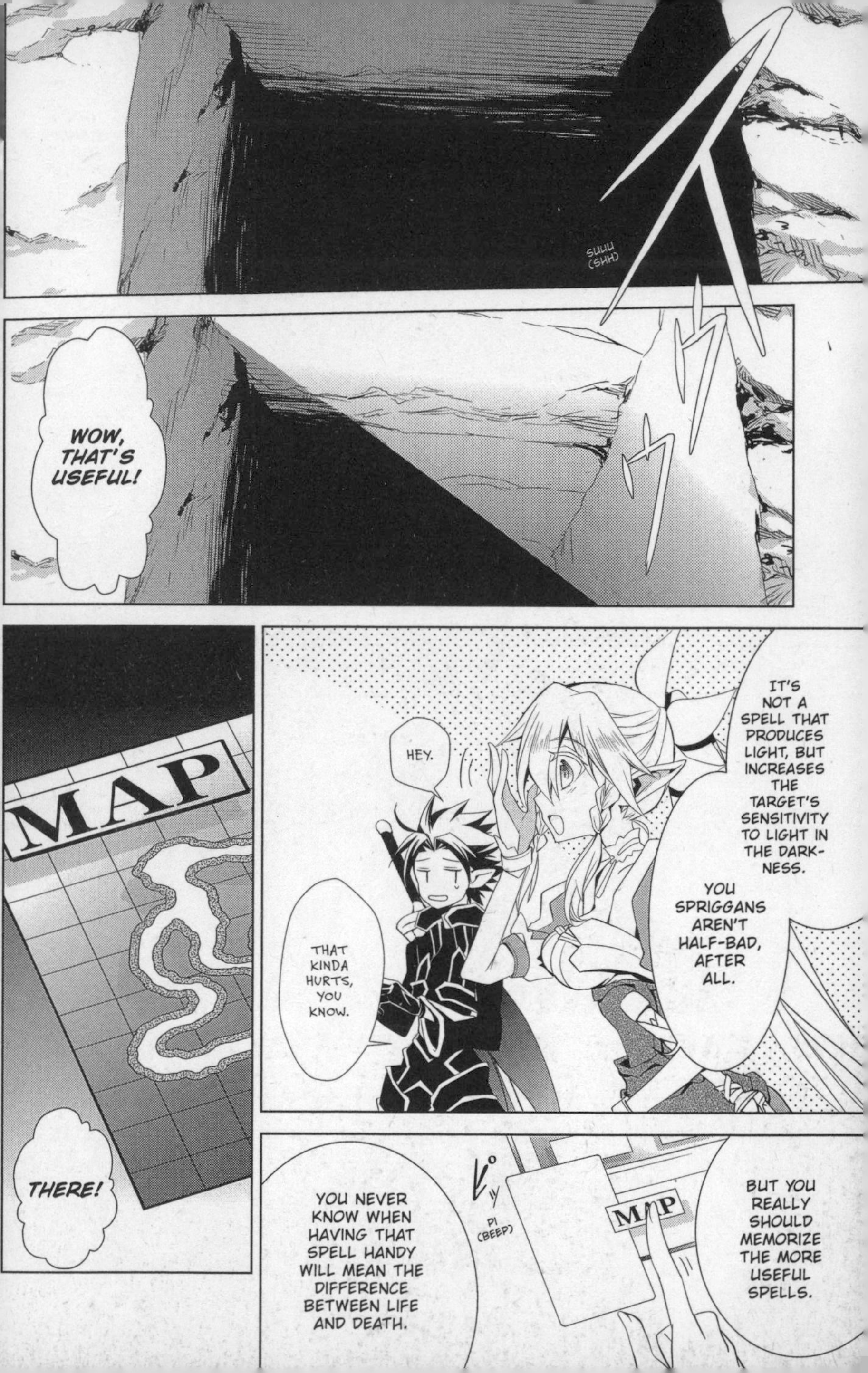
SUUU (SHH)
WOW, THAT'S USEFUL!
IT'S NOT A SPELL THAT PRODUCES LIGHT, BUT INCREASES THE TARGET'S SENSITIVITY TO LIGHT IN THE DARK-NESS.
YOU SPRIGGANS AREN'T HALF-BAD, AFTER ALL.
HEY.
THAT KINDA HURTS, YOU KNOW.
BUT YOU REALLY SHOULD MEMORIZE THE MORE USEFUL SPELLS.
MAP
PI (BEEP)
YOU NEVER KNOW WHEN HAVING THAT SPELL HANDY WILL MEAN THE DIFFERENCE BETWEEN LIFE AND DEATH.
MAP
THERE!

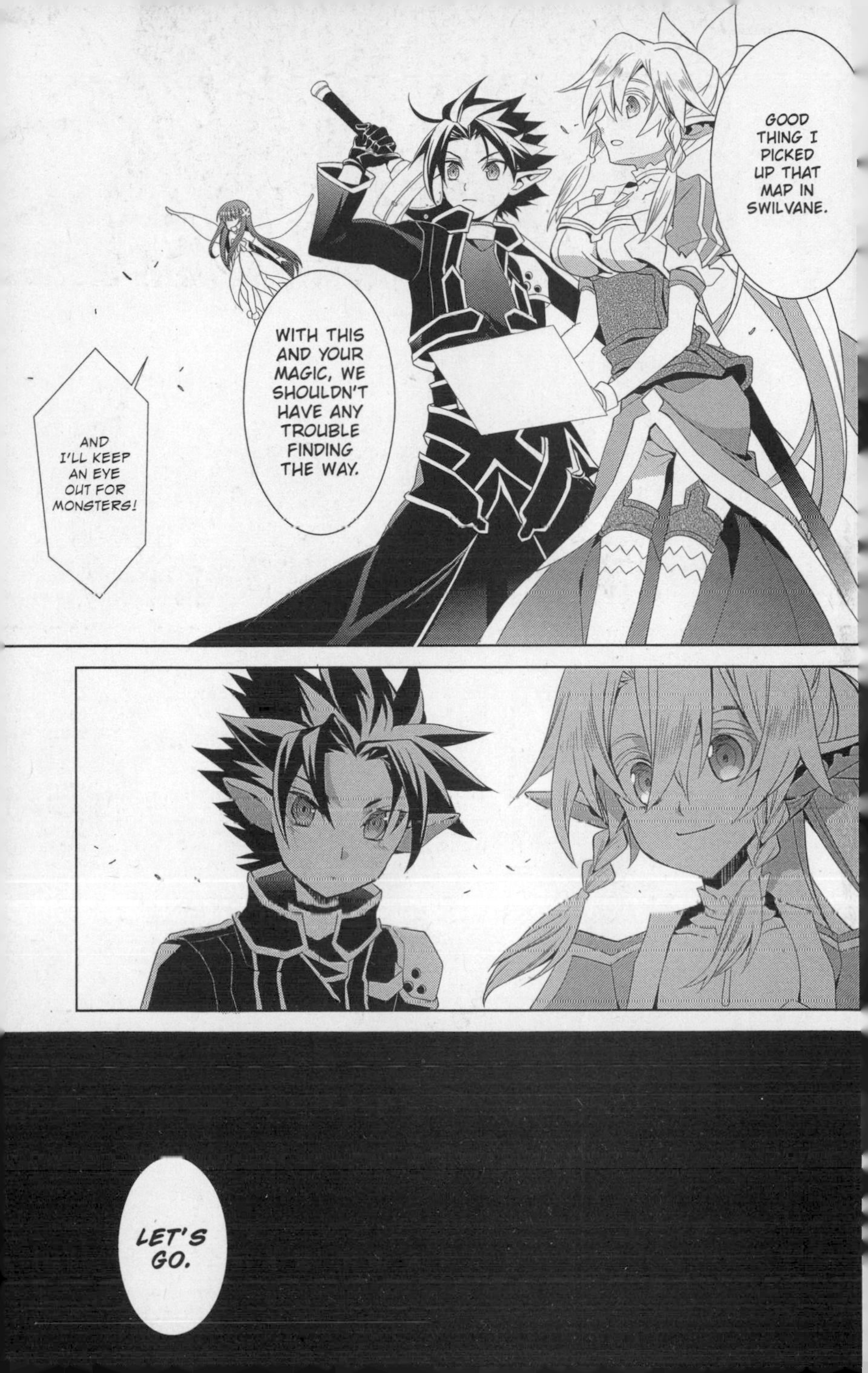
GOOD THING I PICKED UP THAT MAP IN SWILVANE.
WITH THIS AND YOUR MAGIC, WE SHOULDN'T HAVE ANY TROUBLE FINDING THE WAY.
AND I'LL KEEP AN EYE OUT FOR MONSTERS!
LET'S GO.

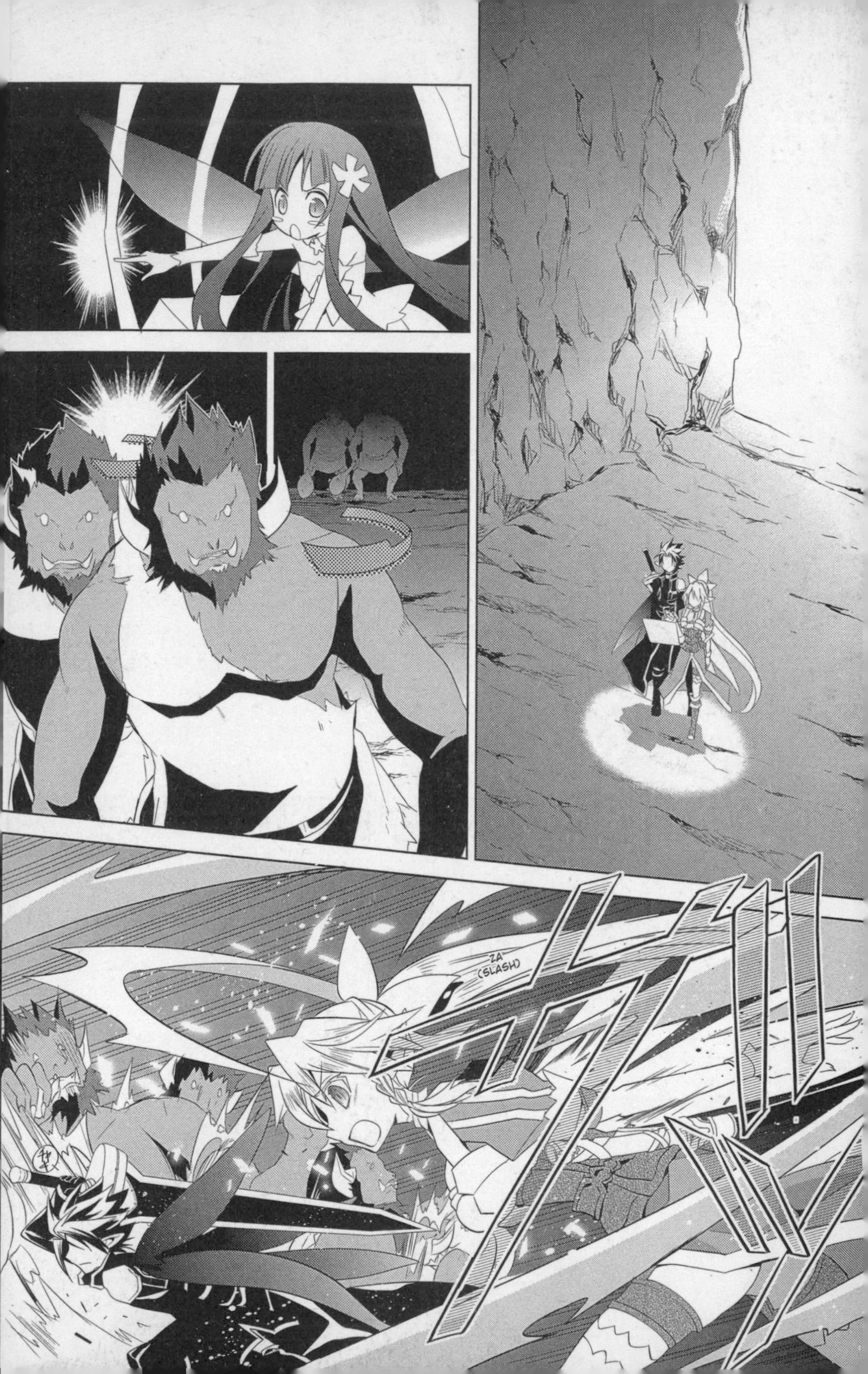
ZA
(SLASH)

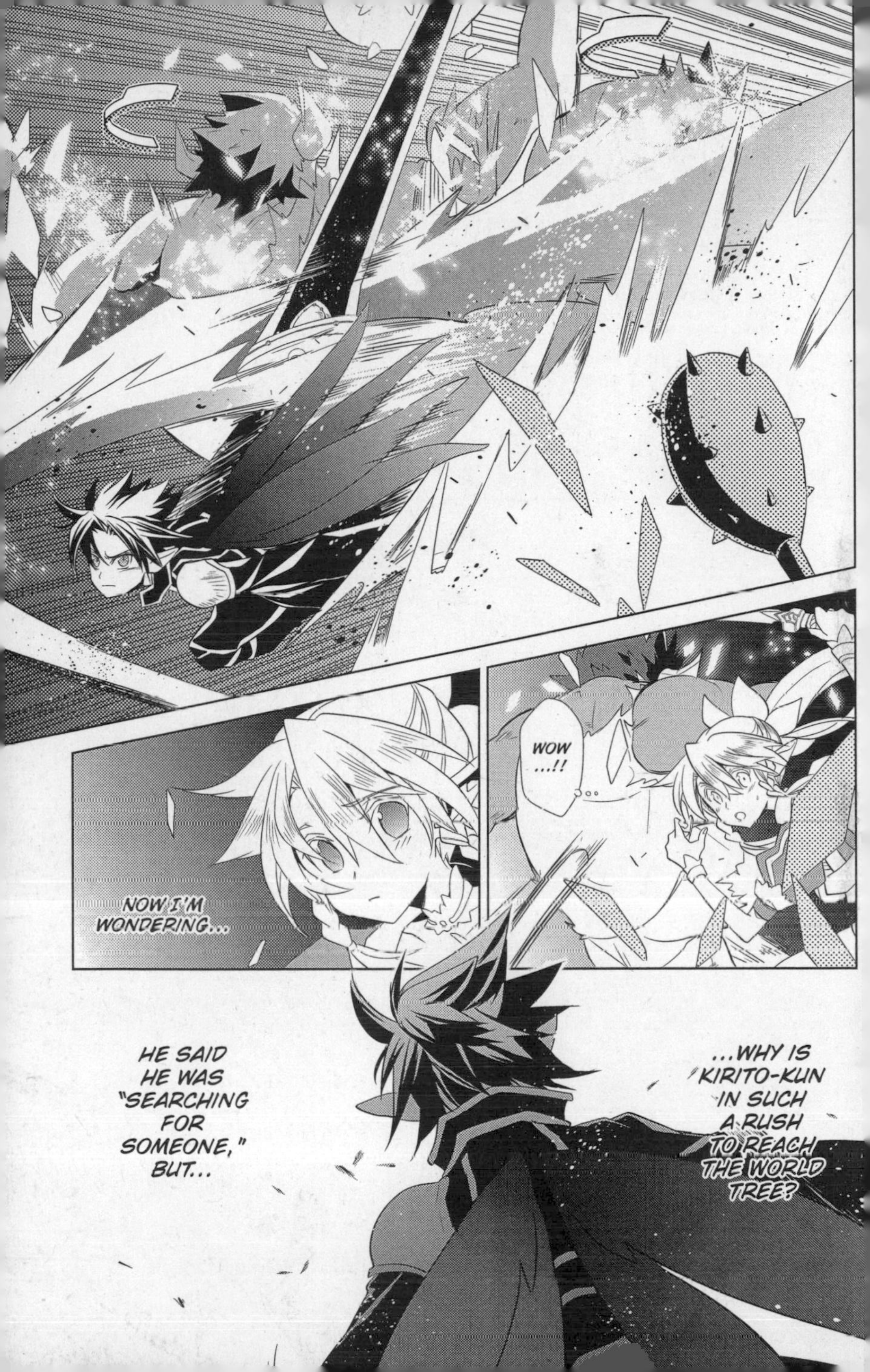
WOW ...!!
NOW I'M WONDERING...
...WHY IS KIRITO-KUN IN SUCH A RUSH TO REACH THE WORLD TREE?
HE SAID HE WAS "SEARCHING FOR SOMEONE," BUT...

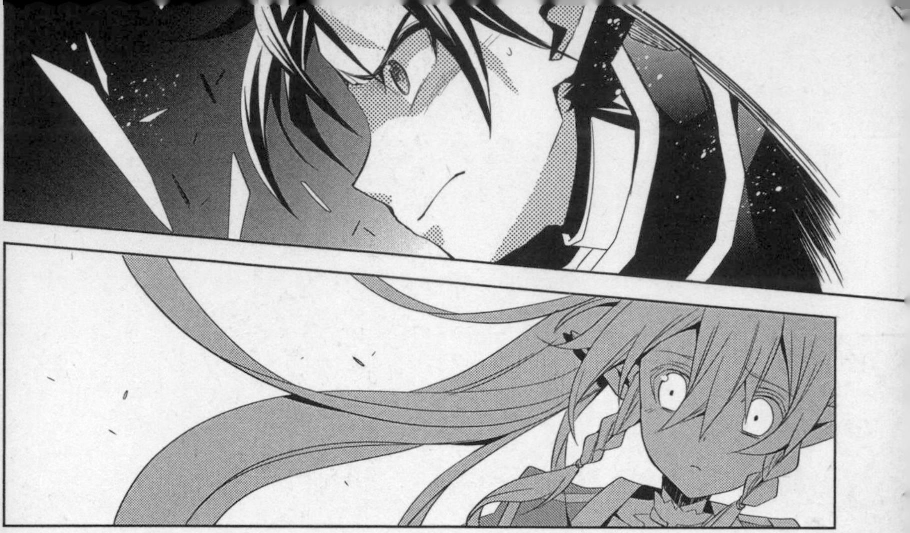

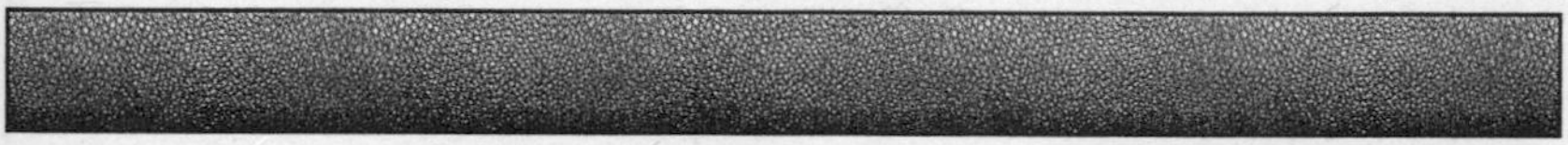

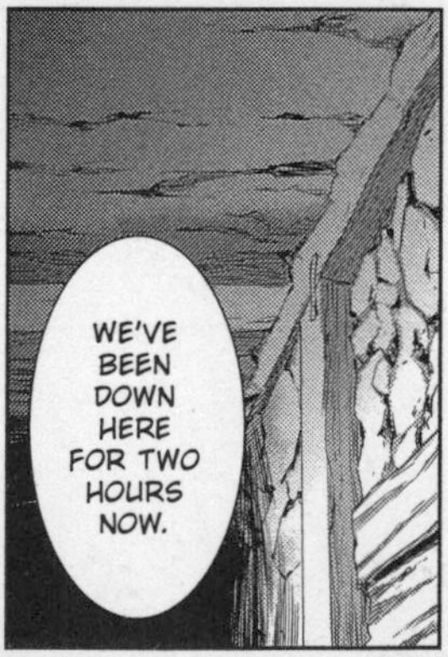
WE'VE BEEN DOWN HERE FOR TWO HOURS NOW.

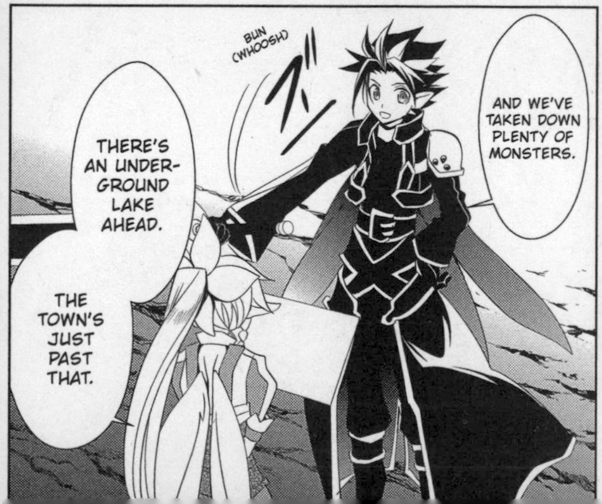
AND WE'VE TAKEN DOWN PLENTY OF MONSTERS.
BUN (WHOOSH)
THERE'S AN UNDER-GROUND LAKE AHEAD.
THE TOWN'S JUST PAST THAT.

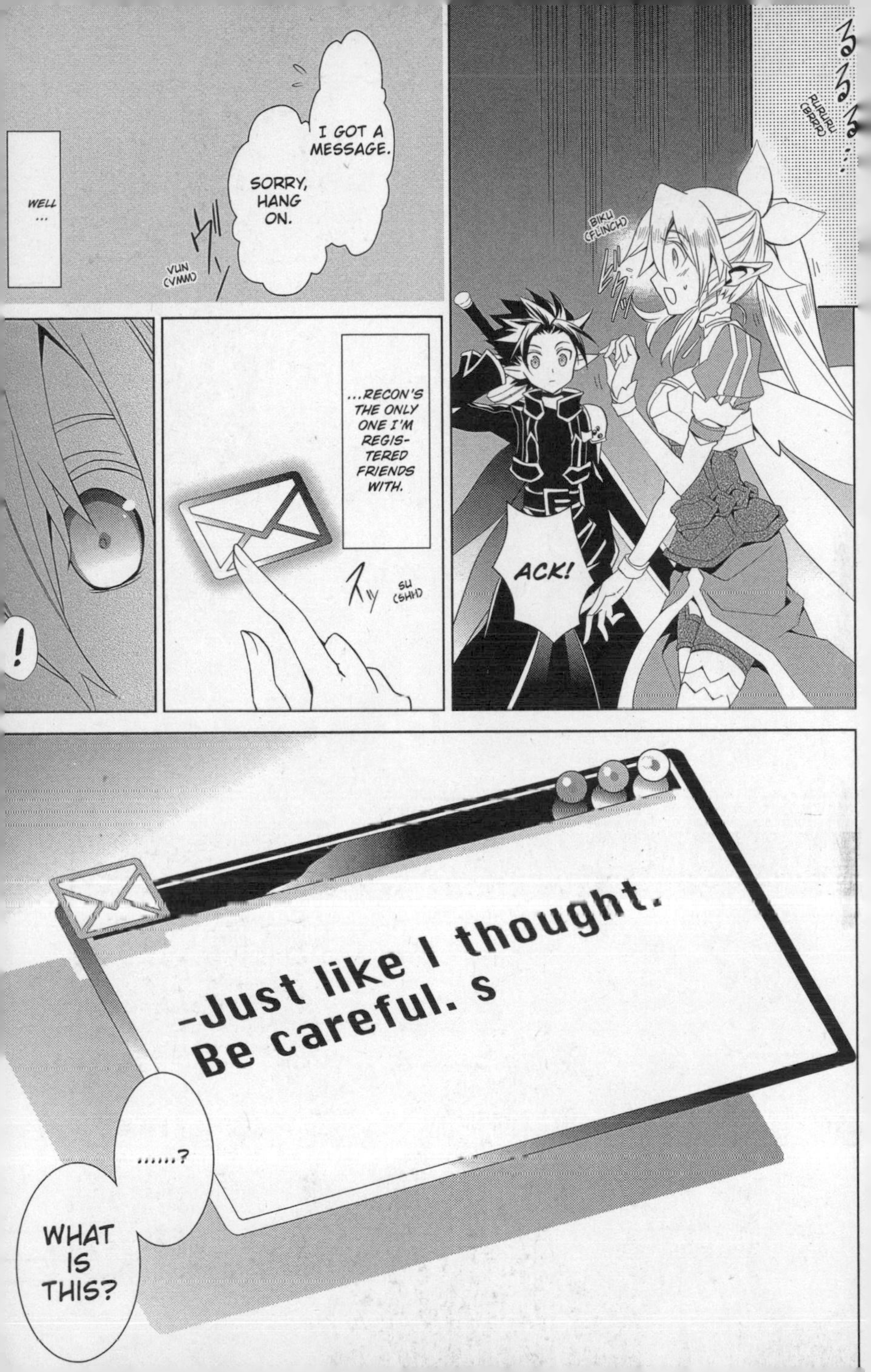
RURURU (BRRR)
BIKU (FLINCH)
ACK!
I GOT A MESSAGE.
SORRY, HANG ON.
VUN (VMM)
WELL...
...RECON'S THE ONLY ONE I'M REGIS-TERED FRIENDS WITH.
SU (SHH)
!
-Just like I thought.
Be careful. S
......?
WHAT IS THIS?

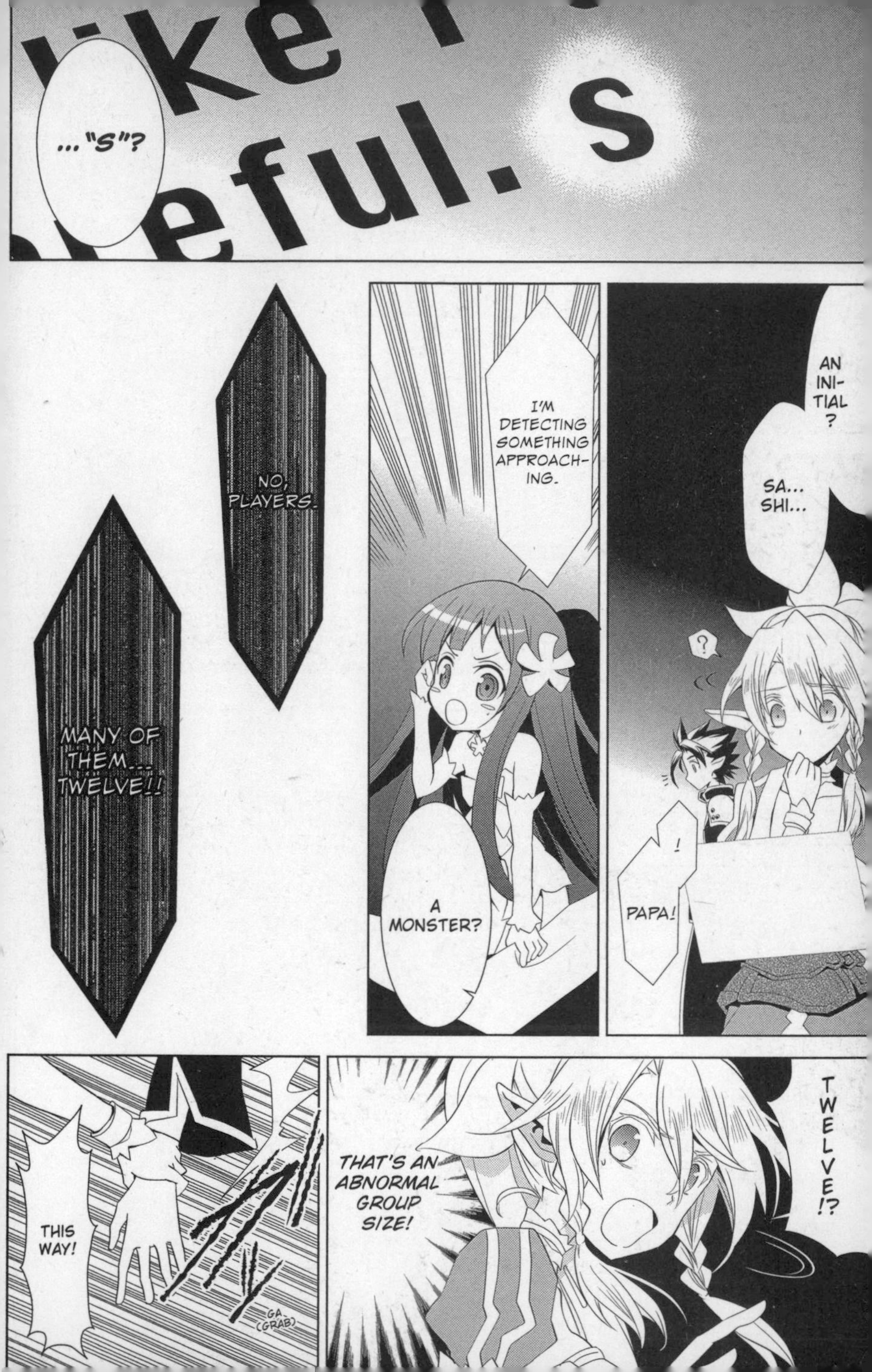
ke
eful. S
..."S"?
AN INI-TIAL?
SA... SHI...
?
!
PAPA!
I'M DETECTING SOMETHING APPROACHING.
A MONSTER?
NO, PLAYERS.
MANY OF THEM... TWELVE!!
TWELVE!?
THAT'S AN ABNORMAL GROUP SIZE!
THIS WAY!
GA- (GRAB)

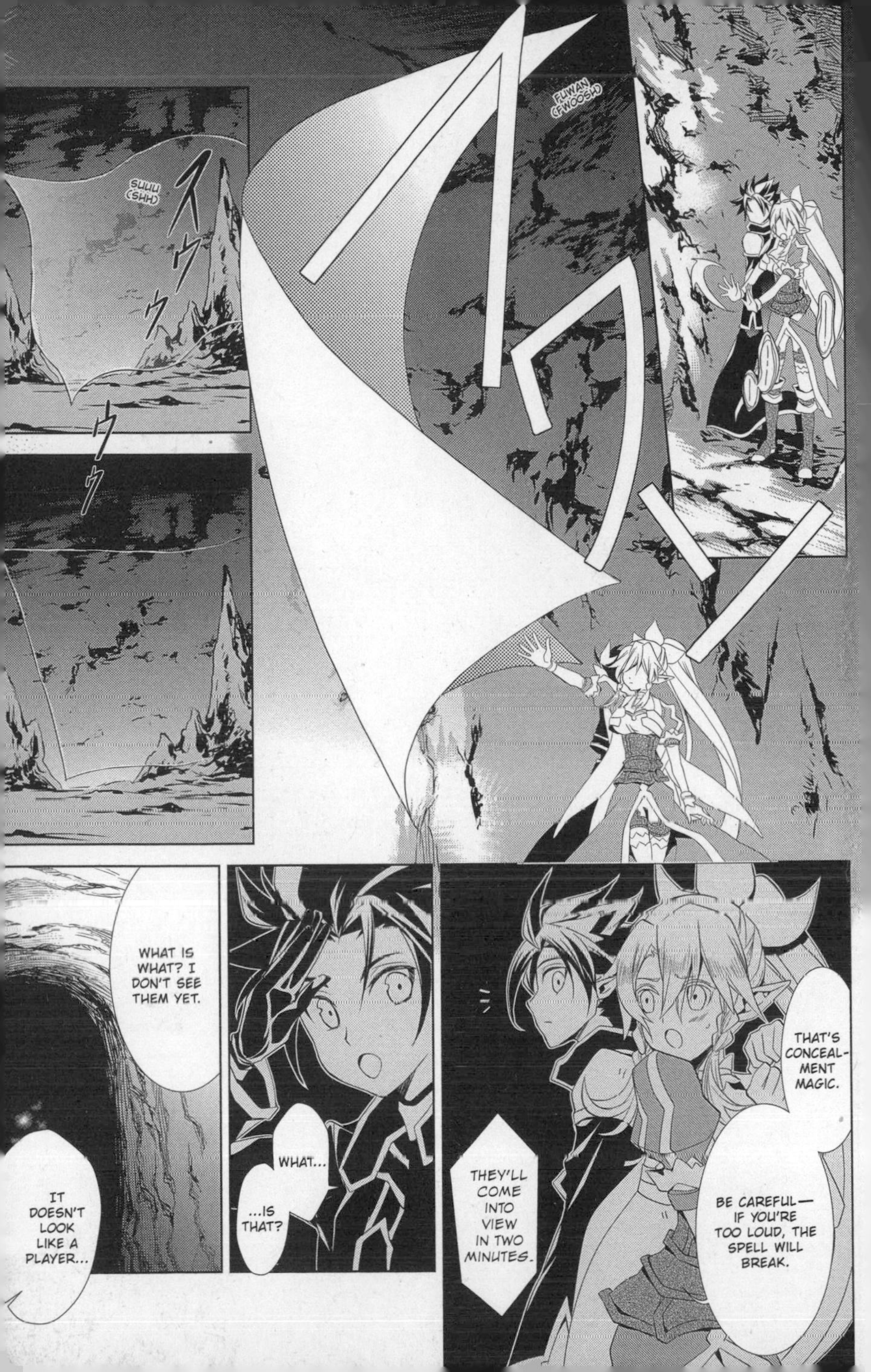
FUWAN (FWOOSH)
SUUU (SHH)
THAT'S CONCEAL-MENT MAGIC.
BE CAREFUL— IF YOU'RE TOO LOUD, THE SPELL WILL BREAK.
THEY'LL COME INTO VIEW IN TWO MINUTES.
WHAT...
...IS THAT?
WHAT IS WHAT? I DON'T SEE THEM YET.
IT DOESN'T LOOK LIKE A PLAYER...

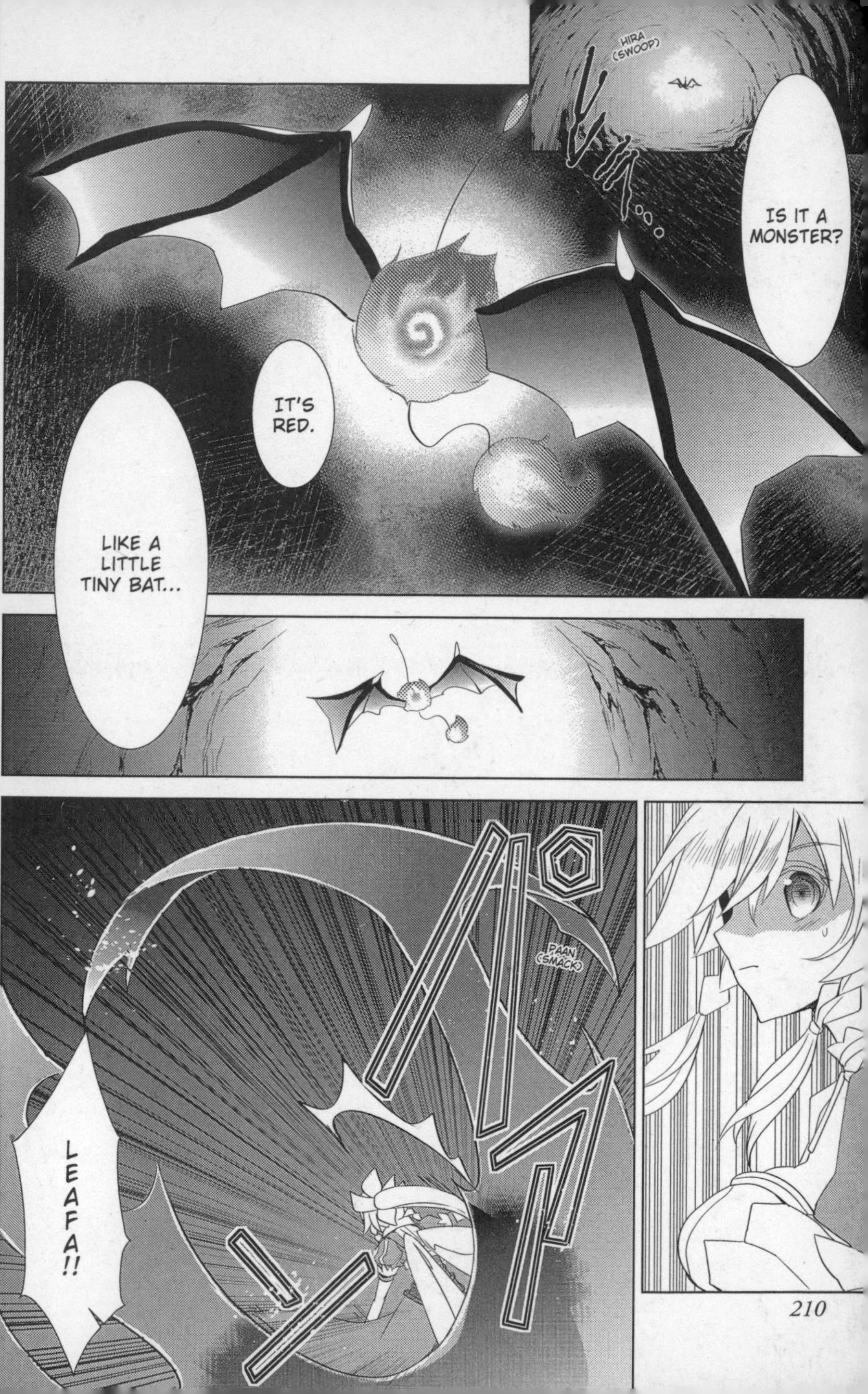
HIRA (SWOOP)
IS IT A MONSTER?
IT'S RED.
LIKE A LITTLE TINY BAT...
PAAN (SMACK)
LEAFA!!

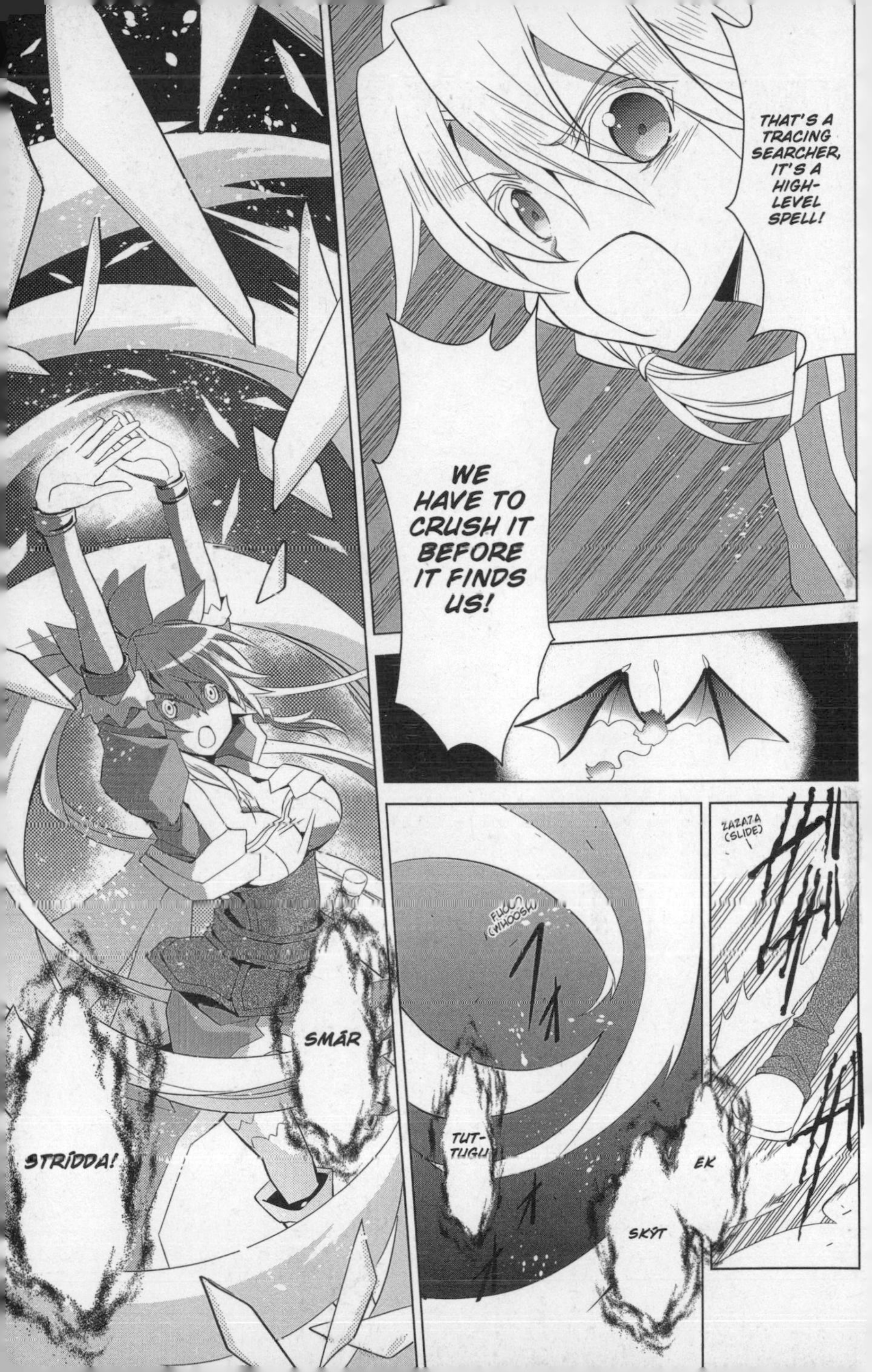
THAT'S A TRACING SEARCHER, IT'S A HIGH-LEVEL SPELL!
WE HAVE TO CRUSH IT BEFORE IT FINDS US!
ZAZAZA (SLIDE)
FUOO (WHOOSH)
TUT-TUGU
EK
SKÝT
SMÁR
STRÍDDA!

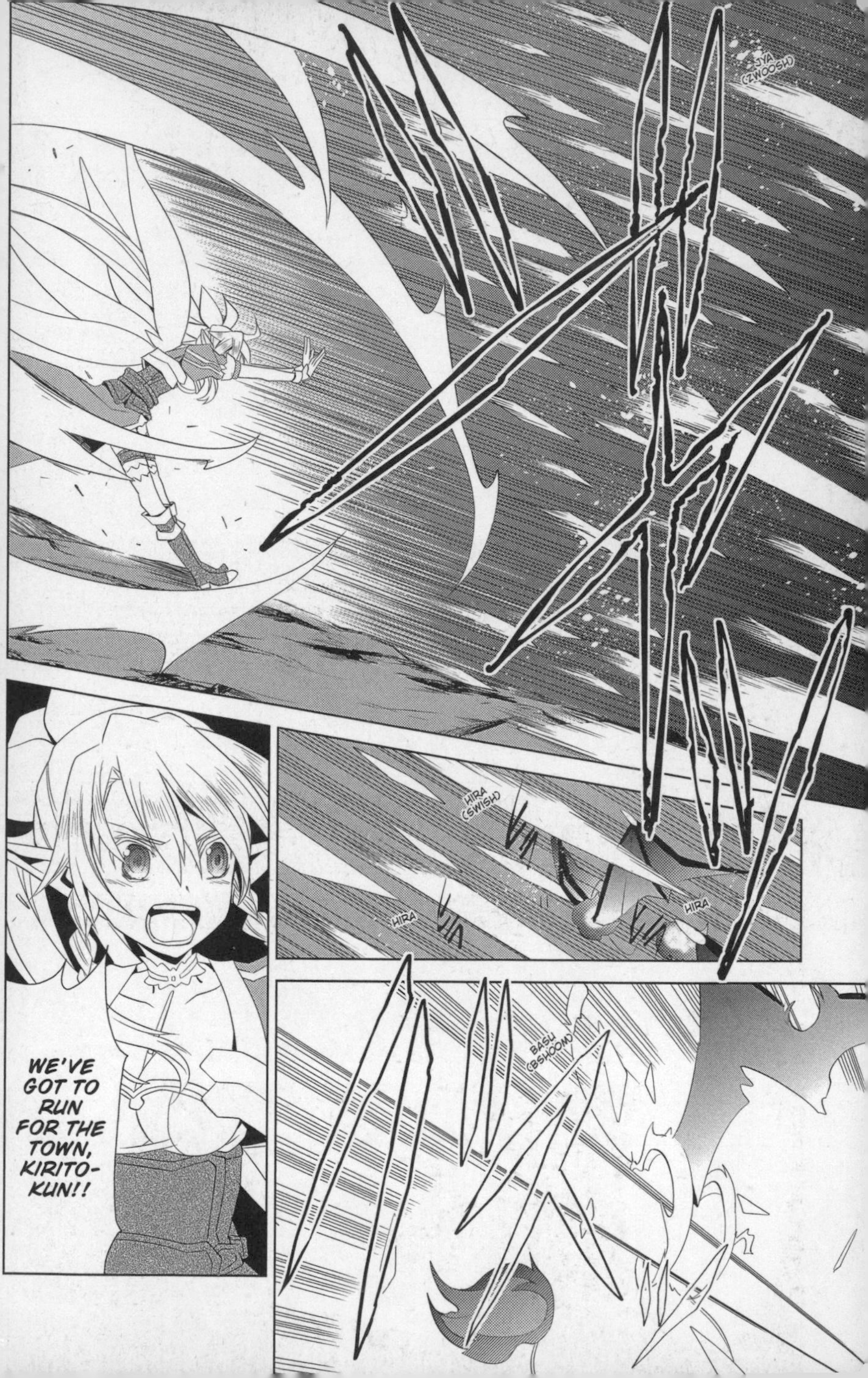
JYA (ZWOOSH)
HIRA (SWISH)
HIRA
HIRA
BASU (BSHOOM)
WE'VE GOT TO RUN FOR THE TOWN, KIRITO-KUN!!

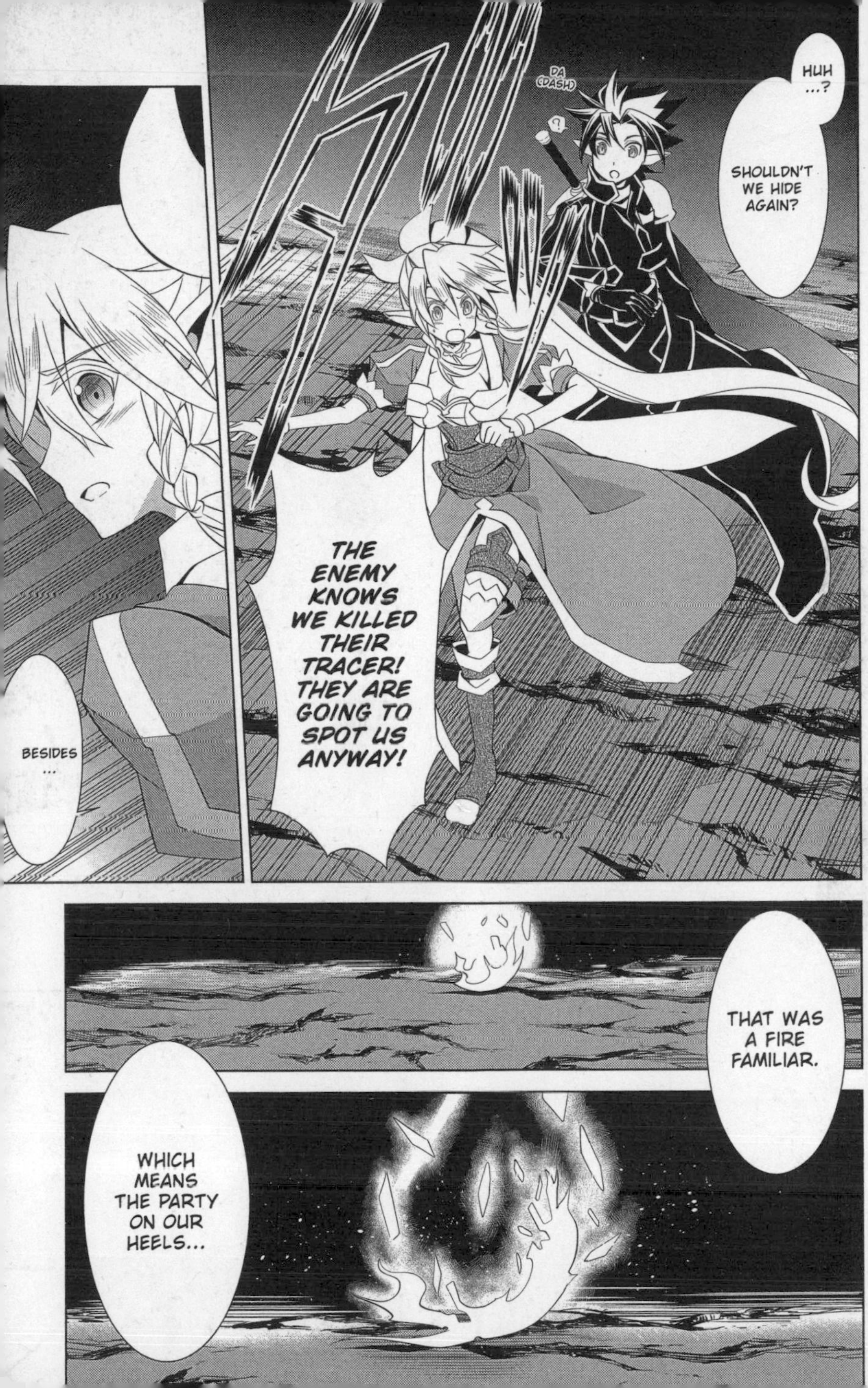
HUH ...?
SHOULDN'T WE HIDE AGAIN?
DA (DASH)
THE ENEMY KNOWS WE KILLED THEIR TRACER! THEY ARE GOING TO SPOT US ANYWAY!
BESIDES ...
THAT WAS A FIRE FAMILIAR.
WHICH MEANS THE PARTY ON OUR HEELS...

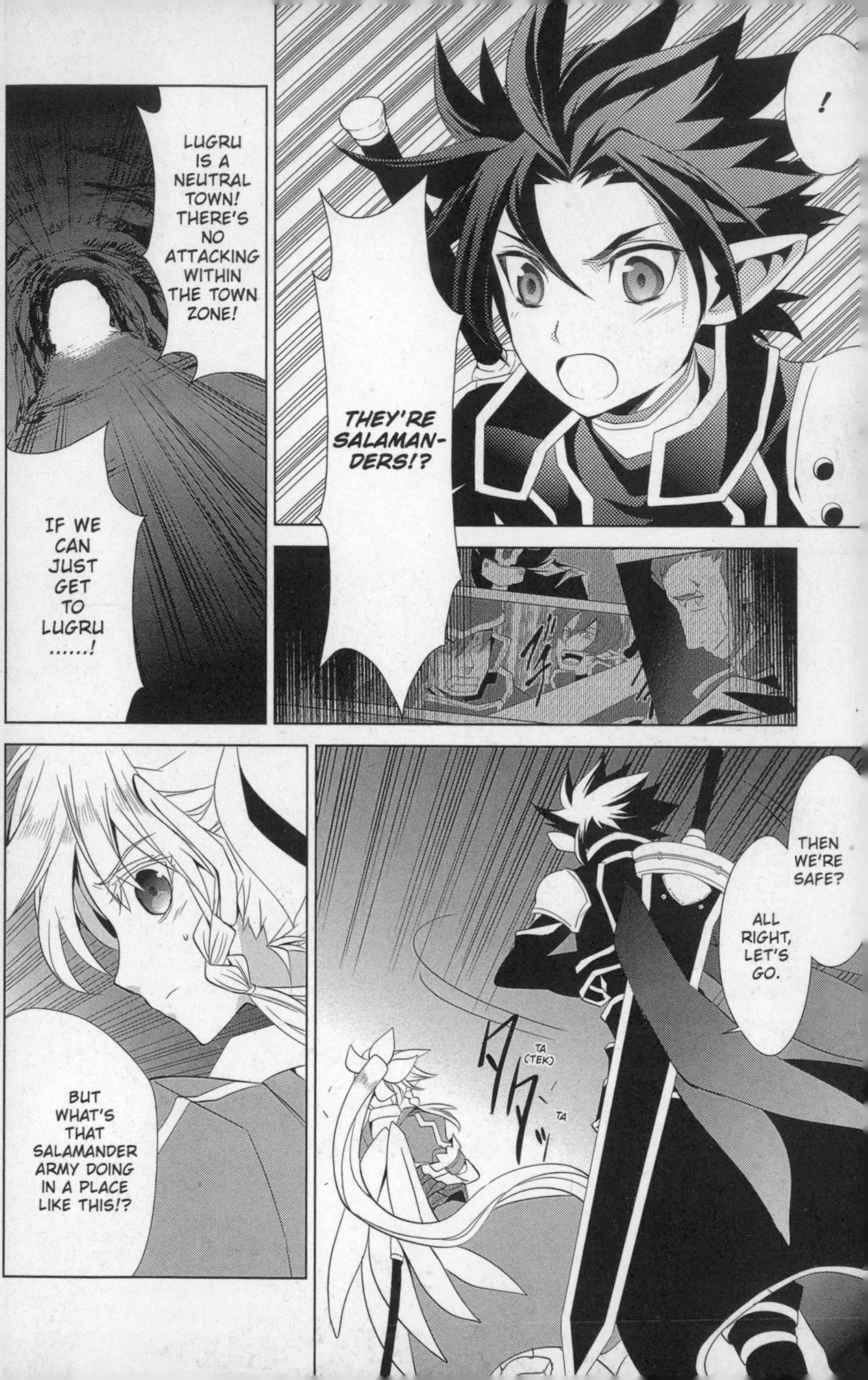
!
THEY'RE SALAMANDERS!?
LUGRU IS A NEUTRAL TOWN! THERE'S NO ATTACKING WITHIN THE TOWN ZONE!
IF WE CAN JUST GET TO LUGRU ......!
THEN WE'RE SAFE?
ALL RIGHT, LET'S GO.
TA (TEK)
TA
BUT WHAT'S THAT SALAMANDER ARMY DOING IN A PLACE LIKE THIS!?

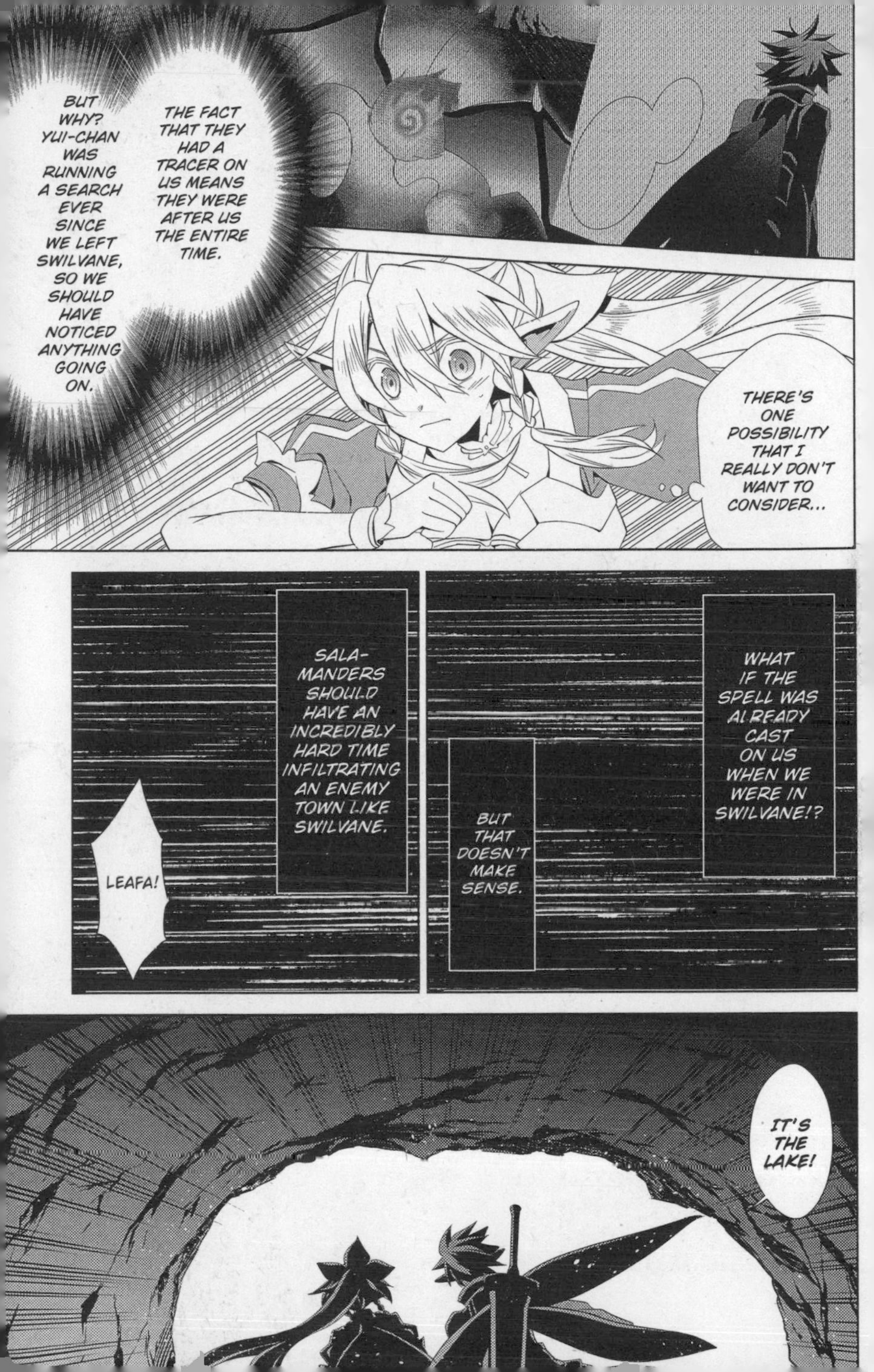
THE FACT THAT THEY HAD A TRACER ON US MEANS THEY WERE AFTER US THE ENTIRE TIME.
BUT WHY? YUI-CHAN WAS RUNNING A SEARCH EVER SINCE WE LEFT SWILVANE, SO WE SHOULD HAVE NOTICED ANYTHING GOING ON.
THERE'S ONE POSSIBILITY THAT I REALLY DON'T WANT TO CONSIDER...
WHAT IF THE SPELL WAS ALREADY CAST ON US WHEN WE WERE IN SWILVANE!?
BUT THAT DOESN'T MAKE SENSE.
SALA-MANDERS SHOULD HAVE AN INCREDIBLY HARD TIME INFILTRATING AN ENEMY TOWN LIKE SWILVANE.
LEAFA!
IT'S THE LAKE!

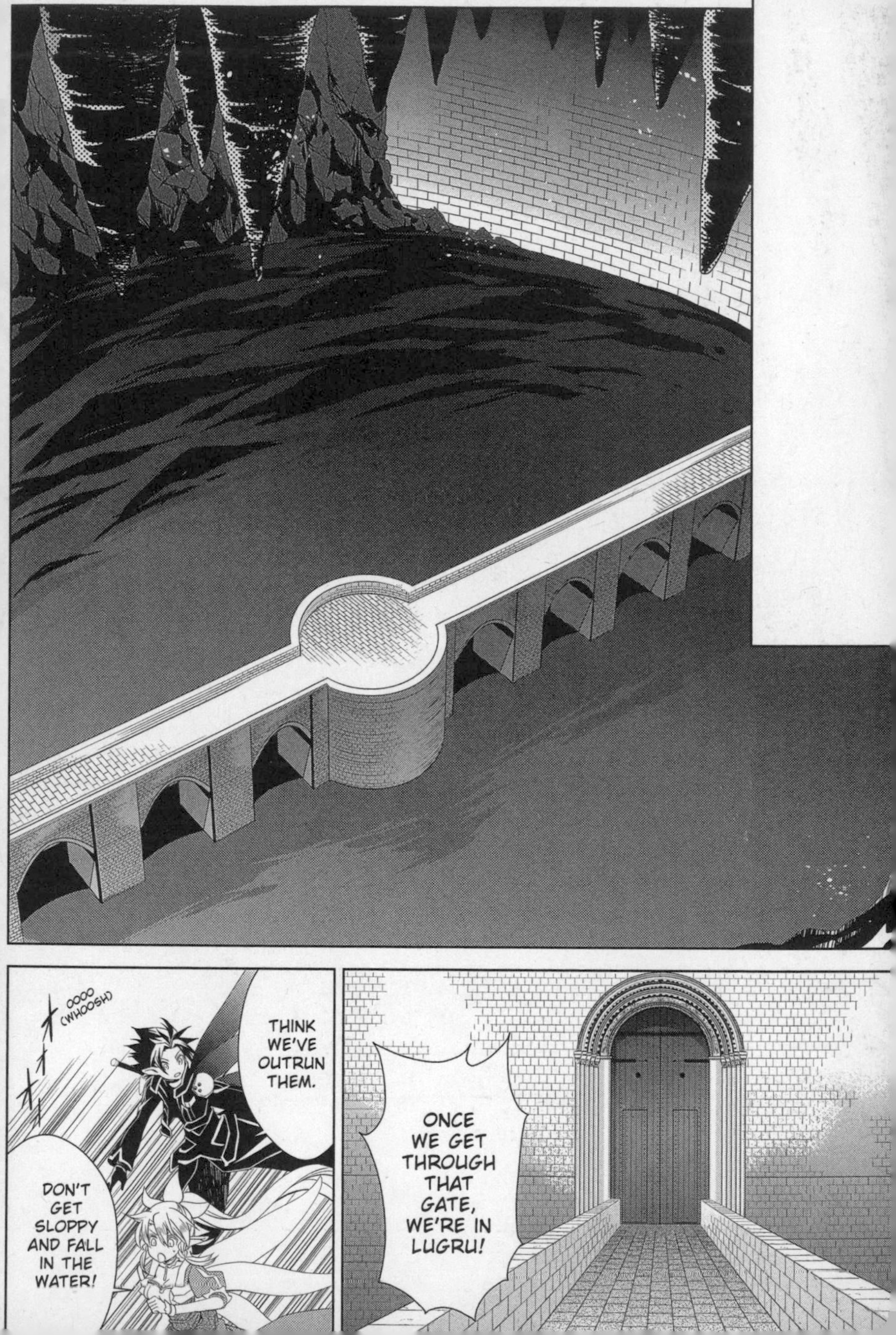
ONCE WE GET THROUGH THAT GATE, WE'RE IN LUGRU!
THINK WE'VE OUTRUN THEM.
OOOO (WHOOSH)
DON'T GET SLOPPY AND FALL IN THE WATER!

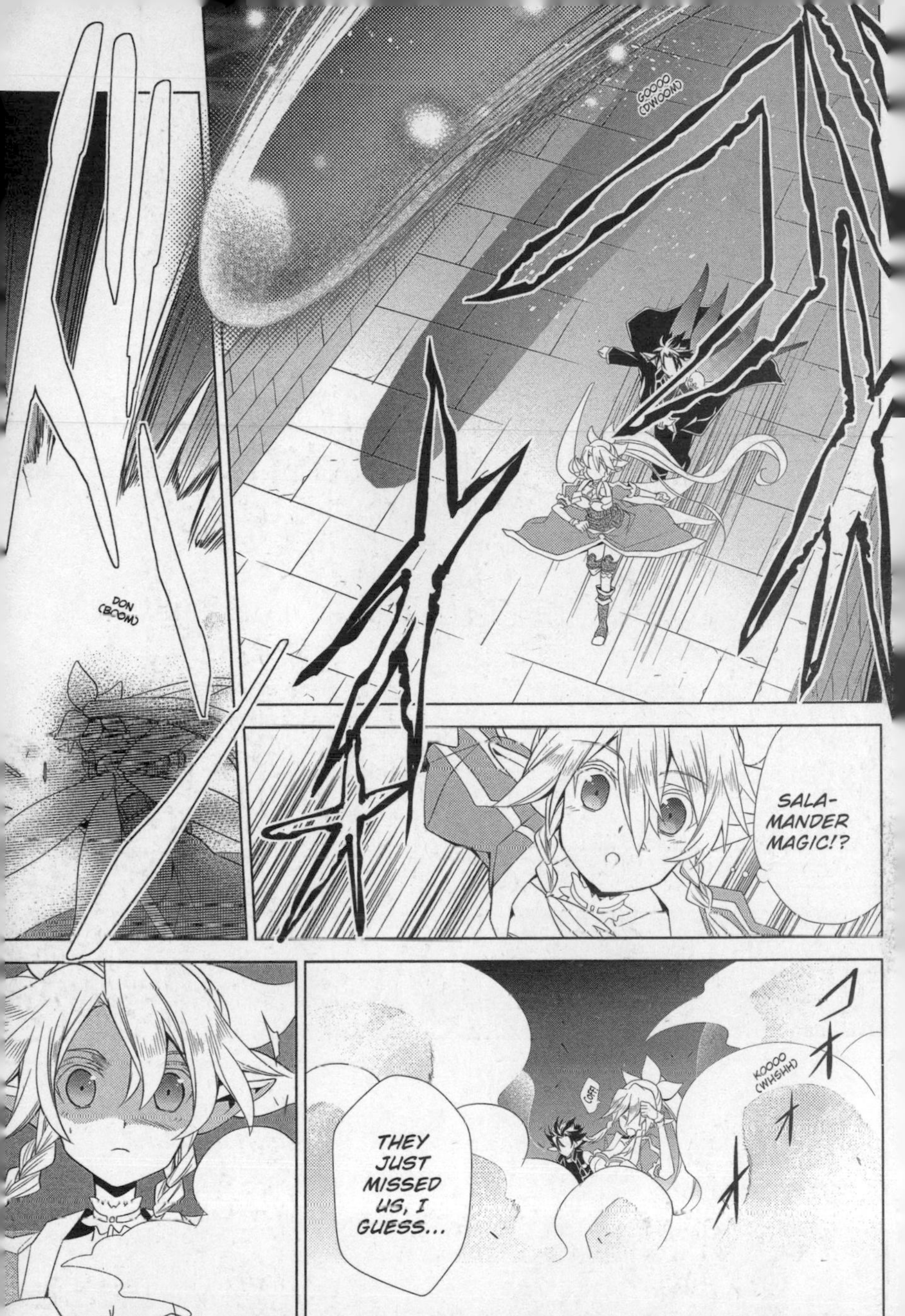
GOOOO (DWOOM)
DON (BOOM)
SALA-MANDER MAGIC!?
KOOOO (WHSHH)
COFF!
THEY JUST MISSED US, I GUESS...

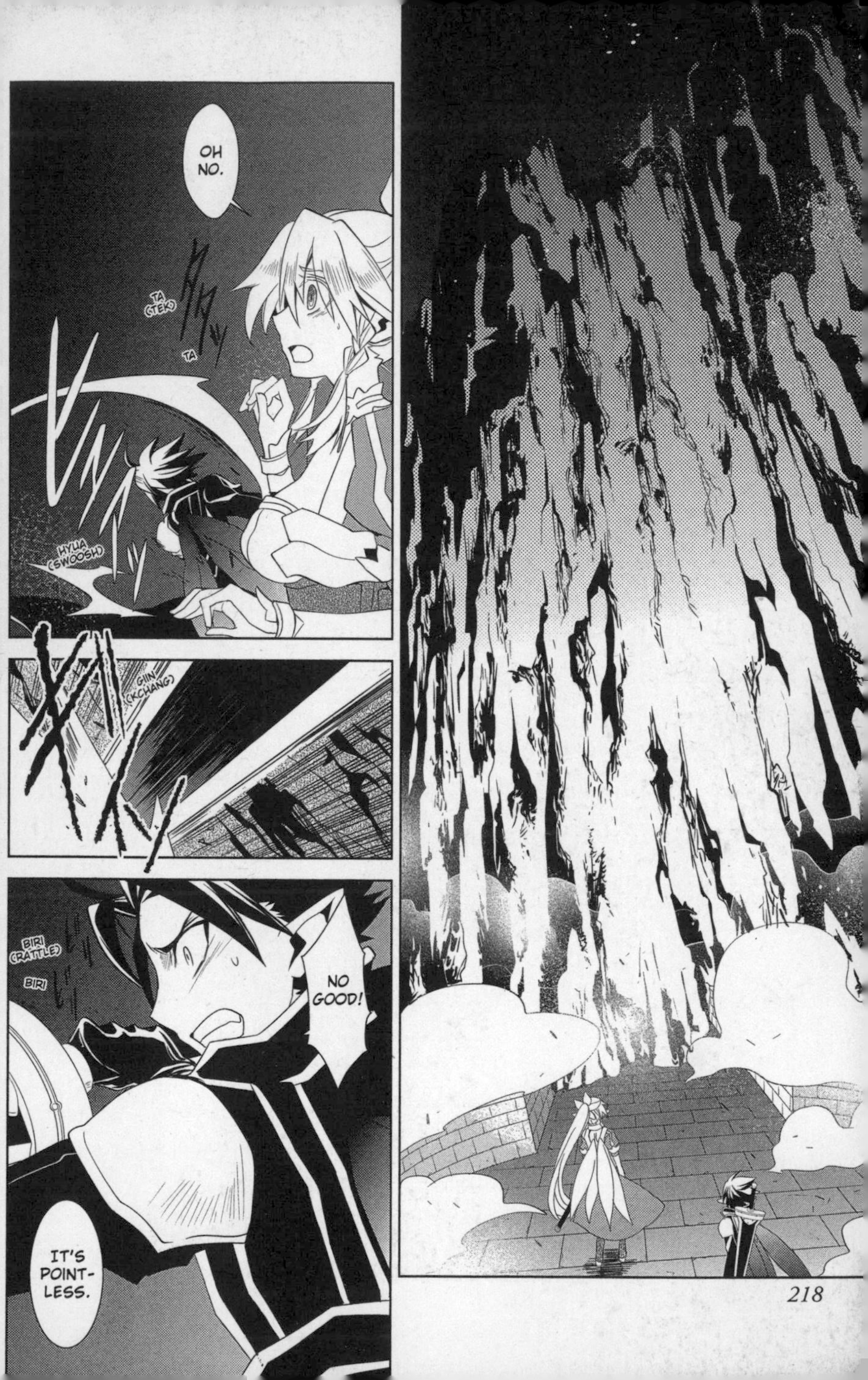
OH NO.
TA (TEK)
TA
HYUA (SWOOSH)
GIIN (KCHANG)
NO GOOD!
BIRI (RATTLE)
BIRI
IT'S POINT-LESS.

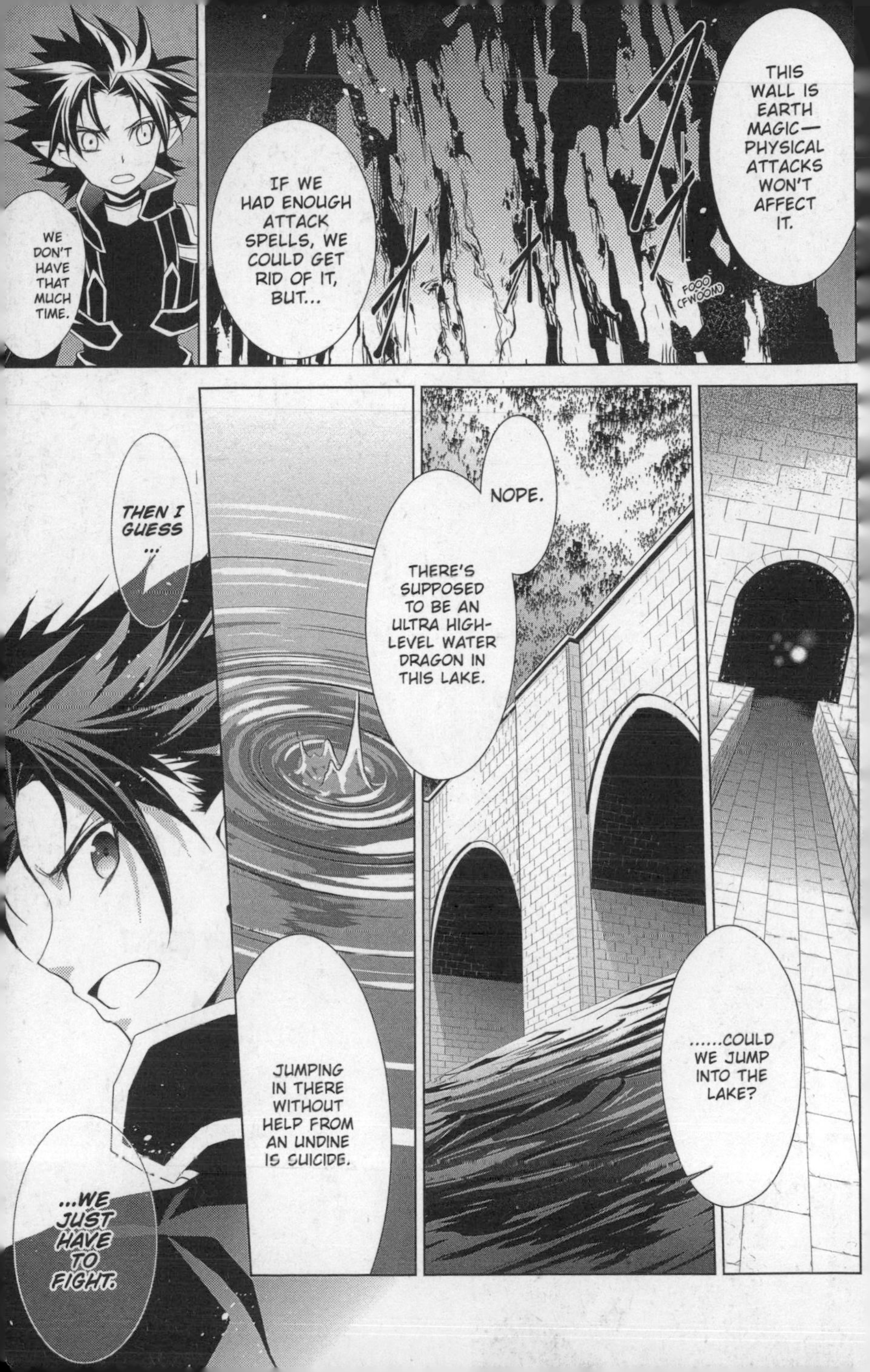
THIS WALL IS EARTH MAGIC—PHYSICAL ATTACKS WON'T AFFECT IT.
FOOO (FWOOM)
IF WE HAD ENOUGH ATTACK SPELLS, WE COULD GET RID OF IT, BUT...
WE DON'T HAVE THAT MUCH TIME.
......COULD WE JUMP INTO THE LAKE?
NOPE.
THERE'S SUPPOSED TO BE AN ULTRA HIGH-LEVEL WATER DRAGON IN THIS LAKE.
JUMPING IN THERE WITHOUT HELP FROM AN UNDINE IS SUICIDE.
THEN I GUESS...
...WE JUST HAVE TO FIGHT.

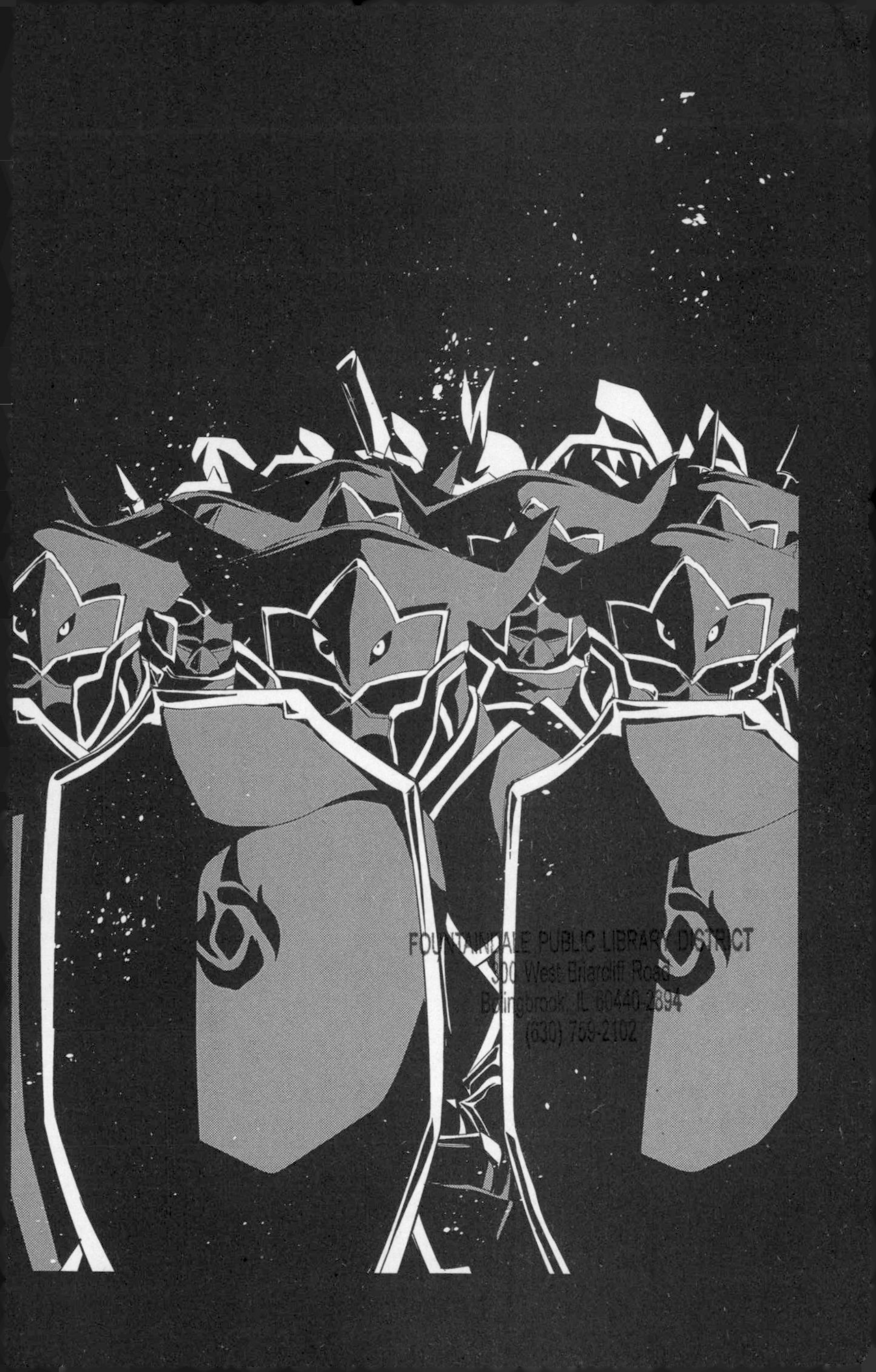

SWORD ART ONLINE
FAIRY DANCE

To Be Continued in the Next Stage...!!

AFTERWORD MANGA

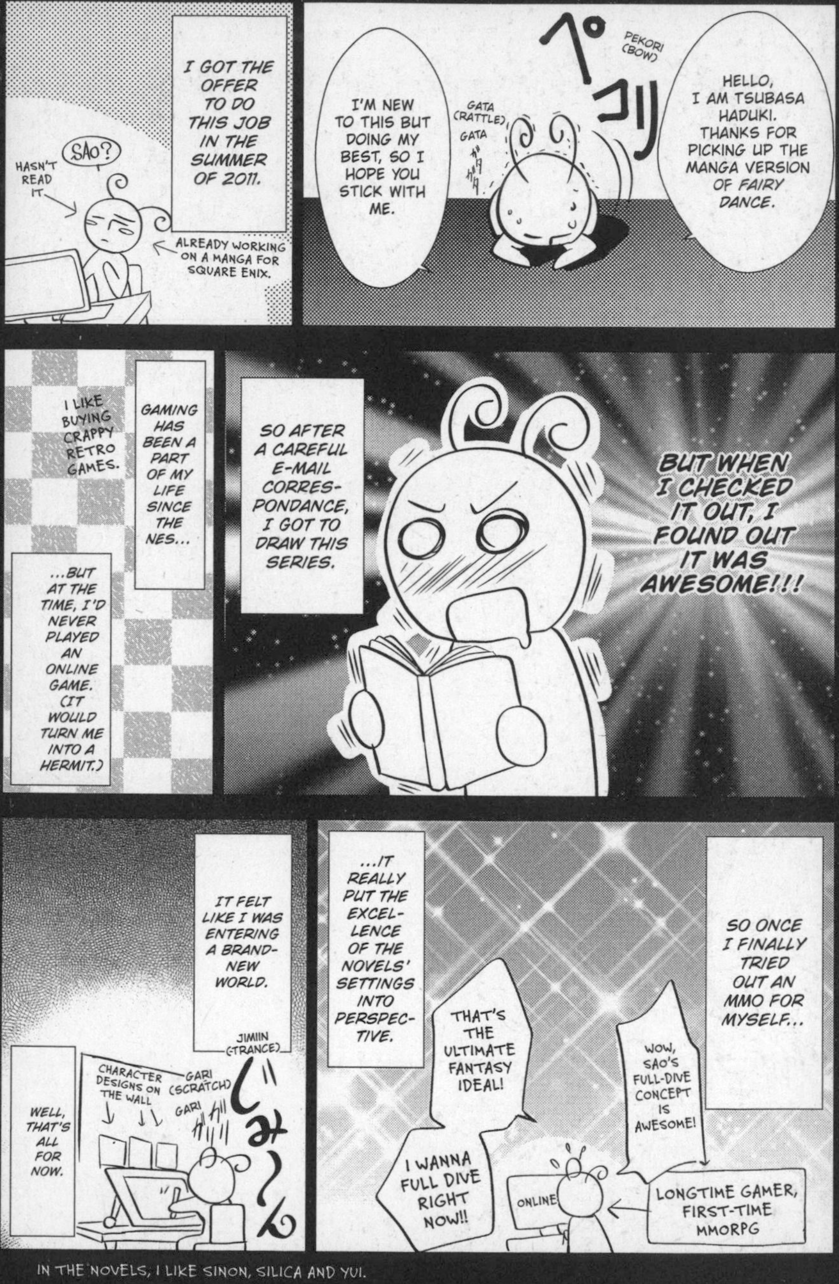

HELLO, I AM TSUBASA HADUKI. THANKS FOR PICKING UP THE MANGA VERSION OF FAIRY DANCE.
ペコリ
PEKORI (BOW)
GATA (RATTLE) GATA
I'M NEW TO THIS BUT DOING MY BEST, SO I HOPE YOU STICK WITH ME.
I GOT THE OFFER TO DO THIS JOB IN THE SUMMER OF 2011.
SAO?
HASN'T READ IT.
ALREADY WORKING ON A MANGA FOR SQUARE ENIX.
BUT WHEN I CHECKED IT OUT, I FOUND OUT IT WAS AWESOME!!!
SO AFTER A CAREFUL E-MAIL CORRES-PONDANCE, I GOT TO DRAW THIS SERIES.
GAMING HAS BEEN A PART OF MY LIFE SINCE THE NES...
I LIKE BUYING CRAPPY RETRO GAMES.
...BUT AT THE TIME, I'D NEVER PLAYED AN ONLINE GAME. (IT WOULD TURN ME INTO A HERMIT.)
SO ONCE I FINALLY TRIED OUT AN MMO FOR MYSELF...
WOW, SAO'S FULL-DIVE CONCEPT IS AWESOME!
LONGTIME GAMER, FIRST-TIME MMORPG
ONLINE
THAT'S THE ULTIMATE FANTASY IDEAL!
I WANNA FULL DIVE RIGHT NOW!!
...IT REALLY PUT THE EXCEL-LENCE OF THE NOVELS' SETTINGS INTO PERSPEC-TIVE.
IT FELT LIKE I WAS ENTERING A BRAND-NEW WORLD.
JIMIIN (TRANCE)
GARI (SCRATCH) GARI
CHARACTER DESIGNS ON THE WALL
WELL, THAT'S ALL FOR NOW.

IN THE NOVELS, I LIKE SINON, SILICA AND YUI.

SPECIAL THANKS

RIONA
CORAL

TOMOAKI IKEDA
MITSUHIRO ONODA
SAORI MIYAMOTO
TAKASHI SAKAI

EMIRI NIHEI
MASAOMI ITO
KOBAYASHI

REKI KAWAHARA
ABEC

KAZUMA MIKI
TOMOYUKI TSUCHIYA

THE STAFF OF THE SWORD ART ONLINE ANIME SERIES

MORE
SCENES

001

SWORD ART ONLINE fairy dance

art: tsubasa haduki
original story: reki kawahara
character design: abec

special comment

original story: reki kawahara

THE *FAIRY DANCE* STORY IS LARGELY BASED AROUND SOMETHING I COULD NOT DEPICT IN AINCRAD, FOR OBVIOUS REASONS: THE SHEER, PURE FUN OF PLAYING AN MMORPG. THE RUSH OF SHOOTING OFF POWERFUL MAGIC SPELLS, THE FREEDOM TO FLY THROUGH THE OPEN SKIES, AND THE EXCITEMENT OF LOGGING IN TO AN ALIEN WORLD.

I'M SURE IT WAS VERY DIFFICULT TO PORTRAY IN COMIC FORM, BUT HADUKI-SAN'S FLOWING AND ENERGETIC ARTWORK HAS CERTAINLY DONE IT JUSTICE. I'M VERY MUCH LOOKING FORWARD TO READING THROUGH THE ENTIRE THING TO EXPERIENCE KIRITO AND LEAFA'S ADVENTURES IN ALFHEIM ALL OVER AGAIN.

CONGRATS ON FINISHING THE FIRST VOLUME!

REKI KAWAHARA

CONGRATULATIONS ON THE BOOK COMING OUT!
abec
CONGRATS!

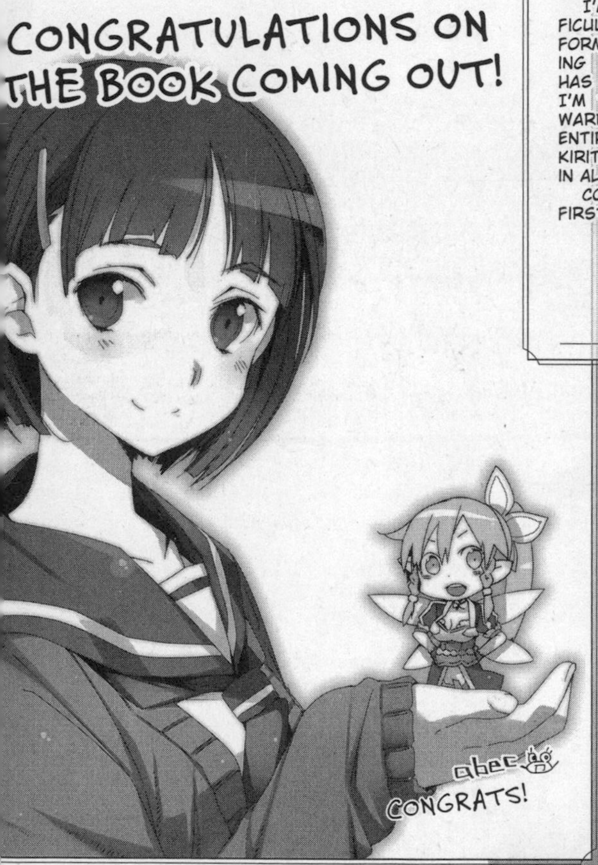

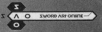

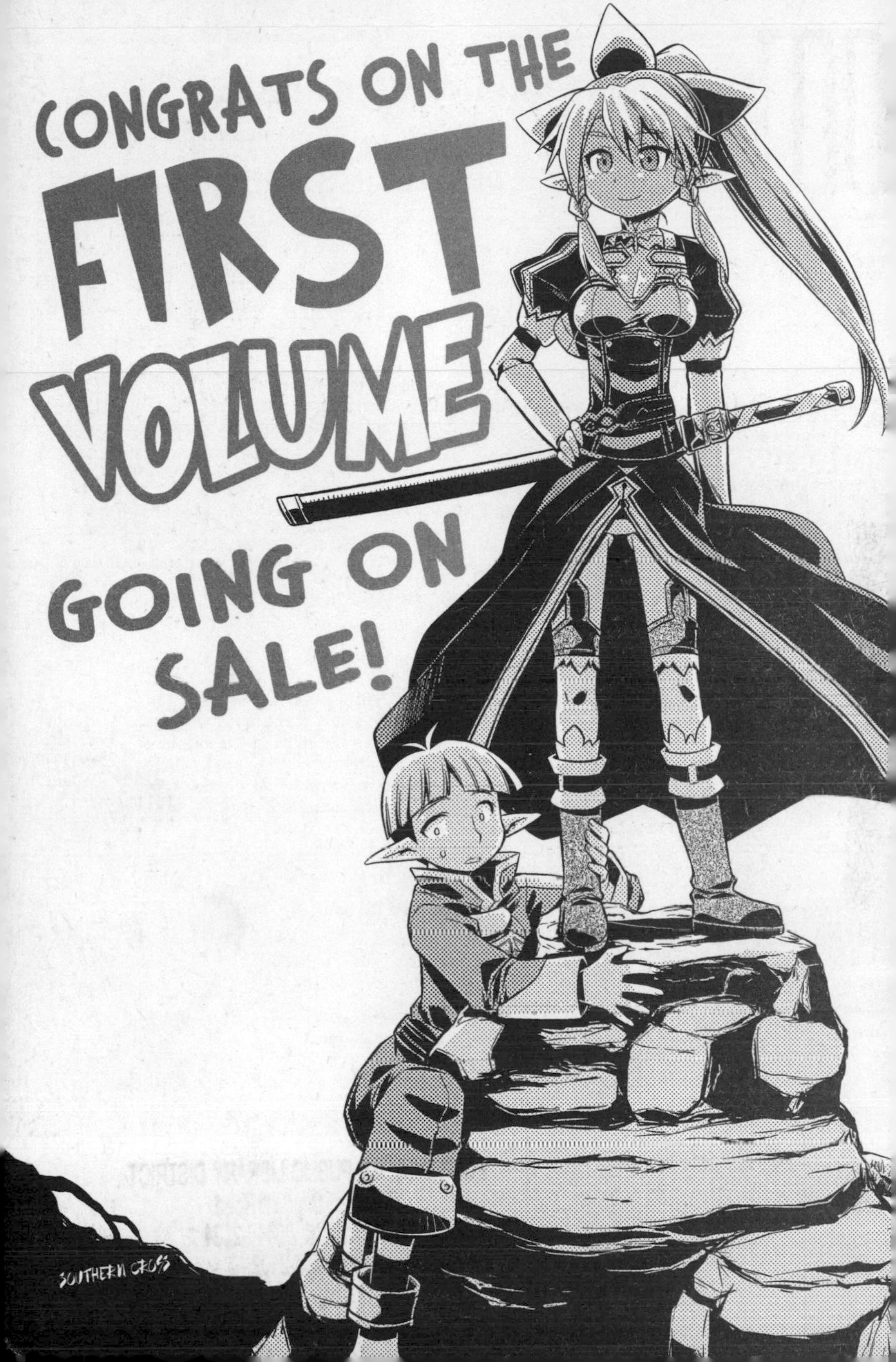
CONGRATS ON THE FIRST VOLUME GOING ON SALE!
SOUTHERN CROSS

SWORD ART ONLINE: FAIRY DANCE ☐1

ART: TSUBASA HADUKI
ORIGINAL STORY: REKI KAWAHARA
CHARACTER DESIGN: ABEC

Translation: Stephen Paul • Lettering: Lys Blakeslee

SWORD ART ONLINE: FAIRY DANCE, Vol. 1
© REKI KAWAHARA/TSUBASA HADUKI 2012
All rights reserved.
Edited by ASCII MEDIA WORKS
First published in Japan in 2012 by KADOKAWA CORPORATION, Tokyo.
English translation rights arranged with KADOKAWA CORPORATION, Tokyo, through Tuttle-Mori Agency, Inc., Tokyo.

English translation © 2014 by Hachette Book Group, Inc.

Yen Press
Hachette Book Group
1290 Avenue of the Americas, New York, NY 10104

www.HachetteBookGroup.com
www.YenPress.com

Yen Press is an imprint of Hachette Book Group, Inc. The Yen Press name and logo are trademarks of Hachette Book Group, Inc.

First Yen Press Edition: June 2014

ISBN: 978-0-316-40738-0

10 9 8 7 6 5

BVG

Printed in the United States of America